CAPTURED BY TEXTS

Puritan to Postmodern

Images of Indian Captivity

GARY L. EBERSOLE

CAPTURED BY TEXTS
Puritan to Postmodern
Images of Indian Captivity

University Press of Virginia
Charlottesville and London

THE UNIVERSITY PRESS OF VIRGINIA
Copyright © 1995 by the Rector and Visitors
of the University of Virginia

First published 1995

Library of Congress Cataloging-in-Publication Data

Ebersole, Gary L., 1950–
    Captured by texts : puritan to postmodern images of Indian
captivity / Gary L. Ebersole.
        p.   cm. — (Studies in religion and culture)
    Includes bibliographical references (p.   ) and index.
    ISBN 0–8139–1607–0 (cloth : alk. paper). — ISBN 0–8139–1606–2
(pbk. : alk. paper)
    1. Indian captivities.   2. United States—Religion—History.
3. United States—Social conditions.   I. Title.   II. Series.
Studies in religion and culture (Charlottesville, Va.)
E85.E24   1995
973'.0497—dc20   95–12129
                                                                          CIP

Printed in the United States of America

CONTENTS

PREFACE

A FEW EXPLANATORY REMARKS are due to the reader. In this study I have retained the original spelling and punctuation in the texts cited, although these are often archaic and irregular. This was done in order to preserve something of the flavor of the original text. Modernizing texts such as these would run the danger of artificially making them seem too familiar and close to us today. I have avoided the use of *sic* except in those very few instances in which a misunderstanding might otherwise have resulted.

The Garland Library of Narratives of North American Indian Captivities, a reprint series of 311 titles in 111 volumes, selected and arranged by Wilcomb E. Washburn, has been used as the reference base in this study. The reader will find references such as (*Garland* 54:21) within the text, indicating vol. 54, page 21, of the reprint series. Although several titles often are included in one volume of this series, the referent text will be clear. Full bibliographical information and full titles may be found by consulting the *Garland* series.

I have retained the term *Indian* to refer to the peoples of the Americas throughout this study. Few of the authors of captivity tales distinguished among the diverse groups of Native Americans before the nineteenth century and even then the criteria used were often haphazard. Most importantly, though, because this is a study of popular imagery, it is important for us to understand the extent to which Native Americans were lumped together by most persons. Moreover, this is not intended as a study of the history of the representation of the Indian; other excellent works exist on this topic. My goal has been to see how the figure of the Indian and the white Indian function over time in captivity tales.

Several friends and colleagues kindly read and offered critical advice on earlier drafts of this work. My deepest thanks go to Richard Gardner, Frank Reynolds, Catherine Brekus, and Davíd Carrasco. As always, I owe a special thanks to Noriko for her love and support. This work is dedicated to our children—Maiko, Koji, Jun, and Kentaro—as they continue to create and recreate their own identities in the world.

CAPTURED BY TEXTS

Puritan to Postmodern

Images of Indian Captivity

INTRODUCTION:
RECAPTURING THE
MEANING OF TEXTS

My earliest impressions of the Indian race, were drawn from the fireside rehearsals of incidents which had happened during the perilous times of the American revolution; in which my father was a zealous actor, and were all inseparably connected with the fearful ideas of the Indian yell, the tomahawk, the scalping knife, and the firebrand. In these recitals, the Indian was depicted as the very impersonation of evil—a sort of wild demon, who delighted in nothing so much as blood and murder. Whether he had mind, was governed by any reasons, or even had any soul, nobody inquired, and nobody cared. It was always represented as a meritorious act in old revolutionary reminiscences, to have killed one of them in the border wars, and thus aided in ridding the land of a cruel and unnatural race, in whom all feelings of pity, justice, and mercy, were supposed to be obliterated. These early ideas were sustained by printed narratives of captivity and hair-breadth escapes of men and women from their clutches, which, from time to time, fell into my hands, so that long before I was ten years old, I had a most definite and terrific idea impressed on my imagination of what was sometimes called in my native precincts, "the bow and arrow race."
—Henry Schoolcraft

MY EPIGRAPH comes from a famous nineteenth-century Indian agent and ethnographer. He was not alone in having formed his image of the Indian from captivity narratives—for centuries virtually every European and American did so to some extent.[1] It would be erroneous, however, to assume that the only thing cap-

tivity narratives did was to convey and perpetuate stereotypes
about the American Indians. Since the seventeenth century, tales
of captivity have been used in the Euro-American world in diverse
ways as vehicles for reflection on larger social, religious, and ideological issues. This situation continues today as the theme of
Indian captivity appears in ethnographies and in novels and films.

The cultural work of captivity tales has not been simple or
uniform; thousands of these tales have circulated and served as
discursive sites for the meaning-making activities of diverse communities over the centuries. But they have not evoked a single
response, nor have they presented a consistent image of the Indian,
as Schoolcraft seems to suggest. In fact, the responses of readers to
captivity narratives have been remarkably diverse, as have the
representations of Indians, whites, and white Indians (persons of
European descent who live with Indians and who come to look
like, act like, and even assume an Indian identity). These different
responses were, of course, due in part to the distinct ways in which
the tales were narratively cast and the authorial intention behind
each telling, but they were also a result of the different needs,
interests, and reading practices readers brought to the texts.

Although scholars have often noted the importance of the literary topos of captivity, they have not always agreed about the
precise role it has played in American cultural history. In their
introduction to a modern anthology of captivity narratives, James
Levernier and Henning Cohen write:

> When Rip Van Winkle failed to return from a hunting trip into the
> Catskills, it was assumed that he had been "carried away by the
> Indians." The assumption was fairly safe. During the French and
> Indian Wars, which ended about the time Rip disappeared, possibly
> as many as two thousand captives were carried to Canada by the
> Indians as war prisoners. Countless others were adopted into Indian
> tribes and lost forever to white society. The Indian captivity was a
> massive historical reality. It helped to shape the national character,
> it provided substance for the artistic imagination, it defined basic
> issues in the white culture, and it was made to serve a variety of
> purposes, not all of which were noble.[2]

Here the "massive historical reality" of Indian captivity refers
not only to the cumulative historical incidents of non-Indians
who had been abducted by Indians but also to the rich narrative
and imaginal activity that has taken place around the topos of

captivity. The captivity narrative has been a major vehicle for reflecting upon the meaning of the European occupation of the captured space of the New World as well as upon the ways in which humans are captured by the space (sociocultural, linguistic, and geographical) they inhabit. This study will focus largely on narrative representations of captivity, but with attention to their historical setting and to the contemporary reading practices brought to bear on these texts.

First, a word about abductions as a fact of life on the shifting frontiers of America is in order; then, we need to get a preliminary sense of the dimensions of the "massive historical reality" of the captivity narrative as a genre (i.e., the number of such tales that were printed and circulated over time); and, finally, we must consider captivity as a general situation in order to appreciate how and why it could become a way to reflect on the human situation.

Exact numbers are hard to come by, but clearly many hundreds of persons experienced Indian captivity over the centuries. Some were held for a matter of days, others spent many years among the Indians. Still others (how many we will never know, but certainly the number is large) went native and never returned to the white world. Indians seem to have abducted individuals for two main reasons. First, captives were frequently taken for their ransom value. At times, for instance, funds to ransom or redeem captives became almost a regular budget item for some colonial governments. Many other funds were raised privately or through donations. In the political struggles between the British and the French in North America, Indians were paid by the French for prisoners delivered to Canada. Second, captives were often taken to replace individuals who had died prematurely or who had been killed in accidents or skirmishes. Some captives were adopted to assuage the grief of a mother who had lost a child, but more often captives were taken out of practical labor considerations. Some captives were harshly used as forced laborers or slaves, but many were adopted into Indian families and assumed the social prerogatives and duties of the deceased.[3] In some cases, they were given the name of the deceased. The practice of taking captives for the purpose of adoption predated European contact, but the decimation of the native population from diseases introduced through contact and the resultant cultural disruption no doubt increased the collective need to resort to this means of maintaining the critical mass of individuals required to sustain Indian forms of social existence.

OLIVE OATMAN.

Figure 1. Former captive with tattoos. From R. B.
Stratton, *Life among the Indians* (1857). (Photo
courtesy of the Everett D. Graff Collection, The
Newberry Library)

Captivity was not a negative experience for everyone. For some
individuals, captivity opened up hitherto unimagined opportunities and lifestyle choices. Some individuals enjoyed a newfound
freedom, unknown in the white world. This was obviously the case
with many black slaves, but others, too—indentured servants,
battered wives, overworked young boys, and young women—also
realized an independence or a new social identity among the Indians that literally opened new worlds to them.[4] To note this fact is
not to suggest that captivity was a welcomed event; rather, it is to
bring to our attention the remarkable adaptability and practical
decision-making abilities of ordinary men and women who were
sometimes able to turn events over which they originally had no

control to their own advantage. Unfortunately, very few of the captives who went native left written accounts of their lives.

There is also considerable evidence that returning to the white world after living with the Indians was easier said than done. Captives who had spent a considerable period of time with the Indians, especially those who had been abducted as children, frequently had taken on an Indian identity. Not only did they dress and talk like Indians, they thought like them, shared many of their values, and, as many observers report, even carried their bodies differently. Some of the former captives also carried facial or bodily scars that marked them for life as white Indians. For those who had truly gone native, Indian culture had been internalized in ways which were not easily shed.

Returning captives often faced widespread prejudice and racism in white society. Many never found themselves completely accepted or fully reassimilated. Some returned captives left the white world out of a sense of disappointment, frustration, or disgust and returned to their Indian families and friends. Others found a niche as cultural intermediaries of one sort or another—as Indian traders, interpreters, guides, and assistants to government agents—but they largely remained on the margins of American society.[5]

Abductions by Indians were so common at times in American history that they came to be accepted as a part of life on the frontier. The following news item, for instance, appeared in the *Pennsylvania Gazette* in 1780, reporting the abduction of a prominent businessman and his entire family:

Philadelphia, May 3d. By a gentleman who arrived yesterday afternoon from Northampton County, we have the following disagreeable intelligence, viz.: On Tuesday morning, the 25th ult., Mr. Benjamin Gilbert's house and mill, on the Mahony, about 4 miles above Gnaden Hutten, 28 miles from Bethlehem, were burnt, and the whole family, viz.: Benjamin Gilbert and his wife, lately married, Andrew Huger, a daylabourer, and two or three persons going to the mill are either killed or carried off. Another son of Mr. Gilbert, with his wife and child, who lived half a mile higher up on the creek, are also missing, and his house burnt. Samuel Dodson's daughter, going that morning to fetch some meal, has not returned, and it is supposed that she fell into the hands of the murderers likewise. The families around them were ignorant of the whole until all was over; they saw the smoke, but as they knew Mr. Gilbert was clearing some land, they supposed the fire was from that; the barn was left, the horses gone, one bull and one cow stab'd and half burnt, the other cattle running in the fields. The report of but one gun was heard, which was in the house, and discharged itself in the fire.

Of this public notice the historian Frank Severance, writing in 1904, pointed out that "this abduction of a numerous and prominent family ocasioned little if any further comment in the press. It was war, and an expected condition of the times."[6] If the abduction itself generated little comment in the press, however, the story of the subsequent experiences of the Gilbert family members while in captivity was one that was eagerly awaited and widely consumed when it appeared in print in 1784 and in new editions in 1785, 1790, 1848, 1890, 1904, and 1975.

In 1780 Indian captivity was, if not a banal occurrence, at least a commonplace on the frontier. It should not be surprising that the newspaper notice had no lasting impact. News, like most human experience, is by its very nature ephemeral; it registers only briefly, then fades into a homogeneous sequence of similar events. An incident transformed into a story, though, comes to have human interest by its being opened to and imbricated in a shared discourse. In turning an abduction into a tale, the experience of one individual is linked to the life experiences of others. Walter Benjamin spoke to this point when he noted that "an experienced event is finite—at any rate, confined to one sphere of experience; a remembered event is infinite, because it is only a key to everything that happened before and after it."[7]

If abduction by Indians was a fairly common occurrence on American frontiers, this fact alone cannot explain the tremendous popularity of captivity narratives over the centuries. Readers were drawn to captivity tales because of the power the very idea of captivity held over them—a power composed of a mixture of fascination and dread. In order to understand something of this elemental fascination with captivity, we need to reflect on the situation a captive faced and the imaginal possibilities this offered (and offers) people.

Captives are human beings in extremis, that is, in situations of grave danger and heightened vulnerability. They are suddenly carried into an alien world and cut off from the normal support systems of family, friends, church, and the larger society in which they had lived. They are abruptly and rudely faced with an immediate threat not only to their physical survival but also to their psychological and sociocultural integrity and identity. Captives are confronted in an immediate and pressing manner with a series of critical issues concerning human existence that most people have to face only indirectly and over time. Tales of Indian captives provide other persons with a rare glimpse of humans forced to rely on their own abilities and resourcefulness in order to survive in an alien world.

Captivity represents an ultimate boundary situation where human existence, identity, and ultimate meaning are called into question as the captive's world is turned topsy-turvy and his freedom and autonomy are stripped from him, along with his social status, clothes, and other cultural accouterments and markers. Frequently the captive undergoes various forms of degradation, as he is reduced to abject poverty, subjected to great physical deprivation, extreme hunger, and psychological stress, and divested of all status and power. Among other things the captive is forced to confront and acknowledge the essential elemental needs of the human-body-as-boundary.

The phrase "body-as-boundary" as used here refers to the limiting condition that embodiedness entails phenomenologically. In many cultures (and certainly in the West) human existence and personal identity are fundamentally defined by the boundary marked by the surfaces of the body. Yet even in waking consciousness, we are often not fully aware of our bodies. In captivity, however, the human body is brutally brought to the attention of the captive as both the fragile container of life and, in the form of a corpse, as the cold, empty marker of death. In captivity (as in war) one's body is experienced in more fundamental ways than previously. In extremis, one becomes acutely aware of the body as the site of pleasure and of pain, of refreshment and exhaustion.

The body is also known more immediately than before as a boundary of fundamental exchanges: severe hunger and thirst reveal the integrity of the body to be fragile and dependent upon the intake of nourishment; at the same time, the body is experienced extruding blood, pus, bile, entrails, embryos, dashed brains, excrement, and vomit. Moreover, in the world of the alien Other, strange sights, sounds, odors, and tastes assault the captive's senses, while dreams, flashbacks, hallucinations, and uncontrollable screams, sighs, tears, and tremors emerge from inside.

In such situations, the body is a painful register of the shattered or porous boundaries of inside and outside, self and other, past and present. The body is seen and experienced as a boundary whose integrity is ever in danger of being violated by being pricked, slashed, gashed, crushed, clubbed, scratched, scalped, bitten, burned, penetrated, painted, scarred, and tatooed. As embodied persons, we normally experience pleasure and pain individually, yet captivity reveals that, because of the social nature of human beings, the case is more complicated and more ambiguous than it appears at first sight. The exposure of the body as a site of pain and suffering makes claims on others that are ontological, epistemological, and moral in nature. The power of Shylock's poignant appeal, "If you prick us, do we not bleed?" comes from this social extension of the body-in-pain.[8] I will return to this important topic and to the variety of ways in which the authors of captivity tales dealt with it.

In the extreme conditions faced by the captive, the body's potential for serving as a symbolic site also emerges into consciousness as new and unwelcomed power relations are inscribed on it through binding, scarification, scalping, mutilation, painting and through the bruises, blisters, and bleeding resulting from forced labor, forced marches, and beatings. Similarly, social differences (class, occupation, gender, age) are displayed through various cultural markings made on the body and in the myriad (and initially seemingly bizarre) cultural forms of presentation of the body. In these ways, the captive comes to know firsthand something of the politics of the body, for his body is transformed into a site that, to borrow Charles Long's pithy phrase, could be "signified upon" by others.[9]

For Europeans used to signifying the Other rather than being the object of signification themselves (and for whom this arrangement was assumed to be the natural order of things), the historical presence of so many captives and white Indians provided an important, albeit unsettling, cultural moment for reflection on these and related issues. For instance, the validity of the primitive-civilized dichotomy, so important to the Enlightenment, was called into question, especially when so many individuals reverted, both willingly and under duress, to savagery. The integrity of the individual as an ontological category was called into question by the presence of persons who had apparently undergone radical identity transformations on the frontier. The specter of environmental determinism (and, indeed, *avant la lettre*, cultural relativism) haunted the physical and imaginal space called America in the ghostly and ghastly figure of the white Indian.

The historical reality of Indian captivity, coupled with the very idea of captivity sketched briefly above, led to the composition of narratives dealing with the experiences of persons while with the Indians. When the captivity of Mary Rowlandson in 1676 or that of the Gilbert family in 1780 was narrated in written form, these captivities became more than mere incidents in history; they became stories. Such stories are never objective or neutral accounts; they are always structured and informed in specific ways in order to give a shape and a meaning to the captivity.

Yet, like all tales, those about captivity were not merely retrospective attempts to make sense of what had happened to an individual. Many of the narratives were designed to lead the reader to reflect on larger issues of the meaning of life. Moreover, at times captivity narratives also helped to shape the expectations of persons who had been captured as to what would happen to them while they were among the Indians. In this way, such texts informed the experience of captivity of these individuals. But, even more importantly, the experience of every person who was abducted was intertextually (or narratively) informed to a greater or lesser extent. Among the Puritans, captivity was an important metaphor used to describe the ontological and spiritual condition of humankind before the first New England Puritan was ever captured by Indians.

The continuing abductions of individuals on the frontier and the rich imaginal activity that took place around such captivities resulted in the composition and printing of a large number of narratives in the Euro-American world. The reason for this is at once obvious and profound: captivity tales allowed readers (and auditors) to reflect on deep existential issues: What does it mean to be human? What is the proper situation of human beings in the world? Telling these tales enabled people to enter imaginatively into an ultimate boundary situation. Part of the goal of *Captured by Texts* is to demonstrate how the reading practices earlier generations brought to bear on captivity narratives were part of a spiritual regimen of self-examination and moral improvement.

A modern checklist of American Indian captivity narratives compiled by the Newberry Library of items either based on fact or presented as factual accounts lists almost two thousand items published before 1880. If fiction were added, the number would be much greater. Scholars have long noted the importance of the captivity narrative in American literary history and its crucial role in initiating an American literature. Of the four best-sellers in America from 1680 to 1720, three were captivity narratives; the fourth was Bunyan's *Pilgrim's Progress.* A century later in the five-year period from 1823 to 1837, only four works sold over a hundred thousand copies—three novels by James Fenimore Cooper and James Everett Seaver's *A Narrative of the Life of Mrs. Mary Jemison* (1824).[10] The Cooper novels (*The Pioneers, The Last of the Mohicans,* and *The Prairie*) include captivity as part of the plot, while the Jemison story is a pure captivity narrative.

Thousands of captivity narratives, both factual and fictional, were published over the years, enjoying a wide readership on both sides of the Atlantic; some were reprinted many times. It has been suggested that the genre's popularity waned in the nineteenth century, but, as we shall see, this was hardly the case. To be sure, with the disappearance of the North American frontier, no more whites were being carried off in the aftermath of Indian raids; thus, new authentic captivities were no longer available. Yet even when Indian captivity was no longer a historical reality, it remained a popular theme in fiction and, more recently, has become so in film. Moreover, actual captivities are still found in the twentieth century, though the frontier has shifted to South America and the Amazonian rain forest. Captivity narratives have continued to be written, republished, anthologized, and recast in new forms for new audiences. The "White Indian Series" of popular Western novels published by Bantam Books, of which there are over twenty volumes, and the continuing popularity of the captivity topos in romance novels are indicative of captivity's remarkable staying power in our own century.[11]

Why this sort of tale rather than any other should have enjoyed such popularity over the centuries remains a problem to be more fully answered. Afterall, at their most basic level these narratives all tell the same tale—on the frontier someone (usually a white, occasionally a black) is captured and carried off into the Indian world. The details are to some extent different in each case (although it will be the stereotypical scenes and characters which will bear our attention below), yet the central story remains largely the same: the author or the protagonist is snatched from his or her home and forcibly carried off into an alien culture, into the world of the Other. There the captive undergoes a series of ordeals or adventures while living among the Indians and later escapes or is ransomed and returned to civilization. Occasionally the captive chooses to remain with the Indians permanently or for an extended number of years and his or her story is obtained by an interviewer.

So why, then, is it that captivity tales have enjoyed such remark-

able staying power over the centuries? A few preliminary suggestions based on the results of my own study may be offered. Clearly,
one of the sources of the sustained popularity of captivity narratives was people's desire to know what captives had done under
situations of great duress. How had they coped with the Job-like
sudden reversal in their fortunes? with the pain and the shock
accompanying the loss of family and friends? with isolation, alienation, and the fear of death? Similarly, many other readers wanted
to learn whether the Indians had abused the captives, taken sexual
liberties with them, or treated them kindly. In other words, it is
undeniable that in some instances readers read such tales because
they wanted to know what happened to the captives.

Yet in and of itself this element does not take us far toward explaining the persistence of the topos, since so many of the captivity narratives are filled with stereotypical scenes and characters.
Indeed, most works held out little or no suspense concerning what
happened; not only were many of the tales completely predictable,
the title pages frequently gave away the plot and the ending. Yet,
significantly, this apparently did not inhibit their sales; after all,
the title pages were designed to sell the work. Cumulatively, these
facts suggest that readers did not consume captivity narratives
primarily to obtain information. I suggest that, for a start, we take
the functions or uses of stereotypes in these works as a serious
subject for study, rather than using them as an excuse to dismiss
the works in which they are found as examples of bad literature. If
we abjure our responsibility as scholars and move on without
really studying the captivity narratives, we will miss other important aspects of the cultural work these texts performed.

In order to understand their significance, we need to take these
works as they are, warts and all, and to study how other readers
have read them. Rather than merely condemning the presence of
stereotypes, we need to study the ways stereotypical representations of Indians and others permitted authors to tell their stories.
In so doing, these writers were able to make specific claims on
their readers. In this regard, Jane Tompkins's point, made in connection with the sentimental novel, holds equally well for the
captivity narrative:

> The presence of stereotyped characters, rather than constituting a
> defect in these novels, was what allowed them to operate as instru-
> ments of cultural self-definition. Stereotypes are the instantly rec-
> ognizable representatives of overlapping racial, sexual, national,

ethnic, economic, social, political, and religious categories; they
convey enormous amounts of cultural information in an extremely
condensed form. As the telegraphic expression of complex clusters
of value, stereotyped characters are *essential* to popularly successful narrative. . . . Their familiarity and typicality, rather than making them bankrupt or stale, are the basis of their effectiveness as
integers in a social equation.[12]

Stereotypical characters and scenes carry an affective load as
well. Stereotypes convey value and information less through conceptual or intellectual forms than through their emotional color-
ing. Authors strategically employ a variety of different stereotypes
in order to manipulate and direct the responses of readers. This is
an important ingredient in the larger cultural work of the captivity
narrative.

It would be equally wrong to assume that the primary appeal of
captivity narratives was to the salacious appetites of readers. A few
works may have sought to titillate the reader (as do some Hollywood films), but from the seventeenth century down to the
present, the captivity tale has been viewed by both authors and
readers primarily as a vehicle of moral improvement or spiritual
instruction. For most readers, captivities were paradigmatic tales
of ordinary men and women dealing, often heroically, with seemingly impossible situations. The topos provided striking illustrations of the vicissitudes of life that allowed them to raise pressing
questions (and to offer answers to these) concerning theodicy, the
meaning of suffering, and identity.

Captured by Texts is a study in the history of religions, although
I hope to speak to students of literature and American cultural
history as well. As a historian, I will seek to understand the local
meaning of captivity for earlier generations of readers by recon-
structing the narrative strategies and structures informing specific
tellings, as well as the reading practices that informed the reception of texts of a given sort and the ways these reading practices
functioned in the lives of readers. Since we are dealing with a large
body of texts from over three centuries, it will be important to
trace the shared reading practices and the significant differences
among major reading communities over time.[13] Yet as important
as this task is (and I will devote considerable attention to it) the
work of the historian of religions is not finished when that has
been accomplished.

Many years ago Mircea Eliade wrote that in contradistinction to the historian, the sociologist, and the anthropologist, the historian of religions "is attracted to both the *meaning* of a religious phenomenon and to its *history*; he tries to do justice to both and not to sacrifice either one of them." For Eliade, "meaning" here referred to the general or fundamental meaning that informed yet transcended any individual historical manifestation of a religious symbol or rite. He went on to argue that, "the greatest claim to merit of the history of religions is precisely its effort to decipher in a [religious] 'fact,' conditioned as it is by the historical moment and the cultural style of the epoch, the existential situation that made it possible."[14] Our facts will be the various tellings and the structures of reception of captivity tales found over three centuries.

Captured by Texts is, then, a history of storytelling, a study of the narrative, representational, and reading practices used in making sense of captivity. It is also a historical inquiry into the making and remaking of meaning. Scholars (including myself) are themselves implicated in this history by the very nature of their own work and status as culturally and professionally authorized hermeneuts. Virtually all of the authorial voices we will hear are white voices. We do not have any texts that present in detail the perspective of Native Americans on the abduction of whites or on the existence of white Indians. Moreover, because almost all of the first-person narratives are told by returned captives, there is a dearth of information about the many persons over the centuries who decided to remain permanently with the Indians. We do, however, have Native American voices speaking on the spiritual value of storytelling. Thus, before beginning my own story of a specific tradition of telling tales, it may be appropriate to listen to a Native American on the importance of storytelling:

> I will tell you something about stories,
> [he said]
> They aren't just entertainment.
> Don't be fooled.
> They are all we have, you see,
> all we have to fight off
> illness and death.
> You don't have anything
> if you don't have the stories. . . .
> He rubbed his belly.
> I keep them here
> [he said]

Here, put your hand on it.
　See, it is moving.
　There is life here
　　for the people.
And in the belly of this story
the rituals and the ceremony
　　are still growing.
　What she said:
　The only cure
　I know
　is a good ceremony,
　that's what she said.[15]

Captured by Texts has been written in the hope that by exploring "the belly of this story," the history of its tellings and retellings, its lives in the lives of our ancestors and in our own, it might be possible to offer something more than entertainment in the modern sense of that term—something edifying.[16] Writing history and telling tales is one of the few ritual offerings academics like myself still know how to perform, but perhaps even in this humble sort of telling the ceremony will continue to grow.

1

THE CAPTIVATING TEXT:
THE MARY ROWLANDSON
NARRATIVE

THE FIRST Indian captivity narrative published in North America, that by Mary White Rowlandson (ca. 1635–1711), appeared in 1682.[1] It quickly set the tone and established the interpretative frame for most of the earliest narratives by imposing the then-prevailing Puritan version of Calvinist covenantal theology on the historical reality of captivity. It can tell us much about the Puritan worldview and ethos in which the text had its genesis. Read carefully, it can also tell us quite a bit about the reading practices of seventeenth-century Puritans.

Broadly, this chapter will demonstrate how the meaning of a text is socially determined. I shall be concerned with how this tale assumed the narrative form it did, how it found its way into the public sphere, how attempts were made to direct its reading in the late seventeenth century, and, finally, how its relationship to popular devotional texts and devotional practices would have affected its consumption. All reading communities are already intertextually constituted or molded and thus predisposed to engage texts in certain ways. Only when we have reconstructed the world of Rowlandson's text in the late seventeenth and early eighteenth centuries will we be prepared to appreciate the significance of the different ways the captivity topos has been re-presented and reinterpreted by diverse readers over the centuries.

The Seventeenth-Century Rowlandson Narrative

In the original preface to *A True History of the Captivity and Restoration of Mrs. Mary Rowlandson*, Mary is represented as having only reluctantly allowed her narrative to enter the public sphere of the printed word. Moreover, she never appeared in print again—a fact that long led scholars mistakenly to assume that she had died shortly before or after the publication of her narrative.[2] Understanding how and why this female-authored text found its way into print is crucial to our task of answering many of the questions posed earlier, as is the study of how later readers have engaged this narrative. It is, however, a futile exercise to attempt to recover its original or authentic voice, if by this we mean a single informing intention and consciousness that is then deployed as the norm against which later readings are judged.

The published narrative we have is most certainly not the original account of Rowlandson's captivity. To say this is not to suggest that the first edition was noticeably different from the second "corrected and amended" edition (something that it is impossible to know at any rate since no complete copy of the first edition has survived).[3] Rather, we must recognize that accounts of Mary's captivity circulated orally before the composition of her narrative as we know it. The events of Rowlandson's captivity were surely the subject of discussion, both public and private, long before Mary's narrative assumed its written form and was printed. Even during the time the captives were held, periodic reports of their movements and physical condition were conveyed to friends and relatives by "Praying Indians," including John Hoar, the negotiator who eventually gained Mary's freedom. These reports circulated orally in full or in part, sometimes in embellished form, and accompanied, no doubt, by a variety of comments and prognostications. Moreover, after her own return, Mary was certainly repeatedly asked to recount her experiences as a captive in different settings and to different audiences. Each of these audiences would have elicited a slightly different telling, based on factors such as whether the setting was formal or informal, the amount of time available, Mary's mood and energy at the time, and the composition of the audience. Subsequently, members of these various audiences no doubt recounted her tale to others in yet different forms and lengths and with different points of emphasis.

Different persons undoubtedly put their own spin on the tale, interpreting its meaning to their own audiences. As can be readily imagined, given the dramatic nature of the events surrounding the captivity, this process had the potential of getting out of control— out of control, that is, in the sense of generating conflicting (and for some persons, unacceptable) interpretations of what happened and why. The published narrative itself hints that this was indeed the case and that not all of the versions were complimentary in their depiction of this minister's wife.

Relatively few of the facts of the case were disputed. Those that were are minor and will not concern us here. Internal evidence in the Rowlandson narrative suggests, however, that some versions of what transpired between Mary and the Indian "chief" Metacomet, or King Philip, during her stay with the Indians included (not surprisingly, perhaps, given the human propensity to gossip) some rather scurrilous innuendos hinting of a sexual liaison. These whisperings had enough currency that Mary felt it necessary to counter them publicly by writing, "O the wonderful power of God that I have seen, and the experiences that I have had! I have been in the midst of those roaring Lions, and Salvage Bears, that feared neither God, nor Man, nor the Devil, by night and day, alone and in company, sleeping all sorts together; and yet not one of them ever offered the least abuse of unchastity to me, in word or action. Though some are ready to say, I speak it for my own credit, but I speak it in the presence of God, and to his Glory" (*Garland* 1:32).

Elsewhere, Rowlandson counters other gossip to the effect that while in captivity she had sent for tobacco for herself. The tobacco, she insists, was not for herself (though she freely admits to having been addicted to her pipe in earlier years), but was part of the ransom for herself and other prisoners. Below the surface of the narrative, then, one hears hints of other versions of what had happened in the wilderness that circulated in largely uncontrolled—and certainly unauthorized—form as gossip and whisperings. Even as the wife of a well-known minister (or, perhaps, precisely because she was a minister's wife), Mary was not immune from such innuendo.

In order to reconstruct something of the manner in which the published Rowlandson narrative was consumed in Puritan New England in the late seventeenth century, it is important to inquire, however briefly, into the status of publishing there and the role and status of authorship. In addition, we must consider a few of the various forms of cultural discourse through which the New England Puritan worldview was constructed, promulgated, and circulated. No complete copies of the first Boston edition of 1682 are extant, only four leaves having survived. Three copies of the second edition, published the same year in Cambridge, still exist, however. Either this edition or a London reprint has served as the basis of almost all scholarly discussions of the narrative and for the more than forty editions and reprints over the years.[4]

The second edition was entitled *The Soveraignty & Goodness of*

God, Together, With the Faithfulness of His Promises Displayed;
Being a Narrative Of the Captivity and Restauration of Mrs. Mary
Rowlandson. On the title page, this is followed by "Commended
by her, to all that desires to know the Lord's doings to, and dealings
with her. Especially to her dear children and relations. Written by
Her own Hand for Her private Use, and now made Publick at the
earnest Desire of some Friends, and for the benefit of the Afflicted."
This is followed in turn by a biblical passage: "Deut. 32.19. See
now that I, even I am he, and there is no God with me: / I kill and I
make alive, I wound and I heal[;] neither is there any can deliver out
of my hand."

The captivity narrative was published together with a sermon
by Mary's husband that, while not specifically referring to her
captivity and redemption, is clearly related to it. The decision to
publish these two texts together served to strengthen this linkage.
The sermon was announced on its own title page as "The possibility of God's forsaking a people, that have been visibly near &
dear to him; together, with the misery of a people thus forsaken,
set forth in a sermon, preached at Weathersfield, Nov. 21. 1678.
Being a day of fast and humiliation. By Mr. Joseph Rowlandson
Pastor of the Church of Christ there. Being also his last sermon."
The narrative and the sermon were also published under separate
covers, a fortuitous circumstance since two copies of the first
edition of the sermon have survived. We will examine this sermon
later in this chapter.

The publisher had advertised the Rowlandson narrative as forthcoming in the first American edition of Bunyan's *Pilgrim's Prog-
ress* in 1681 as follows: "Before long, there will be published two
Sermons . . . As also the particular circumstances of the Captivity,
& Redemption of Mrs. Mary Rowandson; and of her children.
Being pathetically written, with her own Hand."[5] The second
edition of the Rowlandson narrative was reprinted in London in
1682, where it was "sold by Joseph Poole, at the Blue Bowl in the
Long-Walk, by Christs-Church Hospital," under the title *A True
History of the Captivity and Restoration of Mrs. Mary Rowlandson, A Minister's Wife in New-England.* This was followed on the
title page by the advertisement—"Wherein is set forth, The Cruel
and Inhumane Usage she underwent amongst the Heathens, for
Eleven Weeks time: And her Deliverance from them. Written by
her own Hand, for her Private Use: And now made publick at the
earnest Desire of some Friends, for the Benefit of the Afflicted."
Over one thousand copies were published in the first year.

The differences between the title pages of the Cambridge and the London editions of 1682 offer significant clues to their different anticipated audiences. In Puritan New England, for instance, it was not necessary to identify Mary as the wife of a minister, since she was well known there. The London edition also highlights her cruel treatment at the hands of the Indians, while the Cambridge edition does not mention this, stressing instead the point that her captivity and redemption were to be understood as resulting from God's actions in history. The theological emphasis of the Cambridge title page is unmistakable, whereas the London edition stresses the veracity of the account (*A True History*).

In the seventeenth and eighteenth centuries the title pages of most texts were composed and designed by the publishers themselves, not by the authors. Since the publishers also marketed the books they produced (thus, the location where the books could be purchased or the names of sales agents were almost always listed on the title page), for economic reasons they had to determine the audience for a given work and then pitch it to this audience. In light of this, Amy Schrager Lang's characterization of the title of the Cambridge edition as "the apt if somewhat uninformative title *The Sovereignty and Goodness of God*" must be questioned.[6] If anything, this is a particularly explicit title that would have immediately tagged the text for late seventeenth- and early eighteenth-century readers. The title was the first of several textual elements that were designed to inform their subsequent reading of the narrative proper. This title signaled to the audience that the narrative offered more than a personal tale of suffering and woe; it promised a real-life illustration of the mysterious workings of God in New England. The biblical passage similarly functioned to suggest an appropriate metainterpretation for the events constituting the captivity narrative.

Mary had been captured, along with her children and some twenty others, in an attack on Lancaster, Massachusetts, on February 20, 1676.[7] She was ransomed almost twelve weeks later on May 2, 1676, for goods worth twenty pounds at a site that was to become known as Redemption Rock, in Princeton, Massachusetts. Thus, it was more than five and possibly even six years after her captivity that her narrative appeared in print on both sides of the Atlantic. The account assumed its narrative form and structure sometime in the interim. The fact that the narrative does not mention the death of Joseph Rowlandson in late November 1778 suggests that the text was probably finished before this date or at least had already left Mary's hands.

More important than pinpointing the time of composition, however, is gaining a fuller sense of the elements that influenced the text's narrative contours and its initial reception. Vaughan and Clark have noted that "Puritan authors wove the captivity narrative from several existing literary strands. One strand was spiritual autobiography. . . . A second source of inspiration . . . was the sermon. . . . Third, and perhaps most significant, the Puritan captivity narrative owed much of its tone and content to 'jeremiads'—those peculiar laments by Puritan clergymen (and, again, sometimes by laymen) that accused New England of backsliding from the high ideals and noble achievements of the founders, of God's evident or impending wrath, and of the need for immediate and thorough reformation."[8] These three literary forms do not exhaust the influences informing Puritan captivity narratives, however, for they participated in a broader cultural discourse.

In order to understand the social life of this text among Rowlandson's contemporaries, as well as the genres it participated in, we must approach the Rowlandson narrative not primarily as something new (i.e., as inaugurating a new genre, the captivity narrative), since this status could have been recognized only much later in retrospect, but rather as a text belonging (even if idiosyncratically) to a culturally recognized form of the time.

Charles Hambrick-Stowe has convincingly argued that originally Rowlandson's narrative was "a devotional exercise in the tradition of the journal and the spiritual autobiography, related to the discipline of meditative self-examination. The narrative was 'Now Made Publick at the Earnest Desire of Some Friends, and for the Benefit of the Afflicted.' This is the same rationale that was commonly given for publication of an individual's secret exercises as a devotional manual."[9] In other words, the narrative probably was initially composed for Mary's private use in devotional meditative practice but was subsequently offered to others for the same purpose.

By the employment of meditative practices popular in Christianity for centuries, readers were invited to enter imaginatively into the events and the experience of the captivity through an act of literary anamnesis. This is the key issue in any attempt to reconstruct how such texts were read and employed by Puritan readers. Consequently, it would be a grave mistake to ignore the clear indications that this narrative was intended primarily as a record of the author's spiritual experiences and as a goad to others to adopt similar religious practices and to assume a specific existential and moral stance in the world.

Modern readers are often too anxious to read this and similar texts as recording the author's shifting psychological states while in captivity, even though any discussion of psychology or personality in a modern sense would have been alien to people in this period.[10] Rowlandson's representation and interpretation of the events of her captivity and her affective responses to these were undertaken with a different purpose in mind, as can be garnered from her own words early in the narrative: "And that I may the better declare what happened to me during that grievous Captivity, I shall particularly speak of the several Removes we had up and down the Wilderness" (*Garland* 1:3).

Without some knowledge of Puritan language usage and the ways in which specific sorts of texts were employed in popular forms of devotional praxis, one would pass over such passages all too quickly by assuming, for instance, that "Removes . . . up and down the Wilderness" was merely a quaint way of referring to where Mary had traveled and the incidents that occurred during her captivity. This phrase refers to motion, of course, but to Rowlandson's contemporaries it also conveyed much more, as Hambrick-Stowe notes: "The seemingly off-hand phrase 'up and down' signals that the author is referring to the topos of spiritual pilgrimage, not to mere physical motion. More specifically, the phrase indicates the aimless futility of the movement of the pilgrim's soul before he or she finds the true path to salvation and to heaven."[11]

In the last sermon preached by Joseph Rowlandson, which was published along with Mary's narrative, Joseph pointed to God's "removal" of his affection, mercy, and gracious providence as the cause of the community's difficulties. Thus, in Mary's narrative the terms *remove* and *removal* should not be understood merely as archaic terms referring to the periods of forced movement, followed by periods of pause and the setting up camps. Readers familiar with Puritan rhetoric would have been primed to also hear the deeper sense of *removal* in Mary's text—God's affection had been removed or withdrawn. The growing sense of distance—both spatial and spiritual—the captive had experienced with each successive remove would also have been felt by the reader through the act of reading. The removes in this captivity narrative, which was composed (and presumably read) as a devotional text, traced out the pilgrimage of a soul through the process of reconversion and opening to grace. Given this, when Breitwieser interprets the phrase "we were hurried up and down in our thoughts" in exclusively psychological terms, he misinterprets it because he ignores or discounts Rowlandson's deliberate use of language.[12] In this case, she was clearly indicating that her narrative traced the vicissitudes of her spirit or soul, not only her mental condition.

We can understand how Mary—and, by extension, many of her original readers—used her narrative by paying close attention to her concluding statement:

> The Lord hath shewed me the vanity of these outward things, that they are the *vanity of vanities, and vexation of spirit;* that they are but a shadow, a blast, a bubble, and things of no continuance; that we must rely on God himself, and our whole dependence must be upon him. If trouble from smaller matters begin to arise in me, I have something at hand to check my self with, and say when I am troubled, It was but the other day, that if I had had the world, I would have given it for my Freedom, or to have been a Servant to a *Christian.* I have learned to look beyond present and smaller troubles, and to be quieted under them, as Moses said, *Exod. 14.13. Stand still and see the salvation of the Lord.* (*Garland* 1:36).

Rowlandson had her narrative of God's dealings with her, particularly during "the several Removes [she] had up and down the Wilderness," ready at hand for later times of spiritual trouble and unrest. Moreover, she offered this account of her afflictions and God's deliverance of her to others who might also be suffering.

We cannot understand what this text—or even this last phrase, for that matter—meant to the original audience if we read it in isolation, for any text is composed and consumed within a broader cultural discourse, an intertextual and narrative milieu. The meaning of the narrative to its original readers was not found below the surface of the text, but largely in the readily recognizable and stylized rhetorical patterns employed in telling the tale. Rather than summarily discounting these as patriarchal elements externally imposed on Mary's own narrative (i.e., by assuming that she had an authentic account she was not permitted to tell), I take these rhetorical patterns to be a key to unlocking the meaning of this text.

First I wish to note that the way the Rowlandson narrative was framed in a *material* sense that needs to be taken into account. Unfortunately, only a few of the recent modern editions of the narrative have reproduced the original preface that accompanied it, yet this preface provides invaluable insight into the reasons why the clergy promoted the Rowlandson narrative, how they intended it to be read and understood, and the reading practices most likely brought to bear on it. Even fewer versions have reprinted the sermon that followed the narrative.

In general, then, the events of Mary Rowlandson's captivity were not in dispute in the late seventeenth century; at issue and of much greater import was the *meaning* of these and related events. Mary's captivity came to have great communal significance for the Puritans because (1) it was narrated in an authoritative manner through a biblical interpretive frame (2) that transformed it into an exemplum for the entire community made available in the form of a devotional text (3) issued from a theocratically sanctioned press, complete with explicit guidance as to how it should be read and what the reader should gain from reading it. The particulars of the captivity were properly to be understood by subordinating the specific instance and personal narrative impetus to a larger covenantal account or metanarrative of God's intervention in New England history.

Rhetorical Structures and Strategies

Even a limited formal analysis of the text's rhetorical elements will permit us to see how Rowlandson gave order to what had befallen her in captivity. It is much more difficult to determine the extent to which the Puritan worldview affected her experience at the time since all we have to work with is her account, composed several years after the fact. Yet undoubtedly her experience was mediated by the Puritan *habitus,* in Pierre Bourdieu's sense of the term. Something of this may be glimpsed in several passages where Rowlandson's ongoing interpretive activity while in captivity is represented.

Rowlandson's first sentence temporally and spatially locates the events to be narrated, while introducing some of the actors. Cast in the historical past tense, it draws upon Mary's firsthand knowledge of the events, supplemented with additional information she had gathered later from others. With the third sentence, the scene and action are recreated as seen through the narrator's eyes, though she still retains some distance from the action: "On the tenth of February, 1675, came the Indians with great numbers upon Lancaster. Their first coming was about Sunrising. Hearing the noise of some Guns, we looked out; several Houses were burning, and the Smoke ascending to Heaven. There were five Persons taken in one House, the Father, and the Mother, and a sucking Child they knock'd on the head; the other two they took, and carried away alive" (*Garland* 1:1).

The focus in the next paragraph shifts to the attack upon Rowlandson's house; the scene and action are immediately before her eyes. After recounting how the Indians set the house on fire, she suddenly (and briefly) switches to the present tense: "Now is that dreadful Hour come, that I have often heard of, (in the time of the War, as it was the Case of others) but now mine Eyes see it. Some in our House were fighting for their Lives, others wallowing in their Blood; the House on fire over our Heads, and the bloody Heathen ready to knock us on the Head if we stirred out." Previously Indian captivity had been something known only at a distance and through hearsay. It was something that befell others, perhaps, but, as Rowlandson's use of the past tense suggests, for her it had been at a remove both temporally and spatially rather than a part of her world here and now. The sudden shift in verb tense jars the reader into the present of the scene unfolding through the author's act of recollection. The reader shares this horrific vision narratively conjured up by Rowlandson. (Shortly thereafter, when she has completed her account of the attack, she cites a biblical passage in the present tense, inviting the reader to "Come, behold the Works of the Lord, what desolation he has made in the Earth.")

As the second paragraph continues, Rowlandson provides her reader with the first hint that these events in the recent past were to be understood as something extraordinary. She does this by noting that a simple commonsensical expectation (when strangers approach the house, guard dogs bark and attack) had been violated. In order to explain this "remarkable" situation, she invokes the hidden presence (known only in retrospect) of a superagent (God), who had intervened in history in order to instruct the Puritan community: "We had six stout Dogs belonging to our Garrison, but none of them would stir, though another time, if an Indian had come to the Door, they were ready to fly upon him, and tear him down. The Lord hereby would make us the more to acknowledge his Hand, and to see that our Help is always in him. But out we must go, the Fire increasing, and coming along behind us roaring, and the Indians gaping before us with their Guns, Spears, and Hatchets, to devour us" (*Garland* 1:2).

This is an instance of an extremely important rhetorical strategy: when the natural order of things was apparently inverted or subverted, the Puritans often posited an unseen supernatural agent acting in history as the cause. Puritan providential theology, as propounded in sermons and written works, suggested that God often intervened in history in order to protect, chastise, or instruct his chosen people. Rowlandson's rescripting of the Indian attack, with God as a supernatural agent acting in history with a soteriological purpose, transforms the other apparent actors and agents (the Indians and watchdogs) into puppets or mere adjuncts to the agency of divine providence.

Rowlandson's assertion that God is the ultimate or final agent behind the events of her captivity frequently functions to deny the humanity of her captors. A few examples must suffice. Early in her captivity, an Indian gave Mary a Bible to read. In recounting this act of kindness, Mary ascribes it to God's goodness, not the Indian's: "I cannot but take notice of the wonderful mercy of God to me in those afflictions, in sending me a Bible: one of the Indians that came from Medfield fight and had brought some plunder; came to me, and asked me, if I would have a Bible, he had got one in his Basket, I was glad of it, and asked him, whether he thought the Indians would let me read? he answered yes: so I took the Bible" (*Garland* 1:7).

The operative English cultural understanding of the Indian-as-savage was summed up in the oft-repeated phrase used to describe them—"their tender mercies are cruelties." In a perverse manner the emplotment of the Indian-as-savage functions to deny that any acts of kindness by an Indian could be natural or in character. If and when such acts were performed by Indians, they were assumed by most Puritans to be unnatural; consequently, the Puritans tended to explain them away by asserting that God was the real actor behind the scene. This permitted the Puritans (and many persons in the following centuries as well) to retain their cultural or racial stereotypes intact.

Similarly, when Mary became lost in the woods but was not attacked by other Indians she happened upon, this "wonderful" fact is ascribed to God's intervention, while other acts of kindness are passed over in silence: "My Son being now about a mile from me, I asked liberty to go and see him, they bade me go, and away I went; but quickly lost my self, travelling over Hills and through Swamps, and could not find the way to him. And I cannot but admire at the wonderful power and goodness of God to me, in that though I was gone from home, and met with all sorts of Indians, and those I had no knowledge of, and there being no Christian Soul near me; yet not one of them offered the least imaginable miscarriage to me. I turned homeward again, and met with my Master; he shewed me the way to my Son." Or, yet again, when Mary was given shelter by an old Indian couple, this act of kindness is represented as unnatural or exceptional for such agents. If they acted in this manner, it was no doubt because God had made them do so (*Garland* 1:13, 15).

Alternatively, acts of kindness by Indians were often represented as duplicitous, that is, as apparent rather than real, insincere rather than sincere. During her captivity Mary had witnessed heartless acts of cruelty performed by Indians, including Praying Indians who had joined King Philip's force. She uses her status as an eyewitness, coupled with the operative emplotment of the Indian-as-savage, to charge that the Praying Indians back in Boston were impostors whose civilized demeanor and actions were little more than a facade. Their actions were not to be taken at face value because, according to the structural logic of the Indian-as-savage complex, which had been reinforced by her experience in captivity, such acts were definitely out of character.

The power of this demonization of the Indian was such that it could transform Rowlandson's experience of a scene. The following passage, describing nightfall on the first night of her captivity, is an example of this: "This was the dolefullest night that ever my eyes saw. Oh the roaring, and singing, and dancing, and yelling of those black creatures in the night, which made the place a lively resemblance of hell: And as miserable was the waste that was there made, of Horses, Cattle, Sheep, Swine, Calves, Lambs, Roasting Pigs, and Fowls (which they had plundered in the Town) some roasting, some lying and burning, and some boyling, to feed our merciless Enemies; who were joyful enough though we were disconsolate" (*Garland* 1:3).

Because the Indians were already demonized in Puritan eyes and rhetoric, their actions ("roaring . . . singing . . . dancing, and yelling") transform the woods and the night into "a lively resemblance of hell." Part of Rowlandson's disgust is also a result of what she takes to be the impropriety of the Indians' actions in stealing farm animals and then wasting the meat these provided in a wild orgy, rather than consuming them in a celebration of thanksgiving to God, the Great Provider. Moreover, in her eyes this was not even a proper burnt offering to God since the modes of preparation were mixed and anomolous—"some roasting, some lying and burning, and some boyling." Because the feast was so out of place, Rowlandson found the Indians' reactions that night to be equally inappropriate.

Rowlandson often ascribes a sudden change in her situation to her past acts. The Puritan theological understanding of sin and divine affliction was predicated upon this type of linkage. One example must suffice to represent many others. Mary recalls how on the third day of her captivity, she pondered why she should have found herself in captivity: "The next day was the Sabbath: I then remembered how careless I had been of Gods holy time: how many sabbaths I had lost and mispent, and how evilly I had walked in Gods sight; which lay so close upon my Spirit, that it was easie for me to see how righteous it was with God to cut off the threed of my life, and cast me out of his presence for ever. Yet the Lord still shewed mercy to me, and upheld me; and as he wounded me with one hand, so he healed me with the other" (*Garland* 1:4–5).

The Puritan understanding of divine providence was such that happenings of any sort could be ascribed to God's action in the world. Positive developments were instances of God's mercy; negative developments were instances of divine affliction. Yet if the Puritan religious anthropology held that human beings could never deserve God's mercy, nevertheless most Puritans believed that humans could evoke it through the agency of prayer or through ritual acts of humiliation. For instance, in one passage, Rowlandson recounts how, after she had been separated from her children, in answer to her prayer God let her know that her son was still alive (*Garland* 1:6). Here, as in many other instances, Mary acted out of an understanding of the efficacy of the agency of prayer, which was reconfirmed by the appearance of her son shortly thereafter. For Puritans, the agencies of prayer and Bible reading had predictive capacities. Moreover, by recurring to prayer and Bible reading for guidance, these forms of religious practice informed their daily expectations, actions, and reactions to events. It would not be too much to say that in large measure Puritan life was lived and interpreted through these ordering principles and practices.

Suffering, the Bible, and the Body

In captivity Mary experienced her body as a primary site of divine instruction through physical affliction, hunger, and fatigue. In seventeenth-century New England suffering was sometimes understood to be a sign of election, of divine concern for one's spiritual condition. If properly borne (and interpreted), suffering could be an agency of spiritual improvement. According to Mary's own account, her experience of suffering was mediated through Scripture at the time of her captivity, not only later as she sat down to compose her recollections. She writes, for example:

> Heart-aking thought here I had about my poor children, who were sacttered up and down amongst the wild Beasts of the Forest: my head was light and dizzy (either through hunger, or hard lodging, or trouble, or all together) my knees feeble, my body raw by sitting double night and day, that I cannot express to man the affliction that lay upon my Spirit, but the Lord helped me at that time to express it to himself. I opened my Bible to read, and the Lord brought that precious scripture to me, *Jer. 31.16. Thus saith the Lord, refrain thy voice from weeping, and thine eyes from tears, for thy work shall be rewarded, and they shall come again from the Land of the Enemy.* This was a sweet Cordial to me, when I was ready to faint; many and many a time, Have I sate down, and wept swetely over this Scripture. (*Garland* 1:8).

Here Rowlandson recognizes the extreme conditions she has endured as the immediate cause of her symptoms of physical distress, yet at the same time she always implies that God is the ultimate cause of her pain. In captivity her bruised, undernourished, and extremely fatigued body imposed its existence (and the critical contingency of this existence) onto her consciousness. Experientially, Mary came to know her body as a site of almost constant pain. Her body was present to her in an extraordinary sense and was a painful reminder of the radical limitations of the human condition. This lesson forced her attention back to her dependency on God ("The Lord hereby would make us the more to acknowledge his Hand, and to see that our Help is always in him") and to a reconsideration of the proper divine-human relationship. Most importantly perhaps, Rowlandson's bodily suffering led her to a deepened appreciation of the Puritan understanding of the human condition itself as a form of captivity, for not only was the spirit imprisoned in the flesh but the fallen nature of humankind left all persons captives of sin.

Rowlandson's concern in her narrative is not limited to her bodily pains, however. She also notes how these affected her mental condition, or "Spirit." An abiding concern is to forge a linkage between her experience of her body-in-pain, her shifting state of mind, and how her reading of the Bible affected her spirits and consequently allowed her to bear her afflictions. She seeks to witness to the ways in which specific reading and devotional practices affected her experience. In so doing, she seeks to encourage others to adopt the same practices and, more importantly, to adopt the same religious stance in the face of life's vicissitudes.

Rowlandson avers that the Bible was the most common source of comfort she found in captivity. Without it, her pain and suffering would have been meaningless and unbearable; simple recollection or musing on the past, and on her life before she was abducted, produced only deepened pain and anguish. Her reading practices, as she reports them, were consonant with those engaged in daily by many Puritans. Whenever possible during her captivity, she read her Bible, recited the Psalms, and prayed directly to God; when she was unable to read her Bible for whatever reason, she mentally recalled biblical passages which she then pondered over. When in her reading she came to a biblical passage, or "place," that seemed relevant to her situation, she would pause or rest there, seeking solace for her body and soul.

In Puritan understanding and practice, coming upon such a scriptural passage was taken to be a direct communication from God. Mary's conviction that the words of the Bible were immediately concerned with her situation was a source of great comfort to her, "a sweet Cordial," precisely because her suffering then had a meaning. She professes that in large measure she composed her narrative in order to recall—and thereby humbly to witness to— God's mercy in having shown her biblical passages that had helped to make her suffering meaningful and thus helped her to accept her situation. If we ignore or dismiss this element of authorial intention, we will miss a crucial dimension of the meaning of this text for Rowlandson and her contemporaries. Rowlandson writes, for instance:

> As I sate amongst [the Indians], musing of things past, my Son Joseph unexpectedly came to me: we asked of each others welfare; bemoaning our doleful condition, and the change that had come upon us: we had Husband and Father, and Children and Sisters, and Friends and Relations, and House, and Home, and many Comforts of this life: but now we might say as Job, *Naked came I out of my mother's womb, and naked shall I return, The Lord gave and the Lord hath taken away, blessed be the Name of the Lord.* I asked him whether he would read? he told me, he earnestly desired it. I gave him my Bible, and he lighted upon that comfortable Scripture, Psal. 118, 17, 18. *I shall not die but live, and declare the works of the Lord: the Lord hath chastened me sore, yet he hath not given me over to death.* Look here Mother, (says he) did you read this? And here I may take occasion to mention one principal ground of my

setting forth these few Lines; even as the Psalmist sayes, To declare
the works of the Lord, and his wonderful power in carrying us along,
preserving us in the Wilderness, while under the Enemies hand, and
returning of us in safety again. And his goodness in bringing to my
hand so many comfortable and suitable Scriptures in my distress.
(*Garland* 1:11)

Mary reports her first reading of Scripture after she had been
taken captive as having been immediately after she received a
Bible from an Indian. The scriptural passage she settled on then
was to prove determinative in her experience and understanding of
captivity, as well as her retrospective narration of the same:

I took the Bible, and in that melancholly time, it came into my
mind to read first the *28 Chapter of Deuteronomie*, which I did, and
when I read it, my dark heart wrought on this manner, that there
was no mercy for me, that the blessings were gone, and the curses
came in their room, and that I had lost my opportunity. But the Lord
helped me to still go on reading, till I came to Chap. 30. the seven
first verses: where I found there was mercy promised again, if we
would return to him, by repentence: and though we were scattered
from one end of the earth to the other, yet the Lord would gather us
to-gether, and turn all those curses upon our Enemies. I do not desire
to live to forget this Scripture, and what comfort it was to me.
(*Garland* 1:7)

It is instructive to take careful note of the biblical verses Rowlandson held onto as pertinent to her immediate situation. Deuteronomy 28:1–14 list the divine blessings promised if the people of
Israel obeyed Yahweh and faithfully fulfilled his commandments,
while verses 15–68 present the curses to be visited upon the
people if they failed to keep the commandments or otherwise
disobeyed the will of God. Verses 31–33 must have especially
struck Rowlandson as promised curses that had been realized in
her own situation, particularly after she witnessed the Indian
"waste" of "Horses, Cattle, Sheep" during her first night in captivity. These verses read:

[31] Thine ox shall be slain before thine eyes, and thou shalt not eat
thereof: thine ass shall be violently taken away from before thy face,
and shall not be restored to thee: thy sheep shall be given unto thine
enemies, and thou shalt have none to rescue them.
[32] Thy sons and thy daughters shall be given unto another people,

and thine eyes shall look, and fail with longing for them all the day long, and there shall be no might in thine hand.

[33] The fruit of thy land, and all thy labours, shall a nation which thou knowest not eat up; and thou shalt be only oppressed and crushed away.

The striking parallels point to the rhetorical intention behind Rowlandson's listing all of the livestock that had been taken and slaughtered before her eyes. The immediate parallels she saw proved the predictive powers of Scripture. Precisely insofar as Rowlandson understood her own captivity and suffering as "all these things . . . come upon" her, she could also anticipate that God would keep his further promises found in these verses. It is little wonder, then, that she found consolation in them. The opening seven verses of chapter 30, which she had found to be such a great source of comfort, read:

[1] And it shall come to pass, when all these things are come upon thee, the blessing and the curse, which I have set before thee, and thou shalt call them to mind among all the nations, whither the Lord thy God hath driven thee.

[2] And shalt return unto the Lord thy God, and shalt obey his voice according to all that I command thee this day, thou and thy children, with all thine heart, and with all thy soul:

[3] That then the Lord thy God will turn thy captivity, and have compassion upon thee, and will return and gather thee from all the nations, whither the Lord thy God hath scattered thee.

[4] If any of thine be driven out unto the outermost parts of heaven, from thence will the Lord thy God gather thee, and from thence will he fetch thee:

[5] And the Lord thy God will bring thee into the land which thy fathers possessed, and thou shalt possess it; and he will do thee good, and multiply thee above thy fathers.

[6] And the Lord thy God will circumcise thine heart, and the heart of thy seed, to love the Lord thy God with all thine heart, and with all thy soul, that thou mayest live.

[7] And the Lord thy God will put all these curses upon thine enemies, and on them that hate thee, which persecuted thee.

Passages of this sort, which report actual reading practices and the incidents that occasioned the reader's recurring to the Bible, are very important sources of data for historians of religions today. Among other things, they suggest how wrong it is to assume that the biblical verses that punctuate this and other Puritan texts were retrospectively imposed by a ministerial hand. The practice of reading the happenings in their daily lives through a biblical interpretive frame was very common among the laity for whom, like Mary, Scripture provided not only general guidance but immediate communications from God. Indeed, in a crucial sense, her first Bible reading in captivity was to determine and structure her experience and actions for the rest of her time among the Indians. The immediate parallels between the predictions found in Deuteronomy 28 and what had befallen Mary in the wake of the Indian attack on Lancaster no doubt seemed to her (and, after the publication of her narrative, to many readers) incontrovertible proof that God's hand of affliction was upon her and her community. The Puritans had long styled themselves, both rhetorically and emblematically, as *Judea capta,* but now, for Mary, this was no longer just an emblem or a metaphor—it was a punishing reality. The proof or validation of the aptness of this emblem was found in the suffering and affliction visited upon her body.

I have already had occasion to cite the passage where Mary recalls how the Indians had feasted on the domestic animals they had taken in their raid. This event was also predicted in Deuteronomy, as was the taking of captives, and the scattering of sons and daughters among unknown nations where the parents would lose track of them. A cynic might wonder whether Mary had not made up these events in order to create a fit with the biblical text, but the objective facts of the attack on Lancaster and her subsequent captivity were common knowledge and also verified by other sources. It is, however, no doubt the case that this scriptural text helped to determine what elements and details Rowlandson selected to record because they were held to be significant (that is, to have meaning beyond their mundane facticity).

A few examples must suffice to suggest the manner in which Deuteronomy 28 and 30 structured her text. The most basic parallel was, of course, the promise "Thou shalt beget sons and daughters, but thou shalt not enjoy them; for they shall go into captivity." Similarly striking, given Mary's situation in captivity, were verses 47–48: "Because thou servedst not the Lord thy God with joyfulness, and with gladness of heart for the abundance of all things; Therefore shalt thou serve thine enemies which the Lord shall send against thee, in hunger, and in thirst, and in nakedness, and in want of all things."

Rowlandson confesses in numerous places that before her captivity she had often taken the good things of life for granted rather than thanking the Lord for the blessings he had granted her. For instance, after recounting how delicious she had found a small piece of pork given to her, she writes, "I cannot but remember what a sweet, pleasant and delightful relish that bit had been to me, to this day. So little do we prize common mercies, when we have them to the full" (*Garland* 1:25). Her ongoing litany of the severe deprivations she had suffered was intended less to evoke sympathy for herself than to demonstrate that indeed God's wrath had been visited upon her and New England. Deuteronomy 28:65–66 had promised, "And among these nations shalt thou find no ease, neither shall the sole of thy foot have rest: but the Lord shall give thee there a trembling heart, and failing of eyes, and sorrow of mind. And thy life shall hang in doubt before thee; and thou shalt fear day and night, and shalt have none assurance of thy life."

Rowlandson clearly interpreted her pain and suffering through this biblical frame, yet we need to understand this fact in its fullness, specifically in terms of the ways in which it colored and informed her experience and her narrative activity. The events constituting her captivity, including her suffering and her survival, were held to be a "wonder," a direct result of God's "interposition" in history. As verse 46 had promised, "And [all these curses] shall be upon thee for a sign and a wonder, and upon thy seed forever." Thus, Mary's captivity was an event divinely designed to inspire astonishment and awe in the wider community.

At the same time, however, Rowlandson had not stopped reading her Bible at this point; she had continued until she found comfort in the promise of chapter 30 that the captives would be returned and their fortunes restored *if* they obeyed God's warning and kept his commandments. If the curses promised in Deuteronomy 28 had been realized in New England, then surely the promises of chapter 30 would also be fulfilled.

This understanding helps us to appreciate the paragraph immediately following that cited above, which provides further insight into actual reading practices among the captives. When another female captive, then in the final stages of pregnancy, told Mary that she was bent on attempting an escape, Mary prevailed upon this woman to read the Bible with her for divine guidance before acting:

> Now the *Indians* began to talk of removing from this place, some one way, and some another. There were now besides my self nine *English* Captives in this place (all of them Children, except one

Woman] I got an opportunity to go and take my leave of them; they being to go one way, and I another. I asked them whether they were earnest with God for deliverance; they all told me, they did as they were able; and it was some comfort to me that the Lord stirred up the Children to look to him. The Woman, *viz.,* Goodwife *Joslin* told me, she should never see me again, and that she could find in her heart to run away: I wisht her not to run away by any means, for we were near thirty miles from any *English* Town, and she very big with Child and had but one week to reckon: and another Childe, in her Arms, two years old, and bad rivers there were to go over, and we were feeble with our poor and course entertainment. I had my Bible with me, I pulled it out, and asked her, whether she would read; we opened the Bible, and lighted on *Psal. 27* in which Psalm we especially took notice of that, *ver. ult. Wait on the Lord, be of good courage, and he shall strengthen thine Heart, wait I say on the Lord.* (Garland 1:7)

Rowlandson no doubt found comfort in the fact that "the Lord stirred up the [captive] Children to look to him" because this was one of the prerequisites demanded in chapter 30 for the restitution of the captives.

It is important for us not to ignore the testimony in Puritan texts, such as this, that faith had a bodily effect on individuals, or, to put this another way, that faith affected a person's experience of human embodiment. The evidence suggests that the duress of captivity heightened an individual's awareness of the body-as-limit, while faith in the Bible helped individuals to bear physical and mental suffering by imposing meaning on it. In this situation of "tryal" and suffering, Puritan reading practices enacted a process of spiritual transformation that had an immediate impact on the experience of captivity. In seventeenth-century Puritan culture, when a person found himself in a time of trouble or doubt, picked up and read the Bible, and found a "place of comfort" therein, frequently his spirits were lifted, his doubts were assuaged, or he was better able to understand and to accept his suffering, thus transforming his original physical and mental condition.

With this recognition, we are now able to make an important claim based on our analysis so far: Puritan culture was constituted not only through the theological discourse of the clergy, but also (and more importantly) through a popular form of devotional practice that affectively reinforced the explanatory power of the larger providential discourse in the lives of the laity. Modern readers are sometimes too quick to dismiss the biblical interpretive frame in texts like this as awkward or heavy-handed impositions that repress the authentic voice of the author. Yet the fact that the religious reading and devotional practices of these people shared the same informing structure as the rhetoric they employed signals the presence of a strong worldview.

The devotional reading practices of the Puritans need to be recognized as ritual acts that came to constitute a part of the habitus of this culture. According to Pierre Bourdieu, "The habitus—embodied history—is the active presence of the whole past of which it is the product." Many Puritan texts of different sorts (spiritual diaries, devotional texts, conversion narratives) suggest that when a Puritan adopted a prayerful attitude upon opening a Bible, his or her bodily posture (inclined head, eyes closed, folded palms) was unconsciously assumed, based on the thousands of times this ritualized activity had been performed from childhood on. Moreover, this posture and attitude predisposed the individuals to patterned thought processes and to specific affective states. That is, these were more or less somatically invoked.[13]

Rowlandson's narrative includes repeated references to her private reading practices while in captivity. There are also a few references to communal reading with one or more other persons, such as the times she read the Bible with her son or with Goodwife Joslin. While Mary occasionally reports that biblical passages provided only partial or temporary comfort, she only reports one instance in which she could find none for an extended period of time. This came after a rapid series of disappointments and frustrations for her, as she began to despair of ever being rescued or ransomed:

> I asked them to let me go out, and pick up some sticks, that I might get alone, and pour out my heart unto the Lord. Then also I took my Bible to read, but I found no comfort here neither: yet I can say, that in all my sorrows and afflictions, God did not leave me to have my impatience work towards himself, as if his ways were unrighteous; but I knew that he laid upon me less then I deserved. Afterward, before this doleful time ended with me, I was turning the leaves of my Bible, and the Lord brought to me some Scriptures, which did a little revive me, as that *Isai. 55.8. For my thoughts are not your thoughts, neither are your ways my ways, saith the Lord.* And also that, *Ps. 37.5. Commit thy way unto the Lord, trust also in him, and he shall bring it to pass.* (Garland 1:16)

Even in those rare cases when Rowlandson could not find comfort in the Bible, she nevertheless thanks God that he had never allowed her spirits to sink so low that she had utterly despaired, taken God's name in vain, or contemplated suicide. She understood the vicissitudes of her day-to-day existence in captivity as God's chastening hand, but she never fails to point out that this was always followed by his healing and uplifting hand.[14] Through her devotional practices, including Bible reading, prayer, and self-scrutiny, Mary simultaneously felt (both in terms of mental assent to the proposition and somatically) the bodily and mental fatigue and pain caused by each successive physical "remove" farther into the wilderness as God's temporary removal of his divine grace and mercy. She knew God's chastening rod in the bruises and the beating her body had taken, but felt that she was in part responsible for what had befallen her: "Now had I time to examine all my wayes: my Conscience did not accuse me of unrighteousness toward one or another: yet I saw how in my walk with God, I had been a careless creature. As David said, *Against thee, thee only have I sinned:* and I might say with the poor Publican, *God be merciful unto me a sinner*" (*Garland* 1:18–19).

If Mary's reading of the Bible informed her understanding of her physical and mental condition, however, it is equally the case that the physical afflictions she suffered informed her reading and understanding of the Bible. Only through having suffered did she come to appreciate the full meaning of certain biblical passages. As she notes in an elliptical remark to her reader after recounting the transformation wrought in herself by her experience of extreme hunger: "And now could I see that Scripture verified (there being many Scriptures which we do not take notice of, or understand till we are afflicted)" (*Garland* 1:20).

This important dialectical relationship between the captive's reading of the Bible and her experience of her body in captivity needs to be recognized. A major theme of Rowlandson's narrative is how through her suffering she came to appreciate fully the fallen nature of humanity, her own unworthiness and failings, the vanity of the things of the world, and the emptiness (or gaping maw) lurking behind the false sense of security produced by the material comforts of the world. Her own captivity taught her that when subjected to extreme hunger and deprivation, men and women became animallike—greedy, selfish, ravenous, irrational, unfeeling, and undiscriminating. Mary reports that she had not only become swinelike, willing to eat any scrap that came her way, but also had been reduced to being a "ravenous beast" herself. She also freely confesses that extreme hunger had at times transformed her from being a caring mother and a minister's wife into a cold-hearted, unfeeling, and rapacious person. She had learned first-hand how fragile the line between civilized and savage was. While extreme hunger could lead to degradation and the suspension of any moral sense in the rudimentary fight for survival, physical deprivation and suffering could also lead to a fuller appreciation of biblical truths that had earlier seemed remote and little more than words on a page:

> I cannot but think what a Wolvish appetite persons have in a starv-ing condition: for many times when they gave me that which was hot, I was so greedy, that I should burn my mouth, that it would trouble me hours after; and yet I should quickly do the same again. And after I was throughly hungry, I was never again satisfied. For though sometimes it fell out, that I got enough, and did eat till I could eat no more, yet I was as unsatisfied as I was when I began. And now could I see that Scripture verified (there being many Scrip-tures which we do not take notice of, or understand till we are afflicted) *Mic. 6.14. Thou shalt eat and not be satisfied.* Now might I see more than ever before, the miseries that sin brought upon us. (*Garland* 1:19–20)

Here Rowlandson recounts the terrible awareness of the radical contingency of her existence that extreme hunger had forced upon her. This realization haunted her thereafter; even when she had a full stomach, she was forever denied any sense of satisfaction, for the radical uncertainty of the future had transformed her present into a hollow void. This emptiness could not be filled by physical sustenance any more because a full realization of the ultimate contingency of human existence, marked by the elemental needs of the body, had brutally imposed itself on her consciousness. All of the cultural accruements and confident self-images Rowland-son had once possessed had been shown to be as hollow and empty as her stomach in captivity.

The last passage cited above continues with a biblical verse that encapsulates the operative dialectical relationship found in Pu-ritan society between the practice of Bible reading and how an individual bore the pains of living in the world—God instructs through the Bible and through physical and sensory experience, with each informing the other: "Many time I should be ready to run out against the Heathen, but that Scripture would quiet me again, *Amos 3.6. Shall there be evil in the City, and the Lord hath not done it?* The Lord help me to make a right improvement of his word, and that I might learn that great lesson, *Mic. 6.8,9. He hath shewed thee, O Man, what is good; and what doth the Lord require of thee, but to do justly, and love mercy, and walk humbly with thy God? Hear ye the rod, and who hath appointed it"* (*Garland* 1:20).

The result of this knowledge for Mary Rowlandson, as she witnesses to in her narrative, is that thereafter the world is forever turned upside down. Things that once satisfied her now were seen to be empty, false, or unreliable sources of comfort and security; in times of distress, things that once were disgusting become desirable and actions that earlier were unthinkable become doable. As she notes of the tough horse foot she literally snatched from a child's mouth, "That I may say as Job, Chap. 6.7. *The things that my Soul refused top touch are as my sorrowful meat.* Thus the Lord made that pleasant and refreshing, which another time would have been an Abomination" (*Garland* 1:21).

For persons in dire straits and facing starvation, food is a primary interest. Not surprisingly then, food is one of the most common concerns punctuating this narrative. For our purposes, however, it is the significance (or the absence of it) Mary finds in food as she narrates her captivity that is of import. Following their abduction, she and her youngest child had "not the least crumb of refreshment that came within either of our mouths, from Wednesday night to Saturday night, except only a little cold water." Even when she was finally offered food, she initially found it unpalatable, but this too changed: "The first week of my being among them, I hardly ate any thing; the second week I found my stomach grow very faint for want of something; and yet 'twas very hard to get down their filthy trash: but the third week (though I could think how formerly my stomach would turn against this or that, and I could starve and die before I could eat such things, yet) they were pleasant and savoury to my taste" (*Garland* 1:2, 9).

This is the first of many times when Rowlandson recalls how extreme hunger had caused all of her inhibitions to fall away, while formerly disgusting items became "savoury" and highly desirable. She recalls ravenously consuming semiraw horse liver a few days later, noting, "For to the hungry Soul every bitter thing is sweet." Mary learned that in extremis, culture and cooking were expendable luxuries. As a "bruit-Creature," she came to appreciate bear meat and bear grease, among other things. Food became a constant reminder to Mary of her animal nature, but, significantly, she also accepted whatever came her way as a blessing from God, even if it was but a moldy biscuit (*Garland* 1:10, 13, 19). She explains the fact that the moldy biscuit sustained her existence as evidence of God's grace. For her, God had the power to transform the meanest object into a blessing and an aid to those in distress. While recognizing that her desire to live drives her to eat things she never would have touched before, Mary finally backs away from simply declaring that humans can and will do anything in order to survive. Instead, she presses on to maintain that it was God who had sustained her. It could be argued that this rhetorical move merely keeps her from having to face the truth, but to hold this position requires one largely to ignore the extent to which she inhabited (and had incorporated) the Puritan worldview. That is, one would have to argue that her real experience was outside or independent of the Puritan world of meaning, something that is unacceptable.

For the moment we must content ourselves with Rowlandson's own narrative representations. One time, she recalls, an Indian "gave me also a piece of the Ruffe or Ridding of the small Guts [of a horse], and I boiled it on the coals; and now may I say with *Jonathon, See I pray you how mine eyes have been enlightened, because I tasted a little of this honey, 1 Sam. 14.19.* Now is my Spirit revived again: though means be never so inconsiderable, yet if the Lord bestow his blessing upon them, they shall refresh both Soul and Body." In Mary's mind it was not surprising that Indians ate the disgusting and raw things that they did and even enjoyed such "trash"; they were savages, after all. But that *she* was able to consume such things was remarkable—that is, worthy of notation and requiring an explanation. She seems to have been less willing, however, to accept the possibility that Praying Indians could have scruples similar to hers or that they, too, should recur to the Bible for guidance in the same manner she did. She apparently did not believe that a real conversion by Indians was possible (*Garland* 1:21, 23).

Just as physical, mental, and spiritual pain and suffering could be agencies of divine instruction, so could the act of retrospective narration. "The Lord help me to make a right improvement of his word" was Mary's prayer as she composed her account, a "right improvement," or interpretation, being one that recognized the *real agent* acting in history, the ever-present *agencies* of divine providence and grace, operating even in the form of affliction, and the final purpose behind the unfolding of this covenantal history.

The final message of Rowlandson's narrative is that through her captivity she has seen the hand of God in all that has transpired, leaving her in a state of religious awe and astonishment before the terrible vision. This vision haunts her day and night. When she conjures it up narratively, she does so that it might serve as a cautionary tale for herself and others. The conclusion to her narrative is worth quoting at length. Of special interest is the admission that she had earlier misinterpreted an aspect of Puritan providential theology and had foolishly wished for divine affliction:

> Before I knew what affliction meant, I was ready sometimes to wish for it. When I lived in prosperity; having the comforts of this World about me, my Relations by me, and my heart chearful: and taking little care for any thing; and yet seeing many (whom I preferred before my self) under many trials and afflictions, in sickness, weakness, poverty, losses, crosses, and cares of the World, I should be sometimes jealous least I should have my portion in this life; and that Scripture would come to my mind, *Heb. 12.6. For whom the Lord loveth he chasteneth, and scourgeth every Son whom he receiveth:* but now I see the Lord had his time to scourge and chasten me. The portion of some is to have their Affliction by drops, now one drop and then another: but the dregs of the Cup, the wine of astonishment, like a sweeping rain that leaveth no food, did the Lord prepare to be my portion. Affliction I wanted, and Affliction I had, full measure (I thought) pressed down and running over: yet I see when God calls a person to any thing, and through never so many difficulties, yet he is fully able to carry them through, and make them see and say they have been gainers thereby. And I hope I can say in some measure, as *David* did, *It is good for me that I have been afflicted.* (*Garland* 1:35–36)

Tears and the Wine of Astonishment

In Rowlandson's text human beings are described as being in need of both bodily and spiritual refreshment and rest. I have highlighted the ways in which the body, food, suffering, and various devotional practices are woven into the fabric and design of this narrative. Now we will turn briefly to a consideration of a related symbolic complex of affliction: tears, bread, and wine. All three are found in the concluding and climactic passage cited above, where Mary speaks of the divine affliction she has known as "the dregs of the Cup" and "the wine of astonishment," while she also speaks of bread and tears.

Bread and wine are, of course, basic Christian symbols found in the Eucharist. Rowlandson plays on the essential correlations of bread-body and wine-blood, although here they do not refer to the body and blood of Christ but rather are brought into the profane world. Bread represents the basic food that sustains life (or the body) in the civilized world, as well as the material goods and comforts Rowlandson had enjoyed in New England before her abduction and again after her redemption. Bread is also what she lacked in captivity. As noted earlier, when she had enjoyed "bread" to the fullest, Rowlandson was unaware of her creaturely nature in important ways. Thus, she could even be jealous of those neighbors who suffered and yet patiently bore various afflictions. When the Indians fell upon Lancaster, however, sweeping her away and smashing her previous social world to bits, she was rudely forced to learn two related lessons: bread sustained the physical body, but was insufficient for *human life,* which required the acceptance of the real limitations of the human condition, the full recognition of the power, sovereignty, and goodness of God, and, as a result of conjoining these two, the restoration of a proper divine-human relationship. In Rowlandson's case, she came to this realization through a dialectical reading of her body in extremis and the Bible.

Rowlandson describes her experience of the body as "the dregs of the cup" of divine affliction filled with "the wine of astonishment." She is caught up short by the experience, overcome with the awe and astonishment of encountering God that Kierkegaard would later describe in *Fear and Trembling* and Rudolph Otto in *Das Heilige.* Thus, both *bread* and *wine* are related to the term *affliction,* with its dual references to biblical theology and physical and mental suffering. But Rowlandson also appeals to the metaphor of wine when she speaks of certain comforting biblical passages as "a cordial." Bread and wine are related to comfort through the promise of divine blessings that would follow the people's return to a proper covenantal relationship.

Tears are less obvious symbols in this complex, but are intimately related. Mary mentions tears (her own and the tears of others) several times in her narrative. By noting the first few references to tears we may begin to appreciate the different varieties of tears Mary recognized and their moral implications for her. The first such mention is found in the report that the Indians would not let Rowlandson meet with her daughter, because the girl cried whenever she saw her mother. These are tears provoked by the sundering of a basic familial relationship.

The next reference to tears occurs when Rowlandson summarizes eyewitness accounts from the children in captivity to the effect that when Goodwife Joslin, then in the last stages of pregnancy, was tortured and eventually killed, she had shed no tears but had prayed constantly. Here the absence of any outward signs of fear is taken to be a remarkable sign of the power of faith. Following these references, Mary speaks, in a passage introduced earlier, of her own bruised, bloody, and aching body and of the deep spiritual affliction she had known. "I cannot express to man the affliction that lay upon my Spirit, but the Lord helped me at that time to express it to himself. I opened my Bible to read, and the Lord brought that precious Scripture to me, *Jer. 31.16. Thus saith the Lord, refrain thy voice from weeping, and thine eyes from tears, for thy work shall be rewarded, and they shall come again from the land of the Enemy.* This was a sweet Cordial to me, when I was ready to faint; many and many a time have I sate down, and wept swetely over this Scripture" (Garland 1:8).

At first glance Mary may seem to be inconsistent in this passage, for while the biblical verse she cites recommends against weeping, she reports having often shed tears in response to reading this verse. Perhaps the most important occasion of this was when her son and daughter were freed and returned to her. At that point Rowlandson cites this same biblical passage again with the words "now hath God fulfilled that precious Scripture, which was such a comfort to me in my distressed condition. When my heart was ready to sink into the Earth (my Children being gone I could not tell whither) and my knees trembled under me, and I was walking through the valley of the shadow of death: then the Lord brought and now has fulfilled that reviving word unto me" (*Garland* 1:6, 8, 31–32).

There is a crucial difference between the two types of tears she mentions, however. The former are tears of despair, fear, or frustration shed when a person sees no way out of a distressing situation; the latter are tears of joy and of anticipation of the fulfillment of promises found in Scripture. The latter are shed in joy—and, at times, in fear and trembling—when one has recognized God's power, sovereignty, and goodness and placed one's faith completely in the agency of divine grace, whereas the former tears are pathetic, shed because human agency has proved incapable of saving oneself.

In her narrative Rowlandson implicitly draws a contrast between two attitudes adopted in the face of death. The former is represented by Goodwife Joslin, who faced death calmly in prayer; the latter by one Thomas Read. She writes, "About this time [the Indians] came yelping from *Hadly,* having there killed three *Englishmen,* and brought one Captive with them, *viz. Thomas Read.* They all gathered about the poor Man, asking him many Questions. I desired also to go and see him; and when I came he was crying bitterly: supposing they would quickly kill him. Whereupon I asked one of them, whether they intended to kill him? he answered me, they would not: He being a little cheared with that, I asked him about the welfare of my Husband" (*Garland* 1:16).

Clearly, Rowlandson holds up Goodwife Joslin as the model for emulation. Tears, then, are to be judged by noting what has evoked them or, at times, what has led to their not being shed. This is not always easy to do, however, because there are times when it is difficult to identify the cause of tears. Mary recalls the first time she had shed tears in front of her captors, which occurred only in the third week of her captivity, when her "heart began to faile." By comparing these tears with the others represented in the text, it becomes clear that she intended her readers to see the difference between tears shed in fear and despair and the tears she describes at the conclusion of her narrative, which she suggests are akin to those shed by King David at night on his couch. These latter tears are a form of ritual weeping and of communication with God. They are not tears shed in despair or anxiety over the future, but tears shed out of the deep knowledge of God's power and goodness, tears of gratitude that God's awesome power had not been exercised fully on the sinner. They are the tears of someone who has glimpsed the face of God behind the veil.

Having looked at some of the internal rhetorical structures and symbolic complexes informing the Rowlandson narrative, we may now turn to a consideration of the two texts that framed the narrative proper—the Preface to the Reader and the last sermon preached by Joseph Rowlandson. These texts served as explicit reading guides for the original generation of readers of Mary's captivity tale. As such, they are important sources of information as we try to reconstruct the world of the text and the reading practices brought to bear on it.

The Preface to the Reader

The preface to the narrative proper appears to have been written by one of the "friends" who urged Mrs. Rowlandson to permit its publication. An emerging consensus among scholars points to none other than Increase Mather as the author. The author's precise identity is less important, however, than the fact that he was most likely a member of the clergy, the group whose permission and active support were necessary if the work were to be published in New England. The preface occupies just over three-and-a-half pages of print in the second edition.

The opening of this preface briefly rehearses the military situation in King Philip's War in the week before the attack on Lancaster. In its representation of the historical agents involved, both the colonial troops and the Narraganset Indians are portrayed as having acted out of rational motives. The Indians, who in Puritan writing were often subject to a typologization that denied them any rationality, are said to have retreated "for fear of the English army lying in their own country." When access to their stored food had been cut off, they quite rationally came to see the undefended town of Lancaster as a site where provisions might be obtained with a minimum amount of risk. Similarly, through the open discussion of strategy, the colonial Council of War "consider[ed] what was best to be done," although the author pointedly suggests the unfortunate consequences of misguided human reasoning—"The consequent whereof, as it was not difficult to be foreseen by those that knew the causeless enmity of these Barbarians against the English, and the malicious and revengeful spirit of these Heathen; so it soon proved dismal" (*Garland* 1:2A).

There is no hint here in the opening that a divine hand had been controlling the actors in these events. This is, I think, by design, for by holding the providential interpretive frame in abeyance at this point, the writer is able to sketch with swift strokes a mundane (i.e., this-worldly, or profane) view of the historical situation in New England in 1675, but it is a view that is subsequently to be shown to be superficial and egocentric, rather than of "pious scope." The opening is, thus, filled with the sort of historical detail and human motives one might find in a secular military account, such as that by Benjamin Church (1716). The beginning has none of the exegetical insistence of Increase Mather's *A Brief History of the War With the Indians in New-England* (1676) or *An Earnest Exhortation To the Inhabitants of New-England, To hearken to the voice of God in his late and present Dispensations* (1676).[15]

In the second paragraph the focus shifts suddenly from the general situation to the specific manner in which the family—and most especially the "precious yoke-fellow"—of the Reverend Joseph Rowlandson became embroiled in the war, a turn of events labeled the "most solemn and remarkable part of this Tragedy." The focus at this point is on Joseph Rowlandson, even though he was absent at the time of the attack on Lancaster. It is through his eyes that the reader first returns to see "the Town in flames, or smoke, his own house being set on fire by the Enemy . . . and all in it consumed," his family killed or carried into captivity.

This calamitous turn of events demonstrates the truth of the moral lesson that "all things come alike to all" and that " 'Tis no new thing for Gods precious ones to drink as deep as others, of the Cup of common Calamity; take just Lot (yet captivated) for instance, beside others." However, Per Amicum argues that it is also true that not all suffering is equally remarkable. This tale of suffering and woe—or, better, of divine affliction—is of special significance for the whole Christian community precisely because it is "a Narrative of the wonderfully awful, wise, holy, powerful, and gracious providence of God," operating in and through the affliction visited upon the Reverend Mr. Joseph Rowlandson and his wife. The events surrounding this family's trials and suffering, as opposed to the similar tragedy that had befallen other families in Lancaster, represent a remarkable instance of divine dispensation "not to be forgotten, but worthy to be exhibited to, and viewed, and pondered by all" because of the social position of Joseph Rowlandson and then (and only then) relationally of his wife. "It was a strange and amazing dispensation," Per Amicum declares, "that the Lord should so afflict his precious Servant, and Handmaid." They are "as the apple of [God's] eye, as the signes upon his hand, the delight of his eyes, and the object of his tenderest care" (*Garland* 1:3A).[16]

Significantly, while acknowledged as the author of the narrative, Mary is never mentioned by name in the preface. As far as Per Amicum is concerned, her public persona comes only through her husband. This view of the situation was seemingly held from the beginning. In his diary on February 10, 1676, the day Mary and her children were taken captive, Increase Mather wrote: "A dismal providence this day. Lancaster was set on by Indians. Mr. Rowlandson pastor of the church there. His house was assulted. The Lord now speaks solemnly to ministers, inasmuch as a minister's family is fallen upon, and his wife and children taken by the enemy." On May 3 he noted: "This day Mrs. Rowlandson was, by a wonderful hand of Providence, returned to her husband, after she had been absent eleven weeks in the hands of the Indians."[17]

In the captivity narrative proper, there is no description of Joseph Rowlandson's mental state when he returned and saw his home destroyed and his family members killed or scattered other than one report Mary received that her husband was melancholy. And yet Per Amicum would have his readers take full note of the way God had borne up both Joseph and his wife, as he argues that "it was as strange, if not more, that [God] should so bear up the spirits of his Servant under such bereavements, and of his Handmaid under such Captivity, travels, and hardships (much too hard for flesh and blood) as he did, and at length deliver and restore. But he was their Saviour" (*Garland* 1:A3). While later readers of the captivity have focused almost exclusively on Mary's response to her captivity, the original audience was directed to consider the husband's as well.

We may presume that many members of the New England audience either knew Joseph Rowlandson personally or at least by reputation. His response to the events was felt to be an important part of the larger story, the metanarrative of God's dealing with the Puritan community. While today we do not know what his immediate response was, the New England audience of 1682 would have had this within living memory. Moreover, Per Amicum's association of the biblical figure of Lot with Joseph would suggest that he left the scene of devastation and, without looking back (that is, without questioning God's providence), returned to Boston, where he once again took up his ministerial calling.

Breitwieser has, with particular acuity, pointed to the fact that the preface was intended to be an illustration of "the proper manner of reading" both the captivity narrative and history. He misses, however, the way in which Per Amicum (and Mary herself) seek to employ the well-known meditative technique known as "the composition of place," found in both Catholic and Protestant practice, in describing the scene of the attack. At the same time, he also makes too much of what he takes to be "the usefully maladept type of Lot's captivity" invoked by Per Amicum.[18] Yet this choice of an emblem is apposite, given Per Amicum's goals. One should not expect an exact fit in all details between the biblical story and the Rowlandson case any more than one should in the Puritan use of emblems and typology in general, but it is important that one not forget that Joseph and Mary Rowlandson were themselves emblems for the Puritan community at large. It is inadvisable to view the correspondence between the story of Lot and his wife as having been drawn exclusively with the fate of these two individuals. To understand this better, let us recall the wider context of this biblical narrative because this context would have informed the 1682 audience's intertextual reading of the captivity.

In Genesis 12, Yahweh tells Abram to leave his home and go to the land he will show him. He is accompanied by his nephew, Lot, and their families and servants. The Puritans identified their own emigration to the New World with this exodus and New England with Canaan. In Genesis 13, Abram and Lot separate, as the land between Bethel and Ai can no longer support them both. The movement of some Puritans from the old towns of Plymouth Bay and Boston to outlying areas, where new communities, such as Lancaster, were founded, paralleled this situation. It seems likely that the events recounted in Genesis 14—concerning surrounding enemies having formed new coalitions and initiated warfare in which Lot's family was swept up—would have suggested immediate parallels with the Indian-Puritan situation in the 1670s, and especially that found in the newer outlying towns. Verses 11–12 would have been called to the reader's mind by Per Amicum's explicit allusion to Lot: "The conquerors seized all the possessions of Sodom and Gomorrah, and all their provisions and made off. They also took Lot (the nephew of Abram) and his possessions and made off." In the Genesis account, of course, Abram gathers his own troops and pursues the enemy until he defeats them, rescuing Lot and his family and servants, just as the colonial troops pursued and eventually defeated Metacomet (King Philip), Weetamoo, and their people.

In the Bible, the Genesis narrative concerning Lot is then interrupted until chapter 19 by the story of God's covenant with Abram. That this crucial section comes in the middle of the story of Lot would not have been lost on the first readers of the Rowlandson text, since their own collective identity was based on a revisioning of the covenantal relationship to God in terms of their own community. For the Puritans, then, the allusions to Lot and his wife would have seemed quite apropos, suggesting a sacred history unfolding in New England.

Other parallels would have also suggested themselves. Like Lot's children and sons-in-law, the inhabitants of Lancaster had been forewarned of trouble, yet they had not fled and consequently suffered equally dismal consequences. Events overtook them while Joseph Rowlandson was in Boston seeking armed reinforcements. And if Lot was spared in the general destruction because God kept

Abram and his covenant in mind (v. 29), perhaps Joseph had not been taken and killed when Lancaster fell for similar reasons. Perhaps it was divine providence that had led him out of harm's way to safety in another town. Mary's citation of Psalm 46:8 as commentary on the scene of carnage is telling: "Come, behold the Works of the Lord, what desolation he has made in the earth." The bullets that had rained on Lancaster had been sent by God and the resulting scene of destruction was a message and warning to be pondered on.

When the larger biblical narrative context is taken into consideration, the parallel between Lot and Joseph drawn by Per Amicum does not seem awkward or forced. Functioning as a background text, it effectively foregrounds certain elements of the Rowlandson captivity narrative, while others are relegated to the shadows. Just as the Genesis account does not provide any information concerning what was in Lot's mind after the destruction of his home and family or the transformation of his wife into a pillar of salt, both Per Amicum's preface and the Rowlandson narrative proper leave Joseph's state of mind to the reader's imagination. On the other hand, Mary's account is a sustained testimony of what went through her mind throughout her captivity, tracing all her ups and downs, recurring doubts, and renewals of faith and hope. If Mary identifies herself with Lot's wife, she is Lot's wife with her voice and subjectivity restored along with her life. While guilty of sin, as all human beings are, and, thus, subject to divine judgment, chastisement, and correction, she has also experienced divine forgiveness. The parallel suggested with Lot's wife, then, is not exact, nor is it exclusive. Mary also identifies herself with Job and, perhaps, with the servant who was spared to give an eyewitness account of the death of Job's sons and daughters and the destruction of his property and provisions.

While many modern readers may not like it, Per Amicum insists that this is neither a story of Mary's individual heroism, since mere flesh and blood could not have borne such hardships, nor a story of individual affliction. The narrative was to be read and pondered in the same way as a sermon or jeremiad preached on a communal day of humiliation and fasting. Cotton Mather's *Humiliations follow'd with Deliverances* (1697), which was accompanied by some captivity narratives when it was published, is an example of the manner in which the historical reality of Indian captivity was used in seventeenth-century New England to illustrate the communal covenantal relationship to God. Though this sermon postdates the Rowlandson narrative, it is nevertheless indicative of the type of sermon the first readers of the Rowlandson narrative would have been familiar with. They would have been primed to read the captivity in this way through, among other things, having listened to and read sermons in a similar vein. Thus, even if the Rowlandson narrative represents the first captivity published in North America, it did not create its audience or an audience for the genre from whole cloth. Rather, this text was put into circulation and directed to an audience with particular reading practices inculcated and promoted by the clergy and many other pious persons. The jeremiad form and devotional manuals influenced not only the narrative form and structure of Mary's narrative; they would have also influenced the reading and reception of the captivity.

There is a sustained attempt in the preface, then, to convince the reader that the captivity narrative was to be read in a specific and tightly circumscribed manner. Without proof to the contrary, it seems unwise to assume that among seventeenth-century New Englanders this was experienced as a crass or heavy-handed attempt to repress the individual female voice, as it may seem to some modern readers. For Puritan readers, this type of reading guidance would have been familiar, orthodox, and comforting because it reinforced already operative habits. In an important sense, this text was being presented to readers as being like other well-known devotional works that were spiritually efficacious for the readers if approached and employed in the proper manner.

Similarly, the biblical stories of Lot, Job, Joseph, David, and Daniel, which are also offered by Per Amicum as "bear[ing] some resemblance" to the instances of divine providence and dispensations found in the narrative, were also intended to help the reader to read and ponder the Rowlandson narrative correctly by placing it within a wider, authoritative intertextuality. After invoking these biblical stories, which "represent us with the excellent textures of divine providence, curious pieces of divine work," Per Amicum immediately links Mary's narrative with them: "And truly so doth this [narrative], and therefore not to be forgotten; but worthy to be exhibited to, and viewed and pondered by all, that disdain not to consider the operation of [God's] hands" (Garland 1:A3).

It was not necessary to retell these biblical stories in the preface because their familiarity to the Puritan audience could be assumed. This simple fact is important for us to bear in mind be-

cause today we too quickly forget the extent to which virtually
all significant discourse in Puritan society was constructed and
conducted through intertextual imbrication with biblical stories.
Charles L. Cohen has recently stressed the extent to which Puritans' understanding, reading, and interpretation of the Bible were
shared by the clergy and laity alike. For most Puritans it was
"natural" to think quite literally through biblical stories. This
understanding must be extended to the mental activity involved
in the reading process and practices of the Puritans as well. Insofar
as Puritans internalized these and other strictures offered by their
clergy, not only their public discourse but also their private reading practices would have been subject to a form of self-censorship.[19] The self-censorship involved in the text's composition is,
perhaps, easier to establish than is that which was operative in its
consumption in seventeenth- and early eighteenth-century New
England. Yet by tracing the outlines of the reading practices proposed by the author of the preface, it is possible to suggest something of the way in which some—and perhaps most—early readers
consumed and then used this narrative.

Modern commentators tend to emphasize the psychological
dimensions of the captivity narrative as the source of its power, as
we have seen. Per Amicum, however, recommends it to all those
who "disdain not to consider the operation of [God's] hands" in
such "remarkable providences" in history and who "have pleasure
therein." Reading for such didactic purposes may not appeal to
many readers in the late twentieth century, but we must not
ignore the clear indication that earlier readers *did* find pleasure in
such reading practices. The friends who urged the publication of
the narrative occupied social positions of influence and control
over the definition of what reading practices distinguished "good"
Christian readers from others. As their spokesman, Per Amicum
testifies that these readers sought to bring the narrative to the
public because they "could not but be so much affected with the
many passages of working providence discovered therein." Thus,
these influential readers found most affecting and worthy of recommendation precisely those elements that many modern readers
find conventional, hackneyed, heavy-handed, forced, and artificial. Yet these negative adjectives represent our responses and
evaluations and not necessarily those of earlier readers.

While Breitwieser is right that Per Amicum vividly and con-
cretely sketches "the primal scene of attack" in order to arouse the
reader's horror and then to redirect this emotion, this strategy is

not evidence of some male hegemonic conspiracy. We need to understand how the reader's response was to be harnessed and to what end. For Puritans, death and physical torture at the hands of savages were to be confronted in all their raw horror in order to begin to understand the even more horrible fate that they would confront in the future and for all eternity if a proper covenantal relationship with God was not maintained. The Rowlandson narrative was to be read and reread not for any form of base titillation but for the spiritual good to be gained by considering the lessons for one's own life found in the pious declarations of this minister's wife. The final sentence of Per Amicum's preface is unequivocal in its imperative charge to the reader: "Read therefore, peruse, ponder, and from hence lay up something from the experience of another, against thine own turn comes: that so thou also through patience and consolation of the Scripture mayest have hope" (*Garland* 1:A4).

For Breitwieser, the Rowlandson narrative is a subversive text and a testament to "the discrepancies between feeling and prescribed wisdom" that "legitimates an extension of the discrepancy between feeling and dogma into the present of the text." Similarly, he argues that "Rowlandson's narrative is a realistic work, not because it faithfully reports real events, but because it is an account of experience that breaks through or outdistances her own and her culture's dominant means of representation." Literary realism is, he suggests, best understood as "a transcription of reality's astonishing and at least discursively hurtful impact on systems of coherent representation," a transcription available to us as readers precisely in texts such as Rowlandson's because "the real leaves its mark in the contortions it enacts within the writer's best intentions" to impose the dominant interpretive frame on her experience.[20]

In this reading, ideology seems to be something largely extrinsic to feeling and emotion, something that is brought to bear on these after the fact. Pure raw emotion is denied, repressed, or forced into theologically correct conceptual boxes. Yet surely ideology qua theology in seventeenth-century New England was also involved in shaping and defining individuals' emotions from the start. We fail to capture the historical reality of Puritan society if we dismiss Mary's use of Puritan typologies and biblical interpretive frames as extrinsic impositions that were alien to her experience and her reality. It would be more accurate to say that, in their efforts retrospectively to give meaning to events, Mary and Per Amicum both manipulate culturally available authoritative texts (as one would expect in any discursive situation), and that Mary sometimes applies biblical verses in ways that differ from Per Amicum's. It should not be expected that the manner in which they appeal to and employ what is culturally available will always be the same. When these do not match precisely, we must resist the temptation to declare one author to have been coercive and the other coerced. Unless it can be demonstrated with respect to the Rowlandson narrative that Puritan readers read around, rather than through, the reading structure and interpretive frame the preface proffered, and, furthermore, that they discounted the biblical interpretive frame of the narrative proper as an external, alien, and distorting imposition, it is more reasonable to assume that, for the first readers of this captivity narrative, Mary's authorial voice was inseparable from Per Amicum's and that they were not viewed as being in conflict. Readers in later centuries may have felt free (or perhaps compelled) to employ alternative reading strategies to those proffered by Per Amicum, but there is no convincing evidence that Mary's contemporaries did so.

This fact does not mean, however, that modern or postmodern readers are somehow better or worse readers than the Puritans were; it is only to note that we read the same narrative differently. In speaking of Mary Rowlandson's use of the dominant cultural forms of representation, Breitwieser himself notes that "only a shallow understanding of complicity would lead us to see her desire as an unimaginative or weak capitulation."[21] The narrative was written by Rowlandson, according to the preface, "to be to her a Memorandum of Gods dealing with her" and to ensure that as time passed she would never forget the instances of divine providence she had witnessed. Later there is a veiled allusion that while in captivity Mary had made a vow of some sort, presumably promising to witness publicly to God's wonderful works if she survived captivity and was redeemed. Per Amicum uses this vow as another reason for permitting a woman's text to be published: "No serious spirit then (especially knowing any thing of this Gentlewomans Piety) can imagine but that the vows of God are upon her. Excuse her then if she come thus into the publick, to pay those vows" (*Garland* 1:A3). If the narrative as we have it is in part the product of the fulfillment of a personal vow, the published text is a material trace of a (silent) conversation through prayer, a privileged form of communication with God, through which the author came to feel herself contractually bound to speak to others of God's intervention in human history and in her life.

Improved Fortifications: Sermons and Captivities

In order to gain a deeper sense of the intertextual milieu in which the Rowlandson narrative had both its genesis and its consumption, it is important to appreciate the variety of ways in which texts, in both oral and written form, were employed in Puritan life. Texts of various sorts figured in the daily life of the people—the reading of Scripture in both public and private practices, the singing of psalms, the use of devotional manuals, preaching and printed sermons, and almanacs. It is impossible to treat all of these forms here. Rather, we will look briefly at two relevant sermons—Joseph Rowlandson's last sermon (1678), published along with Mary's captivity, and, in the next chapter, Cotton Mather's *Humiliations follow'd with Deliverances* (1697)—which are representative of the jeremiad, calling the people back to God's ways.

It was a fairly common practice in New England to publish a minister's death sermon (i.e., his last sermon preached) as a fitting memorial to him. Because such a sermon represented the final words of the minister to his congregation, it was felt that this "add[ed] one great circumstance to its solemnity" and significance. Unlike election sermons, the type of sermon most commonly published before 1690, death sermons were (for obvious reasons) not revised and expanded from the preachers' notes prepared for oral delivery before publication.[22]

Joseph Rowlandson's last sermon, printed with Mary's narrative, was directed especially to the inhabitants of Lancaster and Weathersfield, his former parishes. Presumably, these parishioners were something of a captive audience, if you will, since purchasing a copy of the printed sermon was taken as a sign of respect toward the deceased minister. Others outside Rowlandson's immediate flock consumed his and other death sermons as well, but there is little doubt that the readership for this specific sermon was increased by its being conjoined with the captivity of his "yoke-mate," even though Mary had already remarried by the time these texts first appeared in print.

Joseph's sermon was on Jeremiah 23:33, "And when this People, or the prophet, or a priest, shall ask thee, saying, What is the burden of the Lord? thou shalt then say unto them, What burden? I will even forsake you, saith the Lord." The sermon occupies only ten printed pages and reads more like an outline than a full, polished piece. The main lesson of the sermon is that "the Lord may even forsake a People that have been near to him, and he hath been near to." This was a popular theme in the late seventeenth century as the clergy tried to explain the difficulties and reversals the colonies had recently suffered. The theme presented an aspect of the problem of theodicy—why should the elect or Saints suffer, while their enemies prospered?—and sought to discover the sins of the people that had invited disaster. At the same time, Joseph Rowlandson sought to spell out the even heavier divine punishment awaiting a recalcitrant and unrepentant people and to call them to a proper and public ritual of humiliation.

According to Joseph Rowlandson: "God is said to forsake a People two wayes. 1. As to affection. 2. As to Action." The former is characterized by God's discontinuing or taking away his love for a people, a situation styled "a very heavy Judgement, and sad removal." When God has removed his affection, he has "withdrawn himself . . . in respect of his gracious presence," but not of his "general presence," which sustains the entire universe and all life. God's removal of his affection is described as a time "when he takes away merciful and gracious providences . . . vexes [his beloved people] with all manner of adversity . . . ceases to protect them from evils, and enemies, as in times past, and provides not for them, as he was wont to do. When he takes away his Ordinances, and bereaves a people of the glorious things of his house; or takes away his spirit from accompanying them, whereby the glory ceases, and the ordinances are rendered ineffectual for the saving good of a people" (Garland 1:38, 39).

This description of how a chosen people could be forsaken would seem to correspond in many respects to the dire straits in which Mary and the other captives found themselves in the wilderness—unprotected against enemies and suffering at the hands of vexious individuals. Such correspondences, made explicit in the sermons of Cotton Mather and no doubt others, are what made it possible for instances of captivity and redemption to serve as an emblem for the communal plight.

Puritan ministers frequently spoke of the human condition after the Fall as a form of "spiritual captivity," since humans are ever subject to sin and to being tempted away from divine grace. In an important sense, Indian captivity as a historical reality was viewed as an external realization of the ontological condition of all humanity. Physical captivity, then, was to be understood as part of an effort by God to represent the spiritual condition of the people to themselves, or at least to "those wise enough to observe this truth," as Cotton Mather was to put it.

For Mary and her audience, the identification of the root cause

of unfolding events in history (including incidents of Indian captivity) with the spiritual state of the people was both common and
thoroughgoing. Through having heard and read many jeremiads,
the readers of this captivity narrative would have already been
warned by God, through the agencies of Scripture and the clergy, of
the dangerous state, both spiritual and physical, that was created
by irregular or nonobservance of the divine will as expressed in the
ordinances and laws of his church. Moral and spiritual laxity
among the people produced a spiritual distancing from God, which
in turn threatened to prompt him reciprocally to withdraw from
his people. Yet along with these dire threats and warnings came
the promise of divine forgiveness if, while humbly and contritely
observing a communal day or week of fasting and humiliation, the
people recognized that they deserved such divine disfavor. "Judge
yourselves worthy to be forsaken," Rowlandson exhorted his parishioners, "because of your forsaking him. If you judge your selves
worthy to be forsaken, God will not judge you worthy to be forsaken, I Cor. 11. 31."

Note the following description of God's forsaking a people ("the
woefullest day that such a people are wont to meet with"), and
especially the images used by Joseph Rowlandson, which bear
immediately on the ways the original readers would have understood both Per Amicum's and Mary's description of the fall of
Lancaster to the Indians:

> Gods forsaking a People is a sore judgment, in that it exposes them
> to all judgements. Sin is a great evil, in that it exposes to all evil; this
> is a great evil of punishment, in that it exposes to all punishments.
> If God be gone, our guard is gone, and we are as a City in the midst of
> Enemies whose walls are broken down. Our strength to make re-
> sistance, that's gone, for God is our strength. As a carcase without
> life, is a prey to beasts of prey; so are a people forsaken of their God,
> to all their devouring enemies, and to infernal and cursed spirits:
> they are exposed to mischief, and the malice of all their malig-
> nant enemies. When the Lord had forsaken Jerusalem, the Romans
> quickly made a prey of it; when they were destitute of God, their
> habitation became desolate. There is no Protection to a people
> whom the Lord forsakes; but they are perplexed on every side.
> (*Garland* 1:46, 41)

It is instructive to compare this general description of the effects
of the removal of God's affection with the opening passages of the

Rowlandson captivity narrative. Joseph's description of the consequences of the actions of those who "forsake [God] and provoke
him to forsake them also" mirrors the woefully inadequate defensive state of the Lancaster community before the attack, as described by Mary and Per Amicum, and then the utterly defenseless
condition of the captives in its wake as they were "exposed to
mischief, and the malice of all their malignant enemies."

History and circumstance are represented here as emblematic or
symptomatic of a spiritual illness.[23] When one's "guard is gone,"
one is exposed to "devouring enemies, and to infernal and cursed
spirits." These are both internal (i.e., there is an increased susceptibility to sin and temptations) and external enemies and infernal
spirits. In this intertextual reading of history, the Indians, like the
enemy armies of Israel in the Old Testament, are scripted not as
human agents but as ravenous beasts from hell, loosed on the
world by God as they work desolation throughout the land. In this
situation identities and moral definitions become blurred. All
who are caught up in this whirlwind of destruction either lose
their normal nature, or, alternatively, as with the Praying Indians,
reveal their real nature by casting off an assumed mask. External
appearances are no longer to be trusted—dogs still appear to be
"stout" dogs, but fail to act as such in responding to alien pres-
ences;[24] Indians have human form, but sound and act like denizens
of hell; Praying Indians no longer practice Christian virtues but
take up arms against the English and dash out the brains of infants
on tree trunks.

These events surrounding King Philip's War forced the Puritans,
"the visible saints," into a period of intense self-scrutiny and
revaluation of their spiritual status. When Mary writes, "And that
I may the better declare what happened to me during that grievous
Captivity, I shall particularly speak of the several Removes we had
up and down the Wilderness," we must accept her declared intention to report more than a factual history. The sequential unfolding of her narrative account is also to be a spiritual history of God's
dealing with her as evidenced in the events of her captivity, a
history that readers can relive through their devotional exercises.

The extent to which "the wilderness" represented a heavily
value-laden imaginal space for the Puritans is so well known that
it needs no elaboration here. It is enough to recall that in Puritan
discourse the wilderness was never merely topographical space
but rather functioned within a larger symbolic complex of wilder-
ness-civilization that carried a spiritual significance.[25] All of the

texts we have examined had their genesis in a communal search for meaning in the history of the colonies. They were also composed out of elements of a shared social understandings informed most especially by biblical stories.

In both Mary's captivity narrative and Joseph's sermon, we find expressions of the Puritan ambivalence toward and anxiety over their sense of assurance of being a chosen people and thus privileged yet coupled with a nagging sense of doubt that they could ever be worthy of salvation. Joseph warns that even a people who are "visibly and externally near and dear to [God] . . . may be totally and finally forsaken of God." But he also distinguishes between a sinner forsaken and a Saint forsaken. The forsaken saint continues to cry after God, without harboring ill thoughts of him. God's "forsaking of his [chosen people] is but temporary and partial," whereas with an unrepentant sinner it is permanent and complete. In this understanding, the visible saint is truly known only through being severely tested through Job-like affliction. It is in this sense that one must understand the many statements by Mary akin to the following: "Though I thought we should there have ended our dayes, as overcome with so many difficulties. But the Lord renewed my strength still, and carried me along, that I might see more of his power, yea, so much that I could never have thought of, had I not experienced it." Or this passage, frequently cited as providing insight into her psychological state, when she became very depressed: "And here I cannot but remember how many times sitting in their Wigwams, and musing on things past, I should suddenly leap up and run out, as if I had been at home, forgetting where I was, and what my condition was: But when I was without, and saw nothing but Wilderness, and Woods, and a company of barbarous Heathen; my mind quickly returned to me, which made me think of that, spoken concerning *Sampson*, who said, *I will go out and shake my self as at other times, but he wist not that the Lord was departed from him*" (*Garland* 1:4, 16).

This and similar passages should not be understood as points where "the real" has broken through or outdistanced an externally imposed retrospective frame but as attempts by author to describe accurately the spiritual significance of the afflictions she suffered and her reactions under these. Rowlandson's temporary madness is related precisely because she felt that it had been promised in Deuteronomy 28. The passage from Judges on Samson makes the point that this form of madness had its genesis in the misplaced belief that one could escape on one's own without the aid of

God. Just as Samson had not realized that Yahweh had forsaken him, Mary reports how she too had forgotten where she was and her "condition"—her captivity, which was both physical and spiritual.

To appreciate Mary's language, one must have a sense of the world of discourse in which it participated. One must look to the Bible, of course, but also to other texts circulating in the society— sermons, devotional manuals, *The Pilgrim's Progress*. When Mary says that after she came to her senses having run out of the wigwam she recalled a specific biblical passage on Samson that helped her to appreciate more fully her own situation, we need to consider this as an honest account of how she had made sense of what was happening to her. The verse from Judges tells how, unbeknownst to Samson, his strength had left him when his locks were shorn as he slept. In his weakened and powerless state, his eyes were put out by the Philistines. Mary's allusion to this bib- lical tale is appropriate here because immediately prior to the events recounted in the passage cited above, she had been blinded herself, albeit temporarily, when a female Indian threw ashes in her face. The full depth of Mary's biblical allusion comes through only when this intertextual dimension is restored.

It is also necessary to note how both Mary's experience and her retrospective account are informed by the Puritan understanding of the affliction of saints. This affliction was at the heart of the conversion experience, which had a specific structure consisting of increasing alienation from God, a growing sense of helplessness, the emergence of self-repugnance, followed by a sudden rekindling of faith and a renewed sense of hope. The contours of this spiritual experience were rehearsed in public in the conversion narratives of congregants, but even more importantly the experience was also cultivated on a regular, even daily, basis as the core of Puritan devotional disciplines.

As Rowlandson recounts her own captivity, the events compos- ing it are meaningfully ordered and structured by employing the culturally available, readily recognizable, and validated form of the narrative of the soul's pilgrimage to God. Mary's sketch of her restless "going up and down mourning and lamenting" is not merely an objective description of her actions; it translates this physical activity into an external representation of the condition of her (and Everyman's) soul by invoking the metaphor of life as a pilgrimage. Examples of the use of this and closely related phrases abound in Puritan literature. John Winthrop, for instance, wrote in the 1630s, "I went up and down mourning with myself; and later being deprived of my youthfull joyes, I betook myself to God." Elsewhere, he describes how he had "wandred up and downe in this sad and doubtful estate" of incomplete faith before his initial conversion. Thomas Shepard used a similar phrase to warn against reliance on outward or visible means of grace, saying, "Mourn in some wilderness till dooms day . . . walk up and down the world like a distressed Pilgrim going to another countrey, these cannot deliver thee, for they are not the blood of Christ."[26]

For Puritan readers, then, the phrase "to wander up and down" was a shorthand description of a person deluded into no longer believing himself to be captive to temptation and sin. Mary's narrative representation of her momentary delusion, believing that she was back in her house, surrounded by family and worldly comforts, rather than in the wilderness and captivity, skillfully employs the resources of Puritan imagery and metaphor to translate this scene into an emblem. She narratively composes a place, a textual site her readers are invited to revisit in their imaginative devotional exercises. Hers is not a blasphemous text, resisting and protesting Puritan ideology; it is a text that seeks to capture the true human condition and to chart one pilgrim's progress through the "removes" or stages of life in captivity in the wilderness of the world.

In his sermon, as we have seen, Joseph Rowlandson claims that God never completely forsakes a saint; he always provides an opening for the backsliding individual (or community) to find hope and renewed faith in the depths of their affliction. This is why Mary regularly declares that God's mercy was shown to her in various ways even though she was a sinner. In the passage where she recalls how she came into possession of a Bible while in captivity, she tells how God led her through a sense of her worthlessness and utter culpability to a glimmer of hope that sustained her. Mary's narrative, then, traces out the contours of a spiritual journey into dread and doubt and back again to faith. This was a readily recognized movement, representing the unsteady progress of the pilgrim. Here, however, history is seen as a dreadful warning from God to the entire community of the dire necessity to repent, to undergo a reconversion. Mary's captivity is presented as a remarkable instance of a larger hierophantic event, of God's call to New England and his people. Her redemption was taken as a sign that God was loath to abandon the Puritans and that he awaited a sign of repentance in order that he might pour his mercy upon them. Mary's suggestion that even when she was temporarily unable to find comfort in the Bible she never lost her faith in God or reviled him marks her as a saint afflicted, as does her humble admission that "I knew [God] laid upon me less then I deserved." "Consider Gods loathness to forsake us," Joseph Rowlandson intoned.

> This is a thing that he is not desirous of, he doth not willingly afflict us with this sort of Affliction, or grieve us with this grievous stroak. God hath shewed himself loth to depart from those that have departed from him; but hath warned them of his displeasure, that they might stay him. It goes near Gods heart to forsake a People that have been near to him. Methinks I hear him saying thus, "How shall I give thee up, O New-England!" thence speaking to warn us, of our forsakings of him, and to be instructed, why? lest his Spirit depart from us, Jer. 6. 7. "Be though instructed, O Jerusalem, lest my Soul depart from thee, lest I make thee desolate, a Land not inhabited." You may easily stay him, the matter is not so far gone, but you might yet stay him: were we but as loth he should forsake us, as he is to forsake us, he would never leave us. His gradual motions from a people argue his lothness, and unwillingness to leave them. (*Garland* 1:44)

One can read Mary's account as stylized, forced, and conventional—but to do so requires one to deny her an authentic existence. Less obvious, perhaps is the danger inherent in viewing her text, as Breitweiser does, as an "innocent narrative, where countermemory emerges from the silence of being an eternal irony in the heart of the community and teaches those who come after what was really down below."[27] If we fail to attend to the reading and compositional practices consciously employed by earlier generations, we are ourselves liable to fall prey to the sin of pride in assuming that we know the truth that eluded those earlier authors and readers. It would be ironic if we were to find ourselves captured in our own webs of pretension.

2

CAPTIVES OF SIN OR
CAPTIVES OF IDEOLOGY?

If any of you are yet in an Unconverted State; let not your
outward freedom put away the sense of the Deplorableness
and Dangerousness of an Unconverted State; and of the
Depths of Misery they are in, that are Captives to Sin and
Satan.—The Rev. John Williams, 1706

WE HAVE INVESTIGATED the content of Mary Rowlandson's 1682
captivity narrative and context in which it had its genesis and
initial circulation. Here we turn to other Puritan captivity narratives published in the two generations following the publication of
Rowlandson's work. These will include captivity tales told by
Puritan clergymen, including Cotton Mather and John Williams,
as well as others by laypersons. While we will investigate further
the captivity topos within Puritan discourse, careful attention
will also be paid to changes found in captivity tales. Numerous
major changes had occurred in New England between 1682 and
1750, of course, and one might expect to find these mirrored in the
narratives that appeared in these years. Indeed, while one finds
that the clerical use of captivity narratives changes relatively little, texts written by laymen and women demonstrate a great diversity. Some closely resembled Rowlandson's narrative; others were
much less theological in tone and content.

This look at other Puritan captivity tales will allow me to
address fully an issue that hovered over the discussion in the first
chapter: How hegemonic was Puritan ideology in New England?
Did New England captives freely employ the providential interpretive frame in telling their tales, or was this somehow imposed
upon them by the clergy? Was the Puritan religious anthropology
part of an oppressive ideology that, once internalized, produced a
false consciousness among the laity? Or, put another way, were
former captives trapped within the discursive boundaries set by
the clergy?

The nature of the clergy's power, the extent to which the religious elite effectively controlled the cultural discourse in New England, and the question whether this power was hegemonic have long been major points of contention among historians. Kenneth Lockridge and Harry Stout, for instance, have stressed the high level of ideological control found in Puritan culture, although they note that this dissipated especially in the third generation. Other scholars, including Jon Butler and Philip Gura, have pointed to the limits of clerical hegemony.[1] I do not pretend to have definitive answers to these vexed issues, yet they cannot be ignored. How one answers these questions directly affects one's understanding of both the composition and the consumption of Puritan captivity narratives. More importantly, perhaps, it determines one's stance toward the authors and readers of these tales. Were they to some extent captives of Puritan ideology? Were they free to tell their stories, or did they read them as they saw fit? Or were their situations more complex and variable, lying somewhere between these two extremes?

I propose to approach these issues obliquely and in a limited way by paying special attention to the diverse uses to which these tales were put and the diverse audiences they were directed at. At the same time, careful note will be made of passages within these texts that describe reading and devotional practices. These can provide invaluable clues concerning the probable ways in which such tales were consumed and how men and women made sense of the vicissitudes in their lives.

Cotton Mather on Captivity

Nineteen years after Joseph Rowlandson's last sermon, Cotton Mather delivered a sermon in Boston in the spring of 1697 as a "Preparative" to a week-long general fast and humiliation. This sermon was printed the same year, with the full title *Humiliations follow'd by Deliverances, A Brief Discourse on the Matter and Method of that Humiliation which would be an Hopeful Symptom of our Deliverance from Calamity. Accompanied and Accommodated with a Narrative, of a Notable Deliverance lately Received by some English Captives, from the Hands of Cruel Indians. And some Improvement of that Narrative, Whereto is added a Narrative of Hannah Swarton, containing a great many wonderful passages, relating to her Captivity and Deliverance.* The circumstances of the delivery of this sermon make clear that captivity, both as a historical reality and as a theological and literary theme, was deeply implicated in the public ritual practices of New England Puritans. Captivity tales were sometimes strategically employed in such contexts by the clergy in an effort to generate communal spiritual change or reconversion through public fasts and days of humiliation.

In Mather's hands historical events in New England, including Indian captivity, continued to be represented as signs from God of his displeasure with the waywardness of his people, while the redemption of captives signaled the possibility of communal "deliverance from calamity." The taking of captives at this time, however, was prompted by somewhat different circumstances than had been the case in King Philip's War, for this practice had become one aspect of French policy in the ongoing French and English struggle for control of North America. Thus, in the social imagination of the Puritans the threat of captivity came to evoke not only the horror of being carried into the wilderness of the Indian Other but also that of being cast into the blasphemous realm of the papists, where one might be seduced into embracing a false religion.

It is unclear how many copies of the Rowlandson captivity narrative were still in circulation in 1697 (it was not to be reprinted until 1720) or whether it continued to have a wide readership. Thus, we cannot claim with any certainty that Mather's sermon affected the continued reception of that narrative in any direct manner. This sermon shows, nevertheless, that in general the clergy's interpretation and representation of the significance of Indian captivity had changed very little during the intervening two decades. Mather introduces two new captivity tales to much the same intent and purpose as Per Amicum had done earlier with Rowlandson's, while recommending the same reading practices and structures of reception to be applied to such narratives.

Mather took as his main scriptural text 2 Chronicles 12:7: "When the Lord saw that they had humbled themselves, the word of the Lord came to Shemaiah, saying, They have humbled themselves, I will not destroy them, but I will grant them some deliverance." He urged his audience, composed of members of various congregations, to confess their sins (he lists twenty in number), but also to acknowledge, as Mary Rowlandson had done twenty years earlier, that the divine chastisement they had already experienced was less than they deserved. With a rhetorical flourish and regular cadence, he presses this theme as he lists the difficulties they had experienced and calls for repentance:

Have we lost many Thousands of Pounds, by the Disasters of the Sea? Let us Humbly Confess, our Sins have Deserved, that instead of making one Good Voyage, we should have been stript of all the Little that is left unto us. Hath one bad Harvest after another, diminished our Ordinary Food? Let us Humbly Confess, our Sins have Deserved, that the Earth which hath been thereby Defiled, should have yielded us nothing at all. Have Bloody, Popish, and Pagan Enemies, made very dreadful Impressions upon us, and Captivated and Butchered multitudes of our Beloved neighbours? Let us Humbly Confess, our Sins have Deserved, that we should be all of us, altogether given up, unto the will of our Enemies, to Serve our Enemies in the want of all things, and have our Lives continually hanging in Doubt, under their furious Tyrannies. (*Garland* 1:12)

While Mather argues that the entire community deserves the removal of God's affection, and the resultant exposure to the depravations of its enemies, he goes on to say, "And yet, we have had Comforts, to mitigate and moderate, our Troubles: In the midst of wrath, God has Remembered Mercy. Now concerning all our comforts, on our Day of Humiliation, Let us Humbly make that Confession, in Lam. 3.22. 'It is of the Lord's mercies, that we are not Consumed'" (*Garland* 1:13). This same theme was found in Per Amicum's preface, Mary Rowlandson's narrative, and Joseph Rowlandson's death sermon.

The burden of the preparatory sermon is that in the upcoming general fast and humiliation the people had the opportunity to affect their future and to stay the Lord's hand. Through the public ritual of fasting, prayer, and the penitent confession of sin, the community could be assured that God would smile on them again, for Mather held the view, already announced in his title, that "the Truth which Lies before us [in 2 Chronicles 12:7], is, *That when a Sinful People Humble themselves before the Almighty God, it is an Hopeful; and an Happy Symptom, that He will not utterly Destroy such a People.*" He warns, however, that the efficacy of such rituals is not automatic with their performance but rather depends on the mental and spiritual attitude of the people. "Fast is but a Form, an Hungry and Empty Form, if we do not therein heartily Repent of our Miscarriages" (*Garland* 1:6, 20).

For Mather, the human body, too, is an empty hollow form hungering to be filled. Puritan captivity narratives, like Rowlandson's, are filled with passages on the physical hunger captives experienced, but this is finally subordinated to the spiritual lessons hunger has to teach—that in times of ease and plenty people rarely acknowledge the many blessings God has granted them, and that normal human discriminations of what is palatable and what is not collapse under trials and distress. In a voluntary fast, the body is deprived of food in order to turn the mind away from the mundane and toward God, toward the only real sustenance in a world of wonders and woe.[2] The goal of communal fasting is to realize a reconciliation with God, which can only be effected through an "internal humiliation" as prescribed in 2 Chronicles 7:14: "My people shall then humble themselves and pray and seek my face, and turn from their wicked ways." Interestingly enough, Mather explicitly identifies the spiritual process of change that must be effected with that found in individual conversion: "Our Fasts are to Slay our Lusts; those are the Beasts, which are then to be slaughtered. Indeed, whenever a Fast recurrs, we should go the whole Work of Conversion over again!" Through the week of the general fast, the days ritually transformed into a week of sabbaths, Cotton Mather sought to lead the community through a spiritual process of collective reconversion and, thereby, to reinvigorate their communal life in a covenantal relationship with God.

As Mather surveyed history, he found God's hand at work at various points raising enemies and tyrants for "the Vexation of mankind." He ended his sermon by acknowledging the presence in the audience of three recently returned captives, whom he pointed to as "an *Example,* full of Encouragement unto those humiliations" (*Garland* 1:21, 30, 40). Mather concluded his sermon by telling their tale of captivity and escape ("this unexpected occurrence") because, he argued, properly understood their captivity and redemption should spur the congregants to greater fervor in the upcoming general fast.

Mather implies that it was the prayers of the churches that had moved God to effect the safe return of these captives. It was not individual courage and heroism but faith in the power of God that had proved efficacious. While their tale contains "some very Singular Circumstances," finally it is of interest to Mather—and he implies it should also be of interest to the members of the community—only insofar as it promotes the fervor of the people's ritual activity of self-humiliation, prayer, and repentance in the general fast. And this captivity was quite a tale, for one night shortly after having been taken, Hannah Duston, with the assistance of her maid and a young boy, had managed to kill ten of their Indian captors with hatchets as they slept. Duston had then scalped the

victims and claimed the bounty offered by the colonial government in Boston.[3]

Not content to leave the interpretation of these remarkable
events to his audience, Mather supplies an "Improvement," at
once an interpretation and a proclamation of its meaning based on
biblical typology. Mather addresses himself directly to the three
former captives, though this pastoral counseling from the pulpit
would have been overheard by the entire assembly (and later by the
reading audience too). Among other things, Mather wonders out
loud whether it would not be possible to exterminate the Indians,
if only the community humbled itself before God. The message of
the sermon is clearly intended for the entire community, even
when Mather at times speaks directly to the returned captives, as
in a passage where he argues that those who had been abducted
were not being punished for their sins, nor were those who had
been spared captivity somehow less culpable in God's eyes. Indian
captivity was best read, he urged, as a sign or emblem of the fallen
state of mankind: "You are not now the Slaves of Indians, as you
were a few Dayes ago; but if you continue Unhumbled, in your
Sins, you will be the Slaves of Devils; and, Let me tell you, A
Slavery to Devils, to be in Their Hands, is worse than to be in the
Hands of Indians!" (*Garland* 1:48–49).

It is common in the Puritan discourse of this period to compare
Indian captivity with mankind's captivity to sin or the "slavery to
Devils" of those persons who have cut themselves off from grace.
The horrors of Indian captivity were nothing, it was claimed,
compared to those that awaited the unrepentant at the end of time
and the final judgment. Physical captivity, which the Rev. John
Williams called "outward Captivity," was to be understood as an
external symptom of an internal spiritual malaise with a horrible
prognosis—unless, that is, a swift and thoroughgoing program of
repentance and reform was undertaken.

In his sermon, Mather explicitly claims that the people can
affect their own future, even guaranteeing the extermination of
their enemies, if only they would truly humble themselves and
repent. While it is clear that Mather is referring to the physical
extermination of the French and Indians here, we must also recall
that, in the spiritual landscape of the human soul, it was the
various temptations and vices that were to be slain. This understanding of how the inner workings of the spirit can immediately
affect events in the material world was basic to the Puritan ethos.
The full and frank admission of powerlessness and unworthiness

was held to be the first essential step toward realizing power through opening oneself to grace. This power was evidenced by a renewed spiritual energy and a strengthened conviction of the need to act in society in obedience to God.[4]

Mather's reading of recent history was presented at length to the public in *Decennium Luctuosum*. Ostensibly published anonymously, few New England readers would have failed to recognize the author—not only is Mather's style distinctive, the volume included a flyleaf at the end advertising the publication shortly thereafter of two sermons by Mather. Moreover, a lecture delivered by him in Boston on July 27, 1698, and entitled "The Remarkeables of a long War, Collected and Improved," was appended.

Mather argues that it is both "a Duty to God, and a Service to the World, for to preserve the memory of such matters, as have been the more memorable Occurrences in the War," especially since the hand of God was evident in the successful prosecution of the war of extermination against the Indians. He presents brief accounts of the captivity of a number of persons, including James Key, Mebetabel Goodwin, Mary Plaised, Mary Ferguson, and Hannah Dustan, to illustrate the Indians' cruelty. Mather purposefully sensationalized his accounts so that his audience might "with mournful Hearts, look upon the Condition of the Captives in those cruel hands" and be moved to tears and to hatred of the Indians. Once again in his work the Indians function as the agents of God's wrath, as sorcerers of the devil, and as negative examples for the people, who are constantly in danger of reverting to the evils of laziness, lying, and indulging one's children.[5]

In important ways, Mather's work presages the developments in literary form and in the reading practices associated with the sentimental novel in the latter half of the eighteenth century as he conjures up sensational scenes for the moral instruction of his reader. The following passage is illustrative:

How many Women have been made a prey to those Bruitish men, that are Skilful to Destroy? How many a Fearful Thing has been suffered by the Fearful Sex, from those men, that one would Fear as Devils rather than men? Let the Daughters of our Zion think with themselves, what it would be, for fierce Indians to break into their houses, and brain their Husbands and their Chi[l]dren before their Eyes, and Lead them away a Long Journey into the Woods; and if they began to fail and faint in the Journey, then for a Tawny Salvage to come with Hell fire in his Eyes, and cut 'em down with his

> Hatchet; or, if they could miraculously hold out, then for some
> Filthy and ugly Squaw's to become their insolent Mistresses, and
> insolently to abuse 'em at their pleasure a thousand inexpressible
> ways; and, if they had any of their Sucking Infants with them, then
> to see those Tender Infants handled at such a rate, that they should
> beg of the Tygres, to dispatch 'em out of hand. (*Garland* 3:220–21)

In calling his readers to identify themselves with the captives
and their situation, Mather was appealing to familiar reading practices for most persons through their use of any of the popular
devotional manuals of the day. His graphic descriptions of suffering and torture were designed to conjure up the experience of
captivity in the minds of his listeners and readers. Through this
evocation of a vicarious experience of the horrors of captivity, real
and imagined, he sought to attain from his audience an emotional,
as well as intellectual, assent to his propositions and "improvements" of these stories. In no way would he allow apparent acts of
human kindness (or the absence of expected atrocities) on the part
of the Indians or the French to pass as actual indications of the
humanity of these opponents. If, for instance, some Frenchmen
had ransomed English captives, treated them well, or if no Indians
had sexually harassed any female captive, these things were all due
to God's interposition of divine mercy, which had overruled the
respective evil natures of the French and Indians.

Mather argues that the recent war is a "text" or "a Book of some
Consequence," but one that has been laid before those unable to
read it. The text of history requires an expert exegete, a prophetic
reader, "to spell the Divine lessons contained in it" for the people;
Mather offers his services. He continues to press themes that
he had stressed during and immediately after King Philip's War
(1675–76), most especially the danger—both physical and, more
importantly, spiritual—of Puritan settlers' leaving towns with
churches for land in the frontier regions where none existed. The
Reforming Synod of 1679 had perhaps put the point most force-
fully: "There have been in many professors [i.e., congregants] an
insatiable desire after Land, and worldly Accommodations, yea as
to forsake Churches and Ordinances, and to live like the Heathen,
only that so they might have Elbowroom enough in the world.
Farms and merchandising have been preferred before the things of
God."[6]

Using Psalm 107 as his scriptural text, Mather repeatedly challenges his audience with its final verse, which he transposes into a

question—"Who is wise, and will observe these things?" The cumulative effect of this rhetorical strategy is to imply that the reading of this history he proffers is the correct one. The emigration out of the towns and cities was at once a symptom of and an exacerbating factor in the people's having fallen away from God's plan. Consequently, these outlying communities had been subjected to divine afflictions, including Indian captivity. In describing these communities, Mather conjures up an imaginary journey into captivity, the physical journey functioning as a visible sign of the spiritual journey of souls away from God. Just as ministers of the gospel lead parishioners through the correct reading of biblical texts, he proposes to lead his audience through a correct reading of the New England landscape, a spiritual topography that had been inscribed or emplotted with "various and marvellous Dispensations of the Divine Providence." Some of these "dispensations" were to be observed in the ruins of former settlements. "I am to Lead you this day thro' a Spacious Country," Mather said, "which has been on many Accounts, the most Charming part of New-England; and I must herewithal say, *Come, Behold the works of the Lord, what Desolations He has made in that Land.* Syrs, 'Tis time for us, to Observe these Things; and this, not with a meer Athenian, but with a more profitable Observation" (*Garland* 3:203).

Mather then guides his reader imaginatively over the countryside, while pointing out the remarkable fact that churched communities had been spared in King William's War (1689), while those that had fallen to the Indians were in general precisely those that had neither churches nor ministers. Significantly, he does not point out that the same could not be said for the situation fourteen years earlier in King Philip's War. But then, to have done so would have detracted from his representation of what he took to be an explicit text, physically inscribed on the land and carved into the bodies of captives with hatchets, knives, and tomahawks. Mather's spelling of the scene he observes is blunt and unforgiving: the people have suffered poor harvests, massacres, and defeat at the hands of the Indians because, he says, they have abandoned the "Original Design of NEW-ENGLAND . . . to settle Congregations, wherein the Lord Jesus Christ should be known and serv'd according to His Gospel. . . . For This cause, we may Believe it is, that our LORD JESUS CHRIST looking down from Heaven upon these Unchristian Undertakings, Thunderstruck them with His Indignation."

Some persons had apparently ascribed these adversities to Indian sorcery, but Mather railed against this reading of the situation. Had the people carried the Gospel with them, he argued, "all the *Spells* of Hell would have been insignificant; there would not have prevailed any *Enchantment* against a *Gods-Spel* which we have in our Gospel" (*Garland* 3:204–6). Then, without citing her by name, Mather approvingly quotes Hannah Swarton's confession that she had provoked God's anger by "removing to a place of no Gospel for larger Accommodations in the World." Swarton's language echoes that of the Reforming Synod, but similar sentiments were no doubt also found in the public confessions of other captives.

Mather intended the contemplation of the horror of captivity ultimately to be morally rectifying. We miss much of his motivation if we ignore this and, instead, assume that his graphic descriptions were simply elements of a racist rhetoric designed to arouse hatred of the Indians. His graphic accounts of captivity and death at the hands of the Indians are part of a concerted effort to have his audience read this recent history in a way that would alter their lives for the better.[7]

If some of Mather's descriptions were gruesome, the raison d'être for them was similar to that found in the *ars moriendi* of medieval Europe—to bring death and suffering before the eyes of the people so that a full awareness of the human condition would affect the conduct of their lives. Just as the *ars moriendi* was used in meditative and contemplative practices as a part of the preparation for a proper and auspicious death, Mather sought to evoke a specific audience response by confronting the people with the horrible reality and inevitability of physical death, but he also warned of the dangerous consequences of the "death" of religion in the land, saying, "Upon the whole; when a Dead man was thrown into the Grave of Elijha, a Touch from the Bones of the Prophet in the Grave Rais'd him from the Dead. I am desiring, that Religion may be Revived out of the Death which has too much Enfeebled it among us. Behold, Syrs, I have now cast you into the Graves of our Dead Friends; It may be, by wisely observing of them, and the things that have befallen them, we may be somewhat Raised out of our Deadly Security. Let our Observation of these things, give some Life to the practice of Religion among us" (*Garland* 3:223).

"Outward captivity," as found in both the biblical stories of *Judea capta* and in the historical reality of the New England frontier, was understood to be immediately imbricated with the spiritual condition of the community of Saints. Even after having undergone the initial conversion experience, the Saints were ever liable to fall back into the captivity of temptation and sin. If the "divine lessons" of Indian captivity as spelled by Mather were observed, however, these afflictions would be taken by the community as an occasion for humiliation and moral rectification. Puritan captivities, then, could and did function as North American equivalents of *The Pilgrim's Progress*.

The moral of Mather's improvement, however, is not limited to the need for a strong church-state and a reformation among the church members, although these remain central. In delivering his jeremiad (and subsequently in its publication), Mather took the occasion to address briefly a new audience, the children. He was quite interested in pedagogical issues, believing that in part the future of the New England experiment depended upon the proper religious education of children. He also placed great importance on right discipline, order, and governance in the family, as we have seen, viewing the erosion of these as tantamount to going native. After describing the horrors of the torture youngsters had been subjected to in captivity and their deaths, Mather warns the children: "Oh! See that you become Serious, Pious, Orderly Children; Obedient unto your Parents, Conscientious to keep the Lords Day, and afraid of committing any Wickedness" (*Garland* 3:222).[8] Obedience, regular church attendance, and orderly conduct kept the Indians at bay, he avers; moreover, these things kept the children from a worse captivity in sin. This was, no doubt, a lesson spelled for them by their elders day in and day out.

Mather draws a connection between the moral "wilderness" resulting from a disordered family and the ever-present danger on the New England frontier of reverting to savagery. Only by making that connection can we appreciate the extent to which the external events of history unfolding over the physical topography of New England were held to mirror the interior movements of the hearts of the people over a spiritual landscape. Even in looking at outward captivity, Mather's gaze was finally directed to the interior world of the soul.

Though Mather turns to address the children in the audience directly only for a moment, in retrospect this may be seen as a significant moment. Scholars have long noted that the jeremiad took on an ever-heightening rhetoric as time passed, a development due in part to a growing concern over the attenuation of the power and authority of the clergy. As more families like Hannah

Swarton's moved out of the established communities and with the precipitous decline in the number of persons admitted to full membership in the church in many communities, the establishment of a church-state became an ever more elusive ideal.[9] The first generation's dream of establishing "a city on a hill" was no longer embraced by many adult members of the society. Mather's brief address directed to the children represents a subtle yet significant shift of hope from the present generation to a future one. At a minimum, in terms of the telling of captivity tales, this shift was a harbinger of things to come in the nineteenth century, as we will see in chapter 4, when such tales for children, with clear didactic and moralistic intentions, were commonly published and distributed under the imprint of Protestant church presses.

Similarly, Mather's strategy of sensationalizing the captivity situation by focusing on female prisoners was to have unforeseen consequences. While Mather coupled the contemplation (and vicarious experience) of the scenes of horror with the directive that this audience should turn again to God and reform their own lives, it proved relatively easy for authors to uncouple these and to harness the reader's affective response to other ends. At the same time, we must be alert for any evidence that readers themselves sometimes ignored the reading guidance and strictures that Mather and other authors supplied with their texts. That is, we must be open to the possibility (and, perhaps, even probability) that over time some readers read *around* the theological interpretive frame supplied by authors rather than *through* it. By the mid-eighteenth century many readers were joining in a new reading covenant with authors of sentimental literature, which replaced in large measure the Puritan religious anthropology and theology with that informing the cult of sensibility. This will be the focus of the next chapter. Before turning to this, though, we need to look at one final example of the clerical representation of Indian captivity in New England.

The Rev. John Williams on Captivity

When Cotton Mather published his *Good Fetch'd Out of Evil* in 1706, he included a pastoral letter from the Rev. John Williams to captives who were being returned to New England.[10] (Mather reported that *Good Fetch'd Out of Evil* was an immediate success, selling 1,000 copies in the first week.) Williams was himself a prisoner at the time but was not among those being repatriated.

The letter is of special interest because it seeks to guide the captives' actions following their return to Puritan society.

Better than most modern commentators, Williams understood that the meaning of captivity is rhetorically and socially negotiated, not predetermined. Thus, he realized that the manner in which the returning captives told their tales and how they comported themselves would help to determine the broader social meaning of their "affliction," even as these would determine the spiritual consequences of their captivity. Williams's pastoral letter, which John Demos has characterized as "a circle of religious cogitation, around a center of pain," echoes themes found earlier in the sermons of Joseph Rowlandson and Cotton Mather.[11] He urges the returning captives to turn their experience of outward captivity to the spiritual benefit of themselves and their communities:

> What is it that is most upon your heart in your Return? Is it that you may with all Freedom Glorify God, in *bringing forth much Fruit, whereby He may be Glorifyed,* whilst you are again planted in the *Court-yards of our God?* How sorrowful is it, if your greatest design be to see your Friends so long separated from you; to Gain Estates, and recover your outward Losses; and to be free again to go and come as you list! When you return, consult, Luk. 8.39 and see from thence, that it well becomes them who have had Eminent Mercies, to be shewing to others *what great things God has done for them.* Hereby you will be advancing the Glory and Honour of God, the highest, last, and most noble End Man was made for. (*Garland* 4:9)

Williams warns the returning captives not to "think to go shares or partners with God in his Glory," by claiming that their freedom was somehow due to their own efforts or goodness. He counsels them, "It's certain, That he who Glorifies God is one that orders his Conversations aright." In Puritan discourse, "to order one's conversations aright" meant to live a Christian life after conversion, including engaging in the daily practice of private devotions. In this case, it also no doubt meant that the returning captives were narratively to order their captivity tales aright.[12]

Williams charges the members of his temporary flock to acknowledge God as the sole agent of their redemption (in both senses of the term) in both their public and private devotions. From his perspective, the deep spiritual meaning and significance of their captivity was to be determined by their words and deeds upon their return, either by their renewed vocation of witnessing to the glory of God or, alternatively, by their returning to mundane thoughts, tasks, and the pursuit of worldly goods and fame.

Like Mather before him, Williams makes much of the necessity for outward captivity to be sanctified by rededicating one's life to God. "If you come forth as Gold well refined," he intones, "cleansed from all you[r] filthiness, and saved from all your Idols: What a Mercy do you Enjoy! The best Freedom, is Freedom by Jesus Christ from Spiritual Evils. . . . Oh! let it be made evident that you were brought into Captivity for your Good." Puritan representations of captivity often had recourse to Old Testament verses on the Egyptian and Babylonian captivities of the Israelites, but such scriptures were read through the prism of the New Testament. Thus, when the phrase "outward captivity" is discursively employed, it is always in reference to the process of conversion and redemption through Jesus Christ, as in this passage. Indian captivity could be the occasion for realizing true freedom from the fallen state of humankind. In other words, it could be an occasion for sanctification, which would be "expressed in a continued, universal, holy Conversation." Through their conversion (or reconversion), the former captives would become not merely "Hearers, but Doers of the Word" (*Garland* 4:12–14).

Williams was himself released in late October 1706, five months after he wrote the pastoral letter discussed above. He had been a prisoner in Canada since the town of Deerfield had fallen to French and Indian troops in February 1704. Not surprisingly, he wrote (and no doubt spoke) about his captivity after his return. *The Redeemed Captive, Returning to Zion* was printed in Boston in 1707. Appended was a sermon Williams had preached in Boston on December 5, 1706. This captivity narrative was to prove to be one of the most popular of the genre, going through multiple printings over the years.[13]

The reasons Williams gives for bringing his tale to the public, as signaled by the title of his sermon, are orthodox ones: "Reports of Divine Kindness: Or, Remarkable Mercies Should be Faithfully Published, for the Praise of God the Giver." In proclaiming God's providential dealings with himself and the instances of divine mercy he had known personally, Williams sought to "fall in with the design of God, and in an active manner to be giving Him Glory." Moreover, in the dedication of his narrative he declares, "The wonders of Divine Mercy, which we have seen in the Land of our Captivity, and Deliverance therefrom, cannot be forgotten without incurring the guilt of the blackest Ingratitude" (*Garland* 5:92, A2).

In his sermon Williams lists several reasons why the proper retrospective narration of a captivity, as both a form of self-examination and of witnessing to God's glory, was required of himself and others: (1) all things that occur are finally for the honor and glory of God; (2) God has "enjoyned us, to shew forth His Praises in rehearsing to others the Salvations, and Favours we have been the Subjects of"; (3) this rehearsal "will stir up others to bless God"; (4) once having humbled themselves in this manner, others will be better able to advise and counsel the former captives as they return to their communities of faith; (5) the narratives may provoke the recognition of God in others and move them to convert; (6) the works of God in the lives of the captives have been wonderful; and (7) narratively witnessing in this fashion is "a good evidence, that [the captives] regarded and took notice of the Works of God in Mercy" (*Garland* 5:92–97).

Like other Puritan captives, Williams saw God's hand in everything, good or ill, that transpired. His theological views on the absolute sovereignty of God and on divine providence, coupled with the shared assumption that the Indians as a species were naturally and innately cruel, were in concert with those of Cotton Mather. These led him to conclude that it was only God who could have caused the Indians go against their nature by showing compassion for the captives. He writes, for instance, "God hath made such whose Characters have been, that they were such whose tender Mercies were Cruelties; such from whom, one act of pity and compassion could scarce be expected, even such who have delighted in cruelty; to pity & compassionate such who were led into Captivity by them. Made them bear on their Arms, and carry on their Shoulders our Little Ones, unable to Travel. Feed their Prisoners with the best of their Provision: Yea, sometimes pinch themselves, as to their daily food, rather than their Captives" (*Garland* 5:98).

Williams's sermon is especially instructive for us today as we attempt to understand what motivated the Puritans to record the events of their captivities in the specific ways they did; it also provides evidence as to how these texts were intended to be read. Williams argued for the spiritual efficacy of such works as devotional texts. "It is very acceptable to God," he wrote, "for Christians to entertain the report of the experiences of others, to excite their own hearts to glorify God. For if God make it a duty in the receiver to report, it layes the hearer under an obligation, to set such remarks upon the passages of Divine Providence to others, as may be useful to engage their hearts to Glorify God, for the favours and blessings He has bestowed upon others." Later in his sermon he criticizes the reticence of some captives to witness in this way, suggesting that they were guilty of the sin of pride and would "rather God should lose his Glory, then they any of their credit and esteem" (*Garland* 5:98, 103).

Given this situation, it should not surprise us to find confessions of personal weakness, doubt, and vacillation in Puritan captivity narratives. The very act of critical self-examination out of which many of the narratives were generated made it incumbent upon the former captives honestly and humbly to verbalize their own unworthiness to have received the outpouring of divine mercy and grace that they had. Yet some modern commentators have taken such confessions to be yet another symptom of the anxious or neurotic search for evidence of salvation among the Puritans, or to be evidence of the clerical coercion of lay persons as the clergy sought to maintain hegemonic control over all discourse. We need to beware of making such judgments too hastily, however, without having first considered the evidence that some individuals freely and willingly submitted themselves to this form of spiritual discipline.

Captivity Narratives by Laypersons

Having examined several clerical representations of Indian captivity, we now turn to a consideration of captivity tales told by laypersons, paying special attention to the descriptions of their religious practices found therein. This latter point is important because, as we found in studying the Rowlandson narrative, the reports of the religious practices of captives provide important clues to their interpretive activity while in captivity. But before turning to the Swarton narrative, let us cast a glance at a brief letter sent to Cotton Mather by a captive. This letter permits us to glimpse something of the way in which oral and written texts were interwoven in webs of signification in the lives of the Puritans, both experientially and then retrospectively in the continuation of the narrative process.

In *Good Fetch'd out of Evil* and again in *A Memorial of the Present Deplorable State of New-England*, both published in 1706, Mather reprinted a letter, dated September 18, 1703, which he had received from William Clap, a layman then held captive in Canada. The letter opens: "Reverend Sir, The occasion of my now Writing to you is, because I Ly under Vow and Promise, to the Great & Almighty God, to declare & make known his wonderful Goodness and Mercy to me, & likewise to have His Name Blessed & Praised in your Congregation on my behalf." Clap then briefly recounts how he had been taken prisoner by the French and how, on the subsequent forced march to Canada, the party had fallen into such dire straits that the two French guards considered killing and eating him. The letter then continues,

> Then I begged Liberty to Pray unto God, before he killed me; & he granted it me. As I was at Prayer, it struck into my Mind, That I had formerly heard your self declare in your Pulpit, what great & wonderful things had been done by Prayer; Particularly, That it had "Stopped the Mouths of Lions." & that it had "Quenched the Violence of the Fire." So I earnestly begged of God, that He would manifest His Great Power to me, by turning the Hearts of those that were about to take away my Life. The words were no sooner out of my Mouth, but the Frenchman, seeming to have Tears in his Eyes, bid me, "Rise up"; He would try one day longer. (*Garland* 4:44–46)

Here one can glimpse how, when facing imminent death, Clap recalled parts of a sermon he had once heard Mather deliver. As he prayed aloud in front of his would-be executioner, Mather's general declarations on the power of God were applied by Clap to his immediate situation. When the Frenchman, overhearing his pitiful prayer, relented and spared his life, Clap attributed this to divine intervention and subsequently reported this remarkable instance of divine mercy and providence to Mather in Boston. Mather in turn published Clap's letter, adding the following scripture: "Psal. 107. 15. Oh that men would Praise the Lord for His Goodness, and for His Wonderful Works to the Children of Men." With this gesture, Mather effectively denies textual closure, for every remarkable instance of God's working in New England was taken to be a part of an unfolding text that he and the community of Saints were under a covenantal obligation to read and spell.

If Mather felt the need to add an "improvement" to his third-person retelling of the Dustan captivity, he felt no such compunction when "A Narrative of Hannah Swarton, Containing Wonderful Passages, relating to her Captivity, and her Deliverance" was added as an appendix to the printed version of one of his sermons.[14]

This was no doubt because Swarton had so thoroughly taken his directives in his humiliation sermon to heart. There, it will be recalled, Mather had charged Hannah Dustan and the other two returned captives—"you, that have been under the Mighty Hand of God, are to Humble your selves, under that Hand. . . . You will seriously consider, *What you shall render to the Lord for all His Benefits?*" Significantly enough, Swarton ends her own narrative with this same biblical passage, restored to its original first-person form—"What shall I render to the Lord for all His Benefits?"

In many ways the Swarton narrative represents an orthodox Puritan interpretation of the significance of captivity. It is not merely an account of what had transpired during her captivity; it is a public confession of her sins and of the righteousness of the afflictions she had suffered. As such, this text raises the issue of the hegemony of the Puritan theological worldview in a clear fashion. It is possible to argue that it provides important evidence that some people at least did take the interpretive frame proffered by the clergy seriously, even voluntarily employing it during their own acts of retrospective narration. Not all scholars have chosen to view the Swarton narrative in this way, however. Alden Vaughan and Edward Clark, for instance, suggest that the narrative was in fact written by Mather. The reasons given for making this assumption are unconvincing. For example, they take the incorporation of "abundant and precise biblical quotations" to be indicative of a clerical hand, but surely this is unremarkable for a text from this sociohistorical locus.[15]

The Bible was studied regularly by most Puritans, both in collective ritual settings and in private. Indeed, the Bible permeated almost all forms of Puritan discourse, oral and written. To imply that only the clergy had "precise" control of biblical passages is to draw too sharp a distinction between the clergy and the laity on this score. In fact, many Puritans had memorized large parts of the Bible, especially the psalms. Thus, there is no reason to assume that Swarton could not have had ready control of biblical verses. Moreover, there is no indication that Swarton composed her narrative without access to a Bible (she had one in captivity), so she could easily have checked each passage.

The best way to determine whether Swarton could have composed this work is, I suggest, to read the narrative carefully while watching for references to her religious practices in captivity. As in the Mary Rowlandson narrative, these provide invaluable clues to Swarton's own interpretive practices and suggest that this text assumed the shape it did because the interpretive frame and reading practices that the clergy had been inculcating for generations had, in fact, been internalized by Swarton, who found them beneficial.

This possibility offers several advantages over the assumption that only a clergyman could be the author. First, it recognizes the high rate of literacy among the New England Puritans and avoids the error of assuming that only the clergy knew the Bible well. More importantly, though, we do not have to see the clergy as having imposed alien interpretations upon the stories of laymen and women, who were unable to resist this. The laity were not essentially passive, powerless, and voiceless. Thus, there is no compelling reason to assume that Swarton was incapable of putting her own experiences into meaningful communicative form, either because she lacked the intellectual wherewithal or because she could not resist the readings of the clergy. This description of the power situation in Puritan society is too crude to be useful; it is also false. As Norbert Elias, Michel Foucault, Pierre Bourdieu and others have demonstrated, the exercise of power is more subtle and complex. Finally, and perhaps most seriously, though, the Vaughan-Clark position strips the ordinary men and women of their basic human dignity by denying that they, too, could be hermeneuts in their own right.

A text such as Swarton's provides an important test case of the purported hegemony of the clergy. The religious worldview informing this text was not an intellectual structure adopted after the fact and then retrospectively used to order Swarton's tale. Rather, a careful reading of this narrative discloses that Swarton's religious worldview was lived through, and immediately informed, her experience of captivity. In addition, it also provides insight into the intertextual nature of Puritan historiography and of the social construction of Puritan reality. It provides evidence of a highly developed and thoroughgoing form of *conscious self-control* among some members of the laity, rather than of a false consciousness.

Swarton's understanding of the deep meaning of the sudden and dramatic changes in her personal world, "now Bereaved of Husband, Children, Friends, Neighbours, House, Estate, Bread, Cloaths, or Lodging suitable," was not achieved on her own, of course (*Garland* 1:56). This meaning was socially negotiated; it was a result of the imbrication of her tale in the larger ongoing cultural and communal discourse of New England. We also must acknowledge the fact that Swarton would have had a significant incentive to craft and style her account in an orthodox fashion, for by doing so she would have accrued a certain amount of cultural capital.

If in her narrative Swarton follows the pattern recommended by Mather in his sermon, admitting her sins and backsliding, acknowledging that she was punished less than these sins deserved, and publicly recognizing God's mercy and providential assistance even during her captivity, these do not necessarily indicate that she had been subjected to heavy-handed coercion. Rather, one should hear her narrative account as part of a conversion narrative, an important public rite of reincorporation into the society of Visible Saints. In such a ritual occasion and public form of expression, the occasion and existing forms would have helped to shape an individual's account. "When candidates met a congregation to advertise their grace," Charles Cohen tells us, "the expectations of each party influenced the course of events. Churches anticipated that applicants would, or at least should, live up to a well-articulated ideal that combined both subjective and objective notices of regeneration."[16] The Swarton narrative must be understood in these same terms, especially in passages such as the following, which has the ring of a public confession:

> My Indian Mistress, was one that had been bred by the English at Black Point, and now Married to a Canada Indian, & turned Papist; and she would say, *That had the English been as careful to instruct her in our Religion, as the French were, to instruct her in theirs, she might have been of our Religion;* and she would say, *That God delivered us into their Hands, to punish us for our Sins;* And, This I knew was true as to my self. And as I desired to consider of all my Sins, for which the Lord did punish me, so this Lay very heavy upon my Spirit, many a Time, that I had Left the Publick Worship and Ordinances of God, where I formerly Lived (viz. at Beverley) to Remove to the North part of Casco Bay, where there was no Church, or Minister of the Gospel; and this we did, for large accommodations in the World, thereby Exposing our Children, to be bred Ignorantly like Indians, and our selves to forget what we had been formerly instructed in; and so we turned our Backs upon Gods Ordinances to get this Worlds Goods. (*Garland* 1:55–56)

Swarton goes on to ascribe the Indian attack, the resultant destruction, and her own suffering in captivity to divine punishment for her sins. Surprisingly, perhaps, we find the same orthodox reading of her captivity coming from a Christianized Indian, who had been introduced to both English Protestant theology and practice and French Catholicism. Swarton gives no indication whether the Indian woman had intended any irony; if she had, it was apparently lost on Swarton.

Earlier we saw that in Puritan usage the verb "to remove" could imply a change in one's spiritual relationship with God, as well as a physical distancing. This is pertinent here as Hannah recounts how a physical move away from a churched community was also a move away from God and into an existential "wilderness." In this passage one can hear the plaintive voice of a woman, bereft of her family and penniless, trying to come to grips with her situation in perhaps the only (or the best) way which seemed to be available to her. It is, of course, impossible to know whether her expression of contrition was genuine or not, but there is no need to discount it as unusual or to take it to be a sign of clerical rewriting.

Most probably Swarton's narrative was composed for a rite of public confession. Some support for this supposition may be found in the fact that the passage cited immediately above continues with Hannah confessing that she had not been diligent enough in her practice of self-examination while in captivity. "I was so amazed with many Troubles," she wrote, "and hurried in my Spirit from one Exercise to another, how to preserve my self in danger, and supply my self in the want that was present; that I had not time or leisure so composedly to consider of the great Concernment of my Soul, as I should have done; neither had I any *Bible* or *Good Book* to look into, or Christian Friend to be my Counsellor in these Distresses. But I may say, The *Words of God*, which I had formerly heard or read, many of them came oft into my mind, and kept me from *perishing in my Afflictions.*"

Swarton maintains, though, that throughout her ordeal she had placed her faith in God and had at times found solace in recalling pertinent biblical passages, just as she had engaged in earnest prayer after having adopted a proper attitude of humiliation. For instance, she reports, "As, when they threatened to Kill me many times, I often thought of the words of our Saviour to Pilate, Joh. 19. 11. *Thou couldest have no power at all against me, except it were given thee from above.* I knew they had *no power* to kill me, but what the *Lord gave* them; and I had many times Hope, that the Lord would not suffer them to slay me, but deliver me out of their Hands, and in His Time, I hoped, return me to my Country again" (*Garland* 1:55). Swarton's suffering in captivity led her in time to examine her soul and past actions; in doing so, she found herself wanting on any number of scores. In this situation, like Rowlandson before her, she prayed to God and made a vow to reform if God would forgive her and lift his rod from her.

In reading Swarton's captivity as a (re)conversion narrative, one hears echoes of the patterned recitations, filled with confessions of sin, anxieties over whether the confessant could ever merit salvation, and remembered instances of biblical verses that were offered before committees of elders judging the qualifications of applicants for church membership. According to Patricia Caldwell, a student of the Puritan conversion narratives, "Scriptural passages become structural elements of the narrative, and there is, so to speak, an actual movement of the narrator through the Bible, almost as through a physical space. When this movement works well, it provides . . . [a] satisfying literary form by a strong reliance on the creative internalization of scripture."[17]

This "movement of the narrator through the Bible, almost as through a physical space" captures precisely the experience and narrative representation of one's removal from God and the community of Saints and of return or restoration found in the narratives of Rowlandson, Swarton, and others. Time and again Swarton witnesses to the ways in which her own internalization of Scripture "shaped the moral contours of her experience" and her reflections while a captive, or long before she composed her written account. Sacvan Bercovitch has noted that Cotton Mather often "transmutes history itself into a drama of the soul." However, "to transmute history does not . . . mean to reject or to submerge historical details. It does mean that the 'real facts' become a means to a higher end, a vehicle for laying bare the soul—or more accurately, the essential landmarks in the soul's journey to God. And the journey of the soul thus abstracted provides a guide for every man—of any age, any culture, indifferently past, passing, or to come—in the choices he must face, the war he must engage in between the forces of evil and good in his heart."[18]

Though on a less grand scale, Swarton does the same with the events of her captivity as she describes her journey *back* to God. Representing herself as a backslider, she recounts a spiritual journey of reconversion, of her return to the community of Saints, and of her newly found vocation of "declaring the works of the Lord" in her life. The following passage could easily have come from a text in Caldwell's collection of conversion narratives:

> I have had many Conflicts in my own Spirit; fearing that I was not truely *Converted* unto God in Christ, and that I had no Saving

Interest in Christ. I could not be of a *False Religion*, to please men [i.e., her French Catholic captors]; for it was against my Conscience: And I was not fit to suffer for the *True Religion*, and for Christ; for I then feared, I had no Interest in Him. I was neither fit to *Live*, nor fit to *Dye*; and brought once to the very pit of *Despair*, about what would become of my Soul. In this Time I had gotten an *English Bible*, and other Good Books, by the help of my Fellow Captives. I Looked over the Scripture, and settled on the Prayer of *Jonah*, and those Words, *I said, I am cast out of thy sight, yet will I Look again towards thy Holy Temple.* I Resolved, I would do as *Jonah* did: And in the Meditation upon this Scripture, the Lord was pleased, by His *Spirit*, to come into my Soul, and so fill me with Ravishing Comfort, that I cannot Express it. (*Garland* 1:66–68)

This passage is perhaps as clear a statement as one will find in the literature of the period of the way Puritan men and women lived through the Bible. Here the captivity narrative and the conversion narrative are one. The long section from which this passage was taken contains all of the classic elements of the conversion experience, as Cohen has described them. The same "affective cycle" he finds in conversion narratives is also found in full in Swarton's narrative. The characteristic series of emotions individuals passed through in the conversion experience included the following: (1) an initial sorrow over sin intensifies into hate of it; (2) upon realizing his inability to win his own salvation, the individual begins to despair; (3) an awakening of faith transforms despondency into joy and a love of God; (4) this in turn evidences the Spirit's presence and proof of election, which gives the individual confidence in his ability now to follow God's commands. The Swarton narrative matches this description of the way Puritans experienced and spoke about conversion to a remarkable degree. Swarton recounts her growing recognition of her past sins and the despair this occasioned because of a growing sense that she was incapable of achieving salvation ("fearing . . . that I had not Saving Interest in Christ.") This is followed by an awareness of faith, producing a sense of joy, peace, and love of God ("And in the Meditation upon this Scripture ['I am cast out of thy sight, yet will I Look again towards thy Holy Temple.'], the Lord was pleased, by His Spirit, to come into my Soul, and so fill me with Ravishing Comfort").

Swarton's narrative presents her account of what her captivity came to mean to her. Cohen points out, rightly, I think, that to suggest that women who embraced Puritan theology and ideology thereby lost all real power is to misunderstand and misconstrue what the expression of helplessness signified in Puritan society (and, one might add, what this effected in the individual's psyche). "Conversion," he writes, "was a responsive mechanism for instilling a sense of potency in everyone who submitted to God. The search for power ended in the arms of the Lord."[19]

Like Rowlandson before her, Swarton confesses her initial weakness and lack of resolution in the face of death. But she faced not only the fear of reversion to savagery but also that of being seduced into embracing what was considered to be a false faith—Roman Catholicism. The Other here is dual—Indian and papist. "Yet I dreaded going to Canada, to the French," Swarton reports, "for fear lest I should be overcome by them, to yield to their Religion; which I had Vowed unto God, *That I would not do.* But the Extremity of my Sufferings were such, that at length I was willing to go, to preserve my Life" (*Garland* 1:59). However, she goes on to recount how she had countered the arguments and scriptural interpretations offered by the French to convince her to convert to Catholicism by citing other scriptural passages back to them. Similar scenes are found in other captivities from the French and Indian War period, such as the Rev. John Williams's *The Redeemed Captive Returning to Zion* (1707).

Swarton had begun to search for meaning in her captivity through Puritan devotional practices before she was ransomed and returned to New England. She recalls, for instance, "I found much Comfort, while I was among the *French,* by the Opportunities I had sometimes to *Read* the Scriptures, and other Good Books, and *Pray* to the Lord in Secret; and the *Conference* that some of us Captives had together, about things of God, and *Prayer* together sometimes; especially with one that was in the same House with me, *Margaret Stilson.* Then was the Word of God precious to us, and they that *feared the LORD, spake one to another* of it, as we had Opportunity. And Colonel *Tyng* and Mr. *Alden,* as they were permitted, did speak to us, to Confirm and Strengthen us, in the wayes of the Lord" (*Garland* 1:68).

The invocation of the names of specific individuals here is of special note, for it suggests that Swarton anticipated corroborative testimony concerning her religious activities during her captivity. Such corroboration was commonly elicited in the investigation by the church as it sought for visible signs of an individual's conversion. In this passage we can glimpse how, in their own attempt to understand the religious meaning of captivity, the captives appealed to comparable precedents in the Bible. Biblical verses that had provided solace to one individual in private reading or through recollection were apparently shared with the other captives, whenever the opportunity presented itself, in the hope that they would be of comfort to them as well.

Hermeneutical activity, then, was not the preserve of the clergy. Laymen and women actively engaged in the discussion of the meaning of the Bible in terms of their immediate circumstances, the prospects for their eventual return to their homes and for reunion with family members, and concerning their afterlife.[21] The following report by Hannah Swarton comes amidst a long litany of scriptural passages that had provided comfort to her in captivity. She writes, "I had very often, a secret perswasion, That I should *Live to Declare the Works of the Lord*. And, 2 Chron. 6. 36, 37, 38, 39. was a precious Scripture to me, in the Day of Evil. We have *Read* over, and *Pray'd* over, this Scripture together, and *Talk'd* together of this Scripture, *Margaret* and I; How the Lord hath Promised, Though they were *Scattered for their Sins*, yet there should be a *Return*, if they did *Bethink themselves*, and *Turn*, and *Pray*. So we did *Bethink our selves* in the Land where we were *Carried Captive*, did *Turn*, did *Pray*, and Endeavour to *Return to God with all our Hearts*" (*Garland* 1:69–71).

Swarton and her fellow captives shuttled back and forth between what they took to be biblical parallels and precedents and their own situations. The cause-and-effect relationships presented in biblical texts were used to provide a way of comprehending what had befallen them and their families. Similarly, the denouement of certain biblical tales, seized on as relevant, suggested what might lie in their own future. In this way biblical verses were a "Great Comfort" and buoyed the captives' spirits because they were read and understood as promises that God had not abandoned them but would effect their restoration and redemption. Moreover, through reading, praying over, and discussing 2 Chronicles 6:36–39 together, Swarton and Margaret Stilson determined that this promise of restoration and redemption was contingent upon their adopting a specific program of ritual and meditative activity modeled on that prescribed in this biblical passage. They did not need clergy to come to this understanding; they had learned and had full control of a complex set of hermeneutical procedures.

Moreover, while still in captivity, Swarton had already envisioned herself assuming a public voice after her redemption in order "to Declare the Works of the Lord." The "secret perswasion" she often felt was the conviction that she would survive precisely so that she could do this (*Garland* 1:70). This purpose also made the tragic events meaningful and worthwhile rather than merely tragic. Subordinating individual tragedy to a larger divine plan in this way is not incompatible with the recognition of human agents acting purposefully.

At the end of her narrative, Swarton readily acknowledges that human agency played a role in her release—"The means of my Deliverance, were by reason of Letters that had passed between the Governments of New England and of Canada" (*Garland* 1:71)— even while she maintains that the ultimate cause was the merciful action of God. At the time her narrative was composed, Swarton still had two children, aged nineteen and twenty, in captivity. She ends by asking for the prayers of her fellow Christians that her children, too, might be redeemed and restored to her and the community of Saints. At the time of her telling her tale, Swarton had, through her devotional activities, found a certain optimism, a renewed sense of identity, and a public voice in the wake of the tragedy she had passed through.

Putting the story of the traumatic events of her recent past into a readily recognizable and culturally meaningful form had immediate this-worldly benefits as well. Among other things, Swarton could then expect a generally sympathetic response, but, more importantly perhaps, the circulation of her tale provided a means of collectively sharing her grief and of transforming it at the same time. Just as the distress felt following the death of a loved one in war may be mitigated somewhat by the sympathy shown by others and by representing it as a sacrifice for the national good, the pain and grief of many captives was made meaningful by locating it within a larger covenantal metahistory. For captives like Swarton, telling their tales was also a way of bringing something good out of the violence, death, and destruction, because these acts of witnessing might lead others back to Christ. She could assume that many people would hear or read her narrative in a predictable way insofar as they shared similar values and reading practices. For example, in encountering and then pondering a captivity narrative, the hearers or readers were expected to recall relevant biblical passages that would improve the narrative, turning it to their own personal spiritual benefit. Such biblical verses were often provided in the text, either in part or whole; at other times only chapter and verse were mentioned, since it was assumed that readers would either recall the passage from memory or would pause at that point to consult a Bible. Readers could also use their own store of memorized scripture to improve a tale of outward captivity by engaging in Puritan typologies on their own, just as we have seen captives themselves doing while prisoners.

In this manner, the acts of composing, listening to, and reading such captivity narratives were readily assimilated into the daily devotional practices of the Puritans. Captivity narratives were generated and circulated, both orally and in written form, because of theological "enjoynments" to do so and because laymen and women found them of service in their own ritual practices of self-examination, humiliation, and (re)conversion.

Puritan reading practices were, as we have seen, decidedly intertextual. This fact had consequences that bear looking at because the Puritan act of reading works for meditation was very different from the way we consume most texts today. A devotional text was not read linearly in a nonstop fashion, nor was it read in isolation. The goal in reading a devotional text was not to find out what happened next or to follow a storyline to its conclusion. The plots of such works were well known already, since the works were used time and again in devotional exercises. The reading practices and strategies recommended by the clergy—and widely embraced by the laity—continually led the reader to call other texts to mind while reading, most especially Scripture, but also devotional texts, sermons, prayers, and even past discussions among laity in their private devotions.

In this culture a captivity narrative or any other devotional text, then, was never a linguistic object separate into itself; it was, rather, a porous narrative, open to other texts brought into association with it. In their reading practices, Puritans demonstrated an understanding that all such texts—and the potential meanings they carried—were woven from relations drawn with other texts and finally to the Bible as the definitive metatext. As a result, Puritans often read at a much slower pace than we do today, as readers were "enjoyned" to pause over every scene in a narrative—to observe, to ponder, to mentally "compose the place," then to enter imaginatively into the scene in order to be instructed. In devotional reading, every scene was to be read in relation to one's own life and spiritual condition, as Per Amicum had charged the readers of Rowlandson's narrative: "Read therefore, peruse, ponder, and from hence lay up something from the experience of another, against thine own turn comes: that so thou also through patience and consolation of the Scripture mayest have hope."

Seventeenth- and eighteenth-century readers read for a pleasure distinct from that of most modern readers; while the latter may seek a temporary escape or release through reading fiction or even works of nonfiction, the "concernments" of the Puritans were focused on the eternal condition of their souls. They read "good" books because, as John Williams suggested, they believed themselves to be "under an obligation" to instruct themselves morally and spiritually through doing so. This is not to deny that readers may also have found a certain pleasure in conforming their reading practices to those that were culturally validated as good and proper, but Puritans were continually warned against this sort of prideful pleasure. Anything that smacked of smugness, self-congratulation, or self-assurance was subject to sharp criticism.

In addition, both the consumption and the generation of captivity narratives must be viewed within the larger cultural project of Puritan sacred historiography. Through shared reading practices, the affliction of captivity was transformed into spiritual food for thought as captives and readers alike (who were themselves understood to be equally subject to "inward captivity") learned that "to the hungry soul, every bitter thing is sweet."

Captivity Tales in the Broader World

Up to this point we have concentrated exclusively on works written by Puritans. However, Puritans were not the only persons to compose captivity narratives. For comparative purposes we turn our attention to a few selected examples of these other texts. By examining captivity tales told by Quakers, we will be able to gain some sense of whether elements found in Puritan texts were, in fact, parts of a broader cultural ethos not strictly limited to the Puritan sphere. Finally, the introduction of two late texts, by a Puritan layman and a clergyman respectively, will permit us to discern any possible changes that may have occurred in Puritan representational activity after the death of Cotton Mather in 1728.

Jonathon Dickinson (1663–1722) was a wealthy Quaker merchant and slave owner. His captivity narrative, *Gods Protecting Providence Man's Surest Help and Defence* (1699), was originally a journal he had kept on board a ship bound from Jamaica to Philadelphia which floundered in a storm off the coast of Florida in September 1696.[21] The crew and passengers were forced to abandon ship but were then captured by Indians on shore. Dickinson continued to keep his journal in captivity. It was published, with a preface, in the hope that others might profit from the spiritual lessons he had learned.

Though written by a Quaker, this work bears some striking similarities to the Puritan narratives we have already surveyed, including the stated reason for its publication. Dickinson's narrative suggests that the worldview informed by providential theology was not unique to the Puritans; neither was the compunction people felt to witness publicly to the mercies shown to them by God, the burden of his preface.

At the same time, we must recognize that similarities of content and the strategies of representation employed do not imply identity. There are significant differences between Quaker and Puritan texts that deserve attention. James Levernier and Henning Cohen have noted, for instance, that "Quakers shared the Puritan belief that through Indian captivity God manifested his power over human destiny, but not their belief that captivity was a punishment for sin. They also saw the Indian differently. Quakers treated Indians with humanity. They conceived of them as 'savage men' in need of enlightenment rather than as fiends from Hell."[22]

The title page of Dickinson's narrative is instructive. In putting this initial face on the narrative, the printer was obviously influenced by earlier captivity narratives, even though the content of Dickinson's text was in some ways noticeably different. We do not know whether Dickinson had a hand in determining the title, but it is entirely possible that he did not. Not only is a theological interpretive frame proffered in the title, but there are at least three phrases on the title page that suggest a familiarity with earlier captivity narratives and help to establish an intertextual relation: (1) "REMARKABLE DELIVERANCE," located in the center of the page in full caps second in size only to "GODS" at the top of the page, signals the work's theological interpretive frame; (2) "cruelly devouring jawes of the inhumane CANIBALS," which casts the captors as ravenous beasts; and (3) "faithfully related," promising a true and theologically correct account. This title page seems to have been pitched to an audience whose expectations had been shaped by earlier Puritan texts and shared reading practices. The manner in which this Quaker text was presented to the public, then, was affected by the Puritan representation of captivity that dominated the market.

The preface, by an anonymous author, opens with the argument that it is incumbent upon those who have received "signal favours" from God to witness to the protecting hand of providence by publishing accounts of the blessings they had known. As in the Puritan works, we find a desire to acknowledge God's hand in the "remarkable outward deliverances" the captives have known. The author's guiding assumption is that *"The hearts of all men are in the hand of God, he can turn them as he pleases"* (*Garland* 4:1, unpaginated preface). Among the instances he cites are the following: when Indians were about to kill the shipwrecked men and women on the coast, God had moved the native *"Casseekey* (or King)" to stop them; arrows shot at the shipwrecked men had missed their mark; and the wife of a chief had been moved to protect the prisoners.

Much of the preface is devoted to an account of Robert Barrow, an English Quaker preacher and missionary who had heard the call in 1694 to come to Jamaica and South Carolina to spread the gospel. Shipwrecked along with Dickinson, Barrow died of illness shortly after being released from captivity in 1697. He is described as having been a paragon of Quaker virtues, suffering all sorts of afflictions for, among other things, refusing to lie about his nationality when asked by the Indians, although, in order to avoid more severe treatment and possible death, all of the others had claimed that they were Spanish, since the Indians were allied with them. At the same time, the author points out the multiple providences of God, appealing to this agency to explain why some persons had not survived captivity, while others, whom one might have expected to perish more readily, survived (*Garland* 4:3, unpaginated preface). Even before his captivity, Barrow had been imprisoned at least seven times for his religious beliefs, because of, in his own words, the "resolution . . . not to bow a knee to Baal."

Dickinson's narrative proper is punctuated with references to the workings of divine providence, though without the frequency found in Puritan narratives. The citations of biblical passages, so common in Puritan narratives, are also missing. This is not to say, however, that the captives never had recourse to the Bible. Dickinson reports that at one point in their captivity Barrows had encouraged the group by expounding on a biblical passage. Yet, significantly, he provides no indication that the laymen turned to biblical verses on their own in an effort to understand their situation in captivity. As in the Puritan narratives, though, both the Indians and the European enemy (here the Spanish) are described as "Instruments" of the Lord, a rhetorical move that effectively deflects full recognition of their human virtues. Indeed, the thing that most troubled Dickinson and his wife during their captivity was the thought that if they were to die, their child "would be kept alive, and bred up as one of those People" (*Garland* 4:15–16, 80, 45).

The Dickinson narrative proper is a largely mundane account of what had transpired in captivity. This is not to say it was a secular account in the modern sense of the term; as it was sent into the world, the title page and the preface presented a providential interpretive frame to the reader. Yet the structure of the main text is not informed by this.

A brief glance at another Quaker work, *God's Mercy Surmounting Man's Cruelty* (1728), provides additional insight into the areas of overlap and difference between Quaker and Puritan works. The tale of a Quaker woman, Elizabeth Hanson (1684–1737), who had been abducted in the summer of 1724 in New Hampshire by a French and Indian war party, this narrative is much shorter than Dickinson's, consisting of only forty pages. The authorship of this text is something of a vexed question. The only extant copy of the first American edition is missing the title page and the last three pages. The title it is known by today was taken from an advertisement for the text in the *Pennsylvania Gazette* of December 24, 1728. This notice indicates that "the Substance" of the first American edition "was taken from [Hanson's] own Mouth," but by whom is unclear. The title page of the first English edition of 1760 reports that the account was "taken in substance from her own mouth, by Samuel Bownas," a well-known Quaker preacher, who had died seven years earlier in 1753. Yet in his autobiography, published in 1756, Bownas writes, "From thence I went to visit the widow Hanson, who had been taken into captivity by the Indians, an account of which I took from her own mouth, being in substance as followeth," and he proceeds to give a one-page account. He also reports having seen a published version of Hanson's captivity when he was in Dublin in 1740, but he does not claim authorship for this.[24] From this, we can surmise that many persons must have visited Hanson and heard her retell her tale. As with other tales, the kind and the extent of the former captive's participation in the composition and publication of the narrative are unclear. Both the Philadelphia and the London editions are told in the first-person, however.

The opening passage by the anonymous first editor suggests that the narrative was being published in order to "help and assist those that fear [God] and put their Confidence in him," by reporting the remarkable providences of God. Elizabeth had witnessed the mur-

der of two of her children before she was carried off along with a
fourteen-day-old infant, a son aged six, two daughters aged fourteen and sixteen, and a servant girl. She and the rest of her family
were ransomed by her husband a year later, although the eldest
daughter had by then been married to a Frenchman in Canada,
where she decided to remain. Like Dickinson's narrative, this
work does not contain many scriptural citations, although it still
has a strong religious tone. Moreover, one particular verse cited
does not function as an interpretive frame for some aspect of her
captivity, as it would in Puritan narratives; rather, it appears in a
passage reporting that when one of her daughters had been pressed
by the Indians to sing for them, she performed Psalm 137 (*Garland*
6:10).

Like many of the narratives we have seen, Hanson also ascribes
acts of kindness shown to her by the Indian during captivity to
God. "In all," she reports, her Indian master "shewed some Humanity and Civility more than I could have expected: For which
privilege I was secretly thankful to God as the moving Cause
thereof." Elsewhere, Hanson reports that initially her Indian master physically abused her son so much that his own mother-in-law
fought with him over this and moved out of his wigwam. She notes
with undisguised satisfaction that God had intervened and punished the abusive Indian by causing him to fall ill.

At points in the narrative one comes across passages that suggest that Hanson's regular devotional practices were very similar
to those of her Puritan neighbors. She writes, for instance, "My
Mind was greatly exercised towards the Lord, that I, with my
dear Children separated from me, might be preserved from repin-
ing against God, under our Affliction on the one Hand, and on
the other, we might have our Dependance on him who rules the
Hearts of Men, and can do what pleases in the Kingdoms of the
Earth, knowing that his Care is over them who put their Trust in
him; but I found it very hard to keep my Mind as I ought, under the
Resignation which is proper to be in, under such Afflictions and
sore Trials" (*Garland* 6:9–10, 29–30, 18–19).

Within the account, one can also overhear a prayer offered by
Elizabeth as she tried to come to grips with the death of her husband, just seven months after she had been repatriated, while he
was on a journey to Canada in an attempt to redeem their eldest
daughter, Sarah. The narrative ends on the same note as Mary
Rowlandson's, almost fifty years earlier, with Hanson saying,
"The many Deliverances and wonderful Providences of God unto

us, and over us, have been, and I hope will so remain to be as a continued Obligation on my Mind ever to live in that Fear, Love and Obedience to God, duly regarding, by his Grace, with Meekness and Wisdom, to approve myself by his Spirit, in all Holiness of Life, and Godliness of Conversation, to the praise of him that hath called me, who is God blessed forever" (*Garland* 6:36–38).

Like Rowlandson and many others, Hanson turned to her faith in order to make sense out of the afflictions she suffered. We can never know how successful her efforts were, but it behooves us to accept her tale as she offered it, in the sacrificial sense of that term, to the public. In telling her tale, Hanson offered up her afflictions and grief in the body of her text in the hope that both God and her readers would be moved thereby. While not a devotional text in quite the same way Rowlandson's was, this work still sought to instruct the reader and to promote a proper relationship with God.

Memoirs of Odd Adventures, Strange Deliverances, &c. In the Captivity of John Gyles, Esq., published in Boston in 1736, reveals a significant attenuation of various features of the Puritan captivity narrative. Gyles had been captured at the age of ten in Maine, along with his father, mother, and three brothers and sisters. He became quite fluent in the Indian languages in his six years among the Indians and later served as an interpreter for the government. Vaughan and Clark have characterized this distinctive narrative as "part horror story, part ethnography, part natural history, and part sermon," while suggesting that Gyles, "the most secular of the Puritan narrators, may have leaned heavily on a local chaplain for stylistic guidance."[25]

Even the title page is noticeably different—there are neither scriptural citations nor mention of "remarkable providences," only "Odd Adventures" and "Strange Deliverances." And, in lieu of a biblical passage, one finds an extract from Homer's *Odyssey* setting the scene. It is the introduction, though, which best captures the distance of Gyles's text from the Puritan narratives. One learns that it was his wife (and possibly his pastor) who had urged him to employ the theological frame, such as it is, found in the narrative. Yet rather than religious humility, Gyles displays his obstreperous nature, even directly challenging the reader who might dare to criticize his narrative.

There is no indication that Gyles felt any strong impetus to bring his tale to the public for its spiritual well-being. Indeed, resistance to Puritan narrative expectations is palpable, while Gyles's attempts to put a theological interpretation on events are awkward at best. For instance, at one point he proudly recalls how he once earned the Indians' respect by beating up a young male who had been harassing him, and then adds a pious tag almost as an afterthought (*Garland* 6:19).

Gyles's captivity narrative may be compared with *A Narrative of the Captivity of Nehemiah How* (1748), issued by the same publisher. How (1693–1747) had been taken by the Indians in Vermont in 1745, during King George's War, and carried to Canada where he died in prison. This text appears to be a journal he had kept in prison. Like the Gyles narrative, it contains no biblical passages in the body of the text, although the printer placed the first four verses of Psalm 137 on the title page. The religious passages one finds in the text, however, seem sincere. Immediately after he was taken, for instance, How reports, "They then led me into the Swamp and pinion'd me. I then committed my Case to God, and pray'd, that since it was his Will to deliver me into the Hands of these cruel Men, I might find Favour in their Eyes: Which Request, God of his infinite Mercy was pleased to grant; for they were generally kind to me while I was with 'em" (*Garland* 6:3; see also 5, 12).

Moreover, How reports having led other prisoners in daily worship in a form his Puritan forebears would have recognized. "When I had been there a few Days," he writes, "the Captives desir'd me to lead them in carrying on Morning and Evening Devotion, which I was willing to do: We had a Bible, a Psalm-Book, and some other good Books; our constant Practice was to read a Chapter in the Bible, and sing Part of a Psalm, and to pray, Night and Morning."

How's narrative is best known, however, as a source of historical information, for he carefully noted all of the persons he encountered during his captivity, as well as the dates many of his fellow captives died in prison. The journal ends with a notice "By another Hand" of Nehemiah How's own death in Quebec on May 25, 1747. This anonymous writer plays on a common metaphor in suggesting that How "is gone from a Captivity of Sorrow on Earth, to join in songs of everlasting Joy among the Ransom'd of the Lord in the heavenly Zion" (*Garland* 6:13, 22).

A list of subscribers for the How narrative follows, along with the towns they lived in, and the number of volumes each person had subscribed for. In colonial times most published works were printed by subscription, so that the printer was guaranteed his costs would be recovered. However, information on such subscriptions for captivity narratives is rare, making it difficult to judge how many copies of any given title may have circulated. From the published list here, we learn that for this second issue of the first edition there were fifty-two subscribers, who had preordered a total of 312 copies. Forty-eight subscribers took 6 books each; three asked for 7 copies; and one individual took 3. Nineteen subscribers were from Rutland, Vermont; the rest were scattered among twenty-one other nearby towns. All of the subscribers were male; six of them were named How. Nehemiah How's narrative seems to have been published as a memorial of sorts to an esteemed neighbor and relative, not unlike the reasons behind the publication of death sermons of the Puritan clergy. This is significant for it suggests that, even before the American Revolution, it had become acceptable to memorialize individuals in this way.

The final captivity narrative we will analyze, *The Redeemed Captive* (1748), was written by the Rev. John Norton, who had been a captive in Canada with How. It is not so much a story of captivity among the Indians as it is of life in a French prison in Quebec. Norton was a clergyman and this narrative indicates more clearly than most the ways in which Puritan discourse about captivity had changed by midcentury. The title page includes scriptural passages on captivity that are presented as parallels to Norton's own case, yet there is no explicit notice of divine providence at work here. The title page promises that the account will be found to be "both entertaining and affecting," suggesting the extent to which the reading practices and expectations had changed in New England by midcentury. This appeal is precisely to values associated with works of sentimental literature, as we will see in the next chapter. The title page also promises to provide the reader with as much historical information (an account of military preparations and tactics, the articles of surrender) as spiritual improvement.

The narrative proper bears out these observations. Written as a journal with irregular entries of varying length, Norton notes the mundane events unfolding around him rather than observing his soul under the divine affliction of captivity, as earlier Puritan authors would have. Even the single instance in the narrative when Norton mentions that an event had provoked him to recall a scriptural passage is telling, for it is quickly and radically qualified, as he writes, "Those who brought [an illness] into the Prison mostly recovered, and so there were many others that had it and recovered; but the Recovery of some was but for a Time,—many of them relapsed and died. It put me in mind of that Text, Jude, ver. 5,

'I will therefore put you in membrance tho'ye once knew this, how that the Lord having saved the People out of the Land of Egypt, afterwards destroyed them that believe not.' Not that I have any Reason to think ill of those upon whom the Sickness fell, and who died with it. Many of them, I hope, were truly pious and godly Persons. . . . Monday, 20. Jacob Reed died. He was taken at Gorham-Town, near Casco Bay, April 19, 1746" (*Garland* 6: 31).

While this passage suggests that humankind's fallen nature is such that even terrible divine wrath is justified, the sentiment is greatly qualified. Here the fire-and-brimstone of the jeremiad has largely expended its energy; Norton's God is less vindictive, while his own view of human nature is much more positive. In concert with this shift in theology, references to divine providence here are made almost in passing (see *Garland* 6:3–4, 12–13).

Whereas in 1703 the Rev. John Williams had debated the relative merits of Puritan and Roman Catholic theology with his French captors, the reader finds Norton debating the merits of those contending for King George's throne. Although Norton ends his narrative with the expected sentiment—"May I never forget the many great and repeated Mercies of God towards Me"—he more commonly expresses sentiments such as "From this Time [the 16th] to the 23d, there was nothing remarkable happened, only this:—that the Jesuits and some unknown Gentlemen, understanding I was short on it for Clothing, sent me several Shirts, a good winter Coat, some Caps, a pair of Stockings, and a few Handkerchiefs, which were very acceptable" (*Garland* 6:21–22, 40, 28).

In Norton's captivity, the remarkable instances of divine intervention in history are remarkable from a historical perspective largely because there are so few of them compared to seventeenth-century narratives. One might argue that perhaps Norton had been unable to improve his journal before its publication, but the fact that he lived for thirty years after its appearance and, apparently, was never moved to do so suggests otherwise. Rather, this work seems to indicate that the earlier Puritan reading and writing practices had broken down. In the mid-eighteenth century, history was no longer read in the same way it had been only a generation before.

If history (and captivity) had, indeed, come to be narrated and spelled differently, then one can say that Puritans and other readers and writers had not been captured or trapped within an ideology and a discourse. The seeds of change were already found in the works of Cotton Mather and other members of the clergy. By promoting literacy and the reading of the Bible in the daily lives of men and women, as well as devotional practices of self-scrutiny, Mather and others had enabled the people to employ hermeneutical techniques in private that could be extended to other areas and other texts.

By promoting an interior turn through regimens of self-scrutiny in devotional practice, the clergy and others led the people to trace and to read the movements of their souls and to take their own affective responses to be of great import. Neither Mather nor any of his compatriots could have forseen the developments these practices would lead to. It will be the burden of the next chapter to suggest some of these. We have seen, however, that it was in part a change in the devotional praxis of ordinary men and women and in reading practices that effected a broad-based and major cultural change.

3

CAPTURING THE AUDIENCE: SENTIMENTAL LITERATURE AND THE NEW READING COVENANT

> Though our brother is upon the rack, as long as we ourselves
> are at our ease, our senses will never inform us of what he
> suffers. They never did, and never can, carry us beyond our
> own person, and it is by the imagination only that we can
> form any conception of what are his sensations. . . . By the
> imagination we place ourselves in his situation, we conceive
> ourselves enduring all the same torments, we enter as it were
> into his body, and become in some measure the same person
> with him, and thence form some idea of his sensations.
> —Adam Smith

PURITAN CAPTIVITY NARRATIVES—part confessional, part medita-
tional text, and part jeremiad—were dominant for two generations. By the early eighteenth century the Puritan divines' monop-
oly over publication in America had ended, while the American
book trade saw ever-increasing imports of works, both nonfictional and fictional, from England and Europe.[1] Captivity was to
remain a popular literary theme, but it was to be narratively cast in
a different fashion and consumed to different effect. The most
significant development in terms of literary form was the emergence and tremendous popularity of the sentimental novel.

Most studies have overemphasized the discontinuities between
the Puritan works of the seventeenth century and the fictional
captivities of the eighteenth century while ignoring important
elements of continuity. Drawing upon the recent work of J. Paul
Hunter, G. J. Barker-Benfield, and others, I will suggest that the
sentimental novel developed out of the increased emphasis in

the eighteenth century on the affections of the heart—"sentiments"—as the locus of morality. With the appropriation and
adaptation of features of earlier genres, the sentimental novel
represented a newly emergent social reality.

The reading practices discussed in the preceding chapters were
adapted to new ends. The sentimental novel was both a product
and a producer of a new reading community, based on a shared
understanding (which I shall call a new "reading covenant") of
epistemology, human nature, and the moral significance of the
transaction between author, text, and audience. Only after tracing
the outlines of this emergent worldview, with its emphasis on the
moral significance of one's affective responses to the existential
situations of other human beings in the real world and in literature, will we be able to appreciate the cultural role the captivity
topos played at this time.

The sentimental novels that appeared in great numbers from the
1740s onwards, beginning most especially with Samuel Richardson's *Pamela*, were very different from the earlier sorts of texts we
have seen, even as they shared certain elements. The captivity
narratives produced in this period were not limited to sentimental
works, but a large number were cast in this mode. Moreover,
Pamela, the paradigm of virtue-in-distress, was herself a captive
of a sort, suggesting an early link between sentimental fiction
and the captivity topos.[2] In this chapter, two eighteenth-century
works—Edward Kimber's *The History of the Life and Adventures
of Mr. Anderson* (1754) and Ann Eliza Bleeker's *The History of
Maria Kittle* (1797)—will illustrate both the general assumptions
operative in sentimental literature and the way scenes of Indian
captivity functioned therein. Kimber's is one of the earliest sentimental novels to include a captivity episode, while Bleeker's work
represents a famous example of a fictional captivity narrative
presented to the reader as a factual account. Not limiting our pur-
view to works written or published in America may also remind us
that the book market of the late eighteenth and early nineteenth
centuries was transatlantic in nature, since many works of fiction
published in Europe were readily available in America.

It must be said immediately, however, that the distinction commonly drawn between fictional and nonfictional captivities is
problematic. Some of the fictional narratives are based, however
loosely, on an actual captivity (e.g., the many stories of Jane Mac-
Rea), while many so-called nonfictional works have been embellished (some a little bit, others to a much greater extent) with

events and scenes that did not happen. Moreover, narrative stylization in these works often functioned to shape disparate events into
similar tales. The intertextual relations among works were complex—works of fiction constantly borrowed descriptions and even
whole action scenes from earlier travel or journal accounts, while
factual accounts were similarly influenced by fictional descriptions. Many students of the captivity narratives have despaired
over the hybrid character of so many of these texts, preferring
plain, first-person, historical accounts above all others. Yet as
Cathy Davidson has reminded us in a different context, this approach to works of fiction from this period is wrongheaded; works
of fiction helped to create events in history through the very act of
narrative representation, which always included interpretation.[3]

Unfortunately, most fictional captivities have received short
shrift from literary critics and historians. Some critics have been
quick to dismiss many novels as penny dreadfuls, hardly worthy of
critical attention. Richard Van Der Beets, voicing a common prejudice, suggests that "for all practical purposes and with few exceptions, the two-hundred-year development of the narratives of Indian captivity culminates in the travesty of the Penny Dreadful."
Thirty-five years earlier Roy Harvey Pearce had stated as an obvious and indisputable fact, "The first, and greatest, of the captivity narratives are simple, direct religious documents," while
many of the later narratives were, to his mind at least, "mainly
vulgar, fictional, and pathological."[4] Many other critics have found
most of the popular novels to be bad literature and the products of
the hack writer gone wild. These novels are characterized as being
filled with cardboard characters, impossible plot twists, absurd
coincidences, and heavy-handed moralism. Moreover, most modern readers find the plots of sentimental novels to be both predictable and redundant, much as are the story lines of modern romance novels. Such judgments, though, finally tell us more about
the different reading structures and expectations of modern readers than they tell us anything of significance about the meaning of
these texts in the lives (imaginary and real) of earlier readers.

In 1794 Susanna Haswell Rowson, one of the most successful
American novelists of her generation, wrote, "I wonder that the
novel readers are not tired of reading one story so many times,
with only the variation of its being told in different ways."[5] While
Rowson was speaking of the sentimental novel, the genre in which
she worked, her comment is equally relevant to captivity narratives. Rowson's puzzlement is instructive, for she rightly sees that

the fact that a familiar plot remains popular over time is a problem requiring explanation. To her credit, unlike some modern scholars, she does not take the shared general plot to be an adequate explanation of the popularity of the texts. The pleasure readers found (and find) in reading basically the same story again and again was (and is) a function of the specific reading practices and expectations readers bring to them. In this regard, we may recall that many types of narrative, from myths and folktales to children's bedtime stories, are consumed not for their novelty but for their familiarity. As Wendy Doniger O'Flaherty has rightly noted, "People listen to the stories not merely to learn something new (communication), but to relive, together, the stories that they already know, stories about themselves (communion). Where communication is effective, communion is evocative."[6]

The consequences of failing to reconstruct the reading practices of earlier generations while projecting one's own back onto texts are evident in many studies. For example, in a generally excellent study of the literary representations of the American Indian, Louise K. Barnett's discussion of fictional captivities is marred by her uncritical acceptance of the long-standing negative evaluation of sentimental and romantic fiction. "Although the captivity narrative continued to be published successfully during the first three quarters of the nineteenth century," she writes, "by 1800, according to Roy Harvey Pearce, it 'had all but completed its decline and fall.' Its vitality passed at this time into overt fiction in which the horrors and travails of the frontier experience were combined with a complicated romantic plot of English origin. In this amalgam, a set of foreign and artificial conventions was superimposed on the basically real and indigenous captivity events." Jay Fliegelman, in his masterful study *Prodigals and Pilgrims*, slips into this same characterization of the history of captivity narratives as one of progressive degeneration.[7]

This evaluation of the history of the captivity narrative is unacceptable for a number of reasons. First, by privileging the plain first-person Puritan accounts as the paradigm and norm against which all other captivities are to be measured, the fictional narratives inevitably emerge as distorted or corrupt. Moreover, the assumption that the Puritan first-person accounts were objective reports, uncolored by any stylistic or genre conventions is untenable. Barnett mistakenly assumes that at this time in history English literature and American literature were neatly and meaningfully separated. This allows her to assume that romantic con-

ventions were alien to America, while American writers had ready
at hand their own separate cultural idioms and conventions with
which they could narratively represent "the basically real and
indigenous captivity events." She implies that while it may be
acceptable that romantic conventions were imposed on the historical reality of captivity from a distance by foreign writers, this is
unforgivable in American literature, which, in order to be authentic, should capture and represent the historical reality. To put this
another way, Barnett shares the broadly held assumption that
early American literature—or at least the best of it—is realistic.
Yet for readers in the eighteenth century, *Pamela, Clarissa, Tristram Shandy,* and other similar works were all held to be realistic.
Indeed, realism was understood to be one of the hallmarks of the
novel.

For their part, historians of religions have tended to focus their
attention almost exclusively on those texts that are explicitly
religious, ignoring others that are not. Thus, Puritan captivity
narratives, with their informing theological interpretive frame and
explicit biblical citations, have been considered appropriate objects of study, while works of fiction (and most especially sentimental novels) have not. Yet we can learn something about the
social function of religion and of the history of religion in Europe
and America by paying attention to what replaced an explicitly
religious interpretive frame in the narration and reception of essentially the same event or existential situation. Thus, if we find
that the Puritan interpretive frame had largely disappeared from
most captivity narratives by the mid-eighteenth century while
captivity tales continued to be generated in great numbers, then
we need to explore the significance of this fact and to investigate
what replaced the earlier interpretive frame and see how this shift
affected the reception of the captivity story line. Moreover, we
need to understand the continuing attraction of captivity as a narrative topos in different types or genres of literature, as well as to
understand the new questions and concerns that people brought to
these texts. In pursuing this task, we will once again explore issues
of generative occasion and authorial intention, as well as the reading practices and expectations brought to bear on captivities.

The Moral Significance of Sentiments

An appreciation of the socioeconomic and historical developments contributing to the emergence of a "culture of sensibility"

in the eighteenth century, of the reading structures brought to the sentimental novel, and of the horizon of expectations of the readers of such texts will prove much more important in increasing our understanding of the cultural work of the captivities from this period than will a facile appeal to the congenial nature of the theme or to archetypalism. We ignore to our peril the significance of what some scholars have called a paradigm shift in cultural discourse in the decades following the publication of Mary Rowlandson's narrative in 1682, resulting from a convergence of developments in science, physiology, epistemology, and religion.

A number of recent studies have greatly increased our knowledge of the origins and development of sentimental literature. Several important cultural developments in the late seventeenth and the early eighteenth centuries deserve mention here, since they led to the emergence of new epistemological assumptions and new compositional and reading practices. Newton's *Principia* (1687) and his *Opticks* (1704) changed the scientific view of the world. Newton's work had an important impact on the religious worldview of many and affected the literary sphere as well. For our immediate purposes, it is enough to recall that Newton's great intellectual prestige led many to take his work on sensory perception seriously.[8]

In his research into how human beings come to know anything about the world around them, Newton argued for the existence of an organ in the body called the sensorium, the node of all the nerves in the brain. Already in 1675 he had argued that the nerves were solid, rather than hollow, and transmitted sense impressions through vibrations carried to the brain, where they were registered by the sensorium. Significantly, Newton's sensational psychology was promulgated along with an implicit religious worldview. He argued that the human sensorium was a part of God's "boundless uniform Sensorium." Linking these two was to have important consequences. For Newton, the world was a divine book to be read by man, who could know God and his grandeur by discovering the laws at the foundation of the universe. By identifying the sensorium in each individual with the boundless uniform sensorium of God—and by invoking the metaphor of reading nature—Newton was to open the way for a revisioning of human nature, divine providence, and the significance of human affective responses to external stimuli.

The Puritan literature of the seventeenth and early eighteenth centuries was replete with reports of the great variety of wonders, miracles, and instances of God's direct intervention in the world known as "special providences." The Puritans also spoke of God's "general providence," which ordered and structured the universe and maintained its regularity and, thus, functionally was roughly equivalent to Newton's natural laws. In general, however, the Puritans were more interested in appealing to the agency of special providence in order to explain events in history than in proving God's general providence through scientific experimentation. While many seventeenth-century texts besides the captivity narratives regularly invoked special providence as an interpretive frame, such appeals declined noticeably in the literature of the early eighteenth century, the writings of Cotton Mather notwithstanding.

Moreover, at the same time—first among the Cambridge Platonists and then more broadly—the predominant conception of God shifted from that of the excoriating and afflicting God of the Old Testament to that of a more benevolent God. Concomitantly, human nature was also reconceptualized from the earlier emphasis on the fallen and corrupt state of humanity to a more positive view of humans as innately compassionate beings.[9] For our purposes it is most important to note that the new sensational psychology led to a revaluation of the moral significance of human emotional and somatic responses and, by extension, to a revaluation of audience responses to nature, art, and narrative activity.

While this history cannot be rehearsed in any detail here, we can say that Newton's ideas were quickly picked up and extended by many others, including Locke, whom Newton christened "the first Newtonian philosopher." In his *Essay concerning Human Understanding* (1690), Locke dismissed Descartes's idea that humans were born with innate ideas; instead, he characterized the infant as a tabula rasa. All human knowledge, Locke maintained, was gained through sensory perceptions. This sensationalist epistemology was then translated into a pedagogical program by Locke in *Some Thoughts concerning Education* (1693), "a volume whose influence on eighteenth-century English culture and especially eighteenth-century English literature can hardly be overemphasized."[10] Other thinkers and authors soon accepted Locke's views in whole or in part, either extending his ideas or challenging them, but no one could ignore them. Many of the major questions that were to occupy thinkers in the eighteenth century came to cluster around the status and implications of Newtonian-Lockean thought, most especially on the relationship of reason and affect. Discussions of human understanding necessarily led to reconsiderations of human nature, human faculties, the bases of moral systems, and issues related to religious experience.

The major shift in cultural episteme that occurred in the first half of the eighteenth century involved not only a reconceptualization of divinity but also of human nature, familial relations, and education. All of these developments were tied together by a focus on models of sensory perception and the relationship of human sentiments, reason, and morals. George Cheyne (1671–1743), a well-known English physician, is typical of the general acceptance among men of science of Locke's argument that all knowledge was based on experience of the world and, most especially—building on Newton's corpuscular theory of light—that sensory experience was based on motion caused by objects. In 1733 Cheyne wrote, "Feeling is nothing but the Impulse, Motion or Action of Bodies, gently or violently impressing the Extremeties or Sides of the Nerves, of the Skin, or other parts of the Body, which . . . convey Motion to the Sentient Principle in the Brain."[11]

Cheyne is a historically significant figure insofar as he served as an intermediary between the medical and the literary worlds. As Richardson's physician and confidant, he made the latest medical and physiological knowledge immediately available to this novelist. Most importantly, this knowledge informed the early novel, which became a major means of transmitting to the general public an epistemology and moral system based primarily on affect rather than reason. In this cultural milieu, "sentimental fiction, next to the religion with which it overlapped, was to become the most powerful medium for the spread of popular knowledge of sensational psychology."[12]

The Scottish commonsense movement, which I will return to later, represented at once an extension and a challenge to Lockean thought. The figures associated with this school, including Adam Ferguson, Francis Hutcheson, and Thomas Reid, shared Locke's views concerning the moral necessity for parents to educate their children in a proper manner. They differed from Locke, however, insofar as they denied that the newborn child was a complete tabula rasa. Rather, they believed that humans were born with an innate moral sense or affection. As the first edition of the *Encyclopaedia Britannica* said in defining the subject matter and goal of moral philosophy, "Its object is to shew whence our obligations arise and where they terminate. Moral philosophy is concerned not with what he may be, by education, habit or foreign influence come to be or do, but what by his nature or original constituent principles he is formed to be and do, what conduct he is obliged to pursue."[13]

This is a crucial difference between Locke and the Scottish philosophers. Locke emphasizes the agency of early education as determinative in forming an individual's moral character, whereas the Scottish commonsense philosophers assume a moral sense to be a part of human nature. Yet by accepting Locke's sensational psychology, these philosophers were driven to posit a sixth sense in human beings, the affections, but now with an innate, if undeveloped, moral component. This linkage of morality, first with the affective rather than the rational side of humans, had important implications. Among other things, it meant that moral education was to be realized through the affections rather than through reason alone. It is this implication that the writers of the eighteenth century were to take up and run with. The novel was to emerge as a vehicle of rational entertainment and moral edification in two ways—first, by illustrating the cultivation of the main characters' sensibilities in a variety of difficult and trying situations and, second, by evoking a sympathetic affective response in the reader.[14] (This latter fact helps to explain the prevalence of the term *pathetic* in so many titles of the day.)

A few names and titles will suggest the extent to which "sensibility," "sentiment," and "affection" characterized the discourse of the eighteenth century: Francis Hutcheson, *An Essay on the Nature and Conduct of the Passions and Affections with Illustrations on the Moral Sense* (1728); David Hume, *A Treatise of Human Nature* (1739–40); Richardson, *Pamela: or, Virtue Rewarded* (1740) and *Clarissa* (1744); Edmund Burke, *The Philosophical Origins of the Sublime and the Beautiful* (1757); Laurence Sterne, *Tristram Shandy,* (vol. 1, 1759) and *A Sentimental Journey through France and Italy* (1768); Albrech von Haller, *De Partibus Corporis Humani Sensibilus et Irritabilius* (1753), published in English in 1775 as *A Dissertation on the Sensible and Irritable Parts of Animals;* Adam Smith, *The Theory of Moral Sentiments* (1759); Rousseau, *La Nouvelle Héloise* (1761); and Henry Mackenzie, *The Man of Feeling* (1771).

For many people in the early eighteenth century, physiological sensibility and moral sensibility were intertwined or one-and-the-same. This was so because they assumed that the sensorium or the human faculties, however these were understood, had been created by God precisely so that humans might be morally responsible for their behavior. After the Restoration, the Cambridge Platonists had sought to soften various aspects of Puritan theology and thought. Rather than stressing man's sinful nature, they began with the assumption that humans were essentially benevolent beings. These thinkers influenced in turn the Latitudinarians, who also argued that human nature was instinctively sympathetic and that humans were, thus, naturally inclined to virtuous actions. This nature was to be reinforced by self-discipline, however, or refined through education and cultivation. Even Hume, the supreme skeptic, held that all human virtues flowed from sympathy.

Eighteenth-century thinkers and writers differed in their precise evaluations of human moral capabilities and of human nature in general, of course. They also had to address the issues of the great differences that were evident among individuals and peoples; in addition, many people began to address gender differences and in so doing sought to naturalize these. In general, these explanations ascribed differences to environmental factors or innate differences, or to some combination of these. On the one hand, some writers, following Locke, stressed that education and training in morals from an early age was essential. Other persons, however, proffered their own varieties of Calvinist determinism by suggesting, for instance, that individual differences were in large part the results of the endowments God had given each person at birth. Cheyne belonged to the latter camp. He wrote:

> There are as many and as different Degrees of Sensibility or of Feeling as there are Degrees of Intelligence and Perception in human Creatures; and the Principle of both may be perhaps one and the same. One shall suffer more from the Prick of a Pin, or Needle, from their extreme Sensibility, than others from being run thro' the Body; and the first sort, seem to be of the Class of these Quick-Thinkers I have formerly mentioned; and as none have it in their Option to choose for themselves their own particular Frame of Mind nor Constitution of Body; so none can choose his own Degree of Sensibility. That is given him by the Author of his Nature, and is already determined.[15]

Not surprisingly, perhaps, the new sensational physiologies and moral philosophies could be (and were) extended to the social sphere and used to justify and legitimate social hierarchies, class distinctions, gender roles, and even racism. Yet the significance of the scientific evidence was unclear, so that the same fact could be used to argue for both sides of a question. For instance, reports of the ability of American Indians to bear great pain and deprivation were cited by some authors as proof of their relative inhumanity; others, however, used the same reports to cast the Indians as stoics with a developed moral sense.

It is in light of these developments that we can better understand the tremendous upsurge in interest in the eighteenth and nineteenth centuries in recording the manners, customs, and beliefs of peoples around the world, including the American Indians. Gathering and ordering these objective facts, it was believed, would allow one to determine the degree of humanity these people possessed (or lacked). Moreover, the diverse societies provided case studies of the effects of different environmental situations and educational practices on human development. When the third earl of Shaftesbury (1671–1713), often called "the father of sentimental ethics," published a collection of his essays as *Characteristicks of Men, Manners, Opinions, Times,* he was participating in a broad-based discourse of moral philosophy that included subject matter we would now divide among psychology, anthropology, sociology, pedagogy, and politics.

Such investigations into human nature, however, were not limited to works of science, theology, or philosophy. Works of literature also imaginatively (yet realistically) explored the nature of men and women, familial and sexual relations, and the consequences of different socioeconomic systems and situations, and in so doing served as vehicles of moral instruction. For many persons in the eighteenth century, sentimental literature functioned as an adjunct of these fields. *Pamela,* for instance, was sometimes read from the pulpit; others report that people who would never have deigned to read mere novels read *Clarissa* with the same care and in the same contexts that they read the Bible.[16] Richardson's works served as moral guides for generations of readers. In 1755, no doubt in response to market demands, he published a handbook entitled *A Collection of the Moral and Instructive Sentiments, Maxims, Cautions and Reflections Contained in the Histories of "Pamela," "Clarissa," and "Sir Charles Grandison," Digested under Proper Heads.* This instructional manual was extremely influential in the second half of the century. Similar works appeared during the century drawing from the novels of Sterne, Fielding, and others. In fact, Sterne's fictional character Parson Yorick became so popular that Sterne took to publishing volumes of his own sermons under the guise of *The Sermons of Mr. Yorick.*

Because sentimental novels were consumed in this way, informing the religious lives of many persons in the eighteenth and nineteenth centuries, they are important documents for the work of historians of religions, as well as literary critics. In the following pages we will work toward understanding how a work like *Pamela* came to be read from church pulpits and how tears and sighs came to be viewed as "natural revelations" of God's moral expectations for human beings. It was no accident that the sentimental novel, John Wesley's "heart religion," and the Great Awakening in America all appeared in the same decade; all of these developments were a result of, and further contributed to, the heightened value placed on the religious or moral affections.[17]

In chapter 1 we saw how tears and affliction worked in Mary Rowlandson's text. By comparing these and related phenomena with those found in eighteenth- and nineteenth-century sentimental works dealing with Indian captivity, we will be able to glimpse an important aspect of cultural change. Admittedly, sentimental novels do not speak to modern readers; they do not easily give pleasure to us. Instead, the characters and plots seem to be overwrought (both narratively and emotionally), if not impossible to believe as realistic. Writing about these novels in general, Jane Tompkins notes, "What all of these texts share, from the perspective of modern criticism, is a certain set of defects that excludes them from the ranks of the great masterpieces: an absence of finely delineated characters, a lack of verisimilitude in the story line, an excessive reliance on plot, and a certain sensationalism in the events portrayed."[18] Rather than accepting these modern values as normative and then imposing them on these texts, Tompkins has made a concerted effort to recover the aims and practices informing the literary activity of sentimental authors, as well as the perspectives, expectations, and reading practices the nineteenth-century audience brought to these texts. As a result of this and other recent studies, it is clear that many (though not all) works of sentimental literature functioned didactically, conveying a moral message to readers and helping them to evaluate their lives.

Kimber's Mr. Anderson

The History of the Life and Adventures of Mr. Anderson. Containing His Strange Varieties of Fortune in Europe and America (1754), a novel by the English writer Edward Kimber (1719–1769), may serve as an entrée into the heated cultural debate about the social responsibilities of authorship, the operative understanding of the power of narrative representation, the didacticism of sentimental literature, the role of imagination in the reader's creation of the meaning of the text, the role of the cult of sensibility or cultivated emotions in the composition and reception of the novel, and the topos of Indian captivity as an instance of virtue-in-distress.

With this mid-eighteenth-century work, we find the form of the sentimental novel fully developed. (*Pamela* had been published several years earlier, in 1740, and was brought out in an American edition by Benjamin Franklin in 1744.) The title page, however, is similar in layout and appearance to most of the earlier captivity narratives we have seen, thus linking it, at least visually, to those nonfictional texts. Below the title and between two heavy rules, one finds the words "Compiled from his Own Papers"—an epistolary ruse used to suggest that the work is nonfiction. Below this is an excerpt from a verse by Addison:

> ———If there is a Power above us,
> And that there is, all Nature cries aloud,
> Thro' all her Works, he must delight in Virtue,
> And that which he delights in must be happy.[19]

This verse encapsulates the informing religious and moral world-view of the sentimental novel: the virtuous will be rewarded with happiness in the end, even though they suffer terribly beforehand, because divine providence has so ordered the world. At the same time, then, that Kimber's work is linked to the earlier tradition of captivity narratives, this verse marks it as also belonging to the newer genre of sentimental literature.

The title page represents this text to prospective readers through a number of key words—"history," "life and adventures," "strange varieties of fortune," "Power," "Nature," and "Virtue"—all which combine to suggest a true story of the adventures and vicissitudes in the protagonist's life in Europe and America, which, of course, ends happily. At the same time it suggests links to other forms of literature. The word *strange*, for instance, would have evoked a connection with the wide variety of popular works of surprising happenings in the world, such as Defoe's immensely popular *The Life and Strange Surprizing Adventures of Robinson Crusoe*.[20]

The title page also implies that when read, this story of virtue triumphing in the end will lead the reader to a heightened appreciation of God's goodness and providence. Absent, though, is the

Puritan emphasis on the fallen, sinful nature of humankind; instead, one finds an optimism concerning the innate goodness of human beings—at least those "of the better sort." This is characteristic of sentimental literature at large and marks a significant change from the religious anthropology of the Puritans, for, as Herbert Ross Brown rightly noted, "A favorite article in the sentimental creed is the belief in the innate goodness of the heart."[21]

The eighteenth century saw a broad-based reaction against both the Puritan anthropology and that found in Hobbes. The Cambridge Platonists, Lord Shaftesbury, Francis Hutcheson, Henry More, and others argued that spontaneous affections were the true locus of all knowledge and morality. Shaftesbury, for instance, in his *Inquiry concerning Virtue* (1699) had argued, "We cannot doubt of what passes within ourselves. Our passions and affections are known to us. They are certain, whatever the objects may be on which they are employed."[22] He assumed that the sense of right and wrong was "implanted in our heart," but it had to be cultivated, as did the natural recognition of beauty and the odious. Aesthetic taste and moral sensibility were natural capacities, but they had to be cultivated through a disciplined regimen of training involving "labour and pains." More, the Cambridge Platonist, was representative of the age (and in complete agreement with Addison) when he argued that we "relish and savour what is absolutely best and rejoice in it." Moreover, he maintained that natural expressions of human emotion, such as a "lamenting tone of Voice, the dejection of the Eyes and Countenances, Groaning, Howling, Sighs, and Tears" have the power to move others to compassion and sympathy. More himself was to influence John Wesley's theology and "religion of the heart." The Great Awakening and the sentimental novel may both be seen as expressions of the increased cultural attention to the affective side of human life and religiosity.[23]

For persons of sensibility, affective exchanges participated in a moral economy within which the exchange of a shared currency of tears, sighs, swoons, and shudders created value and social relations. Moreover, since spontaneous emotive and physical responses were understood to be natural revelations of God's moral expectations of human beings, they were also signals to persons for action. In the sentimental novel, the innate potential of individuals for making proper value judgments and acting virtuously is realized through a process of education, training, and testing through adversity.

It is the last of these—the testing through a reversal of fortune or unmerited suffering—that both shares some aspects with the Puritan representation of affliction and marks a radical difference. The Puritans employed the metaphor of refining gold in a crucible to represent the positive spiritual transformation that could result if instances of divine affliction were experienced and accepted in the proper attitude of humility. In the sentimental novel, however, the characters are not radically transformed through their experience of affliction; rather, the trying experience, be it captivity or whatever, serves to bring out more clearly or to heighten their innate goodness and virtue. In the sentimental novel, the character of the protagonists is never in doubt and, consequently, neither is the final result. Adversity is an occasion for displaying one's virtue and sensibility to the world and to oneself.

The opening of Kimber's novel confirms the reader's expectations, generated by the title page, of the type of narrative one is about to enter into, even as the author apologizes for necessarily breaking with one of the conventions of biography: he cannot provide much detail concerning the hero's parents and family because as a child he had been "plunged into the deepest calamities of life" and denied this knowledge himself. Nevertheless, the reader is assured, Mr. Anderson's experiences proved "equally capable of affecting the head and improving the heart." The narrator then announces the purpose of this work of fiction, masquerading as historical biography:

> If the narrative I am about to present to the public, insensibly, under the guise of a rational entertainment, steals instruction upon the peruser, and produces benefit to the mind; if it should draw the hard bound tear from the eye of inhumanity; if whilst the souls "that bleed for others woes, that feel for suffering merit's deep distress," lend an attentive ear, or eye, to this strange story; it serves to mollify unfeeling, obdurate cruelty, I shall have my wish, and the trouble I have been at to fashion my friends memoirs, will be well repayed; for I am of the poet's opinion, that
> "One moral, or a mere well natur'd deed,
> Does all desert in sciences exceed." (*Garland* 7:1–2)

In the world of the sentimental novel (that is, among authors, readers, and the characters populating the texts), one finds a supreme confidence in both the revelatory power of emotions and the power of narrative representation to [steal moral] "instruction upon the peruser" by "affecting the head and improving the heart." Kimber's belief—that if he is successful in moving his readers, in drawing "the hard bound tear from the eye of inhumanity" through his narration, then acts of human cruelty in the world will decrease—was widely shared in the culture of sensibility. The stated goal of the act of narration is to effect a moral change in society through affecting individual readers. This authorial intention, based on this understanding of the power of literature to alter the real world, was, significantly enough, still found a century later in sentimental works such as *Uncle Tom's Cabin*.[24]

Kimber's confidence in the power of literature is such that, like Richardson, he implies that it is more efficacious than even sermons. Whereas many persons might experience the message of theological writing or preaching as heavy handed and thus resist it at some level, with fiction ("a rational entertainment") the ethical message is artfully and painlessly transmitted.

Writers of sentimental fiction played an important cultural role in promulgating this new epistemology, which privileged feeling over reason as a guide in discerning virtue and making moral decisions. Sentimental authors shared the view of Adam Smith and others that the imagination played an important role in the moral life, for only through imagining oneself into the situation of another was sympathy fully activated. The pleasure to be derived from the exercise of the sympathetic imagination, however, was twofold. On the one hand, there was the pleasure to be had in aiding another person in distress and in knowing that one had done some good. However, while the operation of the sympathetic imagination involved an element of identification with the suffering of another, at the same time (and somewhat paradoxically) it also involved an element of distancing and of contrasting one's own situation with that of the person in distress. This second pleasure was found especially in the act of reading moving tales, where leisure allowed the requisite time for comparative reflection, even if it was largely unconscious. The *Spectator* put this clearly, noting that "when we read of torments, wounds, deaths and the like dismal accidents, our pleasure does not flow so properly from the grief which such melancholy description gives us, as from the secret comparison which we make between ourselves and the person who suffers. Such representations teach us to set a just value upon our own condition, and make us prize our good fortune, which exempts us from the like calamities."[25]

We have already seen Per Amicum direct the reader of Mary

Rowlandson's narrative to "read therefore, peruse, ponder, and from hence lay up something from the experience of another, against thine own turn comes." What is new here is the heightened attention to be paid to one's visceral responses to narrated scenes. In one sense, of course, this aspect of the reading practices brought to bear on works of sentimental literature was an extension and application of the imaginal activity implied in the Golden Rule. To "do onto others as you would have them do onto you" requires one to project oneself imaginatively into the situation of the other person and then to act out of that assumed position. At the same time, part of the pleasure to be found in the reflective activity the *Spectator* speaks of is a result of the recognition that "there but for the grace of God go I."

Most moral philosophers and sentimental writers concurred that morality and moral action originated in feeling rather than reason. Hume, for instance, maintained, "All morality depends upon our sentiments," not upon reason.[26] What philosophers sought to demonstrate through logical argument the writers of fiction sought to represent through the lives of the characters in their novels. It is important to recognize how developments in philosophy, theology, physiology, and psychology were brought into the real world through works of fiction. Along with sentimentally colored historical pieces, novels helped to shape the expressions of feeling of historical agents. Such works helped to locate affective responses within a moral economy. This fact was recognized by authors throughout the eighteenth and nineteenth centuries. In *Adam Bede* (1859), for instance, George Eliot says of one of her characters, "Hetty had never read a novel . . . how then could she find a shape for her expectations?"[27]

Today we assume that an individual can (and must) learn to control and modulate his or her emotional responses, such as laughter or words spoken in anger, in ways appropriate to the specific time, place, and circumstance. Our ancestors believed the same thing, although they assumed that it was the sensorium, or the moral sense, that needed to be trained or, better, refined, so that the affective and physiological responses (tears, sighs, tremors, fainting) to specific stimuli and situations could be controlled. Once this was assumed, it was a natural next step to suggest that the emotional responses of a person to a given situation were an immediate and accurate expression of moral character.

In claiming for literature the role of inculcating moral values, Kimber participated in an increasingly influential cultural discourse in the eighteenth century that privileged examples from real life in the contemporary world over those from antiquity as effective vehicles in this exercise. Novels, as well as biographies, provided paradigmatic figures for emulation by readers seeking both entertainment and self-improvement. Just as the third generation of New England Puritans had come to accept funeral sermons, eulogies, and even biographies of members of the founding generation as vehicles for instructing others, especially youth, so too many eighteenth-century readers and commentators were willing to acknowledge factual accounts as, potentially at least, morally uplifting.

Vociferous resistance surfaced, however, when some people argued that explicitly fictional tales could also serve proper didactic purposes. They argued that the novel could serve as a vehicle of moral instruction precisely because this form was based on everyday life, not fantasy. The trials and situations faced by the characters in novels were similar, even if heightened, to those readers would encounter in their own lives. Such arguments, however, did not convince many others. One commentator, writing in the *Weekly Magazine* in 1789, expressed a concern he shared with many of his contemporaries:

> I have heard it said in favour of novels that there are many good sentiments dispersed in them. I maintain, that good sentiments being found scattered in loose novels, render them the more dangerous, since, when they are mixed with seducing arguments, it requires more discernment than is to be found in youth to separate the evil from the good . . . and when a young lady finds principles of religion and virtue inculcated in a book, she is naturally thrown off her guard by taking it for granted that such a work can contain no harm; and of course the evil steals imperceptibly into her heart.[28]

The presumption behind the "of course" here clearly demarcates the critical point on which these two camps differed: either readers could be trusted to discern the good and the moral from the seductive or seemingly good and the immoral or they could not be so trusted. Either moral instruction stole upon the reader's mind and heart in the reading of novels, or "seducing arguments" and evil did. It is clear that issues of class and gender lay behind the fears of many of those who were suspicious of the novel and other forms of popular literature. Yet both camps shared the belief that literature had the power to affect the moral fiber of the readers, even if they differed radically in their valuation of this power.

Kimber, like many of his fellow fiction writers, sought to evade

the critical arrows flung at him by adversaries of fiction by assuming the pose of being merely the editor of the papers of an actual
individual. Though a work of out-and-out fiction, *Mr. Anderson*
was presented to the reading public as a factual account. Similarly,
Bleeker's *The History of Maria Kittle* employed the same epistolary ruse. This may be merely an artful (or clumsily obvious)
dodge. On the other hand, this appeal to historicity may also have
been a literary device used to justify the act of narration itself, to
create a narrative voice, and to heighten the reader's sense of
engagement with the story by facilitating the willing suspension
of disbelief or tempering skepticism.[29]

In Kimber's novel, however, unlike the Puritan texts we saw
earlier, no program of ritual humiliation and spiritual reformation
is offered, nor is there a heavy emphasis on the involvement of
divine providence in the protagonist's captivity. Rather, the emphasis is on releasing and developing the innate goodness and
powers of moral discrimination found in persons of sensibility
through their encounters with both virtuous and villainous characters. At the same time, the earlier confidence, epitomized by
Cotton Mather, that the deep meaning of the text of history could
be spelled by human beings, is absent. Instead, Kimber cautions
his reader, "We must not expect that all seeing Providence should,
according to our expectations, always punish even the most degrading and abominable crimes" (*Garland* 7:9–10).

Significantly, the authoritative texts appealed to by Kimber are
inevitably poetic texts, not Scripture. Moreover, the proper locus
of moral attention here is the individual human heart, not the
community or society at large. Through the act of reading, an increasingly private practice, the narrative "steals instruction upon
the peruser, and produces benefit to the mind" by providing paradigmatic existential situations of conflict or real-life problems and
their resolutions. For the modern reader, this understanding of the
spiritual and moral impact of the expected narrative transaction
(indeed, almost a pact) between author, text, and reader must be
taken seriously in order to appreciate the cultural work such texts
performed in the eighteenth and nineteenth centuries. As Davidson has noted, "Psychologically, the early novel embraced a new
relationship between art and audience, writer and reader, a relationship that replaced the authority of the sermon or Bible with
the enthusiasms of sentiment, horror, or adventure, all of which
relocate authority in the individual response of the reading self."[30]
Not surprisingly, this democratization, if you will, of the ability to

interpret texts and to judge affect was perceived by many to be a threat to the patriarchal social order and moral values.

Most important, perhaps, for the authors and readers of sentimental literature, the moral authority and the power of a text were to be measured and verified through the affective responses it elicited in readers. Given that reading was usually done individually and in private, only the reader would be in a position to note and then to evaluate these responses. This situation is in sharp contrast to that associated with the Puritan confessional narrative. There not only was the narrative of the applicant's spiritual responses to specific existential situations in the past subjected to scrutiny by an examining committee from the church, but the individual's oral responses to questions posed by this group were also judged as to their appropriateness. Although there were shaded differences in Puritan conversion narratives at different times and places, as Caldwell has demonstrated, there was nevertheless a communal consensus as to what constituted proper and improper responses to specific types of situations or scenes in life. This consensus was worked out and then reinforced through ritualized public performances as well as through the improvements of such narratives offered by the clergy in the oral delivery of sermons and in print. Both the Rowlandson and the Swarton narratives were, as we saw, circulated with accompanying texts that framed and guided their reception and proper usage.

Yet it must always be borne in mind that the sentimental author had designs on his reader, too. The author assumed that readers would learn about the proper affective responses to specific sorts of situations from his novel and then act on and out of these. Through the act of reading, readers would refine their own sensibilities and display these in their reactions to similar situations as these were encountered in their own lives. And even if many of the wildest episodes were unlikely to be found in the lives of most readers, there was still moral good to be gained through imaginatively entering into and contemplating such scenes. Here the sentimental novel clearly shares a direct continuity with Puritan assumptions and reading practices, as we saw in both Per Amicum's preface, the Rowlandson narrative proper, and the sermons of Mather. This understanding of the didactic value of narrative representation was to continue to be held by many persons down through the late nineteenth century.

In an important sense, though, the sentimental novel represented a significant challenge to the earlier cultural status quo by shifting the ultimate locus of moral authority from the clergy as a group to the individual lay person and from the Bible to secular works of rational entertainment and wisdom. This shift was in part a result of the implicit drive of Protestant understandings of the status and power of the Bible, of religious epistemology, and hermeneutics. Insofar as Protestant thought and practice stressed both the necessity and the efficacy of the individual's immediate encounter with the written revealed word of God, the relationships of reader to text and reader to author (or "Author" in the case of the Bible) were already culturally available for extension to other sorts of texts, including didactic works of fiction.

This is not to say, however, that readers were left to their own devices in reading these sorts of texts. Indeed, the opposite is the case. Readers were given explicit guidance in the novels themselves as to what constituted the proper reactions to specific scenes in real life and in narrative representations. There were, as well, negative examples, which illustrated uncultured, out-of-place, and otherwise improper responses.

The following passage from *Maria Kittle* has frequently evoked derisive comment precisely because modern readers have failed to appreciate the active manner in which the author, as part of her role as instructor and guide in moral sensibility, involved her original audience in imaginatively composing a scene and then empathetically entering into the emotional life of the characters. The husband, Henry Kittle, is returning to his frontier home, where he had left his beloved wife, Maria, and two small children, only to discover that they have fallen victim to an Indian attack:

> As he approached his late happy dwelling, his bosom dilated with the pleasing hope of soon extricating his beloved family from danger; he chid the slowness of the carriages, and felt impatient to dissipate the apprehensions of Maria, to kiss the pendant tear from her eye, and press his sportive innocents to his bosom. While these bright ideas played round his soul, he lifted up his eyes, and through an opening of the woods, beheld his farm: but what language can express his surprise and consternation at seeing his habitation so suddenly desolated! a loud exclamation of amaze burst from the whole company at so unexpected a view—the blood revolted from Mr. Kittle's cheek—his heart throbbed under the big emotion, and all aghast, spurring on his horse, he entered the inclosure with full speed.—Stop here unhappy man! here let the fibres of thy heart crack with excruciating misery—let the cruel view of mangled

wretches, so nearly allied to thee, extort drops of blood from thy cleaving bosom! It did—it did. Uttering a deep groan, he fell insensible from his horse. (*Garland* 20:27–28)

Brown assigns most of the end of this passage to Kittle as a soliloquy, although the punctuation of the 1797 text does not justify this reading. According to him, "Henry Kittle's outburst was too self-conscious to be indicative of anything more than his own egoism."[31]

In Brown's misreading, the text seems very awkward, while the characters come off as pretentious poseurs. Yet the reading practices brought by late eighteenth- and nineteenth-century readers to texts such as this would have made this scene very effective. Brown himself seems to have sensed something of what was involved in the transaction between author, text, and reader in the sentimental novel, although he never put the various clues or pieces together and, as a result, was never able to appreciate the cultural work of such texts or to transcend a condescending bemusement with the seeming silliness of the genre. Only a few pages earlier, he had perceptively noted (although he quickly trivialized his own insight) that sentimental novels often portrayed specific emotional responses in given situations ("swoons, trances, visions, languishings, ecstasies, and a variety of emotional delirium tremens") as proof of the character's sensibility and even spiritual election, a situation not unlike that found in Puritan conversion testimonies and written accounts.[32]

Passages such as that above can only be understood if we take seriously the extent to which the early novel, in many ways seemingly so different from Puritan texts, nevertheless shared a deeper identity, for the sentimental novel developed out of the exploitation of certain shared reading structures and practices. If, for example, one recalls the meditative practice of "the composition of place"—a practice first popularized in Ignatian meditation manuals but widely adopted and adapted in Protestant circles as well in the form of "Occasional Meditation"—one can better appreciate how and why Bleeker composed this scene as she did, confident that her readers would share reading practices which would make it work. In the First Exercise of St. Ignatius's spiritual exercises, the meditator is directed to use his imagination to conjure up "a mental image of the place . . . where the object that we wish to contemplate is present." After "seeing" this place or scene "with the mind's eye," the meditator next seeks to share the "pain, tears, and suffering" of Christ in the Passion, or other emotions from the specific biblical scene. In the sentimental novel, this spiritual exercise is simply applied to nonbiblical scenes and narratives. If Bleeker knew her audience, as any successful author must, then she was cognizant of the expectations and reading practices that the reader would most probably bring to her text.[33]

After having assisted the audience in conjuring up the scene of devastation and death, one that would have been well known to most readers already from acquaintance with earlier captivity narratives and their accompanying illustrations, Bleeker then invites the reader to pause before it, to hold the scene before one's gaze, precisely in order to feel the emotional response of Henry Kittle in one's own body. Brown was more correct than he realized when he suggested that the affective response of the reader was taken to be evidence of one's spiritual condition in much the same way as in Calvinist practice.

In order to demonstrate the tradition that immediately links captivity in the sentimental novel with Puritan captivities, let us recall that a century earlier Per Amicum had also conjured up the scene of a husband (there the Rev. Joseph Rowlandson) returning to the site of his former domestic happiness, only to find it a scene of death and destruction: "At his return, he found the Town in flames, or smoke, his own house being set on fire by the Enemy . . . and all in it consumed: His precious yoke-fellow, and dear Children, wounded and captivated (as the issue evidenced, and following Narrative declares) by these cruel and barbarous Salvages. A sad Catastrophe!" Let us recall, too, Per Amicum's claim that "the works of the Lord . . . are great, sought out of all those that have pleasure therein."

Over a century before Bleeker composed her novel, the affective power of the idyllic domestic scene suddenly shattered by Indian attack and captivity had been fully realized and employed as a didactic device by the Puritans. If Per Amicum and his friends had found the Rowlandson narrative "worthy to be exhibited to, and viewed, and pondered by all, that disdain not to consider the operation of [God's] hand," this was because they were convinced that, "forasmuch as not the general but particular knowledge of things makes deepest impression upon the affections," "those of a true Christian spirit" would necessarily find themselves moved by the account and the scenes recalled therein. That is, Per Amicum also recommended scrutinizing reader responses as a way of evaluating the spiritual condition of individuals (*Garland* 1:A2, A3,

A4). The continuity in the understanding of the narrative and reading processes and the transaction between author, text, and reader found in these works by Per Amicum and Bleeker is undeniable, although the obvious differences in genre and style have heretofore kept us from realizing the full nature of this continuity. These differences, however, now appear to be less significant than the continuity in the reading structures and practices brought to bear on these texts.

The theme of captivity was widely employed in the seventeenth, eighteenth, and nineteenth centuries in diverse literary genres because it represented a striking instance of sudden reversal of fortune, whether this was understood to be divine affliction or not. The theme of the sudden reversal of fortune of the good and apparently blameless was, of course, as old as the story of Job. Yet if it was seemingly guaranteed to evoke a response, the shape and meaning of the response was determined by the then-operative reading practices, narrative conventions, and communal valuations of the expression of specific emotions in specific contexts.

Such an empathetic emotional response by the reader was the goal of sentimental authors. In a letter to one of his own readers, Laurence Sterne, a doyen of the genre, explicitly pointed to the role of the reader in generating the pleasure to be found in novels, such as his *Tristram Shandy:* "A true feeler always brings half the entertainment along with him . . . and the vibrations in him so entirely correspond with those excited [in the novel's characters], it is like reading himself and not the book."[34] Sterne understood full well that the author could only do so much in order to elicit a given response; the reader played an equally important role in bringing certain reading structures to bear on the text.

As a result of this situation, the sentimental novel worked only so long as the author and the audience shared the same practices and expectations. If such novels do not work for us today, it is because we no longer identify with the emotional lives of the characters, not because Kimber and Bleeker were bad writers. The words on the page have not changed, but reading practices have. Puritan readers—who had already affirmed the moral imperative of observing the movements of their souls, participated in the tradition of writing spiritual autobiographies and journals, and learned to read themselves through devotional practices of intense self-scrutiny—would have readily understood the assumptions shared by the authors and readers of sentimental novels even if they finally could not have embraced them.

The sentimental novel, then, no less than the Puritan captivity narrative, provided rational entertainment insofar as the emotional responses evoked in the reader were subjected to intense scrutiny as a part of a practice of self-examination. Reading done in this manner was an efficacious path, it was held, leading to the cultivation of one's sensibilities and powers of moral discrimination. Not everyone shared this understanding of the moral benefits of novel reading, as we have already had occasion to note. Many commentators (not all of them male) doubted that the young and female readers would have the wherewithal, the reading skills, and powers of discrimination needed to distinguish corrupting literature from morally uplifting works. We have also alluded to the beginnings of a significant shift in epistemology and ethical thought in the English-speaking world related to the intellectual movement that came to be known as Scottish commonsense philosophy. This involved a shift from an explicitly Calvinist providential view of history to an increased emphasis on natural religion.

Many of those who doubted the claims made for literature as a vehicle of moral education feared that works of fiction threatened to seduce or captivate the hearts and minds of the "weaker sex" and youth. The common usage of terms such as *captivate* and *captivating* in the ongoing, sometimes boisterous, cultural discourse over the relative merits or demerits of fiction in general is worth noting in passing. In railing against novels and other forms of fiction, some opponents had appeal to imagery redolent of the Puritan rhetoric on the dangers of temptations and sin. One editor argued, for instance, that novels "are written with an intent to captivate the feelings, and do in fact lead many on to the path of vice, from an idea that they are within the pale of gallantry." Another male opponent of fiction, wrote in the *Massachusetts Magazine*, "But too many [readers], especially persons of warm passions and tender feelings [i.e., females], are too apt to be captivated with everything which drops from [Sterne's] descriptive, though loose and unguarded pen, and, in swallowing the nectar, to swallow what is enflaming and poisonous." This writer employed, no doubt unconsciously, phallic images that would seem to invite a Freudian analysis themselves, even as they hint at the sexual politics involved in this debate, often just below the surface.

Richardson presented a standard counterargument by suggesting that because the new novel was rooted in the everyday world it represented reality in ways other forms of fiction, such as romance, had not. He called the novel "a new species of writing, that might possibly turn young people into a source of reading different from the pomp and parade of romance writing, and dismissing the improbable and marvelous with which novels generally abound, might tend to promote the cause of religion and virtue." The contest between these positions was not settled quickly, however. Over a century later, in 1853, Margaret Fuller concurred with the critics who found fiction to be seductive and captivating, although she was willing to accept it if certain conditions were met. "But it is only when some effort at human improvement is robed in its captivating garb that fiction should be tolerated," she wrote.[35]

With this general introduction, let us look more closely at our two selected novels. The protagonist of Kimber's *Mr. Anderson* is Tom(my) Anderson. The novel is told in the third-person past tense, with an omniscient narrator. It opens with the editor-narrator recalling that Tommy's parents had been "above the common rank." In May 1697, as Tommy (then aged seven) waited on a doorstep in London for his father, who had gone inside on business, he was abducted by a sea captain. With this incident, Kimber invoked the fairly widespread and highly publicized incidents of child abduction in the British Isles earlier in the century. The kidnapping functions as a device to get his protagonist to America;[36] at the time it would have represented a realistic touch.

Kimber then proceeds to tell a typical sentimental tale of class and virtue denied yet triumphing in the end. We learn that onboard the ship, a slaver headed for America, Tommy was sexually abused by the captain. When they arrived in Maryland, Tommy was immediately sold to a planter, Mr. Barlow, a mean-spirited, abusive man in his own right. Mrs. Barlow, on the other hand, was "a woman of sense and humanity, of many extraordinary endowments, and a mother" (*Garland* 7:1–2).

As in so many sentimental novels, one finds maternal love, virtue, warmth, gentleness, and a nurturing nature counterposed to male brutality, insensibility, and baseness. Equally sharp contrasts are drawn between virtuous individuals and dastardly reprobates throughout the novel. Of special note, however, is the moral anthropology shared by the sentimental novelists and readers, including the belief that the character and moral fiber of individuals were ultimately a matter of temperament. The character, or mettle, of individuals was tested and tempered on the anvil of adversity and suffering. If temperament was inherited, however, it was so along lines distinct from genetic inheritance (e.g., we are told that the sweet daughter, Fanny, had her mother's temperament and nothing of her father's). Moreover, innate goodness had the power to establish bonds of affection that transcended biological relationships—Mrs. Barlow cannot help but feel maternal toward Tommy, who naturally reciprocates, while Fanny and Tommy recognize each other to be soulmates, not merely playmates. Indeed, we are told that all those with any sensibility readily discerned that Fanny and Tommy were almost "twins from the same womb," while the crude and uncultured Mr. Barlow was oblivious to any elective affinities.

The moral anthropology of the sentimental novel owed something to the Calvinist belief in predestination but was not limited to this theological understanding. Like the Calvinists, sentimental novelists and readers believed that a person's innate virtue would necessarily attract the attention of the divine (even if this was often delayed) and ultimately lead to the virtuous being blessed. Some, but by no means all, sentimental novels promised that virtue might well be rewarded in this world, rather than being withheld until the afterlife. Indeed, as we shall see shortly, Kimber claims that the natural activities of the virtuous would prove to be not only economically viable but profitable. There was an inherent economic rationality, then, in virtuous activity—men of good character and sensibility got the goods and the girl.

Persons of sensibility naturally resonated to each other, producing or evoking mutually recognizable physiological and emotional responses. Both their speech and actions disclosed their true nature, their innate goodness and virtue, to others of a similar temper or nature, while those who did not share these qualities were blind to their existence in others. As a consequence, persons of the latter sort rarely recognized the true character and value of persons of refined sensibility. As was to be expected, then, in a woman of refined sensibility and cultivated mind, Mrs. Barlow immediately recognized Tommy's "promising genius, and a softness and good nature of disposition, that would have melted any heart, but that of the villain who had him in his power." Kimber repeatedly emphasizes the innate goodness of his main character, Tommy, and then proceeds to create scenes in which this goodness is readily recognized by others of refined sensibility, no matter how low Tommy's present station or how wretched his material conditions.

We must note, though, the importance attached in the novel to literacy and education in cultivating innate qualities of mind and moral discrimination. Mrs. Barlow, for instance, ignores the ex-

press commands of her brutish husband and secretly teaches little
Fanny, her daughter, and Tommy to read "prettily." After they had
quickly exhausted her "female collection of the politest authors,"
a more substantial library was supplied by a family friend, a Scottish clergyman. The children studied with a neighbor, another
Scottsman, Mr. Ferguson. In time Tom "became a proficient in the
Latin and French, in all the useful branches of the mathematics,
spoke and wrote correctly and elegantly, and acquired such addi-
tions to his native dignity of soul and sentiment" that everyone
"stood amazed at him" (*Garland* 7:10, 26).

Education, then, was of value in developing and refining one's
"native dignity of soul and sentiment." We may assume that the
reading of novels of rational entertainment also was felt to contribute to this end. The seemingly minor detail of these educated
gentlemen being Scottish is in fact significant, since it suggests
(albeit anachronistically within the time frame or historical setting of the novel) Kimber's endorsement of Scottish commonsense
philosophy. The influence of Lord Kames, whose *Principles of
Morality and Natural Religion* (1751) had appeared three years
before the publication of Kimber's novel, can clearly be sensed
informing the moral of this tale.[37]

Kimber occasionally uses his novel as a vehicle for criticizing
the moral hypocrisy of England and many Christians. For instance, in speeches by Mrs. Barlow, Tommy, Mr. Ferguson and
others, he repeatedly rehearses the theme that a person's worth
and character are not to be measured by financial or social status
but by integrity and industry. After Tom and Fanny have grown
into young adulthood, a different love appropriate to their age
develops between them. Because they have been raised almost as
brother and sister, they realize that they need to know how Tom
came into the family and what their true relationship to each
other is. They implore Mr. Ferguson to enlighten them. Instead of
immediately complying, Ferguson tells the history of his own fall
from a high estate into poverty and even serfdom in order to
criticize those who judge people by exterior trappings rather than
on their merits. He also instructs them on the morally deadening
effects of the hurried life in the cities, as people scramble to make
ends meet. Finally, Ferguson tells Tommy and Fanny of his father-
in-law, who, through no fault of his own, had been cast into
debtor's prison "through the merciless principles of revenge, of a
few creditors, who yet were church goers, and every day repeated,
'Forgive us our debts, as we forgive our debtors' " (*Garland* 7:36).

This pathetic tale leaves everyone in tears. When Mrs. Barlow happens upon this scene and finds the participants all weeping, Ferguson hastens to inform her that it had been "their sensibility . . . which had cast them into such disorder." Mrs. Barlow's response reflects the shared assumption in the cult of sensibility that affective responses revealed one's character: " 'I'm glad of it, cry'd the excellent woman; shedding tears for others woes, betokens a goodness and nobleness of nature, that I hope my children will never be deficient in.' "

Then a series of sudden reversals of fortune are introduced, which are each in turn turned completely around as the force of Tom's goodness overcomes all adversity. Mr. Barlow is intent on marrying his daughter to the doltish and uncouth son of a wealthy neighbor, a plan that throws everyone into the depths of despair, although he is oblivious to the entreaties and tears of his wife and daughter. Tom is exiled to a distant plantation as an overseer, but ever true to himself—hardworking, honest, diligent, kind, and considerate—the plantation is soon more profitable than it had ever been, since even the slaves love to serve him (*Garland* 7:40).

Tom is then sold to an Indian trader and seems doomed to a life in the distant wilderness, separated from Fanny and civilization. As Tom and the trader, named Matthewson, leave the plantation on horseback, he has Tom recount his life story. Matthewson is deeply affected by it (and, thus, the reader learns he is a man of sensibility), sets Tom free, and adopts him as his own son. Tom's narrative of his sad history—like the novel itself—evokes the sentimental cycle of emotional responses that witness to the character and temper of each character. As a result, Tom wins a new relation, patron, and friend. Like Ferguson before him, Matthewson sees that Tom's innate goodness and character will ultimately lead him to success.

Sentimental characters are inevitably captivated by each other, as they are enmeshed in a social—even cosmic—world of affect, a world spun out of emotive webs of signification. Kimber expresses as much in the following passage:

> There is a certain somewhat, in certain countenances, that pre-possesses us in the favour of the wearers at first sight, an openness, and ingenuity, and an amiableness, that immediately strikes the beholder—such was Tom's, and that and the many noble instances he had given of his sentiments and his fortitude, had quite captivated his master, so that he really began to look upon him as a son.

The mingled starts of joy, gratitude, and love towards this generous man, which inspired Tom's breast, at the conclusion of this speech, no words can paint—it actuated his whole person, it heaved his bosom—it flushed his face, and deprived him of utterance. (*Garland* 7:99)[38]

Predictably, when Matthewson is killed, Tom inherits all of his property and quickly becomes the most successful Indian trader in the country. Indian captivity is introduced into the novel as yet another (though certainly not the last) sudden reversal of fortune precisely when the tide seems to be turning in his favor. The reader is addressed directly at this point: "Thus behold a reserve of fortune—he, who but a small space of time before, was happy, and employed in making others so, is now strip'd naked, bound with thongs, and a spectacle of triumph and reproach to a barbarous gang of savages!" (*Garland* 7:140–41).

This familiar scene of the captive being carried off to an unknown fate functions in this sentimental novel as one of many reversals that the protagonist undergoes in the course of the tale on the way to his reward—economic security, social status and respect, and domestic bliss. It is impossible to rehearse all of the vicissitudes of the hero's life thereafter as they are played out over the next hundred pages. Suffice it to say that they all follow the same pattern. One incident bears mention in passing, however, since the introduction of divine providence here is representative of its function in many works of sentimental literature. At one point, after a battle with pirates on the Atlantic, Tom discovers that one of the prisoners he has taken is none other than the man who had kidnapped him as a child years before. As Tom recounts his history to the crew, the sailors' "resentment at so base, so wicked an action, carry'd them out into exclamations against the villain, and the captain added—how just is providence—who has permitted you to see the miserable death of your persecutor! I am convinced that, in crimes of an enormous nature, heaven most commonly punishes the criminal even in this life" (*Garland* 7:156–57).

Tom eventually wins his Fanny, rescues the long-suffering Mrs. Barlow from her life with her abusive husband, and they all return to England. The novel ends with the reader being assured that "Mr. Anderson and his lovely Fanny are still living, and, tho' now in the decline of life, experience that love founded on good sense and virtue can never know decay, and that providence ever showers down blessings on truth and constancy. "Oh! never let a virtuous mind despair; / For heaven makes virtue its peculiar care" (*Garland* 7:287–88).

The History of Maria Kittle

Captivity was only one of many trials and turns of fortune the protagonist of *Mr. Anderson* had to triumph over; in Ann Eliza Bleeker's *The History of Maria Kittle* captivity structures the entire work. This epistolary novelette first appeared in the September 1790 edition of the *New York Magazine,* where it was described as "a pathetic story, founded on fact." It was republished posthumously as a part of the author's collected works in 1793 and then under separate cover in 1797 and 1802. Like Kimber, Bleeker employed an epistolary ruse to present her fictional tale as factual. She seems to have fooled some persons, at least in the modern period.[39]

The tale is recounted in a long letter from the author to her friend, Susan Ten Eyck. For our purposes, the reasons given for retelling this tale are of interest. Addressing Susan, the author says: "However fond of novels and romances you may be, the unfortunate adventures of one of my neighbours, who died yesterday, will make you despise that fiction, in which, knowing the subject to be fabulous, we can never be so truly interested. While this lady was expiring, Mrs. C——V——, her near kinswoman, related to me her unhappy history, in which I shall now take the liberty of interesting your benevolent and feeling heart" (*Garland* 20:3). Here the facts of the captivity are presented as having passed orally from Maria, the former captive, to a relative, who in turn recited them to Bleeker. In her own turn, Bleeker proposes to relate this tragic and pathetic history to a friend in writing (although ostensibly in an intimate, private form) out of a conviction that she will be able to interest her correspondent's "benevolent and feeling heart." The author of the letter assumes her friend to be a suitable audience for the story precisely because she expects her to be properly affected by it.

The epistolary form adopted here is not without an important consequence for the readers of Bleeker's work. In gaining access to this intimate correspondence, the real, secondary, readers of this "pathetic history" become the recipient of the letter, the primary reader. The epistolary form permits Bleeker to implicate the reader in an already established relationship. Just as the author knows Susan Ten Ecyk to be a person of highly developed sensibilities and, thus, feels confident that she can accurately predict what her friend's reaction to the narrative will be, the external implied reader of the published text is also presumed to be a sentimental reader who shares the author's benevolent assumptions and reading practices. This opening paragraph establishes a certain complicity, or, perhaps, a covenant between the reader and the author. The author will retell the story of Maria Kittle in a manner appropriate to the reader's sensibilities and expectations while, for her part, the reader will reciprocally acknowledge or repay the author's confidence by affectively responding in the anticipated manner. This is, of course, reminiscent of the way Per Amicum introduced Mary Rowlandson's narrative to the reader. There, it will be recalled, Per Amicum asserted that he and other friends of the author "could not but be so much affected" by the narrative when they read it. Significantly, he then went on to charge the reader—"if thou gettest no good by such a Declaration as this, the fault must needs be thine own" (*Garland* 1:3, 4A). In both cases, it is assumed (or asserted) that the reader's response to the captivity narrative could (and would) itself be read as an indication of the reader's character, moral sensibilities, and spiritual condition. Those who were affected and responded in the expected and valorized manner would thereby show themselves to be members of a select society, while those who did not so respond would demonstrate their coarser and baser nature.

Maria Kittle possesses almost all of the essential elements of a sentimental work, although its genesis as a magazine piece means that many of these appear in compressed form. The protagonist, Maria, is described as having been a fair-haired child of universally recognized excellence of character and mind:

> Her promising infancy presaged a maturity of excellencies; every amiable quality dawned through her lisping prattle; every personal grace attended her attitudes and played over her features. As she advanced though the playful stage of childhood, she became more eminent than a Penelope for her industry; yet, soon as the sun declined, she always retired with her books until the time of repose, by which means she soon informed her opening mind with the principles of every useful science. She was beloved by all her female companions, who, though they easily discovered her opening elegance of manners, instead of envying, were excited to imitate her. . . . it is no wonder that she soon became the reigning goddess among the swains. (*Garland* 20:4)

Utterly desirable as she blossomed into womanhood, Maria nevertheless developed the good sense not to reciprocate the universal attentions paid to her by men. Instead, she recognized only "one Mr. Kittle, whose merits had made an impression on her heart," for "although not handsome . . . his learning and moral virtues more particularly recommended him to her esteem" (*Garland* 20:5). Here, atypically, their mutual attraction was not opposed by either of her parents; neither does one find a doltish but wealthy suitor forced on the daughter by her father or the figure of the handsome rogue. Instead, Maria and Mr. Kittle were soon married. Thereafter, "they resided in the tranquil enjoyment of that happiness which so much merit and innocence deserved." Bleeker then proceeds to sketch quickly the blissful marital state this couple found in a pastoral paradise on a farm on the New York frontier, while asserting that their excellent qualities of character and heart won universal recognition, even from the Indians:

> The indigent, the sorrowful, the unfortunate were always sure of consolation when they entered those peaceful doors. They were almost adored by their neighbours, and even the wild savages themselves, who often resorted thither for refreshments when hunting, expressed the greatest regard for them, and admiration of their virtues.
>
> In a little more than a year they were blessed with a daughter, the lovelier resemblance of her lovely mother: as she grew up, her graces increasing, promised, a bloom and understanding equal to hers; the Indians, in particular, were extremely fond of the smiling Anna; whenever they found a young fawn, or caught a brood of woodducks, or surprised the young beaver in their daily excursions through the forests, they presented them with pleasure to her; they brought her the earliest strawberries, the scarlet plumb, and other delicate wild fruits in painted baskets. (*Garland* 20:6)

The paradisiacal state described here is one in which economic competition, cultural conflict, and disputes over land and hunting rights have no place. The actors are not historical agents with their own often conflicting interests and desires so much as pure representations of superior nature and virtue. The Kittles' only activity is to bring joy to themselves and others by constantly displaying themselves; the other actors are members of an appreciative audience whose role and pleasure is to observe and acknowledge the superior qualities and virtues of the main characters.

In the sentimental novel, however, such blissful scenes of domestic happiness and universal harmony are sketched only as a prelude to some sort of calamity. Given the protagonists' highly developed sensibilities, they often have premonitions of impending doom, even when there are no dark clouds on the horizon. The narrative representation of such premonitions, which today often seems artificial and contrived, only reinforced the sentimental reader's expectations. Moreover, by responding in the appropriate way to the realizations of these calamities the reader's own sense of identity and self-worth as a person of developed sensibilities were confirmed.

In the sentimental novel, a state of blissful existence is established only to imply that it is unsustainable in this world. There is, then, something of a mythic quality to such texts because they all rehearse the story of the Fall, but with one crucial difference—the protagonists are innocent and undeserving of the fate that befalls them. In *Maria Kittle* we learn that Maria had long sensed that the couple's fortune was too good to be true. Paradoxically, the experience of perfect bliss almost inevitably produced a sense of foreboding. "When they sauntered over the vernal fields with the little prattler [Anna] wantoning before them collecting flowers and pursuing the velvet elusive butterfly, Maria's cheek suffusing with rapture, 'Oh my dear,' she would say, 'we are happier than human beings can expect to be; how trivial are the evils annexed to our situation! May God avert that our heaven be limited to this life!'"

Similarly, immediately before the Indian attack on the family's home, Bleeker records a conversation between Henry Kittle and his brother as they were out hunting:

"Peter," said Mr. Kittle, casting his eyes around the lovely landscape, "what a profusion of sweets does Nature exhale to please her intelligent creatures! I feel my heart expand with love and gratitude to heaven every moment, nor can I ever be grateful enough. I have health and competence, a lovely fond wife whose smile would calm the rudest storm of passion, and two infants blossoming into perfection; all my social ties are yet unbroken—Peter, I anticipate my heaven—But why, my brother[,] do you turn pale? what dreadful idea stiffens your features with amazement? what in God's name ails you, Peter? are you unwel? sit down under this tree awhile."—To these interrogaties Peter replied, "Excuse my weakness, I am not unwel, but an unusual horror chilled my blood; I felt as if the damps

of death prest already round my soul; but the vapour is gone off
again, I feel quite better." (*Garland* 20:6–7, 10–11)

When Peter was slain by an Indian's bullet later that day, the
reader is told that he had "sunk down encompassed with those
deadly horrors of which in the morning he had a presentiment."
Such presentiments of impending doom were not limited to the
characters in sentimental works of fiction. Many of the readers of
Bleeker's narrative would also have had a presentiment of sorts of
the horrors to come as a result of their presumed acquaintance
with earlier captivity narratives. The authors of captivity narratives quickly developed a repertoire of "tragical" scenes, including, among others, the Indian attack on the virtually defenseless
family home, an infant snatched from its mother's arms and its
brains dashed out, forced marches through briars and brambles,
and running the gauntlet. Thus, when Bleeker describes the Indian
attack on the Kittle farmhouse, she has recourse to images well
known to her readers from earlier captivity narratives and illustrations. The scenes of horror she conjures up (a husband falls and is
scalped before his family's eyes; a pregnant woman is killed and
the fetus cut from her womb and mutilated), so unsavory and
needlessly gruesome for many readers today, had become almost
stylized iconographic glyphs by the late eighteenth century. These
were, in spite of Bleeker's disclaimer to the contrary, motifs in a
fabulous tableau. Although ostensibly a historical account set in
the everyday world, this captivity was told in a manner that located these scenes within a fabulous intertextual world of meaning ordered by the sentimental reading structures.

While it is difficult to know with any precision how late eigh-
teenth- and early nineteenth-century readers reacted to or pro-
cessed such images, the text itself contains hints of the variety of
intertextual relations being invoked by the author. We have already had occasion to speak about the genre expectations brought
to bear on a work of sentimental literature such as this, but it is
also essential that we not ignore the instances of authorial invocation of biblical tales. Understanding such intertextual allusions
will help us avoid some of the misunderstandings of sentimental
literature that have long been transmitted as accepted wisdom.

Maria Kittle must be read through an intertextual lens that includes the Bible. Whereas biblical parallels were frequently drawn
in Puritan texts and always made explicit therein, here they are far
fewer in number and often implicit, or indicated by brief allusions.

At least three biblical tales are brought into an intertextual relation with the history of Maria Kittle—Abraham and the sacrifice of Isaac, Job, and Lot and his wife. The following scene, for instance, is styled on the Genesis 22 account of the sacrifice of Isaac, although Bleeker adds an interesting twist:

> The Indian that guarded Maria was stooping down to drink, when a loud rustling among the leaves and trampling attracted his attention; he listened awhile seemingly much alarmed, then starting up suddenly, he flew to Maria, and caught hold of her hair, aiming his hatchet at her head: the consequence was obvious, and her fate seemed inevitable; yet, with a stoical composure, she folded her arms across, and waited the fatal stroke with perfect resignation; but while the weapon was yet suspended over her, chancing to look around, he perceived the noise to proceed from a large deer, whose antlers were entangled in the branches of a thicket. . . . [Maria] knew not whether to esteem her late deliverance from death a happy providence or protraction of misery. Observing the spotted trout, and other fish, to dart sportively across the water, she could not help exclaiming, "Happy! happy animals! you have not the fatal gift of reason to embitter your pleasures; you cannot anticipate your difficulties by apprehension, or prolong them by recollection; incapable of offending your Creator, the blessings of your existence are secured to you: Alas! I envy the meanest among ye!" A gush of tears concluded her soliloquy. (*Garland* 20:36–37)

While this scene replicates the Genesis account in some ways, Bleeker subverts a too easy identification of the two. If Abraham obeys God's command and Isaac is compliant in following his earthly father's orders, Maria is equally the model of perfect resignation. Yet her Indian captor is no Abraham, while the plot element one might call "the promise of children" is inverted. The structural relations found in the Genesis account are not perfectly replicated here and, consequently, the intertextual situation is more complex than one might first imagine.

The power of the scene of the sacrifice of Isaac in the biblical account comes in large part from the fact that in entering into the covenant with God, Abraham had received the promise of innumerable progeny in this world. Since Isaac represented an essential link in the immanent fulfillment of this promise, his death would preclude the anticipated result. In *Maria Kittle*, however, Maria is perfectly resigned to dying precisely because she believes that her children, who have already perished, await her in heaven. That is, while "that [domestic] happiness which so much merit and innocence deserved" has been frustrated on earth, the promise of realizing it once again—and this time for all eternity—in heaven is held out (*Garland* 20:6).

There is another important point to note here as well. In the moral economy of the sentimental novel, not every death is a good or auspicious death, nor is every act of resignation recognized as being spiritually efficacious. Perfect resignation in sentimental literature can only be achieved in the fulfillment of one's familial duties. That this is Bleeker's position will become clear if one compares the following passage, describing the Indian attack, as Maria and her two children huddle together in their house, along with her pregnant sister, Comelia, and her husband, and Maria's brother, Henry, with that passage presented immediately above:

> Distraction and despair sat upon every face. Maria and her companions gazed wildly at each other, till, upon repeated menaces and efforts to break open the door, Comelia's husband, giving all for lost, leisurely advanced to the door. Comelia seeing this, uttered a great shriek, and cried out, "O God! what are you doing, my rash, rash, unfortunate husband! you will be sacrificed!" Then falling on her knees, she caught hold of his hand and sobbed out, "O pity me! have mercy on yourself, on me, on my child!"—"Alas! my love," said he, half turning with a look of distraction, "what can we do? let us be resigned to the will of God." So saying he unbarred the door, and that instant received a fatal bullet in his bosom, and fell backward writhing in the agonies of death. (*Garland* 20:18–19)

The resignation of Maria's brother-in-law in accepting the inevitability of death as the will of God here is not represented as being heroic but rather as defeatist. This gesture, prompted by despair, is made in a distracted state; it is not performed with the alacrity borne of the surety of faith. Moreover, this man (he is never named—a fact that defines his identity only through his social role and obligations as the male head of the family) abjures his duty as a husband and soon-to-be father by ignoring the pleas of his pregnant wife and by not defending his family to the end. Bleeker's point is clear: resigning oneself (and possibly others) to death in the face of seemingly impossible odds is not the same thing as either Abraham's or Maria's acts of perfect resignation. The brother-in-law's appeal ("what can we do? let us resign ourselves to the will of God.") is an empty and a foolish gesture, not an act of faith.

This narrative representation by Bleeker of an inauthentic form of resignation is used to draw a sharp contrast with Maria's perfect resignation. To understand more fully how and why Maria could function as a paradigmatic figure of virtue for the readers of this work, one might return to Bleeker's depiction of the scene of horror at the time of the Indian attack on the family home. The unfolding tragedy is played out there at some length by the author in an effort to milk the last drop of affective response from her readers. In this scene, Maria represents the instinct of maternal protection in the face of violence threatening her family; she is also a locus of comfort and consolation in the midst of horror. The scene is drawn in stark black-and-white terms of contrast— innocence versus duplicity, brute force versus soft sentiments, and proper affective outbursts versus the coldhearted response of rocks and stones. Though she could not finally resist the brute force brought to bear on her and her family, Maria is represented as having resisted with all her physical strength. At the same time, she attempted to use her status as a woman and a mother to change the actions of the attackers through moral suasion, based on appeals to the attackers' humanity and feeling. When those appeals failed, she then appealed to the righteousness of God (*Garland* 20:20–23).

Although the Indians had once moved harmoniously within the regular orbit of the Kittle family, they had since unaccountably spun out of control, careening through the once-ordered space of domestic tranquility and leaving havoc in their wake. (Bleeker never explores the possible social, economic, or political reasons for the Indians' recourse to violence, for hers is a history of the heart, not a political history.) The fairweather Indian friend's promise of protection for Maria, now reduced to the hollow offer of life and dancing around an Indian campfire, held no attraction, we are told, for this paragon of maternal virtue.

We must pay special attention to the religious worldview informing the sentimental novel and its consumption if we are to understand the source of the affective power of this "pathetic history." An important part of this informing religious worldview can be glimpsed in the following passage, as Maria and her brother, Henry, are being led away into captivity, after little Anna has perished in the flames when the house was torched:

> Maria, bursting afresh into grievous lamentations, cried, "There, there my brother, my children are wrapt in arching sheets of flames, that used to be circled in my arms! they are entombed in ruins that

breathed their slumbers on my bosom! yet, oh! their spotless souls
even now rise from this chaos of blood and fire, and are pleading our
injured cause before our God, my brother!" He only replied in sighs
and groans; he scarcely heard her; horror had froze up the avenues of
his soul; and all amazed and trembling, he followed his [Indian]
leaders like a person in a troublesome dream. (*Garland* 20:24–25).[40]

In this speech Maria expresses a common religious belief informing sentimental literature: the souls of the innocent are immediately transported to heaven after death. If the ideal of domestic tranquility and bliss cannot be realized in the world, then it
will be in the afterlife. Over a century earlier Mary Rowlandson
had expressed a similar belief that the souls of some of the dead
(most notably her sister) were immediately carried to heaven,
although she did not share the belief in the innate goodness of
people. For the Puritans, proof of election, such as it was, was to be
found in the conversion experience.

In the scene above, however, Bleeker again implicitly critiques
the male view of the situation at the time of the attack and the
action that flowed from it. In the wake of the horrors of this
world, Henry is described as disoriented and distracted. He is
incapable of responding appropriately to either the scene before
him or Maria's affecting speech—"horror had froze up the avenues
of his soul." On the other hand, in spite of her relative weakness in
terms of brute physical strength, Maria (and by implication, perhaps, women in general) emerges as both stronger and more clear-
sighted than many of the men because of her faith.

Some feminist scholars have noted a new matriarchy emerging
in nineteenth-century Anglo-American culture, and one finds
clear indications of elements of this ideology in this late eighteenth-century work by Bleeker. But one also finds that some
males are also represented as persons of acute sensibilities. Bleeker's description of Mr. Kittle's reaction to his discovery of the
charred bodies of his sister-in-law and his infant son may be cited
in this respect. If this husband and father was not at home to
protect his family at the time of the Indian attack, his emotive
response to the scene of carnage clearly indicates that had he been
there, he would not have given up without a fight, as his brother
had.

In passages such as this, Bleeker links the ideology of proper
domestic relationships with the standard plot elements of Indian
captivity, which wrench the family apart. The heroic characters
are precisely those who endorse these family values to the hilt,

actively resist those who would destroy the family, and who are thrown into deep anguish if and when this occurs. Understood in this way, the scenes of horror and the detailed descriptions of the various characters' reactions to the events around them, which threaten to destroy their world of meaning, function to inculcate a constellation of social and theological values and to reconfirm the reader's understanding of virtue.

Since it is the informing religious worldview, however, that finally holds the sentimental work of fiction together as a didactic vehicle, let us return to the two other instances of biblical inter-textuality invoked by Bleeeker. First, there is the promise of a Job-like restoration made to Maria at one point in the narrative. As always, Bleeker brings this biblical text into strategic play in a discursive field where other elements, not always found in the Puritan narratives, are also invoked. Most importantly, one finds an increased emphasis on a woman's duty to provide consolation to her family members, even when she herself is suffering.[41]

On the forced march into captivity, Maria, "with the dignity of conscious merit in distress," refuses to accept any food from her captors, who have murdered her children. She is urged to do so by her brother, Henry, who "tried to touch her feelings on a softer key—'Remember, Maria,' said he, 'you have a tender husband yet living; would you wish to deprive him of every earthy consolation? Would you add affliction to affliction?'" He goes on to suggest that her husband would surely rescue them and she would soon be restored to a scene of domestic tranquility, where "soft sympathies shall wash away your sorrows; and after a few years, who knows but the smiles of a new lovely progeny may again draw a paradise of happiness on you" (*Garland* 20:33, 34). Maria was suitably affected by this speech, the reader is told, and thus saved from a suicidal despair.

In the biblical story of Job, he, too, is blameless yet suffers terribly, losing all of his sons and daughters. At the end of the tale, God restores Job's health, wealth, and gives him a new family. Readers of the Book of Job today usually do not focus on the deaths of Job's children or the other persons, however, nor do they of-ten comment on the tale's improbable denouement or question whether this restoration really sets matters aright or is morally satisfying. Like Maria, many readers accept the improbable so that they, too, may go on with life without becoming bitter or cynical. Or, to put this another way, they are willing to pay attention to certain aspects of a narrative while ignoring others.

In the climactic scene of the reunion of Maria and her husband,

Bleeker implies that, indeed, the death of their children was something that could be overcome and that a new family would replace
the old. In the meantime, civility and feeling friends combine to
provide a sympathetic audience of persons who all understand
that "the eloquence of sorrow is irresistible." In this lachrymos
environment, people weep for joy and weep in pain, until the
distinction becomes blurred as "the house of joy seems to be the
house of lamentation" (*Garland* 20:67, 65–66).

Bleeker invokes one final biblical image elsewhere in her tale.
While Maria is still held captive, a fiery meteor flies through the
sky, striking terror into the Indians' hearts. This is followed by a
tremendous earthquake, which Maria associates with the biblical
tale of Lot and his wife fleeing Sodom.

> This was a terrible scene to Maria, who had never been witness to so
> dreadful a convulsion of Nature before; she started up and fled from
> her savage companions towards an eminence at some distance,
> where dropping on her knees, she emphatically implored the protec-
> tion of Heaven: however, she was followed by an Indian and Henry;
> the latter, highly affected with her distress, taking hold of her trem-
> bling hand, "But why, my sister!" said he, "have you fled from us? is
> the gloom of the forest more cheering than the sympathising looks
> of a friend?" ["]No, my brother!" replied Maria; "but the tho't was
> suggested to me, that the supreme God perhaps was preparing to
> avenge himself of these murderers by some awful and uncommon
> judgment, and I fled from them as Lot did from Sodom, lest I might
> be involved in the punishment of their guilt." (*Garland* 20:41)

It will be recalled that Mary Rowlandson had identified herself
with Lot's wife at one point, looking back to what had been and
longing for her friends and family. Here, however, Bleeker has
Maria identify herself with the fleeing Lot, escaping from the divine punishment visited upon the abominable sinners. The power
of this identification is weakened by Bleeker, however, as she
notes that not only Maria but the "ignorant" Indians as well had
assumed that the earthquake had been divinely sent. While the
author seemingly glimpsed an element of cultural relativism here,
she did not follow it up. While the biblical tale of Lot is invoked,
then, it is to very different effect from its use in the late seventeenth century.

Here we must, I think, appreciate what had happened in the
culture at large in the century since Mary Rowlandson's captivity

narrative first appeared. While most members of the original audience for Rowlandson's or Hannah Swarton's captivity narratives shared a religious worldview and theological interpretive frame brought to bear on the text, along with communal forms of public confirmation of the spiritual significance of an individual's movements of the soul (e.g., in the rite of publicly presenting conversion experiences), by the late eighteenth century the interpretive community was more diffuse and less churched. It was in this situation that both the authors and publishers of sentimental literature helped to create a new sense of community by establishing a new covenant, if you will, with their readers, an understanding between them, based on a shared set of values, reading practices, and genre expectations.

What needs to be stressed at this point is that by making the act of reading almost a rite of renewal of this covenant, the authors and publishers of novels and other forms of sentimental fiction were able to exploit for commercial purposes the demand they created. The act of reading sentimental novels and responding in predictable, stylized, patterned, and valorized ways assured the reader of her own worth and refined her moral sensibilities. Just as Renaissance handbooks of etiquette and related forms of self-improvement had enjoyed phenomenal success in an earlier age, in the late eighteenth and nineteenth centuries, didactic fiction helped to fill the undiminished desire of readers for bettering themselves.

It is difficult for us, perhaps, to believe that works that were not overtly religious could have functioned in this way, but the evidence is overwhelming that this was the case. One need not and should not assume, however, that such didactic works of fiction replaced the Bible or other explicitly religious forms of instruction for many readers, only that they often supplemented these. For those for whom traditional Western theistic religion was no longer a viable option, didactic sentimental works sometimes shared pride of place with works of philosophy as sources of ethical guidance. Thomas Jefferson, for example, once proclaimed: "The writings of Sterne [constitute] the best course of morality that ever was written."[42]

There is another major difference between Puritan forms of writing and this type of didactic fiction. In sentimental literature, the characters are represented as ideal types, totally innocent or wholly depraved. This form of characterization ensures that the reader will readily identify with the good characters and that their

sympathy will be heightened as a result of the undeserved suffering and afflictions visited upon them. This is different from what
one found in, say, Rowlandson's narrative. There, if Puritan readers identified with Mary, it was because her spiritual trials and
doubts were readily recognizable, while the comfort she found in
Scripture was promised to all. Even a minister's wife was human,
with all that entailed, given the Puritan religious anthropology.

On the other hand, the sentimental novel is at one level a
fabulous morality play, with the protagonists' moral status clearly
demarcated. The characters do not really change during the tale;
as moral actors, they are either already fully developed, with their
moral nature firmly established, or else their natural qualities and
moral sensibilities are developed through education. Given their
natures, the characters react to events and to the calamities that
befall them in the only way possible to them as members of a
specific type. Secondary characters, on the other hand, are largely
undeveloped. As a result, readers are able to maintain a certain
distance from the horrors inflicted upon these figures. Like the
deaths of the sons and daughters of Job, for instance, the death
of Maria's brother-in-law evokes little emotion compared to the
death of little Anna. The brother-in-law's death serves a contras-
tive purpose within the narrative, as we have seen, distinguishing
a spiritually efficacious form of resignation from a futile one.

Each atrocity affecting one of the main characters provides an
occasion for Bleeker to put a speech, not unlike a Shakespearean
soliloquy, into his or her mouth, which expresses the character's
emotional, mental, and moral state. In the moral economy of
the sentimental novel, this narration of emotional responses frequently provides the occasion for consolation to be found in the
communion of souls indulging in "the luxury of sorrow" (*Garland*
20:39). That is, anticipating an important component of psychoan-
alytical cures, the act of narrating the horrors and suffering one has
endured is held to be the key to coming to terms with these, but in
works of sentimental literature this is so only—and this is a
critical caveat—if the audience for the narration is an appropriate
one, composed of similar persons of deep sympathy and heartfelt
feeling. As a result, works of sentimental literature often carefully
describe the scenes of the narration and reception of affecting
tales.

Maria Kittle contains several instances of persons narrating the
events of their captivity. It will be instructive to take note of the
situations in which such narrative activity occurs and provides

consolation, as well as of the proper deportment of the audience. The following, for example, describes how Maria encountered an inappropriate audience when she was carried into Montreal as a prisoner, an audience who did not deserve to hear her story of suffering precisely because they did not know how to react properly to it: "The throng of people that came out to meet them, threw Maria in the most painful sensations of embarrassment; but as the clamours and insults of the populace increased, a freezing torpor succeeded, and bedewed her limbs with a cold sweat—strange chimeras danced before her sight—the actings of her soul were suspended—she seemed to move mechanically, nor recollected herself till she found she was seated in the Governor's hall surrounded by an impertinent, inquisitive circle of people, who were inquiring into the cause of her disorder, without attempting any thing towards her relief" (*Garland* 20:45–46).

Such unsympathetic persons literally left Maria cold and she retreated into a sighing soliloquy, rehearsing her story of virtue-in-distress to herself. This remarkable passage clearly indicates the critical need persons of sensibility felt for a proper audience for the narration of an affective tale of captivity or whatever misfortune has befallen them. If "the actings of [Maria's] soul were suspended" temporarily, this was a direct result of the absence of a sympathetic audience. But when a benevolent Englishwoman approached Maria, the "soft impulses of nature" (i.e., the refined feminine natures they shared) created an immediate sympathetic bond and a concert of tears (*Garland* 20:49).

Recognizing a sister of refined sensibilities ("This tenderness, which Maria had long been a stranger to, relaxed every fibre of her heart: she again melted into tears; but it was a gush of grateful acknowledgment, that called a modest blush of pleasure and perplexity on Mrs. D——'s cheek."), the Englishwoman led Maria to a couch and poured her a cordial. Over the next few days Maria largely regained her health and was persuaded to receive visitors. Bleeker's description of Maria provides useful "ethnographic" information for us today as to the proper deportment in this situation. Among her visitors, Maria discovered a former neighbor, Mrs. Bratt, who also had suffered captivity at the hands of the Indians. Echoing the Book of Job, Maria spoke to her, saying, " 'I dare not ask after your family; I am afraid you only have escaped to tell me of them.'—'Not so, my sister,' cried Mrs. Bratt; 'but if you can bear the recollection of your misfortunes, do oblige me with the recital.' The ladies joined their entreaty, and Mrs. Kittle complied in a graceful manner. After some time spent in tears, and pleasing melancholy, tea was brought in" (*Garland* 20:49).

Then, after the women walked a bit in the garden, Mrs. Bratt was next persuaded to tell her own story, which shared much with Maria's and generated yet more tears. Following this, the hostess next "accosted the other stranger," saying, " 'Dear Mrs. Willis, shall we not be interested likewise in your misfortunes?'—'Ah! do (added Madamoiselle V.) my heart is now sweetly tuned to melancholy. I love to indulge these divine sensibilities, which your affecting stories are so capable of inspiring.'—Maria then took hold of Mrs. Willis's hand, and pressed her to oblige them.—Mrs. Willis bowed. She dropt a few tears; but assuming a composed look, she began" (*Garland* 20:52, 56–57).[43]

These women represent the ideal audience for the sentimental captivity narrative. The readers of works such as *Maria Kittle* became members of this audience themselves, "interested" in the misfortunes of their sisters. Their hearts "sweetly tuned to melancholy," they, too, "loved to indulge these divine sensibilities," which the narratives generated. If today we are unable to join this lachrymose community of readers, we can nevertheless imaginatively reconstruct the reading structures through which this community constituted itself, creating a shared world of meaning through communal mourning. "The eloquence of sorrow is irresistible," Bleeker wrote, speaking for generations of readers past, present, and future who shared in "the tender contagion [which] ran from bosom to bosom" (*Garland* 20:47, 65). Historians of religions must recognize this cult of communal ritual weeping for what it was and in all of its complexity.

At the same time, it would be historically inaccurate to assume that this sentimental point of view was held exclusively by women. Adam Smith, for instance, devoted considerable effort to the task of providing a philosophical grounding for a feeling-based system of morals. In *The Theory of Moral Sentiments* (1759), Smith provided, among other things, the philosophical justification for the moral efficacy of literary scenes such as Bleeker's portrayals of the tearful narration and reception of tales of suffering and sorrow. Those who have suffered, Smith wrote, "by relating their misfortunes . . . in some measure renew their grief. Their tears accordingly flow faster than before. . . . They take pleasure, however, in all this, and it is evident are sensibly relieved by it, because the sweetness of the by-stander's sympathy more than compensates the bitterness of their sorrow."[44]

Critics and historians in the nineteenth and twentieth centuries had long accepted Hawthorne's dismissive characterization of female sentimental authors as "scribbling women," but even the important revisionist work of feminist scholars will be incomplete until the religious and cultural work of the sentimental novel is located in the center of the larger context of eighteenth- and even nineteenth-century philosophical and theological thought.

4

REBINDING THE BONDS:
MIXED MOTIVES AND BODIES
IN CAPTIVITY NARRATIVES,
1750–1900

Books, and the readers of books, have done much to bewilder
and perplex the study of the Indian character. The Egyptians
embalmed their dead in myrrh and spices, but the blessed art
of printing has given us a surer and less revolting method of
preserving and transmitting to posterity, all that is truly valuable in the plaudits of virtue, worth, and honor. . . . Books
thus became a more permanent memorial than marble . . .
till the boundaries of letters have well nigh become coexten-
sive with the world.—Henry Schoolcraft (1851)

IN THE PERIOD from 1750 to 1900, the authors of captivity tales
employed diverse narrative strategies to depict human pain and
suffering. Many authors participated in the cultural process of
gendering the human body and social relations so that gender
emerged as an important marker in the natural order of the social
world. The following types of bodies are found in captivity narratives published through the end of the nineteenth century: the
religious afflicted body; the tortured body, used to prove the savage
and hardhearted nature of the Indian; the sentimental female body
as virtue-in-distress; the hermetically sealed body of the male hero
or patriot; the sexual body; the asocial body of the recluse, a
symbol of perfect Christian resignation; and the body of the innocent, pious child.

Many of the captivity narratives from this period mix elements
of the providential interpretive frame and the sentimental novel;
others introduce new motives for composing and publishing such
tales and seek to convey different messages. Information on the

motives for publishing these works can be culled from the narratives proper and from prefaces or introductions, where these issues were often explicitly addressed.[1]

Although the intention to witness to God's providence did not disappear, it was cited much less commonly as a motive for recording and then publishing a captivity account. Even when the author, editor, or publisher explicitly gives this as his motive for publishing a story, a thoroughgoing religious worldview, such as that found in the Mary Rowlandson narrative, rarely informs the tale in the ways or to the extent it had in the late seventeenth and early eighteenth centuries. Perhaps the most conspicuous differences in the narratives published from 1750 to 1900 are the virtual absence of biblical passages and the noticeably different representations of the body-in-pain and human suffering. In this period fewer and fewer individuals read their lives and human suffering through the Bible in the same way and with the regularity their ancestors had.

One finds no directives addressed to the reader that these captivities were intended to be used in private devotional practices. Instead, readers are commonly invited to contemplate specific scenes in the captivity narratives cast in the sentimental mode. Even when religious motives for telling the tale are mentioned, the substitution of sentimental reading practices necessarily altered the reader's experience of the text and thus its meaning. In this period captivity was no longer identified with the theological understanding of the human condition as that of being fallen, corrupt, and bound to sin; rather, it came to serve more diverse metaphorical and rhetorical purposes. In the nineteenth century the emphasis on the moral efficacy of the sentiments evoked by scenes of suffering was, at times, replaced by an indulgence in sensation for nonmoral purposes, including mere titillation. In such texts, the body-in-pain becomes a spectacle and the reader a voyeur.[2]

While frequently more than one reason for publishing is given, one can nevertheless distinguish the following major kinds: to provide religious instruction to adults; to inculcate morals in children; to record (or memorialize) the histories of American heroes and heroines, which are then offered to subsequent generations as paradigmatic figures of courage, virtue, and self-sacrifice; to affect government policy toward the Indians; to record geographical and ethnographic information; to provide enjoyment; to earn money for the former captive and his or her family; and, occasionally, to authenticate the curative powers of "snake oil" medicines.

Religious Captivities and the Attenuation

of the Providential Interpretive Frame

The captivity narratives from the second half of the eighteenth century that mention the author's desire to witness to God's goodness and providence are mixed narratives—that is, they are not pure Puritan narratives of the sort we have examined. These texts are either cast in part in a sentimental mode or they do not contain a central informing religious intention. Nor is the human body represented as a site of divine affliction. Instead, the captive's body is of interest as the locus of affective responses to external stimuli or as it evokes sympathy or other affective responses in others.

Two late eighteenth-century narratives by female captives are representative texts of this sort, since both shared a modified providential interpretive frame combined with sentimental elements. The brief work *A True Narrative of the Sufferings of Mary Kinnan* (1794) is narrated in the first person, although two third-person paragraphs by an editorial hand precede the narrative proper. The opening paragraphs promise the reader a typical sentimental tale of domestic bliss shattered and then restored, complete with a religious moral reminiscent of that found in Puritan captivities:

> Whilst the tear of sensibility so often flows at the unreal tale of woe, which glows under the pen of the poet and the novelist, shall our hearts refuse to be melted with sorrow at the unaffected and unvarnished tale of a female, who has surmounted difficulties and dangers, which on a review appear romantic, even to herself. Her history will not, perhaps, be without its use. It will display the supporting arm of a Divine Providence: it will point to the best and surest support under danger and adversity: and "it will teach the repiner at little evils to be juster to his God and to himself." (*Garland* 21:3)

Whereas Puritan captives traced the movements of their souls, Kinnan (1763–1848) rehearses her somatic responses to specific events. For instance, describing her involuntary response to the memory of the Indian attack four years after the fact, she says, "At the recollection, my bosom heaves impetuous; the cold sweat of fear stands on my brow; and the burning tears of anguish glistens [*sic*] my eye." Equally revealing is her depiction of her response to the murder of her husband and daughter before her eyes. She does not say that divine providence has taught her an invaluable lesson through her suffering; rather, she reports that in extremis she had found strength and faculties within herself that she had not previously known she possessed. On occasion, Kinnan does appeal to divine providence (e.g., when a snake bites one of her captors during their forced march, causing the Indians to pause for several days and allowing her to recover her strength). She also suggests that prayer had helped her to achieve a state of calm resignation, but she also voices a sense of pride in her self-sufficiency not found in Puritan texts (*Garland* 21:4–8).

Interestingly enough, one of the few aspects of Indian culture that elicited any public comment from Kinnan was the failure of Indian women to serve as the agents of civilizing their men and ameliorating their rough and violent natures, something the prevailing Western gender ideology held to be a part of woman's natural role. Like most of her compatriots, Kinnan believed her assumptions concerning human nature and gender to be universally valid rather than culturally specific. As a result, the fact that the Indians did not fulfill her expectations was remarkable and served to disqualify them in her eyes as being civilized. Kinnan's narrative ends on a religious note with a proclamation that her afflictions in captivity had, in fact, been a blessing in disguise. She urges her reader to put her trust in God, as she had, and to adopt an attitude of spiritual resignation in the face of life's vicissitudes (*Garland* 21:8–9, 14–15).

In 1796 *A Narrative of the Captivity of Mrs. Johnson* was published in New Hampshire, forty years after the author had been captured by Indians when she was nine-months pregnant. It is free of a providential frame; indeed, the reader is almost one-third of the way through the text before encountering the lines "Six days had now almost elapsed, since the fatal morn, in which we were taken, and by the blessing of that Providence, whose smiles give life to creation, we were still in existence," and "the same Providence who had brought us so far, and inclined our savage masters to mercy, continued my protector." While recording her suffering in great detail, including how she gave birth to a daughter (whom she named Captivity) on the forced march, she never characterizes her experience as divine affliction. When Johnson finds herself refreshed one morning after having unexpectedly slept well, for instance, she attributes this to nature rather than to divine intervention (*Garland* 23:40, 45, 38).

The absence of an informing providential interpretive frame

enabled this author to recognize the humanity of her captors in a manner her Puritan ancestors had been unable to. At one point, for instance, she recalls that when the Indian band was suffering from dire hunger and forced to shoot a horse for food, they still shared the best cuts of meat with her, an act that "certainly bordered on civility." Elsewhere she notes that she never was shortchanged by them, nor suffered any cruel treatment. In the enlarged edition of 1814, the author, then an elderly widow living with her daughter, Captivity, and her family, used the occasion to lament publicly over the shabby treatment she had received from the family of her second husband following his death, treatment that she "sometimes found almost as painful to be borne, as my savage captivity" (*Garland* 23:33, 50–51, 75–76, 1814 ed., 127).

Other late eighteenth-century captivity narratives display even less of a religious intention. The preface to *A Narrative of the Captivity and Sufferings of Benjamin Gilbert and His Family* (1784), for example, seems to promise a tale illustrating divine providence, but in spite of the expectations thus raised, there are no references to divine providence in this third-person account. Whereas Indian captivity had earlier been understood as a form of divine affliction, here only a perfunctory nod is made in this direction in the preface, and even that disappeared in subsequent editions. Instead, one finds that this nonfictional account has been influenced by sentimental forms. The author's goal is to provide moral instruction to his readers by "interesting [their] Feelings in the Relation of the many Scenes of Affliction the Family were reduced to" (*Garland* 15:6).

This same pattern of later editions de-emphasizing the original religious motives given for publication is found in the publishing history of *Narrative of Mrs. Scott and Capt. Stewart's Captivity.* One can still hear echoes of earlier religious captivities in the third edition of 1784, which is advertised as "A True and Wonderful narrative of the surprising Captivity and remarkable Deliverance of Mrs. Frances Scott." And the publisher's preface, addressed "To the serious and pious Reader," promises "many remarkable and surprising Instances of the infinite Goodness of Divine Providence," which "may be a Means not only of gratifying the Curiosity, but of serving the spiritual Interest of the Reader." The publisher also included a number of biblical passages that he found to be "very applicable to the unhappy Person who is the Subject of the following Narrative." Nothing of this preface or its intention was retained in the subsequent editions of 1799, 1800, and 1811, however (*Garland* 16:iii–iv, v).

References to divine providence were equally perfunctory in numerous other nineteenth-century captivity narratives. In *Narrative of the Captivity and Sufferings of Mrs. Hannah Lewis* (1817) there is only one reference to God's having aided the author in captivity. Moreover, rather than attributing her escape to divine providence, she credits her son with having cleverly convinced the Indians that he had gone native and thus did not require constant supervision (*Garland* 36:8, 23–24).

Eunice Barber's *Narrative of the Tragical Death of Mr. Darius Barber, and His Seven Children* (1818) is representative of the polemical tales of horrible suffering at the hands of the Indians that end with a stylized and conventional acknowledgment of the justness of the divine affliction the author had experienced. While the author refers to the "interposition of Divine Providence," expresses gratitude for the goodness of God, and wishes that as a result of her affliction she might now truly recognize her sinful nature, these religious sentiments are merely added as an appropriate final statement.

Moreover, bodily pain and suffering have little or no religious significance in the Barber narrative. The bodies of others subjected to torture are described in great detail, but these grisly descriptions serve as evidence of the savage nature of the Indian. The longest description of the body of a captive concerns another female captive, who had already been a prisoner for two years when Eunice Barber met her. It is a stereotypical sentimental sketch of female virtue-in-distress, copied almost verbatim from another text. Barber concludes her description by reporting, "Every thing [about her appearance] conspired to confirm and to make her story interesting" (*Garland* 36:13, 15).[3]

In some captivities from this period, however, one senses a deeper religious understanding of past suffering. Zadock Steele's *The Indian Captive* (1818) was published to "preserve in memory the sufferings of our fathers" and to witness to God's divine providence in preserving the author after he had been captured at Royalton, Vermont, on October 16, 1780. Almost forty years after the fact, Steele had not forgotten his suffering in captivity or the cruel treatment he had received from the British, which he found worse than that meted out by the Indians. Yet he seeks to declare how he had turned his suffering to positive account by locating his pain and suffering in a universal religious framework and thereby gained a renewed sympathy for the less fortunate (*Garland* 36:3).

Another narrative written long after the fact seems almost anachronistic in the extent to which a religious interpretive frame in-

forms it. *An Interesting Narrative* by Anne Jamison, a pamphlet of
twelve pages, sold for three cents when it was published in 1824.
Jamison, then in her eighties, had given her account orally to an
editor, who reports that she "earnestly desired me to publish the
following Narrative of God's dealing with her, during five years of
her weary pilgrimage; that her numerous offspring and others
might be excited to acknowledge God in all their ways, patiently
submit to his chastening rod, and fully put their trust in him,
through the Lord Jesus Christ even in the most gloomy and afflictive dispensations of his Providence" (*Garland* 37:1).

Printed forty-six years after Jamison had been captured, the
narrative reads more like an early eighteenth-century captivity
than a nineteenth-century one, as she sees God's hand in all of the
events composing her life. This last phrase is chosen deliberately:
the meaning of her life is retrospectively composed in the manner
it is precisely under the ordering aegis of her providential theology.
Jamison's narrative is repeatedly punctuated with such phrases as
God "saw fit to let the Indians attack our fort twice during the
summer," "God in mercy prevented the Indians from destroying
our boats," and "a holy and righteous God saw fit to continue, and
increase our affliction." In many respects this work is a throwback
to an earlier age.

John Leith's captivity (1831) was given orally to an editor when
Leith was seventy-seven years old. A former white Indian, he had
spent eighteen years in captivity after being taken as a teenager.
The religious interpretation he places on what had befallen him
("The design of the following work is to show the providence of
God, in guiding his creatures through life, although their situation, at times, may be, to all appearance, dismaying, perilous
and almost insurmountable" [*Garland* 47, unpaginated preface]) is
clearly one he supplied retrospectively long after the fact, probably
as a result of his religious conversion.

Orphaned early in life, Leith had been an indentured servant
from the age of seven and seems to have received little religious instruction as a child. At twenty-four, after several years in captivity
he married another white Indian, who had been raised among the
Shawnee since infancy. Given the length of his life among the
Indians and presumably his intimate knowledge of their lifeways,
it is surprising that he makes no mention of any aspect of Indian
religion or even any native cultural practices.

Leith converted to Methodism in 1793 after attending a series of
sermons and meetings held by circuit riders and then experiencing

a long period of personal turmoil and intense spiritual struggle. His detailed account of his prolonged conversion experience is told with much more energy and passion than the section on his life as a captive, caught between the Indian and white worlds in Ohio (*Garland* 47:72–85).

A very different captivity is *The Contrast; or the Evils of War, and the Blessings of Christianity*, an anonymous work of utopian fiction published in London in 1830. Presented as a modern parable, this antiwar piece is cast as a first-person retrospective narrative of how the protagonist, Paul, had been captured and adopted by Indians in western New York. Eventually, he and an Indian friend, named Naka, hear about an idyllic, pacific Christian community of Mohawks living deep in the wilderness, and they set off to find it. In this work the noble savage of the Enlightenment is transformed into a primitive or pure Christian, while Paul and Naka are not so much captured as they are captivated by the harmonious community of Christian love they find in the wilderness. They settle with the Indians, introduce them to European technology, marry and raise families, and rise to positions of respect within the community. In sum, the figure of Paul Placid is a piece of European reverie or spiritual nostalgia about returning to paradise (*Garland* 47).

The Recluse, Perfect Resignation, and the Bible

Two other captivity narratives with strong religious overtones from the first half of the nineteenth century merit attention. Both proffer a theology of resignation to the will of God as the only guarantee of true consolation and happiness in the wake of life's vicissitudes, espoused by a recluse who had lost his family in an Indian attack. These tales represent a defensive effort by conservative Protestants to counter the rise of a broad cultural movement loosely based on a spiritualizing of nature, as found, among other places, in John Filson's 1784 biography of Daniel Boone.

Narrative of the Massacre of My Wife and Children (1835), attributed to Thomas Baldwin, is a curious work. The title page indicates the thrust of the narrative, concerning Baldwin, "who since the melancholy period of the destruction of his unfortunate family, has dwelt entirely alone, in a hut of his own construction, secluded from human society, in the extreme western part of the State of Kentucky." A woodblock print of Baldwin shows him seated on a boulder. He has shoulder-length hair, a receding hair-

NARRATIVE
OF THE
MASSACRE, BY THE SAVAGES, OF THE WIFE & CHILDREN
OF
THOMAS BALDWIN,
Who, since the melancholy period of the destruction of his
unfortunate family, has dwelt entirely alone, in a
hut of his own construction, secluded from
human society, in the extreme western
part of the State of Kentucky.

"Great indeed, have been my afflictions; but, as it was the will of Heaven, I
ought not to murmur, but to say like him, whose afflictions were still greater, " the
Lord gave and has taken away, and blessed be his name."

Annexed are some well written Moral Instructions, of the venerable BAL-
DWIN, to the bereaved and afflicted, how and where (from his own experience)
they may find support and comfort amid the *severest trials* that may attend them
in this "miserable world," and how to prepare themselves for endless enjoyments in that which is to come.

MARTIN & PERRY—PUBLISHERS—NEW-YORK.
1836.

Figure 2. The forest recluse, symbol of male Christian resignation.
(Photo courtesy of the Edward E. Ayer Collection, The Newberry
Library)

line, a furrowed brow, a full moustache and beard. Wearing a shawl and holding an open Bible in his hand, his half-closed eyes are cast down, apparently not focused on anything, a detail indicating that he finds no consolation or solace in nature, but only through the Bible (fig. 2). The wilderness here provides isolation from the vanity of the world and society. The caption suggests a parallel between Baldwin's citation and that of Job: "Great, indeed, have been my afflictions; but, as it was the will of Heaven, I ought not to murmur, but to say like him, whose afflictions were still greater, 'the Lord gave and has taken away, and blessed be his name.'" This is followed by a brief advertising blurb: "Annexed are some well written Moral Instructions, of the venerable Baldwin, to the bereaved and afflicted, how and where (from his own experience) they may find support and comfort amid the *severest trials* that may attend them in this 'miserable world,' and how to prepare themselves for endless enjoyments in that which is to come." Also attached is a large foldout print of seven stereotypical scenes from the captivity, serially numbered and briefly annotated (fig. 3).

The narrative purportedly had been taken down from Baldwin's oral account by an anonymous editor the previous year. The eighty-five-year-old recluse recounts how he and his family (a wife and three children) had followed Daniel Boone to Kentucky in 1780, settling near Boonesboro. Baldwin's description of the death of his wife and child and the torture of another son are graphic, yet his story of his own brief captivity is unremarkable. Providentially, his young daughter had died shortly after being captured, since by "taking the hapless victim to himself," God saved the child from the inhumane treatment the savages would surely have meted out to her and the horror of having to marry an Indian. The last five pages of the twenty-four-page narrative are devoted to a monologue on the Bible and religion as constituting the only source of consolation to be found in this world of woe. The following passage is representative:

> "Should you now wish to know, from what source I have been able to obtain consolation and support in the midst of my sorrow, I would point you to that sacred book"—the old gentleman here pointing to the octavo Bible, lying upon his table, and which bore the marks of having been faithfully read—"from that" he continued, "I think I have obtained that comfort, and drawn that instruction, in my most sorrowful moments, which no human being could impart. It has taught me that the many sore afflictions of

Figure 3. Stereotypical scenes of Indian attack and abduction. From *Narrative of the Massacre, by the Indians, of the Wife and Children of Thomas Baldwin* (1835). (Photo courtesy of the Edward E. Ayer Collection, The Newberry Library)

which it has pleased my blessed Father in heaven to make me the subject, was intended for my spiritual good! . . . How much more real happiness might be experienced by that portion of my fellow-mortals who are continually complaining of their afflictions, and the miseries to which they are daily exposed, in this 'miserable world,' if they would seek to draw it from its only proper source. It is unreasonable for them to expect to be truly happy in this frail world unless they be truly pious, and reconciled to the will of God." (*Garland* 52:18–19)

In 1840 another narrative of a Christian hermit was released in New York. *Narrative of the Extraordinary Life of John Conrad Shafford* is an anonymous work about the events that had led this man to live as a hermit in Canada for over fifty years. The gist of this tale is given on the title page: "Shafford early emigrated to Canada, and was induced first to prefer a lonely life in consequence of being deprived of an only child, a beloved daughter, who, when but 15 years of age, was taken prisoner and carried off a captive by the Indians, and who, although she was three months after redeemed by her afflicted father, yet in consequence of the most shameful and beastly treatment she had received from the merciless savages, she expired a wretched victim of their barbarity, three weeks after her liberation." The blurb continues, promising that the narrative would prove that the Indians did not treat white female captives as well as other writers had falsely suggested.

This fictionalized tale may well have been inspired by a newspaper announcement of the death of a local eccentric known as the "Dutch Hermit," but it is also clearly indebted to the Baldwin captivity. In addition to being identical in length, it shares many similar elements: the author claims to have stumbled across the hermit in the deep forest and convinced him to share his history with him; the old man had become a recluse many years earlier after losing his family in an Indian attack; the recluse has long white hair and beard; and he points to the Bible as his only source of consolation. Here, however, the author also invokes the pathetic figure of an innocent and helpless white woman (Shafford's daughter), held captive and brutalized by savages, in order to counter the romantic portrayals of the noble savage. The daughter's cruel treatment, sexual abuse, and suffering are used to cast the Indians as unfeeling brutes, while the narrative representation of the female body-in-pain is dedicated to evoking outrage at the Indians (*Garland* 56:14–19).

These two narratives share the same constellation of constituent elements—Indian captivity, a shattered situation of domestic bliss for a father and husband, the survivor's adoption of the life of a recluse in the woods, an emphasis on the Bible as the only source of comfort and defence; and the recommendation to the reader to adopt an attitude of spiritual resignation to the will of God. While these recluses live in the midst of nature, nature is not represented as sacred, nor is it a locus of comfort and consolation. Rather, the wilderness here holds the place it had in biblical theology as a place, free of the vanity of the world, where one did penance for one's sins or engaged in other forms of asceticism.

The theological concept of the corrupt and fallen nature of man, coupled with the understanding of this world as a world of woe, made the recluse or hermit a powerful and melancholy spokesman for Christian values and an otherworldly orientation based on the Bible. The immediate impetus to the publication of these fictional narratives seems to have been the danger some persons perceived in the popular heroic image of Daniel Boone and the representation of the spiritual power of regeneration found in nature as promoted by John Filson in his biography of Boone, a work that Richard Slotkin has called "the first nationally viable statement of the myth of the frontier."[4]

Filson, a surveyor and land speculator, published *The Discovery, Settlement and Present State of Kentucke* in 1784. The first part of this work, a promotional piece seeking to sell land in Kentucky to settlers, deals with the commercial potential and utilitarian value of the land. Filson charged, not without reason, that most previous narrative descriptions of the American frontier had been based on secondhand knowledge at best and often on complete ignorance. In contrast, he promised his readers only the facts, either from his own firsthand observations or those of three eminent settlers of his acquaintance—Daniel Boone, Levi Todd, and James Harrod. Filson supplies a signed and notarized statement from these three men certifying the veracity of his descriptions. Filson assured his reader that all of his descriptive information "of general utility" was being provided in a "disinterested" fashion. But, as Robert Lawson-Peebles has noted, "if there is no such thing as an artless language, it follows that descriptions of the environment are never merely empirical. They are strategies which encode the interests and concerns of the writer as well as the physical nature of the terrain, the climate, and so on. As those interests and concerns change, so do the strategies of description."[5]

While Filson's main text is today almost forgotten, his life of Boone, included in an appendix, was to prove to be one of the most influential tales in both the United States and Europe over the following century. (It still informed Walt Disney's cinematic re-telling in the twentieth century.) While the "structural plan and argument of *Kentucke* are modeled on those of the Puritan narra-tives and histories," Filson also employed aspects of the prevailing sentimental understanding of human nature to create in Boone a male hero sufficient unto himself.[6] In his narrative Filson blended elements of sentimental anthropology, an environmental deter-minism, the nostalgia for a natural paradise, and an appeal to divine providence.

Slotkin argues that Filson's narrative is a myth insofar as it gathers together all of the significant elements of the frontier in the colonial period into a single literary form and the figure of Boone. This tale is also linked to the historical destiny of the United States and the designs of divine providence. Filson skill-fully utilized the reading practices of his readers, who had become well acquainted with the sentimental novel, in order to get these readers to identify with Boone and to imagine themselves into his adventures.[7]

Filson asserts that the scenery of Kentucky, emplotted with the scenes from Boone's life, must be read as both a historical and a prophetic text. In this he shares the Puritan view that "Prophesie is Historie antedated; and History is Postdated Prophesie: the same thing is told in Both."[8] Land and lives (topography and biog-raphy) past, present, and future are intertwined in a manner that promises the creation of a new community of individuals and self-made men on the frontier.

In the opening sentences of the biography, Filson offers his mix of sentimental anthropology, divine providence, and the idea of a national destiny: "Curiosity is natural to the soul of man, and interesting objects have a powerful influence on our affections. Let these influencing powers actuate, by the permission or disposal of Providence, from selfish or social views, yet in time the myste-rious will of Heaven is unfolded, and we behold our conduct, from whatsoever motives excited, operating to answer the important designs of heaven" (*Garland* 14:49).

This passage works only insofar as the reader is led to accept a logically linked series of causal relationships—all men are natu-rally curious and attracted to "interesting objects"; these objects naturally "have a powerful influence on our affections" and evoke involuntary responses from persons of sensibility; since God created the world and everything in it, he must necessarily have intended these natural phenomena and topographical features to evoke precisely these affective responses. Here nature is transformed into an agency of realizing God's plan for human salvation, or, to put this another way, nature is subsumed under a providential interpretive frame that has been linked with eighteenth-century sensational psychology. Moreover, Filson claims that no matter what selfish motives persons may have had (or will have in the future) in moving into Kentucky and clearing the land, these actions are part of God's divine plan.

Filson continues his opening paragraph, using the inclusive pronoun "we" to draw the reader into sharing a retrospective view of Kentucky, a gaze akin to Yahweh's in the Genesis creation account, where he surveys his creation and declares it to be good: "Thus we behold Kentucke, lately an howling wilderness, the habitation of savages and wild beasts, become a fruitful field. . . . Here, where the hand of violence shed the blood of the innocent; where the horrid yells of savages, and the groans of the distressed, sounded in our ears, we now hear the praises and adorations of our Creator; where wretched wigwams stood, the miserable abodes of savages, we behold the foundations of cities laid" (*Garland* 14:49–50). This is a fairly typical example of a retrospective survey of an emplotted and transformed scene. By inviting the readers (and, in terms of his contemporary audience, Filson hoped his would-be customers) to share his sweeping retrospective view of the land—what it was, now is, and could be—Filson implies that they could also participate in this sacred history.

In the second paragraph, Filson shifts the narrative voice into the first-person, with Boone ostensibly telling his own tale, including his captivity. The effect of this rhetorical move is significant: in Filson's hands not only is the history of the white invasion of Indian lands transformed into a sacred history, but Boone, who was present at the founding moment, is presented as the mythical figure of the culture bringer. In myths, culture bringers are transitional figures; they introduce dramatic change into the world, but then have to leave it themselves. After performing their foundational creative or transforming acts, culture bringers disappear into the landscape, often becoming specific topographical sites. In Filson's 1824 *Life and Adventures of Colonel Daniel Boon*, Boone is described as having moved farther into the wilderness each time new settlements were established (*Garland* 14:20–24). A trace of his mythical acts of foundation remain, however, inscribed on the land in the name of the first white settlement, Boonesboro.

Once this structural logic is understood, it is easy to appreciate why, as more and more white settlers moved into Kentucky, Boone had to be portrayed as continually moving farther west in order to live alone in "a perfect wilderness." Boone's life of isolation in the wilderness is clearly not an expression of spiritual resignation, as we saw in the Baldwin narrative. Rather, his captivity and adoption into the Indian tribe are used to explain his unique nature, his transformation into a noble savage; and by definition a savage can only live in the wilderness ("savage," let us recall, is derived from "sylvan"). While Boone leads white settlers into Kentucky, he himself can no longer live comfortably in a populated settlement, but must move off into the wilderness where he can enjoy "the chase." As a culture bringer, he brings change, alters the landscape, and establishes a new order, but then he moves on.[9] Filson's Boone is a mythical figure—a white Indian-as-culture-bringer.

The Gendered Bodies of American Heroes and Female Captives

In the wake of the American War of Independence, and again after the French and Indian War and the War of 1812, captivity narratives were used to feed a growing desire among American readers for homegrown heroes and heroines. In these narratives, the hero's body is not a site of divine affliction but is selflessly offered up for the greater good of the nation's citizenry. At the same time, scenes of suffering are narrated not only to move the readers to tears of sympathy but often to develop a profound respect for these heroic men and women, models of patriotic self-sacrifice.

One example of this trend is the short captivity *The Remarkable Adventures of Jackson Johonnot, of Massachusetts* (1791). A former footsoldier in the Continental army, Johonnot maintains that a traditional religious motive lay behind his decision to bring his story to the public's attention, but this is mixed with the expectation that sentimental reading practices would be brought to bear on his tale. Addressing his reader directly, he writes, "As the dispensations of providence towards me have been too striking not to make a deep and grateful impression, and as the principal part of them can be attested to by living evidences, I shall proceed, being confident that the candid reader will pardon the inaccuracies of an illiterate soldier, and that the tender hearted will drop the tear of sympathy, when they realize the idea of the sufferings of such of our unfortunate country folks as fall into the hands of the western Indians, whose tender mercies are cruelties" (*Garland* 18:3).

While the title page notes that the text had been "written by [Johonnot] himself, and published at the earnest request and importunity of his friends, for the benefit of American youth," the narrative does not provide moral guidance for this readership. Instead, it warns young men against foolishly enlisting in the military with dreams of glory and false hopes of realizing easy fame and fortune, as he had done. Johonnot does not represent himself as a model of Christian piety or resignation but as a loyal and patriotic citizen willing to risk his life in order to protect the residents on the frontier. He harnesses the traditional religious motives for recording and publishing a captivity tale to a new cult of nationalism and patriotism (*Garland* 18:5, 17).

Similarly, other captivity narratives were published as part of an effort to memorialize American heroes. Moses Van Campen's *A Narrative of the Capture of Certain Americans, at Westmoreland* (1780?) was composed, according to the author, because "my Mind was so struck with the rare specimens of Enterprize, Bravery, and Conduct which were exhibited in these little Adventures" (*Garland* 13:2).[10] This attitude is characteristic of a broader cultural movement away from seeking paradigmatic figures exclusively in the Bible or in antiquity and toward lifting up native heroes. Historical societies grew rapidly in number in the United States after the Revolutionary War. The Massachusetts Historical Society, founded in 1793, was the first such state society; by 1860 there were 111 historical societies in the United States, almost all publishing their proceedings.

After it was first submitted to the Society of the Cincinnati in Connecticut, David Humphreys's *Essay on the Life of the Honorable Major-General Israel Putnam* was presented to the general reading public in 1788. "An essay on the life of a person so elevated in military rank, and so conversant in extraordinary scenes," he asserted, "could not be destitute of amusement and instruction, and would possess the advantage of presenting for imitation a respectable model of public and private virtues" (*Garland* 19:iii–iv). This text illustrates the emergence in the late eighteenth century of a new literary type—the self-contained male hero—which served as a counter to the representations of the sentimental male.

Humphreys voices concern over what he feels to be the deleterious consequences of the explosion in the number of sentimental historical romances and purported histories of scenes from the Revolutionary War written by persons far removed from the actual scene of battle. He sees his own historiographic activity as a necessary corrective to this deplorable situation and promises to provide the reader with the real meaning of recent American history by presenting an objective account. Significantly, in this history the true source of General Putnam's courage and heroism is found in his natural constitution.

Humphreys rails against the danger that romantic historical fictions pose to the social order. They threaten to undermine the moral foundations of the nation by finally leading the good but easily duped citizens of the republic to lose their faith in historical writing and, consequently, in the truth. The "mischief" caused by fictional works of history was such that "the easy-believer of fine fables and marvellous stories will find, at last, his historical faith change to scepticism and end in infidelity" (*Garland* 19:8–10).

Humphreys holds the inculcation and maintenance of public morality to be the responsibility of the historian. The cultural work of historical biographies is to promote the reader's "historical faith." Significantly, this moral crusade for truth is linked with a strident opposition to the core assumptions held by many persons in the culture of sensibility, most especially the belief that one's moral sense is activated and then cultivated only by responding to external sensory stimuli. Humphreys's male hero, General Putnam, needs no such external goad; he is constitutionally virtuous:

> Courage, enterprize, activity and perseverence were the first characteristics of his mind. There is a kind of mechanical courage, the offspring of pride, habit or discipline, that may push a coward not only to perform his duty, but even to venture on acts of heroism. Putnam's courage was of a different species. His undaunted feelings depended, less than the feelings of most others, on external objects, adventitious aids, or the influence of example. He stood alone, and collected within himself, always possessed intrepidity equal to the occasion. His bravery, that appears to have been constitutional, never for a moment deserted him in the trying situations. (*Garland* 19:17–18)

Putnam is cast as an ideal hero, a man of refined sensibility but one who is cool rather than emotionally heated and who acts out of his innate character. The moral nature of this hero is hermetically sealed, as it were, within the hero's body, a body quite distinct from the tremulous sentimental body.

This depiction of the heroic male was in part a reaction against certain sentimental representations of the moral role women play in culture. Most especially, it denies that men need to be reformed by women, who smooth the rough edges of their harsh or brutal nature. The male hero Humphreys presents as a model for emulation is not subject to swooning, groaning, or any involuntary affective responses to the scenes of life and death, pleasure and pain, or unwarranted suffering which he encounters. Rather, Putnam's character was

> a species of cool, deliberate fortitude, not affected by the paroxism of enthusiasm, or the phrenzy of desperation. It was ever attended with a serenity of soul, a clearness of conception, a degree of self-possession and a superiority to all the vicissitudes of fortune, entirely distinct from any thing that can be produced by the ferment of blood, and flutter of spirits. . . . The heroic character, thus founded on constitution and animal spirits, cherished by education and ideas of personal freedom, confirmed by temperance and habits of exercise, was completed by the dictate of reason, the love of his country and an invincible sense of duty. (*Garland* 19:18)

Humphreys argues that it was this innate character that had allowed Putnam "to pass in triumph through the furnace of affliction." He makes no appeal to any external agency, including divine providence, in this regard. Here, the providential interpretive frame has completely vanished, and in its place one finds a controlling set of gender constructions. The male hero is self-contained and in control of his reason and his libido, while the female is emotional and weak, with her only defense against violence being her ability to appeal to the sympathy of others precisely by displaying her feminine virtues and her pitiful vulnerability. The myriad representations, in nineteenth-century works of literature, in prints and paintings, in sculpture, and on the stage, of women on their knees, with eyes lifted up and hands clasped in prayer in a gesture appealling for mercy before a raised tomahawk, participated in this process of constructing new gendered bodies.

These distinctive gender traits inform the descriptions of General Putnam and Mrs. Howe. Putnam is represented as having been fearless and ever in control of his senses, even when faced with overwhelming odds on the battlefield or the immediate prospect of being burned at the stake by his Indian captors. His calm demeanor and silent courage then were such that the Indians soon came to believe him to be a god, or at least to be under the direct protection of the Great Spirit. With the flames licking around Putnam, as he was bound to the stake, he was stoic and resigned to his death, regretting only that he would be separated from his wife and children. Physical pain held no power over him. Finally, when Putnam was miraculously saved at the last moment, it was not by the agency of divine providence but through the "interposition" of a French officer, who had earlier been the recipient of the kind solicitude of the general (who always recognized individuals of like class). Thus, Putnam's character is represented as having ultimately been the source of his own salvation (*Garland* 19:62, 69–70).

Humphreys introduces a second captivity tale into his narrative as well, that of a Mrs. Jemima Howe. As a counterpoint to the male hero, he sketches her in the complementary terms of a sentimental heroine in distress. Unlike General Putnam, she does not so much act as react to events and the actions of others around her. Her face and body are a text to be read by sensitive observers, for a record of her suffering has been inscribed in her features. One of the dictums of sentimental moral anthropology was that the innate virtue of a person of sensibility would not be adversely affected by the vicissitudes of life; rather, a person's character would be strengthened by such testing. Yet if the inner person could not be changed by adversity, it was widely believed that the effects of having experienced scenes of horror and suffering were registered externally in one's carriage and on one's body—in scars, in a furrowed brow, in the look of one's eyes. All of these were assumed to be clear markers of a person's moral character and personal history. Thus, when Mrs. Howe is introduced for the first time, a discerning eye could read her sad history in her facial features. She is not hysterical (a popular image of the female) but someone who has composed herself and thus who is prepared to narrate an engaging story, even as her body has been textualized:

> Distress, which had taken somewhat from the original redundancy of her bloom and added a softening paleness to her cheeks, rendered her appearance the more engaging. Her face, that seemed to have been formed for the assemblage of dimples and smiles, was clouded with care. The natural sweetness was not, however, soured by de-

spondency and petulance; but chastened by humility and resignation. This mild daughter of sorrow looked as if she had known the day of prosperity, when serenity and gladness of soul were the inmates of her bosom. That day was past, and the once lively features now assumed a tender melancholy, which witnessed her irreparable loss. She needed not the customary weeds of mourning or the fallacious pageanty of woe to prove her widowed state. She was in that stage of affliction, when the excess is so far abated as to permit the subject to be drawn into conversation without opening the wound afresh. It is then rather a source of pleasure than pain to dwell upon the circumstances in narration. Everything conspired to make her story interesting. (*Garland* 19:74–75)[11]

The sentimental female body is morally instructive precisely insofar as it is "interesting" to others. In the late eighteenth century, this term meant that the scene of the former captive narrating her tale had the power to attract the attention of others and to evoke a sympathetic response from them. Insofar as Howe's body-in-pain and her mind have been composed (and thus her person and history transformed into a stable body-as-text), her narrative has the power to interest other persons and to evoke their moral sensibilities. Howe is described as having come to terms with her past suffering and loss so that her affliction is no longer painful to recall, especially when she has a congenial audience of persons of like sensibility. The pleasure to be found in narrating one's past pain and suffering here is not understood as a stage in the grieving process; rather, it comes from the knowledge that the moral sensibilities of the audience can be sharpened and instructed through the affective transaction involved in the act of narration. By sharing her sad story of suffering and woe, the former captive contributes to the softening of the audience's hearts and minds and to the further cultivation of their tenderhearted humanity. In giving expression to her pain and suffering, she provides the opportunity for her listeners' sympathy to find expression as well. Innumerable examples from history demonstrate that intense pain can be borne and can even be a source of ecstatic pleasure for the sufferer when it is located within a meaningful structure. The paradox represented by the composed body-in-pain has fascinated people over the ages.

Overdetermined gendered bodies are found in other captivity narratives from the late eighteenth and early nineteenth centuries. *French and Indian Cruelty* (1757), the story of Peter Williamson's captivity, was one of the most popular captivities in this period and was regularly reissued down through the nineteenth century. Initially, Williamson published his tale in order to move his readers to sympathize with his plight as a wounded veteran and former captive and thus to open their purse strings. By telling and selling his story, he hoped to earn enough money to set himself up in some kind of gainful employment. He seems to have been much more successful in this endeavor than most former captives because he managed to earn a living from sales of his narrative and other writings while exhibiting himself in Indian costume at his coffeeshop in Edinburgh for many years until his death in 1799 (*Garland* 9).

Williamson's tale is representative of works that offered various sorts of captivity to readers. Mrs. Howe, for instance, was represented not only as an Indian captive but also, à la Pamela, as a helpless and vulnerable female captive in Montreal, where she had to ward off unwanted sexual advances from two Frenchmen. Other tales tell of individuals who had been kidnapped and sold into virtual slavery, or of persons who had fallen into poverty through circumstances outside their control and been forced to become indentured servants or otherwise lost their freedom, autonomy, and social position. Whatever the case, such tales sought to evoke the sympathy of readers for the plight of the protagonists and the sufferings they experienced. In doing so, they sought to exercise and cultivate the reader's moral imagination.

The remarkable popularity of Williamson's captivity narrative over the years was due in no small part to his skillful appeal to multiple audiences and their reading practices. He appealed at once to religious sensibilities, sentimental ideals, and the anti-French and anti-Indian feelings that had been stirred up in the Anglo-American world by the French and Indian War. He claims to have been kidnapped as a child of eight in Aberdeen, imprisoned onboard a ship, and sold as an indentured servant in Pennsylvania. In his twenties he had managed to gain his freedom, married, and was living on a three-hundred-acre farm on the Delaware River. In his own words, he was at this time "blessed with an affectionate and tender Wife, who was possessed of all amiable Qualities to enable me to go thro' this World with that Peace and Serenity of Mind, which every Christian wishes to possess." Predictably, his idyllic domestic life was soon destroyed by an Indian attack (*Garland* 9:10).

Williamson describes various sorts of torture he was subjected to in captivity and claims to have borne these in silence by putting his faith in God. Like many other writers before and after him, he narrates scenes of the infliction of pain and suffering, including Indians dashing the brains of infants on rocks and butchering pregnant women, as a means of demonstrating the inhumanity of the Indians and the French, who were hardhearted and unmoved by "the Tears, the Shrieks, or Cries of these unhappy [and innocent] Victims."

The ubiquitous scenes in Indian captivities of infants, children, and women being "knocked on the head" with a tomahawk when they cried or moaned frequently do not reflect actual occurrences. These scenes are too common and too stereotyped to inspire any confidence in their actuality. Such scenes were composed of two elements designed precisely to evoke sympathy for the victims and hatred for the Indians: the victims are inevitably depicted as innocent and helpless, and the savages are unmoved by their tears or cries, as any person of feeling and moral sensibility would be. Such scenes, then, were constructed with an understanding of the moral significance of the circulation of feeling in sentimental reading practices; they were part of the currency in the economy of feeling and sympathy in the eighteenth- and nineteenth-century culture of sentiment.

Time and again Williamson describes the suffering of a poor captive alone among the Indians only to conclude with such an observation as "to all which, the poor Creature could only vent his Sighs, his Tears, his Moans, and Intreaties, that to my affrighted Immagination, were enough to penetrate a Heart of Adamant, and soften the most obdurate Savage. In vain, alas! were all his Tears." While the savages were portrayed as unfeeling brutes, Williamson represented himself and other white males as persons of sensibility. In the culture of sentiment, heightened sensitivity could itself be a source of intense, albeit "exquisite," pain, as in the following passage, describing a party of soldiers as they discovered the female captive, beloved of the captain, naked, bloody, and bound to a tree:

No Heart among us but was ready to burst at the Sight of the unhappy young Lady. What must the Thoughts, Torments, and Sensations, of our brave Captain then be, if even we, who knew her not, were so sensibly affected! For, oh! what Breast, tho' of the brutal savage Race we had just destroy'd, could, without feeling the most exquisite Grief and Pain, behold in such infernal Power, a Lady in

the Bloom of Youth, bless'd with every Female Acomplishment
which render'd her the Envy of her own Sex, and the Delight of ours,
enduring the Severity of a windy, rainy Night! (*Garland* 9:19, 45)

Here Williamson recreates a typical sentimental scene of female
virtue-in-distress, a scene guaranteed to evoke "the most exquisite
Grief and Pain" in the spectators and readers. He continues, addressing the reader directly, a device that evolved from oral forms
such as the jeremiad and other kinds of preaching. Like Cotton
Mather before them, preachers in the Great Awakening and the
Second Awakening in America directly challenged their audiences
to contemplate scenes of death or the suffering of souls in hell.
Williamson asks his audience to gaze on this scene of an innocent
female body-in-pain and to respond appropriately, which now
means in gendered terms:

Behold one nurtur'd in the most tender Manner, and by the most
indulgent Parents, quite naked, and in the open Woods, encircling
with her Alabaster Arms and Hands a cold rough Tree, whereto she
was bound with Cords so straitly pull'd, that the Blood trickled from
her Finger Ends! Her lovely tender Body, and delicate Limbs, cut,
bruis'd, and torn with Stones and Boughs of Trees as she had been
dragg'd along and all besmear'd with Blood! What Heart can even
now, unmoved, think of her Distress, in such a deplorable Condition? having no Creature with the least Sensations of Humanity
near to succour or relieve her, or even pity or regard her flowing
Tears and lamentable Wailings!

As the woman's lifeless form is restored to consciousness, "eagerly fixing her Eyes on her dear Deliverer, and smiling with the
most complacent Joy, [she] blessed the Almighty and him for her
miraculous Deliverance." The pitiful tale she proceeds to tell of
her captivity proves to be a "pleasing, painful Interview" (*Garland*
9:45, 46).

It is, perhaps, hard for us today to appreciate how and why such
pain and grief could be considered pleasing, interesting, or beautiful. But throughout the eighteenth and nineteenth centuries, the
readers of works of sentimental literature undoubtedly found such
scenes to be so. The "pleasure" spoken of here was usually not
located in immediate sensory perceptions but was the result of
reflective activity. Philosophical and epistemological support for
such a position was found, among other places, in *A Treatise of*

Human Nature, where Hume held that "no passion of another discovers itself immediately to the mind. We are only sensible of its causes or effects. From *these* we infer the passion: And consequently *these* give rise to our sympathy."[12] Whatever the precise source of support for the widespread understanding of the moral efficacy of sentimental reading practices, however, it is important to recognize that Williamson's captivity narrative found a ready audience not only because it was linked to "the metaphysics of Indian-hating and empire-building" but because it was linked to sentimental reading practice. The scenes of death and suffering were effective because of the widely shared understanding of how reading such works could be a form of rational entertainment and a means of moral improvement.[13]

Readers of such captivity tales seem to have come from all socioeconomic levels of society, including the lowest. A few captivities sold cheaply on the streets have survived and may be taken to be representative of a much larger number of similar works. *The Travels and Surprising Adventures of John Thompson, who was taken and carried to America, and sold for a Slave there:—How he was taken Captive by the Savages.—With an Account of his happy delivery, after Four Months slavery, and his return to Scotland* (1761) is typical. This work was pilfered almost directly from the Williamson narrative, with only the name of the author and a few other details altered. It was no doubt the product of a modest scheme to make some quick money on the street.

At times the purchasers of such street literature could have an oral account of the author's captivity along with the printed pamphlet. *A full and particular Account of the Sufferings of William Gatenby,* a short pamphlet of only eight pages from 1784, for instance, announces that "if any person has a desire to have any further particulars, by applying to the said Hawker of this paper, they may have their curiosity satisfied with the greatest pleasure." The author authorized the street hawker to sell his narrative, "hoping all well-disposed christians will contribute a trifle to my relief, by purchasing this small book." The hawker apparently took a share of the sales receipts (*Garland* 9:24).[14]

While Humphreys held the moral edification of the people to be the sacred duty of the historian, other authors offered captivity narratives to the public as suitable material for the poet, the novelist, the playwright, and the moral philosopher. *A Brief Narrative of the Captivity and Sufferings of Lt. Nathan'l Segar* (1825) is an example of a work which had these multiple audiences in mind. This edition is a reissue of a work originally penned by Segar

(1755–1847) in an effort to gain full compensation for his military service in the Revolutionary War and his captivity in Maine. The editor argues in the introduction that the work is of both local and national historical interest. Moreover, because it accurately represents the respective characters of the Indian and the frontiersman, it is an important chapter in the history of the moral development of man. "The character of the aboriginal inhabitants of this country is a curiosity in the history of human nature," he writes, "and is falling among the antiquities of moral remains and monuments. The station of the settler, the pioneer of the forest, is also singular and interesting." Figures such as Segar "are men, the incidents of whose lives are frequently of the most romantic cast, and whose habits are, from necessity, often so peculiar as to furnish a fine theme for contemplation and description of the novelist, the poet, the historian, and the observer of human nature" (Garland 37:5, 3).

It was believed that the tales of captives, who had been deprived of the company of civilized persons and the amenities of civilization and forced to live in virtual isolation, were both "amusing and instructive" when they were compared with "the condition of him who hears around him the din or the arts and mingles in the bustle of the busy and social scene." Captivity tales, especially those based (however loosely) on fact, were offered as an invitation to readers to engage in an inquiry into the human condition and, with the comparative knowledge gained, to meditate on the blessings and the costs of civilization. Still other tales were presented as affording the reader "an opportunity of observing the mind of man in its progress from the original savage to civilized life; as well as in its retrograde movements from civilization to the savage state" (Garland 37:4; 26:25).

The presence of large numbers of white Indians in these centuries could not be ignored and led to a wide variety of responses, including some efforts to explain the phenomenon scientifically and others to explain it away. Some persons maintained that the divide between the "primitive" and "civilized" man was the result of an evolutionary process; others claimed that there was an ontological distinction between the savage and the civilized peoples. The possibility that the distinction between these states had not yet been finally won was both fascinating and frightening and has stimulated fictional explorations of "going native," ranging from Cooper's Leatherstocking Tales and Conrad's Heart of Darkness to Burroughs's Tarzan.

Some fictional captivities attempted to mediate between hard history and fiction as narrative vehicles of moral improvement. James Russell's pocket-sized novel *Mathilda; or, The Indian's Captive* (1833) was offered to the public as a means of chasing away the reader's despondency and "unmerited grief," of furnishing amusement and moral instruction, and of demonstrating the workings of divine providence in history. The form and style of the work were crafted with the female reader's delicate sensibilities and susceptibility to seduction in mind. Russell claims to have obtained the outline of his tale firsthand from a former female captive who became the model for his heroine. In apologizing for his limited literary skills, he also claims (unconvincingly, it must be said) that he himself had been abducted and made an Indian captive "at an age when the human mind is most susceptible of improvement" (*Garland* 51:iii).

If Russell claims that his work is not deserving of the designation "novel" because it is based on fact, the editor of *Sketches of Aboriginal Life* (1846), the inaugural volume of a series of historical romances called "American Tableaux," defends the moral efficacy of fiction. He boldly claims that while not "authentic history," works of historical fiction alone could bring the past to life and speak to readers (*Garland* 62:iii).

History and fiction were blurred genres in the first half of the nineteenth century. While many persons were deeply concerned over the negative social consequences of works of fiction and historical romances, others considered these forms to be more truthful and better vehicles of moral instruction than factual historical accounts, insofar as well-written works of fiction were more apt to evoke sympathetic responses from readers. Our present generation was clearly not the first to recognize the literary nature of history.[15]

Female Heroines, Maternal Instinct, and Redemptive Suffering

A large number of nineteenth-century captivity narratives illustrated ideal gender roles and virtues. We have seen how female captives served as historical instances of feminine virtue-in-distress. Such figures were usually passive, waiting to be rescued by male heroes, while the narrative scenes of these suffering innocents were designed to evoke sympathy in the reader or, at other times, a ferocious anger and thirst for revenge against the cruel and inhuman savages who had inflicted such suffering on the women.

We will now turn to a representative selection of captivities

Figure 4. Typical image of a mother's appeal for her innocent child. From *Narrative of the Captivity and Extreme Suffering of Mrs. Clarissa Plummer* (1838). (Photo courtesy of the Edward E. Ayer Collection, The Newberry Library)

from the second half of the nineteenth century in which the central themes are a specifically female heroism, associated with maternal instinct, and redemptive suffering by women and children. Such texts are generally a mix of religious sentiments, a historiographical impetus to record examples of female heroism, and the prevailing gender constructions. *Miss Coleson's Narrative of Her Captivity Among the Sioux Indians!* (1864), an anonymous work of fiction, is representative of the inexpensive novels then widely available. While not a pure work of sentimental literature, it shares many of the same informing values, as selected structural elements of the sentimental genre are incorporated in a tale otherwise reminiscent of earlier religious narratives of suffering, providential escape, and heroism. The author relies upon the reader's familiarity with and affirmation of the values of sentimental literature in crafting his characters and his depiction of the Indians.

This novel employs negative stereotypes of the Indians throughout, most importantly in descriptive scenes and "factual accounts" of savage Indian customs and brutal atrocities—innocent women tomahawked, "mutilated in a shocking manner," and scalped; infants' brains dashed out against trees or rocks; cannibalism; captives forced to run the gauntlet; and sadistic acts of cruelty and torture. The prevailing white cultural constructions of gender and gender roles are also invoked to further damn the Indians as uncivilized. Indian women, for instance, are represented as possessing some of the attributes of female feeling and sympathy, although in insufficient measure. If Pocohantas had once been able to intercede successfully on behalf of Capt. John Smith, the Indian women here have largely lost their powers of moral suasion. The wife of the Indian chief protests without success against her husband's forcing Miss Coleson to watch the torture of a white male prisoner.

The characterization of all Indians, regardless of age or sex, is uniformly negative. Indian children lack the charm, intellect, and moral aptitude of their white counterparts; moreover, their education and even their forms of play are declared to be such that the limited potential the Indian children begin with is never developed. In sum, Indians are found to be closer in nature to animals than to civilized human beings, since "their sense of hearing, sight and smell, are much more acute than those of white people, and enables them to distinguish objects at an incredible distance" (Garland 79:36–38).

In a descriptive passage dictated by the joint values of refined femininity and sentimental mores, the author introduces another incidental character—a young woman, born of a Canadian mother and an Indian father—who helps Miss Coleson escape. This woman's inherited nature as a "mixed Blood" is used to explain both her good looks and her kind civility. Yet while the immediate mutual sympathy this young Indian maiden and Miss Coleman feel for each other signals the recognition of a certain shared nature, the young woman's share of Indian blood finally keeps her from spurning Indian society for civilization.

A mysterious male figure, who suddenly appears as Miss Coleson is attempting to escape, kills her pursuer, and assists her to return to the white world, is introduced in the conventional terms of a sentimental romantic hero—polite, solicitous of female needs, desires, and delicate nature. Physically, he is dark and ruggedly handsome, with a "roman nose and fine intelligent countenance." With this physiognomic validation of the man's good character and trustworthiness, Coleson is certain that she is in good hands (Garland 79:38, 45).

Although Coleson undergoes "unbearable suffering and fatigue" in captivity, she is never too tired to respond to the beautiful and the sublime in nature in a manner appropriate to a woman of her sensibilities. The body of the sentimental heroine is not only a site of suffering, it is also always atingle, sensitive to the scenery and persons around her:

> Notwithstanding the pain in my limbs, and the fatigue of drawing my sledge, I could not help remarking on the loveliness of nature peculiar to these northern latitudes, and which seemed sufficient to dissipate every sensation of pain and weariness; such a rare combination of frost and sunshine, without being seen and felt, could hardly be imagined. The wind, which had blown fiercely all the morning, came to a perfect lull in the afternoon; even the deep roar of the pine woods hushed to a gentle murmur—and as we walked along, our hair, our faces, our eyebrows, and even our eyelashes, were as white as a powdering of snow could make them—while the warmth of the sun gave a sensation of peculiar purity to the air. (*Garland* 79:34)

Even under the extreme duress of captivity, this sentimental and romantic heroine's refined sensibilities are both irrepressible and indestructible. If this portrait seems artificial, unnatural, and unrealistic to modern readers, this was not the case for nineteenth-century readers. In the face of many counterexamples of captives, both male and female, having gone native, the author of this work seeks to deny the very possibility of this happening to anyone who was truly civilized. Coleson had little thought of escaping, not because she could ever be reconciled to a savage life, but because she was so moved and taken by the remarkable sights and extraordinary experiences of captivity that she forgot all else temporarily (*Garland* 79:33).

In both works of fiction and nonfiction the sentimental heroine is frequently paired with the complementary male hero. This is the case even in male adventure stories, which became very popular in the second half of the nineteenth century. Cheap novels, such as Sylvester Crakes's *Five Years a Captive Among the Blackfeet Indians* (1858), mix tales of western adventure with racial stereotypes, information on Indian life and customs, sentimental scenes, and occasionally even religious sentiments. The figures of the heroic rugged frontiersman and the lone cowboy owe much to Filson's Daniel Boone and Cooper's Leatherstocking Tales, as they find life in nature to be spiritually rewarding and invigorating. The following passage illustrates the mix of romanticism and male freedom in the wilderness:

> In the wild roaming of the hunter, amid the freedom of the forest, mountains, hills, and valleys, there is a species of ennobling adventure and enlarged liberty that is calculated to fill the soul with admiration for the vast and grand in nature—where the looming of the hoary mountain, the roaring of the river, the whispering of the forest, and the murmuring of the gentle rivulet, speak, in accents bold and grand, the praises of that God who commanded, and they stood fast. Cut off from of the conventionalities of civilized life, the trapper feels somewhat like Robinson Crusoe, on the island of Juan Fernandes. (*Garland* 74:19)

Like Daniel Boone before him, John Dixon, the hero-narrator, found his life as a hunter and trapper to be "actually captivating." His own condition as a captive mirrored the human condition in important ways, while his response to captivity was a model of and for living with life's vicissitudes. In this way, the author manages to combine a standard Christian moralism, a sentimental male-female relationship, and an action-packed male adventure story (*Garland* 74:19, 36). Although he makes no appeal to divine providence, he presents a familiar rationale for telling a captivity tale—by presenting the utter degradation of the heathen Indian, he will rekindle the reader's gratitude for having enjoyed the civilizing influence of Christianity.

The introduction of the character of Roxana, a female captive, permits the author to portray ideal male-female relationships, as well as her eventual "beautiful death." Dixon acts as the noble civilized male, ever attentive in the midst of savagery and unfeeling cruelty to the needs and the nature of the suffering incarnation of female virtue-in-distress. Selflessly, he vows to stay among the Indians in order to nurse Roxana back to health until such time as he can lead her back to civilization. Theirs is not a sexual relationship, however; the hero's reward is in serving this paradigm of female purity and humility (*Garland* 74:157, 170).

Roxana, who is dying of consumption, is presented as a model of perfect Christian resignation in the face of her illness, pain, and suffering in captivity. The beautiful death of a pale, innocent woman (or, alternatively, a child) was a popular theme throughout the nineteenth century, guaranteed to evoke tears in the readers' eyes and to turn their thoughts to the power of purity in the world. Because the Bible had promised the meek would inherit the earth, nineteenth-century authors frequently used pale, sickly, pious women to illustrate this truth for millions of readers. The figure of the innocent woman suffering in captivity immediately suggested itself as an ideal model of perfect resignation to the will of God.

In *Two Months in the Camp of Big Bear* (1885), a first-person narrative, Theresa Gowanlock and Theresa Delaney seek to correct incomplete and inaccurate accounts of their captivity that had appeared in the press, including the suggestion that they had been sexually violated. These Canadian women style themselves as being content with Victorian ideals of womanhood; Gowanlock even suggests that only the memories of her domestic life "within the sacred precincts of the paternal hearth" had kept her from sinking into despair during her captivity. This phrase captures the extent to which the patriarchal ideal of domestic life had taken on religious overtones in the nineteenth century. For her part, Delaney invokes divine providence to explain what had befallen her, while justifying the publication of her tale for reasons found earlier in Adam Smith's *The Theory of Moral Sentiments:* "I look upon the writing of these pages as a duty imposed upon me by gratitude. When memory recalls the sad scenes through which I have passed, the feeling may be painful, but there is a pleasure in knowing that sympathy has poured a balm upon the deep wounds, and that kindness and friendship have sweetened many a bitter drop in the cup of my sorrow and trouble" (*Garland* 95:6, 5).

When Delaney recalls how she had become an object of the male gaze, she invites the female reader to imagine herself into her situation. She assumes that the leering gaze of the male voyeur is universally known by women, as the female body is exposed to the male "naked eye." Interestingly enough, this lurid feeling of being exposed and watched is then compared to the knowledge that one's actions are being watched by God:

> Imagine yourself seated in a quiet room at night, and every time you look at the door, which is slightly ajar, you catch the eye of a man fixed upon you, and try then to form an idea of my feelings. . . . I know of no object so awe-inspiring to look upon, as the naked eye concentrated upon your features. Had we but the same conception of that "all seeing eye," which we are told, continually watches us, we would doubtlessly be wise and good; for if it inspired us with a proportionate fear, we would possess what Solomon tells us i[s] the

first step to wisdom—"The fear of the Lord is the beginning of wisdom." (*Garland* 95:117–18)

In an 1854 anthology of captivity narratives, *Heroic Women of the West*, the editor, John Frost, claims that the blessings then enjoyed by the American people were a direct result of the toil, suffering, and heroism of the first settlers, including pioneer women. The stories of the latter provided, he maintained, "the most splendid examples of that [female] spirit of self-sacrifice and devotion which can only be prompted by disinterested affection" (*Garland* 66:8). The symbolic complex of female self-sacrifice, "disinterested affection" or selfless action, and redemptive suffering took on a religious aura in the nineteenth century. Whereas men might at times be motivated by visions of glory to perform acts of courage, women's heroism was understood to be of a purer nature, precisely because female acts of courage and self-sacrifice were assumed to be selfless. Female maternal instinct and love led to egoless actions in which all thought of oneself was overridden by concern for the welfare of others.

The representation of female virtue expressed spontaneously in a time of need was found in innumerable works of literature. In many captivity narratives women often willingly risk their own lives and suffer physical pain in order to protect their children and husbands. In Margaret Hosmer's *The Child Captives*, issued in 1870 by the Presbyterian Publication Board, one finds the following example: "Beyond her power of suppression, [Mrs. Bright] uttered a shriek of horror, which redoubled its agony when she saw [the Indians] approach the bed of her husband. Instinctively she sprang before it to save him, and received in her own breast the ball of a pistol lowered and pointed at him by the leading savage. She fell, and covered his face with her own lifeblood" (*Garland* 83:45).

In *The Capture and Escape* (1870), Sarah Larimer presents herself as always having been motivated by maternal love. In describing how she had successfully escaped from the Indians, carrying her small son, Larimer says that only a mother's love could have driven her to act as she had. Her text, like so many others, is heterogeneous, drawing at points on structuring devices found in earlier captivity narratives, including sentimental and religious ones. The following passage, lifted directly from the manuscript of Fanny Kelly, a fellow captive, deals with the death of Kelly's young daughter, Mary.[16] While it goes on at undue length for modern sensibilities, nineteenth-century readers apparently enjoyed the "luxury of pain and grief" such as this scene produced:

> The body of little Mary had been found pierced by three arrows, and she had been scalped by the ruthless knife. . . . When discovered by a traveller, her body lay with its little hands stretched out, as if she had received, while running, the piercing, deadly arrow. None but God knew the agony of that young heart in its terrible extremity, and surely He, who numbers the sparrows and feeds the ravens, was not unmindful of her in that awful hour, but allowed the heavenly kingdom, to which her trembling soul was about to take flight, to sweeten, with a glimpse of its beatific glory, the bitterness of death—even as the martyr Stephen, seeing the bliss above, could not be conscious of the torture below. (*Garland* 84:113–14)

The understanding informing the composition and reception of scenes such as this was that the pain and suffering visited upon innocent children won them immediate entry into heaven, without their having to wait for the Second Coming. Moreover, the children's memory of their pain was graciously erased by God, who, at the moment of death, granted them a foretaste of the blissful eternal life in heaven that awaited them. Like Harriet Beecher Stowe's depiction of Little Eva's death, the death of little Mary also participated in what Jane Tompkins has called "a pervasive [nineteenth-century] cultural myth which invests the suffering and death of an innocent victim with . . . the power to work in, and change, the world."[17] The significance of Mary's death is presented to the reader as follows:

> Of all strange and terrible fates, no one, who had seen her gentle little face in its loving sweetness, the joy and comfort of her adopted parents' hearts, would ever have predicted such a barbarous one for her. But it was only the passage from death into life, from darkness into daylight, from doubt and fear into love and endless joy. Those little ones, whose spirits float upward from their downy pillows, amid the tears and prayers of broken-hearted friends, are blest to enter into at heaven's shining gate, which lies as near little Mary's rocky, blood-stained pillow in the desolate waste as the palace of a king; and when she had once gained the great and unspeakable bliss of heaven, it must have blotted out the remembrance of the pain that won it, and made no price too great for such delight. (*Garland* 84:115)

Kelly structured her own account of her captivity in large part by drawing a sharp contrast between her expectations of what the family's migration westward would be like and the reality they subsequently encountered. She writes of having set out on the journey "with high-wrought hopes and pleasant anticipations of a romantic and delightful journey across the plains, and a confident expectation of future prosperity among the golden hills of Idaho." Even life in a tent was experienced as an enjoyable extension of homelife before the Indian attack destroyed her family (*Garland* 85:12–14).

Chapter 16, "Scenes on Cannon Ball Prairie—Reflections," is a sustained meditation on the landscape of captivity, blending memories of her childhood and mother, her present state of captivity, and the uncertainty of the future into a general religious statement about human life. Because it encapsulates so many of the cultural values of the time, it bears our careful attention. Kelly narratively sketches the contours of her emotional responses to the landscape, noting each change and shifting shadow. "Well do I remember my thoughts and feelings when first I beheld the mighty and beautiful prairie of Cannon Ball River," she writes. "With what singular emotions I beheld it for the first time! I could compare it to nothing but a vast sea, changed suddenly to earth, with all its heaving, rolling billows; thousands of acres lay spead before me like a mighty ocean, bounded by nothing but the deep blue sky. What a magnificent sight—a sight that made my soul expand with a lofty thought and its frail tenement sink into utter nothingness before it!" (*Garland* 85:154).

As memories of the past roll over Kelly, the landscape before her—"heaving, rolling"—comes to resemble her own body through an affective affinity. Nature and its scenes could move persons of sensibility in the same way that witnessing the suffering of other persons did. As a result, it was believed that one's affective responses to changes in the scenery and landscape, if carefully noted, could provide moral instruction. Kelly participated fully in the culture of sentiment and invited her reader to share her vision and experience of the landscape and the human condition. Most importantly, she invokes the cult of motherhood, with its emotional complex of selfless love and pain in her didactic reverie:

> I stood and marked every change with that poetical feeling of pleas-
> ant sadness which a beautiful sunset rarely fails to awaken in the
> breast of the lover of nature. I noted every change that was going
> on, and yet my thoughts were far, far away. I thought of the hundreds
> of miles that separated me from the friends that I loved. I was

recalling the delight with which I had, when a little girl, viewed the farewell scenes of day from so many romantic hills, and lakes, and rivers, rich meadows, mountain gorge and precipice, and the quiet hamlets of my dear native land so far away. I fancied I could see my mother move to the door, with a slow step and heavy heart, and gaze, with yearning affection, toward the broad, the mighty West, and sigh, wondering what had become of her lost child. (*Garland* 85:155)

The vision of her mother, conjured up by the landscape, overwhelms Kelly. In a similar situation in captivity almost two centuries earlier, Mary Rowlandson and Hannah Swarton had been moved to lament the fact that they had failed to keep the sabbath, had been less than ardent in their prayers, or had forsaken a churched community to pursue a desire for more farmland. Kelly, though, is moved to lament her failure to appreciate the sacrifices her mother had willingly made for her. We are in the realm of the cult of motherhood:

Mother! what a world of affection is comprised in that single word; how little do we in the giddy round of youthful pleasure and folly heed her wise counsels; how lightly do we look upon that zealous care with which she guides our otherwise erring feet, and watches with feelings which none but a mother can know the gradual expansion of our youth to the riper years of discretion. . . . How deeply then we regret a thousand deeds that we have done contrary to her gentle admonitions! How we sigh for those days once more, that we may retrieve what we have done amiss and and make her kind heart glad with happiness! (*Garland* 85:156)[18]

Kelly's thoughts, memories, and regrets lead her to burst into tears, while, her body trembling, she cries out to her mother. She then reflects on her husband's probable captivity, the murder of her daughter, and the utter destruction of their "short, happy springtime of life, so full of noble aspirations." She moves quickly to generalize from her immediate situation, suggesting that all life was full of such vicissitudes. Like so many authors before her, she finds all that has befallen her to be part of a divine plan. If her "cup of calamity," as Increase Mather called it, has been full, she claims that nevertheless she has found peace in a state of perfect resignation before life (and death) as these are known in the world (*Garland* 85:158).

The Angelic Child Captive and the Bible

Captivity tales were absorbed into a new genre in the nineteenth century—juvenile literature. These texts are infused with didactic religious messages and were intended as vehicles of moral instruction. The providential theological interpretive frame survived in children's literature, a fact that is telling—adults continued to teach their children what in many cases they could apparently no longer believe themselves. Most captivities written for children served up the morals that children should always obey their parents, read and put their faith in the Bible, engage regularly in prayer, and be grateful for all of the blessings they enjoyed thanks to their parents and God's goodness. Many also claim that it is the Bible alone that separates the civilized from the savage. A glance at a few examples of such works must suffice here.

In *The Captives of Abb's Valley*, a Presbyterian church publication of 1854, the author recounts the captivity of his mother and other relatives. The author begins with a simple denominational history of the Presbyterians in the United States, but when he turns to the captivity proper, he surrounds it with a covenantal interpretive frame for his young readers. In describing the first day of captivity of his uncle, James, then a small child, he presents all of the elements of a conversion experience found in earlier Puritan captivities—a sense of deep despair, helplessness, and impending doom; acts of earnest prayer, self-abnegation, and humiliation; and the giving up of oneself to the will of God, followed by a pervading sense of tranquility and sudden uncontrollable tears:

> As soon as James got to the foot of the hill, supposing himself entirely unobserved, he kneeled down and engaged in prayer to God. He had been taught this and other duties of religion by his parents; and now he realized as he never had before the privilege of calling on God, and feeling that though unseen He was a friend near at hand; the only friend to whom he could tell his sorrows; the friend that could guide and protect him. It is said in God's word, "Thou wilt keep him in perfect peace whose mind is stayed on thee, because he trusteth in thee." In part at least, this was fulfilled in the case of the young captive. When he had cast himself on God, he rose from his knees in a state of entire tranquility of mind. So great was the change in his feelings, that for the first time since his captivity the tears burst from his eyes, and he wept abundantly. From that hour he felt no troublesome apprehension of evil. (*Garland* 65:51)

Youngsters were instructed in morals through works such as this; they were also given explicit guidance concerning the preferred forms of religious praxis. The lachrymose religiosity associated with American covenantal theology continued to be rehearsed for young readers. The author's mother serves as a model for girls. She is portrayed as having, by the grace of God, saved only two items from the raging fire set by the Indians who had attacked her family's home—copies of the New Testament. These she carried with her throughout her captivity and, the young readers are told, they were the source of great consolation. The ideal child not only read the Bible for her own benefit and spiritual consolation; she also read it for the spiritual edification of others. This young captive, for instance, often read the Bible to her Indian family, even though they could not fully understand it. This scene reflects the situation in many American homes in the nineteenth century, where religious instruction increasingly fell to women as part of their maternal duty (*Garland* 65:82).

Another captivity narrative published for young readers, this time under Methodist auspices, offered a providential reading of history, while making a plea for greater appreciation of the sacrifices made by earlier generations of settlers. *Joseph Brown; or, The Young Tennesseean Whose Life Was Saved by the Power of Prayer* (1856) is remarkable for the explicit manner in which the captivity has been recast to serve primarily as a didactic vehicle illustrating proper religious attitudes, activities, and responses to the vicissitudes of life. The text was composed with the specific reading practices of young readers of the period in mind in order to seduce them back into the author's world of Christian moralistic discourse.

The narrative strategy adopted by the author is intended to steal instruction upon the reader by drawing him or her into a heavily didactic text. The author skillfully draws upon the popular tradition of landscape description, including the practice of guiding the reader to reconstruct imaginatively a scene in his mind's eye. Here, however, this is done precisely as a setup prior to the author's subversion of the romantic view of nature, so popular at this time, by suggesting that another, more terrible, history had been inscribed on the landscape. Here the act of narrating the captivity reinscribes the present bucolic scene with the otherwise invisible traces of a bloody past (*Garland* 67:10–12).

Like their parents or elder brothers and sisters who read sentimental novels, juvenile readers were asked to imagine themselves into the scenes of the characters' family life, captivity, and trials and tribulations. In doing so, they would gain moral instruction and find models for living a Christian life. The editor of this work, for instance, assures adults that this captivity narrative is suitable for children. "The importance of youthful piety," he promises, "will also be impressed upon [the young readers'] minds by seeing it so beautifully exemplified in the case of Joseph Brown." The juvenile readers are asked to imagine themselves in young Joseph's shoes when he is captured: "What would any boy of the same age think now of being in so dreadful a situation, with these savage wretches grinning at him, and flourishing their tomahawks, ready to throw them at his head—first one taking aim, and then another, and still another?"

Lest the reader's imagination run wild—and a vague fear that one might be susceptible to going native, a fear akin to the Protestant religious fear of being tempted into sin, always hovered around the thought of Indian captivity—the author immediately provides the answer to her own question, writing, "Apparently his doom was sealed, and he had nothing to do but to be resigned to the will of God, for he well knew that God was there, and that, unless it was his almighty will, he could not possibly die, but would live to praise him" (*Garland* 67:vii, 36, 37). A whole chapter, entitled "Merciful Deliverance," is devoted to portraying the perfect faith and resignation of little Joseph along the following lines:

> Joseph fell on his knees, his face blanched with terror, turned up to heaven, where God sits upon his glorious throne above the stars, and, his hands firmly clasped upon his beating heart and heaving breast, he remained a few moments in humble, fervent prayer to God. He poured out his young heart, beseeching God to have mercy upon his soul, to accept it for Christ's sake, to wash away his sins in the Saviour's blood, and make him pure, and take him safe to heaven to live with him for ever among the angels; and resigned himself, saying, "O God, thy will be done." (*Garland* 67:38–39)

Like Little Eva in *Uncle Tom's Cabin*, which had been published just four years earlier, this child is an active agent of redemption and salvation on earth, a veritable angel whose exemplary piety inspires others around him to turn back to the Bible, to acknowledge God's will, or to convert to Christianity. The power of faith and prayer, exemplified in this child captive, is such that the hearts of the Indians are miraculously melted, their stern countenances are changed to smiles, and their cruel hatred is transformed into "kindness, love, and pity." Through the agency of prayer, this "young Christian hero" is able to secure the safety and release of his mother and sister as well. With no thought for himself, he offers up "a strong, and deep, and heartfelt appeal, which pierced the sky, and reached the throne of love and mercy." Joseph is also the agent of converting his Indian parents, who were deeply impressed by his life of purity and piety, to Christianity:

> He also prayed for Tunbridge, his adopted father, who had tried his best to save him from the Indians, and risked his own life for him; and this kind but ignorant man's heart was so touched, and the heart of his new [Indian] mother, by the fervent and simple prayers of the white boy, that they, too, wept and prayed with him, whenever they saw him thus engaged, and loved him more and more, for they felt as if the Great Spirit had sent an angel to live with them; and from this captive boy they learned to honor, and obey, and serve God, and to love him too—to adore him and to pray to him: so Joseph's misfortune in being made a captive was thus the means of converting two souls to the knowledge of God and salvation. (*Garland* 67:47–48)

In works such as this, the topos of captivity provides a ready-made boundary situation where, faced with the terrifying prospect of immediate death, a "young Christian hero" imitates the martyr Stephen, drops to his (or her) knees, turns his eyes to heaven, and gives himself up completely to the will of God. Such scenes are legion in the literature of the nineteenth century. This sort of saccharine religiosity and relentless didacticism is alien to the modern sensibility, while the juvenile hero's or heroine's actions are impossible to accept as realistic. Yet we must recognize the power that the figure of the pious innocent child held for millions of nineteenth-century readers, who accepted these literary figures as ideal representations of the fervent religious ideals of the age. Such scenes moved many of these same readers to aspire to the same selfless courage and faith. If the stories are unrealistic, they nevertheless had real-world consequences as they shaped the lives, ideals, and actions of readers.

The power captivity narratives could have over the imagination of children and adults may be discerned in a juvenile captivity written by the Rev. Reuben Weiser, then the president of Central College in Iowa. *Regina, the German Captive; or, True Piety Among the Lowly* (1856) is a retelling of the captivity of Regina

Hartman in eighteenth-century Pennsylvania. It is based on earlier written and oral versions of this tale, supplemented, as Weiser admits, by a bit of poetic license. He first heard the story as a child from his grandmother, who had personally known Regina and her family.

Weiser's work, intended for use in Lutheran Sunday schools, presents Regina as a modern American example of Christian martyrdom. The captivity tale is retold as a means of instructing children concerning the power of faith and the necessity of practicing piety in one's daily life. Only Regina's faith and piety had saved Regina from going native and, as a dreadful consequence, losing all hope of eternal life in heaven. Weiser also teaches (or preaches) the spiritual value of suffering borne in faith and pure resignation to the will of God. He proclaims that his captivity narrative is "sent forth to teach parents as well as children how to live and die happy." But readers are also treated to virulent racist and anti-Indian views (e.g., "The American Indians are fast passing away, and our children should know something about their cruelties, and thus see why God has permitted them to be banished from their native land" [Garland 69: 6–7]). The pernicious ends to which covenantal theology could be put are found from the time of Cotton Mather down to the second half of the nineteenth century. Even more insidious, this theology of racism and hate was frequently promulgated through works designed for children and issued from church presses.

Margaret Hosmer's The Child Captives (1870) is less racist in tone, yet it shares many features with other religious captivities told for juvenile audiences: a covenantal interpretive frame; a model child representing innocence, obedience, and perfect piety; the child's purity and his power of faith—all lead to the reformation or conversion of others. Hosmer assures her readers of the factual basis of her tale as well as its ethnographic accuracy, yet the account is largely fictional. As omniscient narrator, the author supplies all of the characters, including the Indians, with dialogue (e.g., "Me good Indian, me no fight white man; only hunt buffalo, deer, antelope . . . How! how! how!") and presents their silent thoughts. She argues, however, that the sad condition of the Indians is due not to their innate inferiority but to social and political factors:

> The facts are here related with a full sense of the providential care
> that marked [the captives'] course, and an earnest desire to represent

Indian life as it truly is, not totally without humanity and even tenderness of instinct, but sadly and bitterly benighted. In truth, apart from Christianizing influences, they are beset by evils in example and association of far too black and degrading a nature to be mentioned in a book like this. How can it be otherwise whilst, in addition to their native heathenism, they are under the teachings of three missionaries as whiskey, dishonest agencies and the contaminations of bad white men? (*Garland* 83:229–30)

The Rev. J. J. Methvin, a Pentecostal missionary among the Indians, offered *Andele, or The Mexican-Kiowa Captive* (1899) for the "pleasure and profit" of young readers. The theology of redemptive suffering still informs this work: "Trials, conflicts, emergencies, are necessary to arouse and develop the latent faculties of our being, hence we should count it all joy when they come." Unlike many others, Methvin was optimistic about the prospect of civilizing the Indians through the power of the gospel, in spite of their seemingly intractable savage nature. The fact that he had been able to convert Andele, a captive who "had become a veritable Indian with but little trace of civilized life left in him," was proof of this. Still, negative racial stereotypes of the Indians pervade this work (*Garland* 103:3–4, 10, 77).

Hybrid Dime Novel Captivities

Captivities were a staple of the dime novels of the second half of the nineteenth century. Often they combined the western adventure tale and romance genres. Edward S. Ellis's *Seth Jones; or, the Captives of the Frontier* (1860), number 8 of Beadle's Dime Novels, was one of the first really successful western male adventure tales in this format and set the pattern for many others in the following decades. As a transitional hybrid form, it combines elements of the male adventure story, where the hero is a backwoodsman or frontiersman, with elements of the domestic romance. The plot moves toward the discovery of the true identities of the main characters and their eventual marriage, reestablishing an idyllic domestic scene.[19]

The main characters represent "nature's noble-man," the "bloom" of young womanhood, and the rough yet good-hearted hunter-trapper. Much of the action revolves around the efforts to rescue Ina Haverland, a beautiful young woman taken captive by Indians. Ina has taken on certain aspects of the wilderness, rendering her wild yet pale, exotic yet familiar, innocent yet provocative. For most of the tale, Seth Jones is disguised as an uneducated and rough hunter-trapper, but eventually his true identity and his cultured refinement are revealed to the others by the trembling of his body caused by his feelings when the rescue party, returning from having saved Ina, view the Haverland homestead again, where his fiancée is (*Garland* 77:14, 87–88).

Seth Jones marks the beginning of popular works of fiction featuring rough, no-nonsense heroes, who nevertheless have a tender spot for the "female species." *Massasoit's Daughter; or, The French Captives* (1861), issued as number 19 of Beadle's dime novels, has an even more convoluted plot. Announced as "A Romance of Aboriginal New-England," it is set in the colonial period and comes complete with a shipwreck, a sentimental Indian couple (a permutation of the noble savage), forbidden love (intertribal and white-Indian), pirates, and a white female captive. In an inversion of the usual pattern, it is an Indian family whose domestic bliss is shattered by white slavers.

Here there are good Indians and bad Indians, just as there are good and bad whites. The author describes the brawny, muscular body of the Indian male in detail, suggesting the emergence of a market for sexual fantasies related to the exotic and primitive Other. Marie, the white heroine who had fainted at the time of the Indian attack, regains consciousness only to find herself in the arms of a swarthy Indian named Tishquontam. She is carried to an idyllic glade where she finds a wig-wam, the appearance of which "suggested somewhat of a civilized effect." This sylvan scene works as a sedative, diverting Marie's attention from her own suffering and the recent horror she had witnessed. Then she meets Monoma, a beautiful, noble, tenderhearted young maiden of sixteen, who physically resembles most sentimental heroines. The two women immediately recognize the nobility and refined nature of the other and this recognition is instantly sealed by a spontaneous act of sympathy:

> The red maiden . . . advanced to the French girl, and kneeling beside her, took her head tenderly between the palms of her hands, and imprinted a kiss upon her forehead. Marie's heart grew full in a moment. She forgot that her companion was a strange maid, that she was a heathen and of a savage race. She only felt that warm kiss upon her forehead, and saw two tender eyes gazing into her own with a look of sympathy which won her confidence. Marie sobbed

aloud, and, throwing herself upon the neck of the Indian girl, burst
into a flood of tears. (*Garland* 77:33, 35–36)

This affecting scene, recognizably within the sentimental fold,
brings tears to the eyes of even the stoical chief, who has to step
outside to hide them. While Marie is an Indian captive, she has
nevertheless found herself in a familiar world where cultural differences are relatively unimportant; pure emotion and sentiment
translate immediately and effectively across these differences. In
this work, the culture of sensibility is, if not universal, at least
transcultural. In the course of the novel each of the characters
shares his or her own affecting story of pain and loss with their
new acquaintances (and thereby with the reader, who is admitted
to this circle of feeling).

Massasoit's Daughter represents the romanticizing of the American Indian as a "noble savage" through the projection of sentimental values unto some of the natives. The author envisions a world
in which essential identities overcome the differences that separate the Indian and the white. If Tishquontam learns to pray to the
Christian God, his French wife, Blanchette, is called to heaven by
"the Great Spirit"; even the supreme beings of the two cultures are
identified.

Through the eyes of one of the characters, the author further imagines the possibility of a benevolent brotherhood among
whites and Indians. The Abbe Claude, a Catholic priest, captured
along with Marie and her brother, Louis, indulges in a reverie that
is a blend of utopian world theology and latent homosexual fantasy. The scene begins as he awakens in a dimly lit wigwam on the
first morning of their captivity:

A swart savage, holding in his sleeping grasp a huge warclub, lay
close beside the priest, while a dozen more, all apparently slumber-
ing soundly, were dispersed over the wigwam floor; but the Abbe's
gaze fell first upon the form of Louis, encompassed by the brawny
arms of a Herculean Indian. He breathed a silent prayer of gratitude,
as he saw that his youthful friend was sleeping as quietly on the
broad breast of his guard as if suffering and captivity were things
unknown to his experience.

Upon a log, at the wigwam-entrance, reclined a gigantic warrior,
with his weapon—a knotted, jagged, but beautifully polished maple
club—grasped in his sinewy fingers. As the increasing light, falling
between the branches of a forest-tree above, played over the red-

man's features, the prisoner was struck at once with their solemn and devout expression. The copper brow seemed gilded with the morning beams, and a strange seriousness, as of awed thoughts, invested the savage face with a quiet grandeur which drew the admiration of the priest. "Perhaps the Indian prays! and doubtless his prayers—even his untutored prayers—are accepted of the Lord!" (*Garland* 77:38)

We may now summarize the findings of this brief survey of representations of the body in captivity tales from 1750 to 1900. The captive's body in most tales from this period is not the site of divine affliction, calling the errant back to a proper covenantal relationship with God; rather, it is a tremulous, acutely sensitive locus of feeling. This sentimental body, both male and female, is textualized; it resembles a title page that can be read by sensitive observers to disclose the outlines of a person's sad history. The captivity tales of this period are filled with overdetermined gendered bodies—bound, lacerated, naked, and bloody bodies of female captives and innocent children which evoked boundless sympathy and righteous anger. Many of these figures were presented as models of perfect Christian resignation. Female captives, figures of virtue-in-distress, came to epitomize the ideal of perfect Christian resignation as they bore terrible suffering and pain without complaint, looking toward heaven.

The recluse is another figure of perfect Christian resignation found in captivity tales in this period. Living alone deep in the wilderness, with the Bible as his only source of comfort and consolation in this world of suffering and woe, the recluse symbolized perfect resignation to the will of God, while challenging the belief found in nature religion of various sorts that spiritual reinvigoration was to be found in nature. Indian captivity provided an ideal story line for authors who sought to represent the cult of true womanhood. Female captives also provided the occasion for male heroes to display their own sensibilities and character, although, as we saw in the biography of General Putnam, there was a backlash against the claims that the character and courage of men was necessarily provoked and inspired by women, rather than being innate.

Captivity narratives written specifically for children and young adults appeared for the first time. Many of them were published by church presses and were intended for use in Sunday schools; almost all were highly moralistic. The protagonist epitomized the social and religious values of American Protestantism—honesty, obedience to parents, hard work, and the power of prayer and Bible study—while the power of faith, purity, suffering innocence, and piety were stressed. Juvenile captives are angelic and possess the power to convert or otherwise save adults. All such captivities invited their readers to imagine themselves into the situations of the protagonists and thereby be instructed morally.

Thus, captivity narratives were composed and published for quite diverse reasons between 1750 and 1900. Fewer works were written primarily to witness to God's providence, while many more had a historiographic intention. Nevertheless, even this latter motive had a religious dimension, since the communal narration of the national history and the affective responses it evoked contributed to the development of a form of secular religion. In one way or another, most authors of captivity narratives continued to have designs on their readers. Few works were written exclusively to provide entertainment to the reader. At a minimum, there was a nod toward providing some form of rational entertainment or moral instruction, however trite, even in western adventure tales. The captivity topos continued to be a significant cultural resource for imaginative activity, which could be (and was) appropriated and used for various ends and purposes. In and of itself captivity did not mean any one thing; multiple meanings were created in specific retellings and through the specific reading practices and expectations brought to these narratives.

5

GOING NATIVE, GOING PRIMITIVE: WHITE INDIANS, SEXUALITY, POWER, AND THE PROBLEM OF IDENTITY

> Our own existence cannot be separated from the accounts we give of ourselves. It is in telling our own stories that we give ourselves an identity. We recognize ourselves in the stories that we tell about ourselves. It makes very little difference whether these stories are true or false; fiction as well as verifiable history provides us with an identity.—Paul Ricoeur

THE HISTORICAL REALITY of Indian captivity on the American frontiers raised in an immediate and pressing fashion an important set of existential questions that had long haunted the human imagination: Could one lose one's identity? Or, to pose the question positively, was it possible to transform one's self fundamentally and thus escape from the bounded nature of a given sociohistorical identity? Was the self sovereign and stable, or was it subject to fragmentation and dissolution from external factors? Was the vaunted distinction between "civilized" and "primitive" real? Or was it tenuous at best, or even an illusion? Could a person really go native and thereby revert to a state of savagery or, alternatively, return to a primordial paradisiacal state?

These and related questions became increasingly prominent in the cultural discourse of the West in the wake of the age of discovery and European expansion across the globe. As time passed the European historical experience in the Americas revealed a troublesome pattern. In the eighteenth century as the number of whites becoming white Indians grew, it became painfully obvious to many observers that in the New World, cultural assimilation was largely a one-way process—many whites crossed over and became Indians, but few Indians made the opposite movement. This situation was a source of great consternation for many Euro-Americans, since it ran counter to most of their theological presuppositions as well as to the assumption that theirs was an undeniably superior (and infinitely desirable) civilization. In 1747 Cadwallader Colden, the surveyor-general and a member of the King's Council of New York, expressed the puzzlement he shared with many of his age as to what was actually happening on the colonial frontiers when many white captives refused repatriation: "No arguments, no Intreaties, nor Tears of their Friends and Relations, could persuade many of them to leave their new Indian Friends and Acquaintance; several of them that were by the Caressings of their Relations persuaded to come Home, in a little Time grew tired of our Manner of Living, and ran away again to the Indians, and ended their Days with them."[1] Six years later, Benjamin Franklin noted much the same thing:

> When an Indian Child has been brought up among us, taught our language and habituated to our Customs, yet if he goes to see his relations and makes one Indian Ramble with them, there is no perswading him ever to return. When white persons of either sex have been taken prisoners young by the Indians, and lived a while among them, tho' ransomed by their Friends, and treated with all imaginable tenderness to prevail with them to stay among the English, yet in a short Time they become disgusted with our manner of life, and the care and pains that are necessary to support it, and take the first good Opportunity of escaping again into the Woods, from whence there is no reclaiming them.[2]

In *Letters from an American Farmer* (1782) Crèvecoeur, too, addresses the issue:

> By what power does it come to pass, that children who have been adopted when young among these people, can never be prevailed on to readopt European manners? Many an anxious parent I have seen after the last war, who at the return of peace, went to the Indian villagers where they knew their children had been carried in captivity; when to their inexpressible sorrow, they found them so perfectly Indianized, that many knew them no longer, and those whose more advanced ages permitted them to recollect their fathers

and mothers, absolutely refused to follow them, and ran to their adopted parents for protection against the effusions of love their unhappy real parents lavished on them! Incredible as this may appear, I have heard it asserted in a thousand instances, among persons of credit. . . . [Life among the Indians] cannot be, therefore, so bad as we generally conceive it to be; there must be in the Indians' social bond something singularly captivating, and far superior to anything to be boasted of among us; for thousands of Europeans are Indians, as we have no examples of even one of those Aborigines having from choice become Europeans![3]

These statements pointedly testify that the existence of white Indians was a source of great vexation. Too many persons seemed to be captivated by the life of the Indians, lured by the siren song of the primitive in the wilderness. This palpable ambivalence in the face of the primitive Other was not limited to the eighteenth century. From the Enlightenment down to the present, "the primitive" has been a uniquely emplotted and powerful Western symbolic construct. Yet even as the primitive-civilized dichotomy marked the Indians off as radically distinct from Europeans, the presence of white Indians challenged the validity of this distinction.

It is important to study the literary figure of the white Indian and the narrative representations of the process of going native because such tales were (and are) tales about ourselves and who we are. As Ricoeur has said in the epigraph to this chapter, our identity is a function of the stories, historical and fictional, we tell about ourselves. The perspective of the history of religions adopted here focuses not only on the historical facts of Indian captivity (how many individuals were captured in a given period, how many were ransomed, killed, or underwent transculturalization) but more importantly on the imaginal and representational activity carried on around the topos of captivity and the figure of the white Indian. It was, after all, largely through narrative forms (supplemented by pictorial representations and theatrical performances) that the "facts" concerning white Indians were constructed, circulated, and consumed in the West. Only through the careful study of the specific representations of going native will it be possible for us to recover the imaginal explorations of alternative existential possibilities that were available to audiences in earlier centuries.

For millions of readers (and, more recently, moviegoers), captivity tales have been important vehicles for exploring the pos-

sibility of identity transformation. Representations of going native, including those that affirm the process and those that display
abject horror over its very possibility, are responses to a basic
human fascination with the thought of losing or changing one's
identity. In important ways, to lose one's identity and then to
assume another is equivalent to dying and being reborn. Given
this, many Indian captivity narratives functioned as secular equivalents of myths of death and rebirth.

While the very idea of white Indians opened up new possibilities
for reimagining personal and cultural identity and for making the
term *humanity* more inclusive, in actuality this rarely occurred.
More often than not representations of Indian captivity and of
going native were used to reinforce existing cultural categories and
conceptual systems of exclusion. In order to understand why this
should have been the case, it is important to recognize the manner
and the extent to which religious and moral values in the captivity
narratives were related to the broader cultural discourses on race,
class, gender, and male-female power relations. These religious
and ideological values deeply influenced the representations (and,
thus, the meaning) of going native and the understanding of Europeans and Americans of themselves, the Other, and, finally, what
it meant to be human.

For over three centuries, diverse representations of Indian captivity have been an important vehicle for reflection upon the primitive-civilized dichotomy. Through captivity narratives, readers
could imaginatively identify with captives and thus both enjoy the
adventures of white Indians and suffer with them. In the safety of
their own homes, readers could imaginatively explore the possibility of a very different life and existence.

This imaginal activity inevitably led authors and readers into
comparative activities as they were drawn to evaluate their own
lives, society, and civilization in light of the different perspectives
provided by Indian cultures. Not surprisingly, most authors and
readers found their own people, society, religion, and cultural
mores to be superior and preferable, but there were significant
exceptions. Still other captivity narratives employed the authority
gained by the narrator's firsthand acquaintance with Indian life to
criticize aspects of Western society or Christendom, and even to
question the value of the purported blessings of civilization.

Some authors used the tales of Indian captives to evaluate the
quality of human life with and without Christianity and the Bible.
Others explored lifeways where Euro-American gender roles and

sexual mores did not obtain, usually to testify to the superiority of Western patriarchal social structures and values. The topos of Indian captivity provided an occasion for imaginative reflection on issues of race, class, power, and sexuality. Finally, captives' lives among the Indians frequently led to evaluations of the moral and spiritual significance of the wilderness and nature. Often several of these elements were conjoined in a single narrative, forming important symbolic complexes that took on a life of their own.

Indian captivity and going primitive were (and are) associated with other symbolic and narrative complexes and, in this way, they were made to perform different sorts of cultural work. In this chapter a few of the complexes that became associated with captivity will be examined: (1) European technological superiority combined with native naiveté and credulity, leading the Indians to take the white man to be a deity of sorts; (2) white Indians and the cult of motherhood; (3) the Pocahontas complex and male sexual fantasies; (4) female fantasies of the male savage Other; (5) utopian dreams of the noble primitive and of returning to a state of innocence; (6) the Amazon complex, or the association of Zenobia-like martial women and pure maternal violence; (7) sentimental values and the religious ideal of perfect resignation; and (8) male bonding in a world without women, free of the constraints of civilization.

As this list suggests, representations of the primitive Other often involve some element of sexuality, either explicitly or implicitly. Sexuality often figures in instances of cultural contact, in colonial situations, and in various forms of the domination of others (including slavery). In chapter 2 we saw that in the late seventeenth century Mary Rowlandson felt compelled to respond to whispered rumors and innuendos of a sexual relationship with an Indian. By the second half of the eighteenth century, narrative explorations of white-Indian sexual relationships were more explicit and more central to the plot in many texts, especially in works of fiction. The representations of sexual relations found in Indian captivity narratives are always imbricated in larger symbolic and discursive fields.

As the patriarchal family came to assume a heightened importance in the West as a locus of cultural and moral values, many works of literature portrayed ideal family life and gender roles. Yet it is clear that the actual lives of many persons were less than happy. As a result, the trials, tribulations, and afflictions of Pamela, Clarissa, and other literary characters came to express the disparity between the ideal and the real. In this situation, the historical reality of Indian captivity stimulated a flurry of reflections on the fragility of the family, the social order, and civilization. Readers were led to imagine how they might react to radical disruptions of their lives if they were forcibly abducted, carried into an alien world, and stripped of the protection and support offered by family and society. Some works suggested that under duress humans discovered unsuspected wells of courage and strength within themselves; others maintained that only the Bible and faith would sustain them in such situations.

Indian captivity also allowed authors and readers to explore many of the assumptions informing different competing philosophies and theologies. Questions were raised, for instance, as to whether sympathy was a universal human emotion or not, whether female nature was uniform throughout the world or was affected by social factors, whether nature or nurture was primary in the intellectual and moral development of children, and whether nonwhites or members of the lower classes were capable of socioeconomic and moral improvement.

Going Native: The Rational Ruse

Several aspects of the process of going native were unclear and, as a result, became the subject of debate and diverse imaginal activity. If children were essentially blank slates, as Locke had suggested, then it was perhaps understandable that they would be susceptible to identity transformation and to going native, but what of the many cases of adult captives who had also done so? One fairly common response to this question, found in male-authored captivity narratives, was to claim that going native had been little more than a ruse adopted by the captive in order to gain better treatment from his captors or to gain their confidence so that an escape could be successfully effected sometime in the future. The rational ruse claim served two important and related purposes. It served the social needs of the returned captive, and it confirmed the cultural prejudice of readers that life with the Indians could have no attraction for civilized persons.

Like Mary Rowlandson, returning captives often sought to silence criticism and gossip regarding their conduct during their sojourn with the Indians, especially concerning purported or actual sexual relations they had entered into with Indians. The plea made by returned captives that they had only pretended to go native also made it easier for readers to indulge both their own cultural prejudices and fantasies through such narratives without having to admit that personal and cultural identities were fragile constructions and relatively easily shed.

Returned captives often maintained that, given the difficult situation they had found themselves in and the limited options open to them, they had made a rational decision to pretend to have accepted life as an Indian. This explanation allowed people to hold on to the psychologically comfortable assumption of cultural superiority, while it permitted readers to enjoy furtively—and safely—titillating sexual fantasies involving the exotic Other, without having to acknowledge that any real physical attraction was involved.

Memoirs of Charles Dennis Rusoe D'Eres (1800) illustrates these points. Purportedly the author had been captured as a four-teen-year-old by Canadian Indians and had subsequently spent eleven years living with them. He reports that he soon had dressed in Indian fashion, became accustomed to Indian food, learned to hunt and fish with them, joined the Indians in attacks on other tribes, and eventually set himself up in Indian society as a black-smith and profitably plied his trade. Rusoe D'Eres claims that he went native largely as a practical matter, although he also implies that his acceptance of Indian culture was facilitated by the mater-nal attention he had received from Indian women.

The white Indian who, like Rusoe D'Eres, later returned to Euro-American culture and took up the pen to tell his (or her) tale faced distinct pressures in entering the public sphere. On the one hand, like the anthropologist today, his authority to speak came precisely from his having been a participant-observer of life in Indian culture, yet he was under pressure to confirm the ethnic and cultural stereotypes of his readers about the Indians through his eyewitness account of Indian life. This often led to the inclu-sion of predictable scenes of the Indians as blood-thirsty savages engaged in primitive rites of sacrifice and cannibalism. At the same time, social pressures militated that the returned captive represent himself as being morally distinct from and superior to the Indians. As a result, the captive often portrays his participation in savage customs as having been under duress, or at least as having been less than enthusiastic. Rusoe D'Eres's account is typical:

Forty of [the enemy] we took alive, and killed all except ten, who were reserved for future diversion. After the battle was over, we counted among the dead on shore, and in the water, two hundred and fifty, without any loss on our side. Soon after, the forenoon of that day, several of them were most inhumanly slaughtered by the tomahawk and knife, cutting open their bodies, and with their hands scooping up the warm blood out of their bodies, while alive, and drinking it greedily, whooping and dancing merrily, as if partaking of the most agreeable repast. Some of our Indians observing my backwardness to join them, ordered me to do as they did—with which I was obliged to comply so far, as to scoop up blood into my hands, and daubed it over my mouth and face, to make them believe I drank it; they then said I was good man. (*Garland* 25:20–21)

Some captives may well have adopted the ruse of going native in an effort to have their captors lessen their vigilance or to receive milder treatment, but the imaginative and discursive possibilities inherent in the narrative representation of the embedded author as a pretend white Indian allowed the reader, who identified with the protagonist, to participate vicariously in such bloody rites without then having to accept the moral consequences (or the ontological implications) of having done so willingly.

By claiming to have been a pretend Indian, Rusoe D'Eres could at once participate in "hot" bloody rites, while at the same time representing himself as having all the while maintained a rational, analytical, or "cool" detachment from them. Moreover, as the ideal participant-observer, he gains additional authority to speak about the Indians. Rusoe D'Eres draws the reader into such scenes in such a way that, in the act of reading, the reader comes to occupy or share his position as a participant-observer, as in the following description of a bloody sacrifice and torture:

The prisoners who survived, were kept confined without any sustenance, and every day were whipt and tortured, by burning their fingers; forcing them into their pipes, when smoking, and there confining them, until burnt to the bone; whooping and dancing round them—this was their practice day by day, until this scene changed, by a scene more horrible, which cannot be realized by my readers; nothing but occular demonstration can bring this to a proper point of view, to this day, (a recollection of the scene) it being transacted before my eyes, at a period of life, when the smallest impression must make a lasting continuance—even now, makes me to shudder. The manner of sacrifice, is as follows. (*Garland* 25:21)

A detailed description of the various types of torture the prisoners were subjected to, occupying nearly two pages of print,
follows. Having claimed that only an "occular demonstration"
could "bring this [scene] to a proper point of view," the author
proceeds to conjure it up before the reader's mind's eye. As he
narratively recreates the scene of human sacrifice, he constantly
shifts back-and-forth from the past to the present tense, often
within the same sentence. The cumulative effect of this is to blur
the temporal distinction between the narrator's past and the reader's present and between his firsthand participation-observation
and the reader's act of reading.

In other narratives, the protagonist's participation in Indian
raids, the taking of scalps, and other violent activities are also
ascribed to the practical necessity of maintaining the ruse of having gone primitive in order to survive. This explanatory strategy is
found in both nonfictional and fictional texts. For instance, in
Sylvester Crakes's fictional work, *Five Years a Captive Among the
Black-Feet Indians* (1858), which purports to be a factual account
based on the journal notes of the former captive John Dixon, the
protagonist addresses the reader directly concerning this issue,
claiming that he had only pretended to go native in order to protect
a female captive (*Garland* 74:157). Among the many captivities
that deal with the theme of taking-the-first-scalp, John Dunn Hunter's brief account is of note because, although he had been more
thoroughly Indianized than almost any other author, he too felt it
necessary to profess in print his utter disgust with his act. He
notes, though, that after the fact he had been feted and showered
with acclaim by the Indians and attracted the special attention of
the young Indian maidens (*Garland* 39:50).

In captivity tales, the topos of pretending to have gone native
often provided a vehicle for conveying and affirming cultural stereotypes of the primitive as ignorant or naive. In the fictional work
The Life and Travels of James Tudor Owen (1801), the protagonist
tells a series of tales of his adventures, trials, tribulations, and
heroics in his travels around the globe, including his having fallen
into the hands of American Indians. The descriptions and stereotypical scenes of torture and Indian rites and customs, including
that of adopting captives, are clearly based on earlier captivity
tales. Owen claims to have been adopted as a son by the widow of
the chief Onandaga. Later, when the Indians had been stricken by
an outbreak of smallpox, he used his knowledge of their superstitious nature and credulity to his advantage by declaring that

Ishtobooloo, "the god of spirits," had told him in a dream that this plague was a punishment for the Indians' having tortured and killed some captives. He finally made his escape by pretending that the spirit of his adoptive mother, who had died of smallpox, had come to him in a dream, instructing him to go into the mountains in order to intercede on the part of the Indians by praying to Ishtobooloo (*Garland* 25:27, 29–32).

Numerous other narratives have captives employing similar ruses to trick the Indians, who are represented as being slaves to their superstitious beliefs. Two examples must suffice. In a work published in 1859, Nelson Lee claims that his Indian captors came to believe that he was a wizard or holy man because he could make a pocket watch, "the brother or offspring of the sun," talk. The American Indian's religion (and idolatry), like the Hindu's, is based on ignorance and naive credulity. His watch-cum-deity was as believable (and as ludicrous) as other idols:

> The character it became necessary for me to assume, therefore, was that of a missionary, expounding my peculiar doctrines among the heathen. Accordingly, I received it at their hands in an attitude of great humility, and gazed upon it with that air of reverence which may be supposed characterizes the Hindoo kneeling before the graven image of a monkey, wound it up, held it to my ear, listening to the tick, tick, tick, with a solemnity of expression intended to convey the same idea, as if I had said to them in their own language: "Gentlemen Indians, I am now receiving important telegraphic despatches from the other side of Jordan!" Presently, it sounded the alarm. It would have been a curious and interesting picture for an artist, could he have watched the various expressions of astonishment, awe and wonder that overspread their features during the whir and whirl and whiz of the cunning mechanism. (*Garland* 75:125–27).[4]

The idea of the primitive was frequently mixed with nine-teenth-century orientalism—all primitives and pagans were of a piece. They were necessarily ignorant of science and prone to take Western technology, and those who controlled it, as somehow connected to the spirit world. In *Five Years a Captive Among the Black-Feet Indians*, for instance, the author claims that, having no knowledge of firearms, some Indians returned his loaded rifle to him, even as they were about to burn him at the stake. This fantasized scene includes a peculiar takeoff from the Genesis 22 account of the sacrifice of Isaac, accompanied by an appeal to divine providence:

> The faggots were now fired in several places, and the savages were performing their circular gyratory dance, with the usual accompaniments of noise and confusion, when, on raising my eyes in a suppliant attitude toward Heaven, almost the first object that I distinctly comprehended was a very large panther, laying on the limb of a tree, almost directly above us. The idea immediately occurred to me that this was providential, and designed as a means for my deliverance. Knowing the superstition of these wild people, the thought flashed upon me that if I could bring the panther down (with my rifle) in their midst, they would attribute the report and smoke of the gun, and the simultaneous fall of the animal to supernatural agency, and the result might possibly be my deliverance from the tortures of the stake.

The protagonist goes on to report, "From this time the Indians seemed to regard me as a superior being, exerting a kind of supernatural power, and instead of insult and abuse, they paid the greatest deference to my wishes, and in most cases were obedient to my commands" (*Garland* 74:67, 68).

Returning captives, as well as the authors of third-person accounts, frequently report cases of captives having entered a matrimonial arrangement with a native. In point of fact, many captives, both male and female, did marry Indians, sometimes out of love but other times based on more practical considerations of labor needs and the necessity to replace a recently killed individual in a family unit. Not surprisingly, many returned captives profess that they had been disgusted by the prospect of such a sexual relationship, or that they had entered it only under duress. Alternatively, captives sometimes claimed that they took up life with an Indian woman as a calculated move to gain the confidence of their captors and to open up the possibility of escaping.[5]

Apparently some white males at least could engage in sexual relations (real or imaginary) with Indians with fewer lasting social consequences than white women could. There were two very different popular Western images of the Indian female: the repugnant "dirty squaw" and the lovely Indian maiden à la Pocahontas. A number of captivity narratives were built around the figures of the "man of feeling" and the Pocahontas-like female, as Western gender constructions and values were projected onto Indian society as a means of naturalizing and universalizing them.[6] In some cases, the noble savage served as an exemplar of natural nobility and grace.

In a number of works, sentimental heroes reportedly married Indian females in order to avoid hurting the feelings of the lovely maidens smitten with them. Such tales participate in the white male fantasy that white men are sexually irresistible to beautiful, sensuous native women. For instance, in the novel *Narrative of the Singular Adventures and Captivity of Mr. Thomas Barry* (1800), Barry is engaged to be married to the lovely Eliza Wilson in South Carolina. On a trading expedition, however, he is captured by Indians and is about to be burned at the stake when—in a scene indebted to the tale of Pocahontas and Capt. John Smith—he is saved by a lovely Indian maiden, named Oneida, taken to her hut, and nursed back to health. Alas, as a man of feeling, this kindness and female solicitude puts him in a moral bind as he comes to have conflicting emotions and obligations:

> This was the trying moment.—My obligations to the beautiful Indian excited the warmest glow of gratitude in my heart, which was now softened into tenderness by her tears; and, encircled in the arms of a generous woman, who had saved my life, on whose bounty I lived, and without whose assistance it would be impossible for me to regain my liberty—*Eliza* was forgotten—and in this exigence I resolved to comply with the inclinations of my benefactress. Ere we parted, we expressed mutual passion; and in a few days after, we were married, in the presence of all the Indians. Thus, by a fortuitous series of events, I became the husband of *Oneida,* whose love was sentimental and enthusiastic;—but little did she know the keen remorse that racked my soul, when reflection reproached me with the violation of my vows to *Eliza!* (*Garland* 24:30)

In this way, the hero's sexual relationship with a native is given the aura of propriety. Through tales such as this, readers could enjoy their fantasies without having their basic values challenged. If the situation was complicated (and, thus, more interesting in plot terms), nevertheless the reader could be sure that when, on her deathbed, Eliza learned the truth about the moral dilemma her fiancé had faced in captivity, she would recognize his actions to have been above reproach and would forgive him.

John Davenport's narrative of his brief captivity in the War of 1812 is typical of those works in which the male authors admit having contemplated marriage with an Indian, but then go on to deny having actually had any sexual relations. Like many authors who seek to absolve themselves of any moral responsibility for sexual relations with native women by appealing to a form of "the end justifies the means" argument, Davenport first proclaims his utter disgust with Indian women, but goes on to say that he had finally accepted the idea of marriage as a means of effecting his escape. He claims, though, to have been saved from this unsavory prospect at the very last minute.[7]

A Narrative of the Incidents Attending the Capture, Detention, and Ransom of Charles Johnston (1827) similarly explains how practical concerns had led the protagonist to overcome his initial disgust with Indian women. "The prospect, indeed, was not very rapturous, of leading to the altar of Hymen an Indian squaw, already the mother of several children," Johnson writes. "But there was something extremely consoling in the hope, I might say in the persuasion, that such an event would bring within my reach those chances of escape from the savages, and for restoration to my country and friends, which I had thus far vainly exerted myself to obtain" (Garland 43:54–55).

John Jewitt (1815) blends an appeal to divine providence with a claim that he had adopted the rational ruse of going native: "After returning thanks to that merciful Being who had in so wonderful a manner softened the hearts of the savages in my favour, I had determined from the first of my capture to adopt a conciliating conduct towards them, and confirm myself, as far as was in my power, to their customs and mode of thinking, trusting that the same divine goodness that had rescued me from death, would not always suffer me to languish in captivity among these heathen."

Jewitt is at pains, though, to note that his Indian captors were much lighter-skinned, better looking, cleaner, and more cultivated than most other tribes. Under penalty of death, he married a pretty, light-skinned seventeen-year-old, whom he describes as amiable, intelligent, "neat and clean," with soft hair, and teeth of "dazzling whiteness." Moreover, she was possessed of a "sweet-ness of temper and modesty." Nevertheless, Jewitt felt the need to deny that he ever found any pleasure in this arrangement. "With a partner possessing so many attractions, many may be apt to con-clude, that I must have found myself happy, at least comparatively so; but far otherwise it was with me. . . . in my situation, I could not but view this connection as a chain that was to bind me down to this savage land, and prevent my ever again seeing a civilized country" (Garland 28:57, 160–61, 72–73).

Similarly suspect is William Biggs's claim in his privately published account, *Narrative of William Biggs* (1825), that an Indian maiden once had pursued him for several days with the intention of marrying him, while he was not the least bit interested in her. He describes her as "a very handsome girl, about 18 years of age, a beautiful full figure, and handsomely featured, and very white for a squaw; she was almost as white as dark complexioned white women generally are; her father and mother were very white skinned Indians" (*Garland* 37:16).

A white man who married an Indian woman and settled into a domestic life on the frontier was usually looked down on by other whites and disparaged as a "squaw man." In many cases, the depictions of such relationships were colored by an incipient racism mixed with a stark class-consciousness. In captivity narratives, aristocratic gentlemen who fall into Indian hands almost always attract the attention of beautiful native maidens, usually the daughters of a chief, while the "ruder" type of men get the Indian women they deserve (*Garland* 26:126–27). In many works class-consciousness is more important than race. That European class consciousness was not shared by the Indians made little difference in the literary representations.

William Snelling's 1830 account of Charles Hess, an Indian trader who had himself been captured by Indians as a child, is typical of the environmental determinism that informed a widespread understanding of going primitive but atypical in its charitable representation of a white man who opted to remain with the Indians:

> It has often been observed, that men most exposed to hardships, danger, and privation, by the nature of their employments . . . are more attached to their occupations than those of more tranquil habits. No where is this more forcibly exemplified than by the persons actively engaged in the Indian trade. Once fairly drawn in, they are seldom known to leave it. A very short residence among the aborigines learns them to despise the refinement and artificial wants of civilized society, and spurn the restraints legally and conventionally established to bind men to each other. The wild, independent habits of the wilderness are at first pleasing from novelty, and soon become riveted by custom. An Indian wife, and a family of half breed children complete the change; and when they have thus encumbered themselves, they may be considered as chained to their occupation for life. (*Garland* 45:66–67)

Snellings holds a racist view of the Indians, yet perhaps because he was himself a frontiersman, he finds the offspring of mixed marriages between traders and other frontiersmen and Indian women to be "an improvement on the Indian and the white" physically. Less surprisingly, he does not find them to be morally superior, but "in manners and morals . . . on a par with the Indians" (*Garland* 45:85–86).

John Dunn Hunter also felt that "the outsettlers are generally men of indolent, and frequently dissolute habits" (*Garland* 39:17). Charles Johnston argues in his 1827 captivity tale that the ignorant frontiersmen cannot be the agents of the civilizing process, although persons of a higher class could be, if they would settle with the Indians rather than merely observing their customs as a "curiosity . . . so unlike those of civilized men" (*Garland* 43:258).

Social class was for many persons as important as the category of race was to be for others in the nineteenth century, although then they were usually found together. British authors especially found frontiersmen rude and uncouth, in no small part because they frequently intermarried with other races. Environmental determinism was also invoked by some to explain the lamentable moral character of frontiersmen. An anonymous English author, no doubt frustrated by American recalcitrance toward England, wrote in 1812, "The lower order of the white people in the United States of this new world, are, if possible, more savage than the copper-coloured Indians." The propensity of the colonists to go to war with the motherland was also ascribed to their having taken on something of the violent nature of the savage by intermarrying with Indians and blacks (*Garland* 19:26).

Frontiersmen were to become romantic figures in various works of American literature from the early nineteenth century, ranging from Cooper's Leatherstocking Tales and Filson's biography of Daniel Boone to dime novels. However, very few of these heroes were represented as having become romantically involved with Indian women. More often than not, they lived outside the world of domesticity and the restraints or bonds of civilization.

A refreshing comeback to the negative portrayal of the Indian female is found in *The Life and Adventure of David C. Butterfield* (1851), a text that participated in the growing movement of using self-deprecating "western humor" while poking fun at "eastern" artifice and effeteness. Butterfield, a former captive, proudly proclaims himself a frontiersman and challenges the aesthetic values of the eastern elite by championing the natural look in women.

"You know nothing of true natural beauty in your villages and cities," he writes, "it exists only among the artless fair of your mountainous districts, or among the free roving Indians of the far West. Nature never made the model for your city Belle, but deformity cut out the die, and fashion filled the mould" (*Garland* 63:17–18).

Butterfield married an Indian woman and voluntarily joined the Indians, in part because, he says, he could no longer stand the hypocrisy of the missionary for whom he had worked as an interpreter. His ten-year marriage, which produced several children, was stormy and eventually ended, but the couple's marital spats provided him with some of his best material for his brand of western humor. Yet through the veil of humor one can at times glimpse the harsh social realities a mixed-race couple on the frontier faced, as when he writes, "The next day we proceeded towards Ohio, thence to New York state, where some of my friends resided. They were astonished and glad to see me but some turned their noses up at my marrying an Indian. Some said they would rather know I had been burnt, than have taken an Indian squaw;—but I concluded the fire would not have been quite so comfortable as having my hair pulled up hill [by my wife when she was mad]" (*Garland* 39:34).

The White Male Phallic Fantasy

In captivity narratives where the author or protagonist is represented as having adopted the rational ruse of having gone native, sexual relations with the natives are usually described as unpleasant and undesired. Yet if the authors of such texts frequently denied that interracial marriage had actually taken place, other tales of going native provided readers a way of imaginatively enjoying forbidden sexual relations in much more explicit fashion. One distinctive narrative expression of sexual relations with the exotic and erotic Other may be called the white male phallic fantasy. In this widespread fantasy, the white male is represented as being clearly superior to the male Other in all ways, including sexual prowess. The white can run faster, shoot straighter, and fight better than any native, but, most importantly, he proves to be sexually irresistible to beautiful female natives. John Dunn Hunter, for instance, titillates his reader with the suggestion that precisely because he was white, Indian women had found him sexually attractive and showered him with special favors.[8] "These

Indians, particularly the squaws," he writes, "treated me with singular attention, probably on account of my being the only white person they had ever seen: I forbear, however, going into details, because they might by some be considered, as clashing with propriety" (*Garland* 39:71).

The merest suggestion of forbidden sexuality was apparently enough to evoke this male fantasy in the minds of some readers. It would be futile to search for the origins of this fantasy, although versions of it have been in print continually from at least the time of Capt. John Smith's account of Pocahontas. Through the consumption of captivity narratives containing this symbolic complex, the male reader could maintain his moral propriety, while tasting forbidden pleasures in the privacy of his own room.

The discourse of discovery and conquest was laden with sexual imagery of the white male taking or possessing the virgin land. We need not rehearse this well-known story here. In some romantic waking reveries sexual imagery was projected onto the landscape, thus naturalizing male fantasies in a unique fashion. In L. P. Lee's *History of the Spirit Lake Massacre* (1857), for instance, the whole of nature is gendered and sexualized. As the rhythms of the diurnal cycle are provocatively inscribed within the male gaze, the rising and setting of the sun are assimilated to male penetration of the willing female, while, in the best narcissistic fashion, the brilliance of the reclining female body is seen to be the reflection of the male's splendor: "At night, when the visitors of day were not there to see, and the shadowy reflections in the lake clothed it with the soft witchery of spiritland, the chaste moon, attended by the train of modest stars, was wont to come and bathe in the refreshing waters and then trip hastily away before the light of day. And in the morning and evening, it seemed to be the special pride of the lake to glow with the imparted brilliancy of the sun, when he threw her a golden mantle to wear while he enjoyed his rising and setting dip" (*Garland* 72:10).

In 1778 Alexander Kellet claimed that Indian maidens positively desire white men because they are better lovers and know what women want. At the same time, he mixed Indian captivity with the negative moral and ontological evaluation of those who are captives or slaves to their base desires. "Animals in general rather desire to copulate than to propogate," he wrote, "but our Indians seem to reverse this maxim, by their cold treatment of their wives, notwithstanding their love for offspring is so excessive as to replace their lost children by the adoption of captive enemies, the

Whites not excepted. Their women are consequently very prone to European attachments; where they are agreeably surprised by a fondling and dalliance which is quite novel to them, and not the less captivating" (*Garland* 11:20–21).

Kellet's representation of "our Indians" presaged the inordinate interest anthropologists were to have in the following centuries in, to borrow the title of a famous ethnography by Bronislaw Malinowski, "the sexual lives of savages." Thus, the figure of the primitive provided westerners with a way to explore discursively and imaginatively areas that were otherwise largely taboo. It is one of many historical ironies associated with the European contact with Native Americans that the ethnographic knowledge gained of Indian cultures did so little to alter the cultural provincialism of the West. For example, if one assumes for the moment that Kellet accurately represented the social situation of the young Indian female—that she was sexually free before marriage and able to choose her sexual partners, but was not therefore considered to be immoral, since as soon as she married she became monogamous— it is telling that he never seriously considered this understanding of sexual morality as a possible alternative to the prevailing Western sexual mores. Had he done so, he might well have contributed to a significant comparative discussion of the positive and negative aspects of each. As it was, he simply imposed a Western patriarchal value system and condemned the moral weakness of all women, while white males received no moral criticism.

Narrative of the Singular Adventures of Mr. Thomas Barry (1800) is another fictional text in which the white male fantasy is played out. The narrator is captured by Indians and about to be burned when he is rescued in Pocahontas-like fashion by a beautiful Indian maiden, Oneida. The iconography of the scene was well-known: "I beheld a young Indian female on one knee before an old woman, and in the attitude of supplication, while she pointed at me" (*Garland* 24:20). This Indian maiden was "passionately enamored of the object of her benignity." Like Kellet, Barry too avers that single Indian women have sexual freedom before marriage. He claims, however, that he had loved this maiden as a sister—until, that is, he mentioned his desire to escape, reducing her to tears. Out of compassion, he agreed to give in to *her desires* and they made love. Soon thereafter, they were married, a step that resulted in his being granted more freedom of movement. Oneida is presented to female readers as a perfect model of the virtues of the "fair sex." Barry's justification of his actions is a composite of the claim it was all a rational ruse, an appeal to racial prejudice, and sexual fantasy:

> Necessity alone is my only plea of extenuation; and indeed the peculiarity of my situation seemed to admit of no alternative; for probably the tenderness of the Indian would have given place to the most implacable hatred, had I rejected her proffered love; and the consequence would have been my inevitable destruction! . . . My spouse, whose heart had never before felt the influence of the soft passion, enjoyed the pure delight of a virtuous attachment; her happiness seemed perfect; every night she sunk to repose in the embraces of a man whom she idolized, and each morning her bosom thrilled with new endearments. (*Garland* 24:iv, 30–31)

Joseph Priest's *The Fort Stanwix Captive* (1841) mixes a sentimental tale with elements of male fantasies. After Isaac Hubbell had been captured in the Revolutionary War, he was saved from horrible torture and certain death when the sister of the Indian chief interceded and adopted him to replace her recently deceased son. Hubbell quickly established himself as "the equal to their best shots with a rifle," while, in a series of foot races he proved himself to be the fastest man in the entire tribe. As a result of his victory, the chief offered Hubbell the choice of any of his incomparable daughters for his wife, while promising that he would be elevated to the status of chief. The Indian women seem to have come from a European aristocratic mold. "Their teeth, when they laughed, appeared like rows of alabaster, and the forms of their faces such as even a white man would look upon with rapture. The high prominent cheek was not there, nor the flattened nose; these were of the fairest Grecian or Circassian forms" (*Garland* 56:31, 37–38).

Popular dime novels were a common vehicle for feeding male sexual fantasies to readers. *Massatoit's Daughter*, a Beadle Dime Novel (1861), is representative. Both the white male hero and Sameeda, the beautiful daughter of the chief, are described in typical sentimental fashion as naturally the most good-looking, the most intelligent, and the most graceful members of their society; moreover, they are universally recognized as such. Both are persons "of the better sort," aristocrats in their own worlds.

Louis is the handsome white male, magnetically attractive to native maidens, who fall over each other in their competition for the honor of viewing, decorating, and touching his body. He is "skillful in the chase," while Sameeda is "like a young fawn." This metaphor implies the naturalness and innocence of female desire, while hinting that, in the nature of things, the exotic female will fawn over the white male captive-hunter. The image of the native princess as a fawn also preserves Louis's noble character, for no real hunter would pursue a fawn. Instead, in a form of symbolic inversion, here the fawn-female pursues the hunter-male. In this tale, as in so many others, the Indian maiden becomes the means whereby the white male captive effects his escape. She becomes an active agent on his behalf due to her sentimental sensibilities, which are displayed when hearing his sad tale (*Garland* 77:63).

The white male fantasy involving the exotic native female has shown a remarkable staying power. Over the last three centuries, the topos of Indian captivity has provided an ideal plot device for situating the white male hero in an alien world, where he is largely powerless, his body bound, stripped naked (or nearly so), and subjected to the attentions of others. The white male body becomes an object of torture and then the object of female desire. Yet somehow he always manages to triumph over the pain inflicted on him, proving himself to be a real man, and thereby winning the heart and hand of the lovely chief's daughter. The unmistakable presence of this complex in many Indian captivity narratives from the last three centuries is a testament to the captivating hold this fantasy has exerted over the white male imagination—especially when it has been contrasted, implicitly or explicitly, with what was experienced as the real bonds or shackles of marriage in the civilized world.

Boys in the Woods: Male Bonding in
a Natural World without Women

Ironically, the very patriarchal social structures that were designed to preserve and promote the privileged position of the male came to be experienced by some men as a form of imprisonment, severely limiting their freedom and enjoyment of life.[9] For some men, marriage was a form of captivity. Paradoxically, in this situation Indian captivity narratives provided a means of escaping, temporarily at least, their suffocating lives. The figures of the white Indian and the woodsman could embody male fantasies of escaping from the duties and responsibilities of family life, while enjoying a life of adventure, self-sufficiency, and male comaraderie. Female company was available to these figures when they wanted it, but without any of the strings attached in normal domestic relationships.

Many European and American writers criticized the Indians' itinerant lifestyle, which for them symbolized the state of savagery as opposed to civilization. Living off the land through hunting and gathering was identified with individuals and peoples characterized by laziness and a lack of discipline and ambition. In contrast, cultivating the land and owning and improving property were equated with a life of propriety. Yet for many other men the life of hunting, fishing, and trapping in the woods held an undeniable attraction. The great popularity of figures such as Natty Bumpo and Daniel Boone signaled a widespread romantic nostalgia for a natural life of living off the bounty of the land. This nostalgia was frequently conjoined with the fantasy of a world of male comraderie, free of the restraints of civilization and the female domestic sphere. The captivity narrative was readily adapted to the task of representing a life of adventure in the woods, allowing the reader to enjoy imaginatively the adventures of white Indians and frontiersmen. Through the act of reading, readers could imagine an alternative lifestyle and, through identifying with the heroes, temporarily assume a different identity.

There is an undeniable element of escapism in such works, as the male protagonists seek to avoid the "civilizing influence" of women. The image of the self-sufficient woodsman came to be conjoined with a masculinity constructed in opposition to that of the good-natured man of sensibility, who was most at home among females. Many positive representations of life on the frontier refer to the freedom enjoyed by the hunter-trapper, unencumbered by the artificial restraints and niceties of civilization.[10]

White Indians and the Cult of Motherhood

White males have long had an ambivalent attitude toward women, both native and white, especially in terms of their sexuality. However, the figure of the mother has also been extremely influential in terms of the Western male psyche. Maternal figures play a prominent role in numerous American Indian captivity narratives. A number of captives, mostly males who had been abducted as children, speak of the strong influence their adoptive Indian mother had exercised in their ready assimilation into Indian culture and their assuming an Indian identity. Significantly, the critical role of

Indian women played in facilitating the identity transformation appears almost exclusively in nineteenth-century narratives.

A cult of motherhood developed in the nineteenth century in Anglo-American culture.[11] In some narratives the symbolic and value-laden complex of motherhood is combined with the topos of Indian captivity in order to reflect on issues of human identity, family structure, gender roles, moral development, and the significance and universality of human emotions and affective displays. In *Memoirs of Charles Dennis Rusoe D'Eres*, for instance, the author points to the protective nature of the female as having been crucial in facilitating his assimilation into Indian society. He reports that "contrary to my fears, the Indian women used me tenderly in their way . . . fawned over and flattered me, and by this means, I became more familiar with them, and frequently used to run to them for protection, when I thought myself in danger from the men. . . . After being with them about fifteen days, I became in a measure, reconciled to them, and used much familiarity with them" (*Garland* 25:13). Like most of his compatriots, this author assumes that all women are gentler than men. To be sure, many Europeans and Americans still questioned whether Indians were fully human or not. Even in mid-century, many persons held that the Indians "in a moral point of view, seemed but little above the brute creation, and their knowledge rather instinct than reason" (*Garland* 74:53).

Texts such as these appealed to the ideological image of women as agents of the civilizing process. Within the nuclear family it was believed that it was the wife and mother who smoothed the rough edges of the male and otherwise softened or ameliorated the potentially destructive consequences of his brutish nature.[12] This understanding of the proper and complementary roles of males and females in the family promoted the maintenance of the patriarchal value system, while granting a central space (the domestic sphere or hearth) to women in which they exercised enormous influence when the men were abroad in the more public, male world. In projecting these Western gender constructions onto Indian societies, authors could usually rely on the reader's ideological sympathy and acquiescence, based on the general reluctance to admit that "proper" gender roles and relations, were, in fact, culturally relative rather than universal. Male-female roles and power relationships were natural and timeless and thus could not be altered without precipitating social problems of grave moral consequence.

A relatively few authors had positive views of Indian women. A notable exception is found in Harriet M'Conkey Bishop's *Dakota War Whoop* (1863), where it is suggested that if Indian women were allowed to act out of their own nature, rather than under the oppressive domination of men, moral improvement and civilization would surely follow. Bishop uses the captivity narrative as a vehicle for offering, in a deflected or indirect form, a cultural critique of her own society that would have been more difficult for her to make directly. She projects her critical thoughts concerning the gendered power relations found in her own society onto Indian society.

In commenting on the situation of the Indians, and especially of the women, Bishop implicitly (and subversively from the patriarchal point of view) appeals to the very claims of a universal and timeless feminine nature and the cult of true womanhood proffered by many other authors, both male and female. By extending this complex to the Indian, she is able to speak to the inherent contradictions in the phallocentric constructions of proper male-female relations by appealing to the true history of the conquest and white-Indian relations. This bloody history would have been very different, she suggests, had Indian women been granted a more important sociopolitical role. The implication that the same situation would obtain in white society cannot be missed when she writes,

> We are glad that we have comparatively small record to make of [Indian] women being the aiders and abettors of the transactions which brought such dismay to our frontier. As a general thing, they have "fed the hungry and cloathed the naked" when in their power to do so. True, they have been subject to their liege lords, obliged to do their bidding; but whenever left to themselves, we are convinced that the fundamental elements of *true womanhood* live in the hearts which beat beneath their dirty short gowns and rusty old blankets. Remove the shackles which the men inflict upon them, and they would soon arrive to the dignity of white women. (*Garland* 78:170)

John Dunn Hunter also eloquently invoked all of the values associated with the cult of motherhood in order to explain how and why he had been transformed readily into an Indian. While explicitly recognizing many cultural differences between Indians and whites, including differences in gender roles, in social and economic values, and in the expression of emotions, in explaining how and why he had gone native, he appeals to the Western values associated with motherhood and femininity.

After the publication of his narrative, Hunter became a celebrity for a time in London. His reception in the salons of the aristocracy and the wealthy was no doubt due in part to the novelty of a white Indian in their midst, but his image was largely the result of his literary self-presentation. Hunter paints himself as having been a vulnerable, loving child at the time of his abduction. Suddenly deprived of his family and the blessings of civilization and raised among "savages," he had nevertheless somehow grown up to be a man of feeling. This fact needed to be explained, and Hunter obliged, appealing to the reader's sympathetic imagination and to values informing the cult of motherhood. This literary self-figuration allowed women of sensibility to indulge themselves in the "exquisite" emotions of sympathy and pity for this young man while at the same time they could surreptitiously enjoy the tempting aura of wildness and untamed sexuality in this dapper white Indian:

> If . . . the imagination be allowed scope, and a lad of ten or twelve years of age, without kindred or name, or any knowledge by which he could arrive at an acquaintance with any of the circumstances connected with his being, as supposed in the central wilds of North America, nearly a thousand miles from any white settlement, a prisoner or sojourner among a people, on whom he had not the slightest claim, and with whose language, habits and character, he was wholly unacquainted; but, who nevertheless treated him kindly; and it will appear not only natural but rational, that he should return such kindness with gratitude and affection. Such nearly was my situation, and such in fact were my feelings at that time. (*Garland* 39:35)

Hunter provides us with one of the deepest insights into the way in which some Indians at least viewed the phenomenon of whites going native, as well how some Indians characterized the whites. "The accounts of the white people, which the Indians had been very particular in giving me," he notes, "were no ways flattering to my colour; they were represented as an inferior order of beings, wicked, treacherous, cowardly, and only fit to transact the common drudgeries of life. I was at the same time assured, that my transposition from them to the Indians, was for me a most fortu-

nate occurrence; for now I might become an expert hunter, brave
warrior, wise counsellor, and possibly a distinguished chief of their
nation. All this I considered as true, till the arrival of the traders
among us" (*Garland* 39:48).

In captivity tales such as this, the cult of motherhood has replaced appeals to divine providence as the main locus of value.
Hunter, who had taken scalps as an Indian, could well have come
across as a morally despicable character (and was so cast by some
of his enemies and detractors), yet by appealing to the cult of
motherhood and identifying himself with sentimental values, he
emerged (in his own narrative at least) as a very sympathetic
figure. The following passage illustrates this:

> Not long after this, I experienced a painful loss. The squaw who had
> adopted me among her children, and who had treated me with great
> tenderness and affection, was accidentally drowned in attempting
> to collect drift wood, during the prevalence of a flood. This circum-
> stance was the cause of great grief, apparently more poignant to be
> endured than is usually experienced in civilized life; because, the
> customs of the Indians do not tolerate the same open expression of
> feeling, from the indulgence of which the acuteness of grief is
> relieved, and sooner subsides. The Indians regard tears, or any ex-
> pression of grief, as a mark of weakness in males, and unworthy of
> the character of the warrior. In obedience to this custom, I bore my
> affliction in silence, in order to sustain my claims to their respect
> and esteem; but nevertheless, I sincerely and deeply felt the be-
> reavement; and cannot even at this late day, reflect on her maternal
> conduct to me, from the time I was taken prisoner by the Kansas, to
> her death, without the association of feelings, to which, in other
> respects I am a stranger. (*Garland* 39:34–35)

While affirming the sentimental values surrounding motherhood, Hunter also introduces cultural difference in terms of the
public expression and nonexpression of emotions in white and
Indian society. He suggests that, like all persons of sensibility, he
had deeply felt the loss of his adoptive mother, even though he
could not display his feelings as one could in white society. In a
manner that presages modern theories, he recognizes that affective responses are not automatic but rather are culturally constructed and subject to social constraints.

Other former captives who had been abducted as children recalled their childhood among the Indians in glowing, almost idyl-

lic terms. William Filley, for instance, who spent almost thirty years as a white Indian in the mid-nineteenth century, reported that as a child the Indians had doted on him, showering him with affection and gifts. Perhaps most importantly, he also pointed out that Indian parents never used corporal punishment or over-worked their children, as whites frequently did (*Garland* 81:50–51). Any attempt on our part to understand why so many captives refused repartation must take seriously the many reports of Indian child-rearing practices and the sharp contrast these represented to the prevailing practices in America in the eighteenth and nine-teenth centuries.[13]

In white homes, the maxim "Spare the rod and spoil the child" was followed by most parents. In many families, perhaps of neces-sity, children were viewed primarily as a source of labor and were exploited as such. One white Indian, who had been forced by his biological father to watch a flock of sheep alone for long periods of time, recalled that he had voluntarily left his family at the age of twelve and joined an Indian band after the Indians had glowingly described to him a life of hunting, fishing, and riding, and even promised him a pony if he followed them. In his own words, "That looked better to me than herding a bunch of sheep alone . . . [so] the next day I told them I would go."[14]

Dozens of former captives also testified that the moral and ethical instruction they had received from their Indian parents was of great value and even superior to that found in white society; some faulted white Christians for being hypocritical. To cite only two instances, John Bickell, who had spent over four years with the Delaware as a child, wrote:

> The Delawares are the best people to train up children I ever was with. Their leisure hours are, in great measure, spent in training up their children to observe what they believe to be right. . . . as a nation they may be considered fit examples for many of us Christians to follow. They certainly follow what they are taught to believe more closely, & I might say more honestly, in general, that we Christians do the divine precepts of our Redeemer. . . . I know I am influenced to good, even at this day, more from what I learned among them, than I learned among people of my own color.[15]

William Filley unabashedly claimed Indian morality to be supe-rior in general to that found in the white world. Like other former captives, he used his intimate experience and knowledge of Indian

society to criticize Anglo-American culture for its racial hypocrisy. "The pale-faces think it is no sin to steal the red man's
property from his land," he notes, "but to steal from a white man is
all wrong, and deserves punishment. I say, of a truth, they ought to
be punished in one case as well as in the other. If this were not so,
there would be no honesty whatever." Moreover, he argued, "there
are more honest Indians, according to their numbers, than there
are whites. If this is not so, your State prisons would not be so full."

Abducted as a child of five, Filley had later been sent by his
captors to a mission school, where they hoped that he would learn
English and, thus, be able to help them manage their increasing
intercourse with whites. But after three years in this school, which
he hated, and having begged his Indian parents to no avail to let
him drop out, Filley volunteered to become the "captive" of a
Camanche Indian in order to escape from the school and the
authority of the Indians who had placed him there. After he had
been adopted into this tribe, he reports, "At this time I had my first
liberty. How does the reader suppose I felt at my being almost as
free as the deer or the antelope, to stay or go when I wished? If I was
ever happy in my life, I was at this time. It seemed so strange to
me, when I had no one to watch me, I would sometimes sing and
dance, and be almost at my wit's end, to express my happiness"
(*Garland* 81:79, 80, 61–63).

Paradoxically, Indian captivity often meant a new freedom for
individuals as an inferior social identity in the white world was
exchanged for a new one. If, through passages such as this, we can
come to appreciate why some children found freedom in captivity
as an Indian, it is, perhaps, even easier to understand why slaves
and indentured servants also found a world of freedom and opportunity in Indian society. Even though many of the captivity narratives portray the horror of Indian captivity, others speak for the
many white and black Indians who opted not to return and whose
voices have been largely lost to history.

White Women and the Sexual Other

Culture has been defined as the webs of significance we spin and in
which we are then enmeshed. Like all people, the Europeans who
first came to the Americas and their descendants have been captured by texts in numerous ways, enmeshed in the tales they
themselves have spun. Representations of Indian captivity, ranging from Mary Rowlandson's narrative to Hollywood films, con-

sumed as mimetic texts mirroring reality, have all too often made us captive to our own fantasies and fears. Nowhere has this been more obvious than in the literary and iconographic representations of the relations between white women and the male Indian Other. When abduction was still a reality on the frontier, such representations at times colored and structured the experience of actual captivity for some persons and influenced their initial interactions with Native Americans. After having read and heard captivity tales as a child, James Moore had fearfully imagined being abducted long before he was actually taken in 1784. In cases such as this, the experience of Indian captivity was structured to a significant extent by a complex intertextuality in which tales of captivity informed the expectations, hopes, fears, and anxieties of captives as they passed through the reality (*Garland* 65:46).[16]

In the extant captivity narratives, there is a clear difference between male and female accounts of interracial sexual relations, resulting no doubt from the nineteenth-century constructions of gender differences. As we have seen, male captives often claim to have entered such relationships as a calculated means of realizing their escape, yet female captives almost never make this appeal. A notable exception, the case of Sarah Wakefield, actually proves this generalization by illustrating how difficult it was for a woman to get others to accept such a claim.

Wakefield maintained that during her six-week captivity a friendly Indian, named Chaska, had protected her from unwanted sexual advances from other Indians by pretending that he had taken her as his own wife. After her return to the white world, Wakefield found herself "grievously abused by many, who are ignorant of the particulars of my captivity." She was subjected to vehement criticism of her behavior in captivity and to innuendos to the effect that she "loved the Indians" in more than one way. This charge was circulated even more widely after she tried to intervene (unsuccessfully as it turned out) with government authorities in an effort to save Chaska from being executed. Wakefield argued that her motives in pretending to have gone native and married Chaska had been entirely rational, as she had sought thereby to protect herself and her children. This argument did not sell (*Garland* 79:27–28, 15).

Wakefield's case was not helped when she was forced to admit that reports of other actions by her in captivity were true, for these were hardly of the sort that evoked sympathy. She had, for instance, been overheard telling her captors that if she were spared from death, she would kill the other captives. Wakefield pleaded that in captivity her life had constantly hung by a thread and she had had to be ever wary of giving those in the Indian camp who wished her ill even the slightest provocation, excuse, or tidbit of gossip that could be used against her. Her defense rested on the recognition that gossip could be dangerous for a powerless woman—it could cost a captive her life and, equally seriously, it could cost a woman her reputation after returning to the white world (*Garland* 79:29–30, 27).

Clearly, the ruse of going native and marrying an Indian was not a real option for women. While men could enter such sexual relations without necessarily incurring any long-term social stigma, women who had done so faced an entirely different prospect if and when they returned to white society. Given the high cultural value—even sacrality—placed on female chastity and virtue, most women felt they had to protect these at all costs; those who engaged in sexual relations with Indians, willingly or otherwise, were profaned and polluted. Saran Ann Horn expressed the anxiety and pressures most female captives experienced in this connection when she concluded her own narrative with the declaration and disclaimer "perhaps I ought to say, that with reference to a point, of all others of the most sacred importance to a captive female, (with gratitude to my Maker I record it,) my fears [of being sexually abused] were in no part realized" (*Garland* 54:60).

Long before the Cold War, the cry of "better dead than red" (or its equivalent) was on the lips of many female captives. The reasons for this are immediately related to the larger symbolic complex of white feminine virtue, the savage sexual Other, and rape—or, to put this another way, to the symbolics of racial, sexual, and gender power relations. Juliette Kinzie's 1844 account of one woman's reaction to an Indian attack in 1812 on a tiny community near the Chicago River echoes dozens of similar reports in this respect. "The heroic resolution of one of the soldiers' wives deserves to be recorded," she wrote. "She had, from the first, expressed a determination never to fall into the hands of the savages, believing that their prisoners were always subjected to tortures worse than death. When, therefore, a party came upon her, to make her a prisoner, she fought with desperation, refusing to surrender, although assured of safe treatment; and literally suffered herself to be cut to pieces, rather than become their captive" (*Garland* 59:25).

The "heroic resolution" (or the irrational fear) of this anonymous woman was provoked by the power this symbolic complex held over her and presumably many other women. Her image of what Indian captivity meant for a white woman was part of a much broader, powerful cultural symbolic complex. Recently, in speaking of Edgar Rice Burroughs's Tarzan novels, Marianna Torgovnick has argued, "*Abduction* always carries with it the double meanings of kidnapping and rape. . . . The jungle may be impenetrable, but Jane is not. . . . The abduction scene teases and titillates, bringing together the racial and gender subtexts so frequently involved in Western treatments of the primitive."[17] This point has immediate relevance to many Indian captivity narratives.

Whereas actual rape is always forestalled in the Tarzan tales, in American Indian captivity narratives not all of the women are saved in the nick of time by strong white men. In an anonymous 1869 work of fiction (presented as a factual account), which the title page touts as "a Heart Rending Story" that "Will Bring Tears to Every Eye," one finds the female protagonist subjected to the unbridled sexual appetite of the savage male. Designed in part to rally support in the eastern United States for the Indian War on the northwest plains, this work is anything but objective in its characterizations. Yet rather than dismissing this novel as just another penny dreadful, it deserves our attention as a popular (if unsavory) use of the captivity topos, employing readily available racist and gender stereotypes. The villain of the piece is a Kiowa chief named Santana, who embodies raw, untamed male power and sexual desire:

> Santana had brought with him as captives a beautiful white woman—the unfortunate Mrs. Blynn—and her little boy Willie Blynn, the latter about two years and six months old. Mrs. Blynn herself was not over twenty two, and possessed of rare personal beauty. In truth it was this that had caused Santana to spare her, in order that he might add her to the squaws he already possessed; a proceeding that not one of the latter dared object to, without the certainty of having her head split open with the Chief's tomahawk. With almost hellish shrewdness too Santana had spared Willie's life, not that he cared for it, but as he said: "If I kill white squaw's boy, she cry and fret, and then she get ugly! Me want to keep her pooty all the time." (*Garland* 81:22)

The male sexual Other here is unfeeling, selfish, calculating, and domineering—as are innumerable villains of various colors in other works of fiction of the time. In the presence of the helpless young white mother, whose plight would move any man with any moral sense whatsoever to sympathy, Santana's actions are ruled solely by his sexual desire. This characterization of the Indian male as totally evil, cold-hearted, and with a rapacious sexual appetite sets the stage, of course, for the white male hero to make his appearance as the rescuer of the damsel in distress. The author of this tale employs these gender constructions in order to manipulate the feelings of the readers. If in this case the heroine is raped repeatedly by the Indian, this outrage is intended to produce the equivalent emotional response—outrage—in the readers.

The white woman embodies the virtue of maternal heroism *cum* perfect resignation as she endures this "horrible abuse" and "debauch," which otherwise would be worse than death itself, for the sake of her small son. She sacrifices her own bodily integrity for her child's sake. "Indeed, had it not been for her tender solicitude for her child she would have taken her own life" (*Garland* 81:23). Every bodily indignity and every bruise Mrs. Blynn suffers is transformed into a badge of maternal heroism and perfect Christian resignation. Even as she is dying and consciousness is gone, this paragon of maternal self-sacrifice instinctively acts to protect her child. The death scene of this innocent female illustrates the use of stereotypical language and imagery. Italicizing the constituent elements shows how relentlessly these evocative triggers have been employed:

Black Kettle's camp was the first to be attacked [by the cavalry], though all the village was of course aroused. It was just breaking day, and Mrs. Blynn hearing the yells, huzzas, and firing, sprang out, *her heart beating wildly with mingled hope and dread.* Through the cold grey light she peered, and suddenly there came dashing forward a column of U.S. Dragoons guided by Viroqua; who, pistol in hand, fought *like an Amazon.* The thought of being at last saved, completely unnerved the poor mother; and, *bursting into tears,* she was compelled to sit down, sobbing in *trembling,* happy tones:

"Oh Willie! Willie! Mamma and Willie's saved at last! Don't be afraid darling; Mamma will hold you safe!"

The words were yet on her lips, when, *like a wild beast,* Santana *sprang* behind her, *and buried his tomahawk in her head.* He also fired two shots into *the quivering body of his victim* as she *sank back dying.* Another instant and *little Willie was in the monster's grasp, his head dashed against a tree,* and then, *lifeless and limp, the dead baby* was *thrown like a dog upon his mother's breast.*

Most *touching scene* of all, *the mother, even in the agonies of death* retained the idea of *saving her child,* and unconsciously, from the moment of *receiving her death blow,* she had been reaching forth her *wasted arms* as though groping for him in the dark. And now as his body was flung down upon her *bosom,* the same *arms instinctively, spasmodically clasped him* about; never more to let him go—for in this way were *the corpses* found by General Sheridan and his staff. . . . Mrs. Blynn and Willie, with the bodies of the white soldiers, were *carried tenderly* to Fort Cobb, and there *in one grave,* just outside the stockade, mother and child lie *sleeping peacefully* enough after their *terrible captivity and sufferings.* (*Garland* 81:38)

Just as the primitive was widely represented ravenously consuming the "quivering flesh" of sacrificial offerings, readers voraciously consumed the literary and artistic offerings of the quivering bodies of innocent white women and infants sacrificed in the cults of sensibility and true womanhood. The array of stereotypical elements in this death scene was designed to "bring tears to every eye." This affective power came from the intertextual associations these elements invoked as well as from the imagistic associations derived from the plethora of nineteenth-century prints, etchings, paintings, sculptures, and stage performances based on the captivity theme.

Joy Kasson has convincingly demonstrated the existence of a specific cultural matrix of images and values in the nineteenth century that produced works of sculpture characterized by "the interweaving of themes of captivity, female vulnerability, and spirituality with those of dangerous sensuality, loss of identity, and disrupted domesticity." This same matrix structured the reception of such works of art. Works of ideal sculpture, for example, were intended to be viewed and interpreted through the tale behind the specific scene portrayed. Each emplotted work then served as a site of contemplation of the moral lesson displayed before the viewer. Nineteenth-century American works of art depicting bound white women were to be appreciated through the complex intertextuality of captivity narratives and the network of associations the figure of the white female captive evoked.[18]

Female heroism in the nineteenth century was most often of several distinct types, most immediately related to the symbolic complex of femininity or true womanhood. Women who would rather die than have their person sexually violated were highly valorized, but so were those women who embodied the virtue of perfect resignation, placing their faith in a higher power, be this God or a male hero. John Frost spoke for many of his contemporaries when, in 1854, he averred, "The [female] fortitude to suffer is as noble as the courage to dare. Perhaps, patient endurance is rarer than bold adventure" (*Garland* 66:109). In the nineteenth century, the woman who used violent (normally male) means to save herself or her family members was frequently associated with the figure of the Amazon or of martial queens, such as the African Zenobia. Such women, though, usually were portrayed as finally subdued and in chains themselves.

Frost's 1854 anthology of captivity tales epitomizes the nineteenth-century discourse that sought to circumscribe female heroism tightly within the ideals of true womanhood. In this discourse, female heroism was—and by definition could only be—"the heroism of the heart," for female "deeds of daring and endurance are prompted by affection" (*Garland* 66:iii). Whatever the specifics of the case, the actions of women deemed heroic are represented as having arisen out of the desire to preserve their virtue or out of maternal instinct. The vast majority of authors, both male and female, assume that the gender differences, roles, and power relations found in European and American societies are natural. For these authors, recounting captivity tales provided an important means of proclaiming and demonstrating these "natural facts" by providing exemplary instances of male and female heroism in extremis when, it is assumed, all artifice had been stripped away and naked human nature was displayed.

Anne Jamison's 1824 narrative, written when she was about eighty years old, is representative of those captivities that laud a religious form of perfect resignation. Insofar as this ideal resonates with that found in the accounts of Mary Rowlandson (1682) and Jonathan Dickinson (1699), it is an indication of the remarkable persistence of this ideal in Anglo-American society. By the nineteenth century, however, perfect resignation had become preeminently a female religious virtue, an existential stance women could (and should) still adopt in the world. It was also held out as a spiritual mode of being in the world appropriate to other powerless persons, including blacks and children. In contrast, the male exemplars of perfect Christian resignation were limited to the figure of the recluse, who had withdrawn from the commercial world to the forest to seek comfort and solace in the Bible.

Women embody the ideal of perfect resignation by bearing the afflictions of captivity; bodily suffering is a way of realizing a purer

spiritual state. In many nineteenth-century works of literature—
and in many women's lives—the pursuit of a moral and spiritual
sublimity often included women offering their bodies up in the
crucible of this-worldly affliction. The cultural message was clear:
self-sacrifice was to be taken literally by women.

Anne Jamison never faced any sexual threat in captivity, a fact
that gives her tale a special bent. In the absence of the threat of
sexual violence, one finds that other most basic form of violating
the human body—cannibalism—substituted in the account. Jamison claims that her faith, coupled with acts of divine providence,
had preserved her physically and kept her from reverting to being a
cannibalistic savage. Jamison's publisher avers that "she earnestly
desired me to publish the following Narrative of God's dealing
with her, during five years of her weary pilgrimage; that her numerous offspring and others might be excited to acknowledge God
in all their ways, patiently submit to his chastening rod, and fully
put their trust in him, through the Lord Jesus Christ even in the
most gloomy and afflictive dispensations of his Providence" (Garland 37:1).

Jamison and her children had been in a large party fleeing an
Indian attack by floating down the Mississippi on a raft. They soon
had been reduced to desperate straits and faced starvation. Part of
her account centers around how she and her children had survived
through divine providence, as God moved the normally cruel and
hard-hearted savages to assist them (e.g., an Indian provided game
on two days; other "hostile" Indians provided meat on another
occasion). Surprisingly, perhaps, the threat of cannibalism came
not from the Indians but from the only surviving adult male in her
party. Faced with starvation, he had proposed consuming a child
chosen by lot, but Jamison was able to dissuade him by rational
argument. Jamison's embrace of the religious stance of perfect
resignation pervades the entire narrative: "But to prevent despondency, and raise my hope in God; he was pleased to direct my mind
to a chain of reflections, on what he required of me, as a rational
and social creature, and as a professor of his holy religion—That
rather than murmur or complain, I ought constantly to feel and
daily to acknowledge with joyful gratitude, what the Lord had
done for me, a vile unworthy sinner" (Garland 37:9–10).

In pathetic narratives, women who are forced against their will
into sexual relationships with the Indian Other or uncouth men
are usually portrayed as victims who merit sympathy from readers. The theme of virtue-in-distress had been the mainstay of

sentimental literature since Richardson's *Pamela*, of course, but
the captivity narrative offered authors and readers new possibilities for exploring this theme. At the same time, the captivity topos
provided the possibility of creating a variety of evil Others—a
savage, a Frenchman, a crude member of the lower classes—to
contrast with the male hero. The Indian-as-primitive could be
made to embody wild, animal sexuality, while the white male was
moved by sympathy rather than sexual desire.

Through the projection of sexual fantasies and gender and class
constructs onto the primitive Other, readers (both male and female) could imaginatively enjoy forbidden sexual relations, even
while being able to preserve their self-image as sensitive, feeling,
and moral persons. *Five Years a Captive Among the Black-Feet
Indians* is exemplary. Midway through the novel, John Dixon, the
male protagonist who has become a chief among the Indians, hears
about a white female captive in the camp. He discovers her asleep
in a teepee and, as the reader shares his male gaze, he proceeds to
read her history of suffering and woe inscribed in her features. The
scene provides the opportunity for the hero to distinguish himself
as a man of feeling in the presence of this sentimental female-in-
distress as he reacts to her tears:

> Whilst contemplating her appearance as she thus lay sleeping,
> many strange emotions passed through my mind, as to who she was,
> how she had fallen into the hands of the savages, and the miseries
> untold through which she had probably passed since she had be-
> come a victim of their cruelties. . . . all the sympathy of my nature
> was aroused in her behalf. . . . She opened her eyes, and with an
> appearance of surprise, gazed steadily in my face for some time, as
> though doubting the correctness of her senses—her eyes meanwhile
> filling with tears, she covered them with her hands. The eloquence
> of this appeal to my sympathies, so affected me, that in my own
> mind I resolved, if possible, to save her from the farther brutality of
> the savages, or, with her, perish at their hands. (*Garland* 74:99–100)

Dixon, a pretend white Indian, subsequently pleads for the female captive's life in an Indian council, arguing that if she was not
freed the Great Spirit, whom he served and through whose assistance he was able to protect the Indian people, would be angry
with them and send plagues of bears, panthers, and other wild
animals. Even though Dixon and Roxana begin to live together,
theirs is a chaste love, based upon a sympathy of nature. Dixon's

only desire is to nurse and serve this paragon of female virtue-in-distress. He is a special sort of self-sacrificing Christian hero, a moral man of feeling and "friend of suffering humanity." At one point he addresses the reader directly, suggesting that the presence of this "sacred charge . . . had been placed, entirely Providentially, under [his] protective care," for "her humility and trust, (in her Heavenly Protector,) like that of a little child, seemed to flow unbidden and without affectation from her heart" and had inspired him to live a selfless life (*Garland* 74:119).

Roxana's tragic tale is spun out by the author, who conjures up intertextually transmitted images of rape and horror in the reader's imagination. She is represented as a pitiful victim of the brutal sexual appetite of the savage male. When the Indian to whom she is forcibly married is killed in a fight before the marriage could be consummated, the author suggests this was an act of divine providence (*Garland* 74:130–31). Later Roxana is captured by an even more "base and treacherous tribe of savages" among whom she suffers actual sexual abuse. As "a prey (notwithstanding her prayers and resistance to the contrary) to the diabolical passions and caprice of the inhuman wretch who had usurped power over her," Roxana had been subjected to such horrible forms of "humiliation" that she prayed that God would take her life away. Having become a victim of her captor's lust, Roxana despaired of ever returning to her family again. This part of the narrative is telling, for it illustrates the way some authors used an appeal to providence as a cover to introduce titillating material:

> Thus far she had lived in hopes that, by some means unknown to herself, Providence would effect her release from the savages, and enable her again to return to her friends in England. But now, not only were her hopes blasted forever, but even the desire for such an event perished in her bosom. Could the change have taken place by a single volition of the will, she informed me that she would be loth to make it. "For," said she, "what would be my condition on returning home? Could I look [my fiancé] Charles in the face without a blush, or a feeling of conscious shame? never, never! Rather than bear the weight of a sense of this crushing debasement, I would rather, a thousand times, perish in the wilderness, and be forgotten forever." (*Garland* 74:141–43)

If the sanctity of the white female body is obvious here, so is its vulnerability and fragility. For many women, returning to a normal life in society was impossible; a woman's honor could only be recouped through a "beautiful death," characterized by perfect Christian resignation. Such a death is represented as a process of transmutation whereby pure spiritual gold is extracted from the dross of physical existence in the crucible of affiction. Or, better, this sort of death scene, so popular in the nineteenth century, is represented as an apotheosis of sorts, as the "goddess of innocency and purity of thought" is freed from the now corrupted and fallen female body.

> Her calm resignation and humility, under all her trials and suffer-
> ings, gave me a realizing sense of the power of the Christian's hope,
> that I never before had conceived of. . . . During the whole course of
> Roxana's lingering illness, I never heard a murmur or complaint
> from her, or even observed an expression in her countenance in-
> dicative of impatience or anxiety. Her whole being appeared to
> be merged in the good pleasure and will of her Maker, and was en-
> tirely satisfied to abide, with humility, whatsoever His providence
> deemed proper in her case. . . . By means of the long and severe
> chastening to which she had been exposed, her Christian character
> had developed itself in an extraordinary manner, and, like fine gold
> thoroughly purged by the heat of the fire, was void of every impurity.
> (Garland 74:174–75)

Viewed retrospectively from our position in the late twentieth century, many readers will reject the use of theology to transform the tragic result of the prevailing gender constructions and values into a beautiful death. Yet by revealing the pernicious uses to which religious symbolic systems and values can be put, tales such as this may still be instructive, although not in the way the authors intended.

The 1838 and 1839 narratives of Clarissa Plummer and Caroline Harris are characteristic of those largely fictional texts that used purported sexual outrages committed against white women, as well as stereotypical accounts of the brains of infants being dashed out, as a means of exciting anti-Indian sentiment among the read-ing public. Plummer, for instance, reports that in captivity "the most beastly liberties" were taken with the women by the "unmer-ciful savages." She sharply contrasts the moral sensibilities of civ-ilized persons with the lack of the same among the savages, who "could coolly and deliberately dash out the brains of the harmless new born babe." Such creatures were inhuman and thus "it could

not be expected [they] could be moved to pity, or in any way affected by the tears of its distracted mother" (*Garland* 54:11–13).

The husbands here are well-meaning but finally ineffective de-
fenders of the virtue of their wives, though they both valiantly die
trying. With no countervailing power in sight, the natives are, true
to their nature, beastly. In such tales, there is no effort to soften the
characterization of the Indian-as-savage; rather, the Indian appears
as a pure type—the exact antithesis of the man of sensibility.
Thus, Indians are represented as cold-hearted persons who have no
qualms whatsoever about killing children while the weapons of
the weaker sex—tears, sighs, bouts of fainting, supplications made
on one's knees—are utterly ineffective with this wholly alien
Other.

The wilderness abode of the Indian savage is dark and deep—as
dark as his heart and as deep as his moral turpitude. The innocent
female captive is out of place in this hellish world where everything is topsy-turvy—groans are music, cruelty produces delight,
and tears fail to move the captors. A popular poem, cited in Sarah
Ann Horn's narrative, encapsulates the imagery of the symbolic
complex informing such sentimental tales of female virtue-in-
distress:

> At every turn my weeping eyes survey'd
> The deep recesses of the dreadful shade,
> Where darkness tangible, and unconfin'd,
> Reigns uncontrolled o'er cruel savage mind;—
> Where *nature*, sunk in deepest moral night,
> Makes deeds of fiendish cruelty delight,
> And at whose guilty shrine, through circling years,
> Are pour'd, as offerings meet, the captive's tears:—
> Where groans are music in the savage ear,
> And wrecks of peaceful homes his daily cheers:—
> Where sad mementos of my own were found,
> And still my bleeding heart retains the wound.
> (*Garland* 54:35–36)

Still other captivity narratives are contrapuntal to sentimental
tales insofar as the female protagonists enjoy no domestic bliss to
be shattered by an Indian attack. Instead, the heroine is a naive
young woman who, either suffering sexual abuse or seduction by a
deceitful male, is the victim of a rapacious male. One of the
clearest instances of this type of work is the fictionalized *The True*

Narrative of the Five Years' Suffering and Perilous Adventures, by Miss Barber, Wife of "Squatting Bear," A Celebrated Sioux Chief (1872). Very loosely based on an actual event, which had caught the public's imagination and been widely covered in newspapers and magazines, this factual basis serves as a thin guise for a series of fictional romantic and Gothic tales, replete with affecting scenes of female virtue-in-distress. Miss Barber, a naive and idealistic young woman, has foolishly married an Indian, thinking that this would enable her to better spread the gospel among the western tribes. She is soon disillusioned, however, as her husband proves to be abusive and her married life one of drudgery. Worst of all, she discovers that her husband already has several wives.

The author seeks to correct several romantic fallacies, noting, for instance, "the *noble* Indian has nothing but ignoble wives. . . . the 'squaw' is forced, in most cases, to do all the manual labor, [and] is in fact a slave." Moreover, while "romance forms the greater part of the Indian nature . . . like many of their '*white* brethren,' the lover dies in giving birth to the husband." The social commentary here is directed at the white male as much as at the Indian, who is a transparent stand-in for the reprobate rakish male. Like so many other novels, this work warns young women to beware of men who are not what they appear to be.

Physically abused by her Indian husband, Miss Barber also becomes the object of unwanted sexual advances from other men. She is abducted by a French Canadian trader and carried to a cave in the wilderness (obviously inspired by Charles Brockden Brown), guarded by a hideous hunchback, the product of an interracial marriage. However, Barber is "providentially" rescued by an itinerant Methodist missionary and a sensitive Indian maiden. Later she is abducted by yet another Indian trader, whose attentions, she avers, were "of too free a nature to satisfy my sense of propriety." All of the action in this work revolves around the theme of innocence violated, which is replayed in a number of different sites and sometimes with a different cast of characters. The tale ends with the narrator directly addressing the reader: "If my narrative has proved interesting I am well satisfied, but if in its perusal some silly girl may change her mind regarding the noble red men and relinquished all thoughts of going among them, for any purpose whatever, then am I fully satisfied" (*Garland* 86:25, 97, 101).

Only occasionally does the reader of captivity narratives catch a glimpse of women who remained with the Indians of their own accord. The case of Frances Slocum, whose story was told in a melancholic fashion by the Rev. John Todd and many others, may be the most famous instance. Todd, a frequent contributor of advice literature to women's magazines, suggests that Slocum had gone native because she had lacked access to the Bible. In 1891 John Meginness still found "nothing in the annals of Indian history more pathetic and impressive than the story of the captivity, life, wanderings and death of Frances Slocum," yet he was able to appreciate some of the reasons why she decided to remain with the Indians. "Her reasons for not consenting to return were wise as well as strong, when viewed in their true light," he notes. "She would have been an object of curiosity and therefore ill at ease among strangers. Too old to adopt herself to the usages of civilized life, she clearly realized that her new condition would not be a happy one, and she aptly clinched the argument by comparing herself in that event to a 'fish out of water'—meaning that she would soon die." Meginness then continues, quoting one of the many romantic poems inspired by this white Indian. It appeals both to a form of environmental determinism and to nineteenth-century ideals of motherhood to justify Slocum's decision to stay with the Indians. At the same time, Slocum is a spokesperson for the nineteenth-century ideal of "nature religion," as she lives her life close to God in nature (*Garland* 58:69–70, "To the Reader").

In contrast to the highly romanticized and sentimental view of Indian life found in some captivities, a report from 1812, while secondhand at best, nevertheless rings true in terms of the reasons why a young female captive might choose to remain with the Indians. She did so because of the social disgrace and discrimination she would probably face in the white world. A female captive in the Mississippi Valley refused to return when she was ransomed by her father, explaining that "the Indians had disfigured her face, by tattooing it according to their fancy and ideas of beauty, and a young man of them had taken her for his wife, by whom she believed herself pregnant; that she had become reconciled to her mode of life, and was well treated by her husband; and that she should be more unhappy by returning to her father, under these circumstances, than by remaining where she was" (*Garland* 34:150–51).

If this anonymous young woman had been "scarred for life," this was so in a dual sense—the tatoos and scars on her body marked her in Indian society as occupying a specific social position and, thus, helped to mark her new identity; in white society these same bodily markings would have carried a negative moral significance.

She would have been a marked woman as certainly as Hester Prynne was with her scarlet *A*. In white society, she would no doubt have been widely viewed as damaged goods. Faced with this prospect, she made a rational and informed decision to remain with the Indians.

A speech put into the mouth of a white female captive in an 1858 work of fiction puts the situation such women faced in stark terms. It should be read as a critique of the real consequences of the hypocrisy of the moral values of the society and of the hollowness of many appeals to a providential theology. By elevating the moral value of female sexual purity to the level of sanctity, people have perverted both Christian theology and common sense by holding women responsible for events over which they have no control. In this scene the female captive, ill and resigned to dying, is speaking to the narrator, a male captive:

> "All my prospects for life have been blasted, and I have been reduced to a point of degradation that is revolting to my own mind, and that my conscience abhors. And although this has all come upon me without any fault of my own, but in opposition to my prayers, tears and agonized efforts to the contrary, yet the conscious innocence and purity of my life, prior to the dark hour when I became a victim to the unrestrained passions of a savage, condemns the degradation into which I have fallen, and refuses in the smallest degree to relinquish an iota of the sentence: thus rendering life to me a burden.
>
> "It is a truth in theology, no doubt, as well as in common sense, that we are only responsible for that over which we have or may have control. But, as it is equally true that whether degradation be brought upon us voluntarily or in opposition to our best efforts, and by means over which we have, or can have, no influence whatever, purity equally condemns the thing in either case. It is the eyes of purity which are constantly looking in upon this conscious sense of degradation, (although involuntarily), which poisons and renders offensive to my taste, the cup of life."
>
> Such were the candor and truthfulness of these remarks, that I dared not attempt to controvert or gainsay them. I told her that I hoped Providence would so shape our future, that we might have reason to rejoice in the knowledge that "all things work together for the good of those who love and serve Him." Expressing a wish that she might enjoy a good night's rest, I bade her farewell for the night, with thoughts more sombre than those with which I entered the tent. (*Garland* 74:106–7)

Literary critics today may call such popular dime novels trash, but we must realize that they provided an important vehicle for raising significant moral questions and mounting incisive cultural critiques. The moral poverty of appeals to divine providence in this situation is obvious, while the white male's "sombre" thoughts signal a serious questioning of the social viability of the ideal of the man of feeling in a world where a double moral standard for men and women operates. In works such as this, the captivity topos proved to be readily adaptable to this sort of cultural critique by casting these and other issues in sharp relief.

Women and Justified or Domesticated Violence

Some authors used the captivity narrative as a vehicle to reveal the inherent contradictions and tensions created by the high cultural value placed on female sexual purity and the gender construction of women as the weaker species. On the one hand, a woman was expected to protect her purity at all costs, but, on the other hand, she was to be soft and delicate, passive rather than aggressive. For many persons, female violence was something that had to be explained (or explained away).

A Surprizing Account of the Captivity of Miss Hannah Willis (1799) is characteristic of tales of women driven to perform acts of violence. In her retrospective account, the author recalls that, after she had been abducted and carried off to an Indian village, she learned that she was to be tortured and burned at the stake. Stripped naked, tied to a post, surrounded by whooping and dancing Indians, and certain she was about to die a horrible death, Willis swooned and lost consciousness, later awakening to find herself in an Indian hut. There she was soon faced with a painful question long associated with the vulnerability and essential powerlessness of women in white society: Was entering a coerced sexual relationship with a rapacious male indeed a fate worse than death? Or was it an acceptable, albeit unsavory, survival tactic? By dramatically posing such questions in imaginative works such as this, authors broached broader social issues of gender relations, power, and moral responsibility, while exposing the potential for male abuse of power within the patriarchal social system.

Delivered from the fire of the savage stake, Willis found herself cast into the flames of the intemperate passion of another exploitive male, her putative rescuer, a British officer. "I will endeavour to persuade [the Indians] to release you from this cruel alternative [of marrying one of them]," he said, "provided you will promise to

allow me two things,—1st that you will permit me to take what
liberties I please with you while I remain in this country, and 2d,
on my leaving it that you will go with me." Willis considered her
options: "To be given up to merciless savages to be murdered, was
a dreadful thought, and to prostitute myself, altho' shocking in the
extreme, was not so bad as to be tortured, I therefore resolved to
accept his offer" (*Garland* 24:8–9, 12).

Willis does not place her fate in the hands of divine providence
and resign herself to whatever might happen. Rather, she takes
matters into her own hands, locates a knife, and hides it. That
night, when the Englishman has fallen asleep, she plunges the
knife into his chest. The reader is led to view this as justifiable
homicide, as "injured innocence had obtained vengeance." Before
expiring, the man admits that he had intended to use Willis and
then throw her back to the Indians; moreover, he had been guilty
of this crime twice before.

The narrative ends with Willis offering a standard rationale for
telling her tale: "Expecting soon to leave this transitory world,—
soon to be arraign'd before the dreadful tribunal of my maker, I
consented to have this printed, that the world may see that God is
good, just and merciful" (*Garland* 24:10, 12). This effort to encom-
pass an act of female violence within a providential frame is akin
to that of Cotton Mather many years before.

The sentimental novel built on the tradition of Puritan compositional and reading practices, most especially in terms of narratively rehearsing the spiritual and emotional trials and tribulations in one's life. In spiritual diaries, individuals recorded their
trials and temptations and, when appropriate, their triumphs over
these; former captives often did much the same thing. Like Pamela, Willis can only become a model of virtue-in-distress by first
publicly rehearsing the sordid details of the improper sexual advances made to her and then displaying her resourcefulness in
preserving her purity. The audience must know all of the details of
her trials and afflictions before her actions (including her homici-
dal violence) can be seen to have been virtuous and moral.[19]

A brief anonymous work of 1815, *An Affecting Narrative of the
Captivity and Sufferings of Mrs. Mary Smith,* appears to be based
in large part on the Hannah Willis narrative. The intertextual
elements of direct borrowing are obvious, as is the highly stylized
nature of both texts, yet here the constituent elements of the
symbolic complex of the Amazon and pure female violence are
used to a significantly different effect. The Smith narrative is filled

with explicit scenes of the torture and deaths of Smith's husband and three children. More than was the case with the Willis narrative, it is a polemical anti-Indian piece. Having just witnessed the torture and death of her entire family, Smith learns that she is to be spared if she agrees to replace the Indian chief's deceased wife. Neither Willis nor Mary Smith is presented as a model of perfect resignation; neither woman chooses to die rather than to accept the proposals made to them. Instead, each considers trading her body for her life.

At the same time, neither woman enters the arrangement from the start as a deliberate ruse; rather, each acts after a quick consideration of the options available to her. One hears echoes of Mary Rowlandson's early confession concerning what she had done when faced with a similar dilemma—"I had often before this said, that if the Indians should come, I should chuse rather to be killed by them, than taken alive: but when it came to the trial my mind changed: their glittering Weapons so daunted my Spirit, that I chose rather to go along with those (as I may say) ravenous Bears, than that moment to end my daies" (*Garland* 1:2). The ideal held up for women from the seventeenth century down through the nineteenth was obviously easier to mouth in the comfort and security of the city than it was to act out on the frontier. It should not surprise us that some women were reluctant to embrace the ideal of the beautiful death.

The women here are represented as rational beings, rather than as merely instinctual creatures of feeling. Given time to reflect on her situation, each woman weighs her options and the relative risks and costs of each of these, and then decides to take a calculated risk in order to avoid an unwanted sexual relationship. As a result, female violence is represented as a logical and laudable response to the situation each woman faced, not as a bizarre aberration of nature.

The broader cultural symbolic complex that developed around the figure of the Amazon is more clearly in evidence in other works of fiction. *Gertrude Morgan: or, Life and Adventures Among the Indians of the Far West* (1866), an anonymous work of popular fiction, illustrates yet another way the captivity topos, racial stereotypes, and the existing gender expectations could all be used in a specific combination to comment on broader social issues. According to this story, Gertrude was captured in 1855 on her way to California to meet her husband, who had made his fortune there in the recent goldrush. The only member of the wagon train to survive an Indian attack, she reportedly spent the next eleven years among the Indians, but, significantly enough, without suffering any sexual assault from the Indians. The reader is led to understand that this exceptional fact was due to a fortuitous event that had occurred shortly after Gertrude was taken. In a twist on a popular pattern found in male captivities, Gertrude had come to be viewed by the Indians as a sacred (and, thus, sacrosanct) person after she had managed to heal her captor from a gunshot wound.

Gertrude does not, however, escape all unwanted sexual attention. When the Indian warriors are all away on a raid, an escaped mulatto slave, who had gone Indian, attempts to take advantage of her. Gertrude valiantly resists the physical advances of "the ignorant and sensual brute," twice managing to escape her "foe in the very act of clasping [her] in his foul embrace." When "with demon-like rage the monster" leaps toward her, "almost involuntarily" she seizes a spear on which the man impales himself (*Garland* 79:24, 27–28).

It is no accident that the first such black Indian (actually a mulatto) appears as a literary character in a captivity narrative in the 1860s. In the wake of the Emancipation Proclamation and the Civil War, many whites feared that former slaves might seek revenge upon those who had enslaved and exploited them. This general anxiety expressed itself most strongly in the fear of sexual assaults upon white women by men of color, which later fed the crowd psychology behind racial lynchings. With the figure of the black man functioning as the dangerous sexual Other, the Indian could be freed from playing this role. Gertrude declares that while tales of white women being raped by Indians are a mainstay of romances, this never actually occurs in Indian societies. Among the Indians "the crime of ravishing captive women, so common and hellish a vice among civilized nations, is entirely unknown. This statement may dissipate the romance many writers have imparted to their stories of the Indians and beautiful white captive maidens, but it is nevertheless a fact. An American savage will mercilessly butcher white women, but a wild and chivalous [sic] honor deters him from ravishing or scalping them" (*Garland* 79:29). This understanding is in sharp contrast to innumerable opinions offered on the subject over the centuries. In one of the more bizarre extensions of providential theology, one late eighteenth-century author suggested that white women were not molested by Indians because the latter were providentially undersexed (*Garland* 13:5–6).

It is likely that male and female readers (or members of the audience for plays and works of ideal sculpture) responded to the literary figures of violent women differently. Whereas many men found such figures to be unnatural and out of place in their ordered social world and, consequently, imaginatively projected them into the sphere of the alien and exotic Other, some female readers imagined a universal sisterhood through such female heroines. While many men had difficulty acknowledging the presence of such strong women in their own culture and homes, women knew that they were there, even if they had not always found their way into history books.

The sentimental fantasy of female virtue-in-distress in its purest form asserted that the weak and the innocent could gain control over dangerous situations by exposing their vulnerability and helplessness to their persecutors and calling upon their natural sympathy. Women were taught survival skills and strategies based upon the New Testament promise that "the meek shall inherit the earth." Yet in the face of numerous and undeniable real-life instances of the failure of this strategy and, to the contrary, of women effectively using violence, writers and readers had to revaluate the practicality of this defense strategy and the universality and naturalness of Western understandings of gender.

The difficulty in trying to reconcile these two images of the female may be glimpsed in a scene from a mid-nineteenth-century popular novel entitled *The Dreadful Sufferings and Thrilling Adventures of an Overland Party of Emigrants to California*. There, in a story-within-a story, the reader is introduced to Teresa, a young woman happily married to a trader and the mother of a small son. A few years earlier, the young couple had sought refuge in the Texas wilderness from the continual harassment from a spurned suitor of Teresa's.

One day, while her husband is absent on a trading trip, this spurned suitor, Munoz, who has become a notorious bandit, shows up. In this scene, the cultural ideal or fantasy of the power of feminine virtue to reform even the seemingly most reprobate male is played out, even as the threat of maternal-female violence in defense of a child and a woman's own purity is recognized as a real option for the woman. Finally, a noble suicide is presented as a last desperate option should the male offender prove to be without any feelings and, thus, immune to the powers of feminine innocence, vulnerability, and moral appeals. All three of the available cultural resources for protecting the woman and her family are appealed to here—the cult of virtue-in-distress, Christian values, and armed resistance. Fortunately, behind his public persona of a desperado, Munoz is still a man of feeling. Confronted by Teresa's virtue and innocence, he begs her to save his soul and promises to become an honest man again (*Garland* 63:46).

The successful conclusion of the sentimental fantasy of the power of female virtue in times of distress ultimately depended upon the humanity of the male offender. Given this situation, the topos of Indian captivity provided a ready vehicle for casting individuals and peoples as moral human beings, to a lesser or greater degree, or, alternatively, as inhuman and utterly immoral. American Indians could be represented in numerous ways across the spectrum of possibilities, ranging from the cold-hearted savage to the romantic noble savage. In the real world of cultural contact, interracial relations, and male-female sexual and marital relations, the situation was more complicated and messy than the sentimental ideal suggested. Nevertheless, through captivity tales writers and readers were able to explore, imaginatively and critically, society, gender roles and identities, and the possibilities for changing these.

The Utopian Captivity

Far from the American frontier, British authors could thoroughly romanticize life as a white Indian. *The Contrast* (1830) expresses a nostalgia for a Christian utopian world or a paradisiacal state on earth by imagining voluntarily going native as a possible way of returning to this state. Through such works, some writers and readers expressed reservations over the human and spiritual costs of civilization. Convinced that Christendom has lost its way, the author of *The Contrast* imagines an ideal Indian society as a critical counter to Western civilization. In their fallen state, all humans are doomed to a life of violence and bloodletting as long as they do not take the Bible as their guide (*Garland* 47:43).

If our Puritan predecessors had failed to establish a Christian city on a hill in New England, readers were presented with a utopian fantasy in which its sylvan equivalent was found in a spiritual community in a hidden valley of western New York. The Christian Indian embodies a distinct variant of the noble savage— the primitive Christian. As the main character says, "I was now got among a people by whom Christianity was understood and practiced, in more of its native simplicity than I had ever yet witnessed" (*Garland* 47:57).

The Contrast marks one of the last extended expressions of this sort of Christian utopianism, which could only be sustained at a distance from the historical reality of Indian-white relations. The sad history of Christian missions to American Indian peoples was, from the perspectives of both whites and Native Americans, largely a history of failure and misunderstanding, though obviously for different reasons. This history, coupled with the bloody final conflicts and massive dislocations of Indians on the plains in the second half of the nineteenth century, meant that few persons from either side were able to imagine seriously the possibility of a utopian community of this sort.[20]

6

INSIDE THE HOUSE
OF MIRRORS:
THE CONTINUING SEARCH
FOR AUTHENTICITY

The Indians, with their music, dance and ritual, are constantly striving to escape their material lives into the spiritual world. In making a movie we take the material elements of our society and transmute them into a stream of light flowing on to a wall, hoping that it will contain something of *our* spirit. As Takuma [a Kamaiura shaman] said, he and I do much the same work.—John Boorman

Every man has a right to create his own savage for his own purposes. Perhaps every man does. But to demonstrate that such a constructed savage corresponds to Australian Aborigines, African Tribesmen, or Brazilian Indians is another matter altogether.—Clifford Geertz

THE TWENTIETH CENTURY has been unique in terms of the history of the captivity narrative. By the end of the nineteenth century, Indian captivity as a historical reality had disappeared from the North American continent. Captivity, like the great Indian nations and the buffalo herds that had once covered the vast plains, quickly become a thing of the past, the stuff of lore and legend. Yet captivity tales continue to be told in great numbers in novels, short stories, plays, juvenile literature, works of history, historical pageants and reenactments, and films.

We continue to be captured by captivity texts and images from the past, imbricated in a complex intertextual history of narrations and readings that create and recreate diverse and even contradictory meanings of the loss of autonomy, suffering, human identity, and authenticity. The captivity topos continues to be employed as a means of imaginatively reflecting on the possibility of identity transformation and going native, while the wilderness and the Indian-as-Other remain important imaginative constructs through which we project our fears, fantasies, and nostalgias onto the world. Some captivity tales critique aspects of the modern world; others press environmental concerns or theological or ideological agendas.

In the twentieth century, issues of authenticity, which had hovered around Indian captivity from the beginning, have emerged as major points of contention. Authenticity in terms of the reliability of authors and narrators, authenticity in terms of identity (individual, cultural, sexual, and racial), authenticity in terms of the existential situation one assumes in the world. In this chapter, selected works of fiction, films, and scholarly studies will be used to illustrate how the captivity topos has been variously employed to address these issues.

Heretofore, film has not played a role in our study, nor has the work of academics been a major focus. In the twentieth century, however, Hollywood and the academy have both become important arbiters of authenticity and reality through the stories they tell. Ironically, Hollywood, that most inauthentic of all places, has come to produce important vehicles for cultural reflection that have reached hundreds of millions, while the academy has told and analyzed captivity tales in ever more specialized jargon for a small, largely professional audience.[1] Between 1903 and 1970 there were at least twenty-five films that dealt with whites who lived with the Indians or had been raised by them; there were ninety-two films concerning white captives, twenty-two of which featured male captives, while seventy featured female captives.[2]

The main focus here will be on representations of captivity from the second half of the twentieth century. Nevertheless, a brief word about the preceding decades is in order. By and large, in the early decades of the century it was the then-recent history of genocidal violence on the northern plains that was most often remembered and rehearsed in heroic terms in works of historical fiction, in historical scholarship, even the play of children. Today the popular image of the American Indian is composed of a symbolic complex with specific ethnographic details (teepees, eagle-feather headdresses, horse-riding warriors, buffalo hunts, the Vow to the Sun ritual) from the northern plains cultural area—that is, precisely the area where the final Indian wars were fought in the late nineteenth century. In this sort of history of the wild West, the heroes are Kit Carson, General Custer, and Buffalo Bill, while the Indians are merely their foils.[3]

For many persons, the porous nature of the social and cultural boundaries that had existed between whites and Indians on the American frontiers was represented as an unfortunate, if often unavoidable, element of the civilizing process and life on the frontier.[4] White Indians such as John Dunn Hunter and John Tanner virtually vanished from American history texts or were dismissed as impostors, liars, and opportunists. While historians were not unaware of the existence of such persons, they rarely made them the subjects of serious study. To be sure, those who had gone native seldom left a paper trail. A more important reason for this neglect was that white Indians and going primitive went against the "natural" flow in the triumphant tellings of the history of European discovery, conquest, and settlement of the New World. As a result, white Indians were either portrayed as idiosyncratic individuals and historical oddities, or, alternatively, as despicable and immoral renegades or "squaw men."

Carl Coke Rister's 1940 volume of retellings of captivity tales from the southern plains is typical of the way in which racist assumptions distorted the historical vision of many Americanists earlier in this century. According to Rister, cultural contact and conflict in North America had "strengthened certain [preexistent] racial traits" among both whites and Indians, including the Indians' avarice and vindictiveness. Rister denied, of course, that his representation of the Indian was racist or anything other than objective: "If our narrative reveals the nomadic Indian as primitive, savage, and vindictive, and in these respects quite unlike the heroic warrior as pictured by James Fenimore Cooper, it should be remembered that his environment would make him so. . . . the author does not seek to condemn or to condone; he is only interested in picturing the red man as he was, and as he created a cultural problem."[5] Through the 1950s white Indians, too, posed a cultural problem for historians of Rister's ilk and for popular authors and filmmakers.

At the same time, after Indian cultures had been largely destroyed and, thus, were no longer serious competitors to Euro-American culture, the figure of the Indian could be recast and freely incorporated into new pedagogical projects. For instance, a very different image of the Indian was incorporated into programs of moral education for children in the first decades of the century.

A number of major youth groups adopted a version of the noble Indian as a model for the physical, spiritual, and moral education of the young. For instance, Ernest Thompson Seton, the founder of the Boy Scouts of America, designed this organization's programs around activities modeled on Indian life and skills (camping, hiking, survival skills, firemaking, woodcarving). In response to a suggestion from Rudyard Kipling, Seton first presented his ideals in the form of a novel, *Two Little Savages: Being the Adventures of Two Boys Who Lived as Indians, and What They Learned* (1903). In Seton's hands, the Indian became a paradigmatic figure for white children, because he

> was brave; he was obedient to authority. He was kind, clean and reverent. He was provident, unsordid, hospitable, dignified, courteous, truthful, and honest. He was the soul of honor. He lived a life of temperance and physical culture that he might perfect his body, and so he achieved a splendid physique. He was a wonderful hunter, a master of woodcraft, and a model for outdoor life in this country. He was heroic and picturesque all the time. He knew nothing of the forgiveness of sin, but he remembered his Creator all the days of his life, and was in truth one of the finest types of men the world has ever known.[6]

By and large, the values projected onto the Indian by Seton were mainstream Western cultural, moral, and religious values. He propagated this image of the Indian in order to combat what he saw as the enervating aspects of urbanization and modernization. In doing so, he brought together the late nineteenth-century emphasis on physical fitness as a prerequisite for a healthy mind, a belief in the health benefits of exercise outdoors from the Teddy Roosevelt era, and the traditional romantic image of the Indian as noble savage. The Boy Scouts and the Campfire Girls were two of many youth groups that invited children to go native in a controlled program of spiritual, moral, and physical fitness.

Through such organizations, many thousands of children were able to enjoy the life of a white Indian through organized and validated forms of playing Indian. In concert with this growing movement, stories of Indian life and white Indians proliferated in juvenile literature, comics, novels, and later in film. It is important to note that tales of Indian captivity, such as Seton's *Two Little Savages*, and of voluntarily going native were frequently told as part of a larger project of moral education. These stories differed from the nineteenth-century juvenile works introduced earlier in that they did not flaunt the absolute superiority of Christianity and Euro-American culture. Implicitly (and frequently explicitly), Indian culture and spiritual values were affirmed as worthy of emulation, even if the content of what was taught often had little to do with actual Indian societies and religious traditions.

A White Indian Scorned: The Case of Grey Owl

We will turn in a moment to look at John Ford's film "The Searchers" and Conrad Richter's novel *The Light in the Forest* as exemplars of two very different mid-century castings of the captivity topos. First, though, let us recall briefly the meteoric literary career of an Indian author in the 1930s when it was revealed that he was not really (i.e., racially) an Indian. The ways in which the possibility of going native have been imaginatively embraced or, alternatively, denied in this century can provide important insight into the modern and postmodern moments of Western culture.

Grey Owl, whose works were bestsellers on both sides of the Atlantic in the late 1930s, was vehemently attacked as an impostor after his death in 1938. He was born Archibald S. Belaney in Hastings, England, in 1888. As a child he had been infatuated with American Indians, voraciously devouring "boys' novels and the paper-covered penny dreadfuls of the day, these being chiefly stories about Red Indians which had had a great success with boys in the early years of this century."[7] Raised by spinster aunts, the boy had studied everything he could about North American Indians and created an imaginary world into which he frequently retreated, pretending to be an Indian, skulking through the woods, and camping outdoors. Except for the intensity of his interest, he was no different from thousands of other boys of the age.

At seventeen Belaney left England for Canada, where he lived with various Indian groups, learning to hunt, fish, track, and trap as they did. Gradually, he went native—playing Indian for real, if you will—as he lived as a trapper, guide, and forest ranger in the Canadian wilderness. Eventually, he began writing about his life in the woods and the creatures there, becoming a naturalist, a preservationist, and, *avant la lettre,* an environmentalist. In the last few years of his life, he came to enjoy great success with the public as an author and speaker, as he carried a message of the need for protecting the wilderness and wildlife. Through his vivid stories of his life in the wilderness, which recalled for millions of readers a time and a way of life that was fast disappearing when men and the animals all lived as one with the land, Grey Owl became a powerful spokesman for environmental awareness and natural conservation.[8]

Grey Owl was, in many ways, an early incarnation of the ecologically correct Indian, a native appealing to a romantic nostalgia for a simpler, purer life in nature, while criticizing the capitalist values of materialism, property, consumerism, and the exploitation of natural resources for economic gain. Called "an Indian Thoreau" by the press, Grey Owl had quickly come to realize that his voice had greater authority in the white world when people believed him to be an Indian. When he spoke of the immanent destruction of a simpler way of life, for instance, and of the possible extinction of the beaver at the hands of white interlopers who carelessly and senselessly exploited the bounty of the land, upsetting the delicate ecological balance in the wilderness, it was Grey Owl's presence as an Indian that evoked a flood of sympathy from his audiences. As an Indian, he was a living reminder of the recent tragic history of death, destruction, and cultural disruption among the Indians, which had been caused by the whites and the ideology of progress. Yet Grey Owl's very presence, the fact that he and the wilderness he so vividly described had seemingly survived, even if tenuously, held out the promise that perhaps things could still be saved and put right. Grey Owl's editor put his finger on another source of his popularity: "To be an Indian! What he laid claim to, some at least of his English audiences also longed for imaginatively. Through him they could live that existence momentarily."[9]

While people were willing to accept Grey Owl and his message when he was believed to be an Indian, many of them rejected the possibility that he could be an authentic Indian (or even an authentic spokesman for Native Americans) if he was not racially an Indian. This rejection is emblematic (if not symptomatic) of the age: human value, worth, and authenticity were to be determined by race. Blood or genetics, rather than the quality of an individual's life or mind, were what mattered. The vicious posthumous attacks on Grey Owl as a fake and an impostor came precisely in the period when the tragic consequences of racism and the failure of the sympathetic imagination in Germany, the fascist states, and elsewhere were being played out. The ability to imagine oneself into the situation of another person and to sympathize with that person has long been recognized as necessary for moving oneself to moral action. Native Americans wisely spoke of "walking a mile in another's moccasins," while Adam Smith, Hume, and others held the sympathetic imagination to be the basis of morality. The inability or unwillingness to recognize and to respond to the pain and suffering of others is a fundamental contributing factor in the dehumanization or demonization of other human beings.

John Ford's "The Searchers"

John Ford's film "The Searchers" (1956) is a classic western complete with the requisite black-and-white conflict between good and evil, sharply drawn gender roles, an ongoing conflict between the feminine world of domesticity and the fierce independence of the lone itinerant hero, as well as a virulent racism and a horror of miscegenation.[10] The end of the film, however, registers a perceptible shift in the public's view away from a total repudiation of white Indians.

"The Searchers" is based on the novel of the same title by Alan LeMay. The movie concerns a search conducted over many years for a young girl, Debbie, abducted by Comanche Indians in Texas in 1868. The film opens with stirring Indian music in the background. As the credits role, a cowboy ditty introduces the theme of the western hero as a loner and a wanderer ill at ease in the domestic world of women. After the credits fade, the screen goes black. The first visual image to appear is a rear silhouetted shot of a woman opening a door; a yellow light outside illuminates a desert landscape; the sides and the top of the screen (the door frame) are dark. The camera then follows the woman through the door onto a porch and into the light, pans quickly over the landscape of Monument Valley before reversing direction and focusing on the woman, shading her eyes with a raised hand as she searches the plain. The camera then cuts back to her line of sight and picks up a lone horseman in the distance wending his way toward the cabin.

The opening delineates two spaces—the domestic space, which is primarily feminine, and the vast open spaces, the realm of the masculine.[11] A family reunion follows and the main characters are quickly introduced. The lone rider is Ethan (John Wayne), returning to his brother Aron's farm in Texas after serving in the Confederate army in the Civil War. The farm family consists of Aron, his wife, a son, two daughters (the teenaged Lucy and Debbie, aged seven or eight), and Martin (Jeffrey Hunter), a young man who had been adopted as a small child after his family were massacred by Indians.

When Martin comes into the house wearing buckskin, the viewer gets the first hint of Ethan's racial prejudice. Looking critically at Martin, he says with disdain, "A fella could mistake you for a half-breed." Martin naively responds, "Not quite. I'm an eighth Cherokee, the rest Welsh and English, or so I'm told." The movie then moves quickly to set up the plot and establish the characters. Sam Clayburn (Ward Bond), the local preacher and head of the Texas Rangers, informs everyone that Indians have stolen a herd of cattle from a neighbor. He deputizes the men, forms a posse, and they set out to teach the Indians a lesson. When the men come across the slaughtered carcasses of the cattle, Ethan immediately realizes that they have been tricked by the Indians, who had used this ruse to draw the men away from the farms, leaving them defenseless. Ethan and Martin rush back, but are too late; they find the farmhouse and outbuildings burned to the ground and all of the inhabitants killed, except for the two girls who have been taken captive.

Thereafter the horror of miscegenation haunts the film. After giving the dead a decent burial, the men are off again in pursuit of the Indians. Several days later Ethan discovers Lucy's body in the desert, but he refuses to describe the condition of her corpse. The clear implication, conveyed by appealing to the audience's intertextual knowledge and familiarity with earlier tales of Indian atrocities and "what they do with white women," is that she had been raped and mutilated.

This same theme surfaces again in another scene set months later as the search for Debbie has proved futile. Ethan, speaking of Debbie, says, "If she's alive, she's safe. For a while. They'll keep her to raise as one of their own, until she's an age to . . ." His voice trails off, yet the horror is palpable if unspoken.

When Ethan and Martin come across some female captives who have been brought to an army fort, the women are physically scarred and mentally crazed by what they have endured. "It's hard to believe they're white," a cavalryman comments. "They ain't white anymore. They're Comanche," Ethan responds. For Ethan— and, as the hero, he carries the film's burden—a white woman who has had sexual relations with an Indian, even against her will, is no longer a white woman; she has become a dirty savage. Indeed, as far as Ethan is concerned, Debbie is in a sense already dead. "Livin' with the Comanches ain't bein' alive," he asserts.

Later, Ethan denies that Debbie is kin, because "she's been livin' with a buck." He simply assumes that Debbie and her captor, a chief named Scar, have a sexual relationship. Such a sexual relationship would have been highly unlikely, however. Since Debbie had been raised in Scar's family after her abduction, she would have been considered a family member (probably Scar's adoptive daughter) and, thus, any sexual relationship between them would have been considered incestuous. The fact that the screenwriter ignored this is a tipoff that a racist ideological intention has overridden simple ethnographic facts.

Scar is in some ways Ethan's double. His virulent hatred of whites mirrors Ethan's hatred of the Indians, for his own children had been killed by whites. Like Ethan, he too is an outsider in his own society, leading a band of renegades. The theme of the horror of miscegenation is rehearsed again after Ethan and Martin have returned to the Jorgenson farm, where the daughter, Laurie (Vera Miles), is smitten with Martin and has long been trying to get him to settle down with her. When news comes that Scar has been spotted nearby, Martin jumps up to pursue him again and the following dialogue takes place, blending the theme of "a man's gotta do what he's gotta do" with that of the social and ontological consequences of miscegenation for a white female:

Laurie: Martin, you're not goin'. Not this time.

Martin: Are you crazy?

Laurie: It's too late. She's a woman grown now.

Martin: But I gotta go, Laurie. I gotta fetch her home.

Laurie: Fetch what home? The leavin's o' Comanche bucks sold time and again to the highest bidder, with savage breasts of her own . . .

Martin: Laurie, shut up!

Laurie: Do you know what Ethan will do if he gets a chance? He'll put a bullet in her brain. I tell you, Martha [Debbie's deceased mother] would've wanted him to.

In the end, of course, Martin goes after Scar. At dawn, just before the cavalry is about to attack Scar's village, Martin sneaks into Debbie's teepee to "fetch her home." She agrees to go with him, but just then Scar appears and Martin is forced to shoot him, alerting the village to his presence. In the ensuing cavalry charge, Debbie attempts to flee; Ethan spies her and sets off in pursuit, while Martin frantically screams for him to stop. Then, just as the audience expects Ethan to kill Debbie, he scoops her up, saying, "Let's go home, Debbie."

The scene suddenly shifts to the Jorgenson home, where the women on the porch again await the men's return. Laurie rushes out to embrace Martin, while Ethan carries Debbie into the house. Martin and Laurie enter the house hand-in-hand, symbolizing the restoration and renewal of domesticity, as another stanza of the cowboy song, "The Searchers," is heard on the soundtrack:

> A man will search his heart and soul,
> Go searchin' way out there.
> His peace of mind he knows he'll find,
> But, where O Lord? O where?
> Ride away. Ride away. Ride away.

The final shot of the film replicates the structure of the opening one, though with an opposite movement through space. Through the dark portal of the house, the audience sees Ethan silently turn away from the reunion scene and walk off alone into the distance. John Wayne, the epitome of a "real man," had brought the ideology of the classical Western to life on the screen for millions yet again.

"The Searchers" exemplifies the classic western, which represents the Indian as a brutal and rapacious savage. There is no serious attempt to understand Indian culture or to appreciate the perspective of the Native Americans. The Indian functions as a cardboard villain in the heroic saga of the white settling of the West and the civilizing process, as well as an excuse for a sustained diatribe against miscegenation. Yet the audience is left with the feeling that everything will be all right. The Comanche have been killed or herded into stockades and reservations; Martin and Laurie will get married and raise a family; and the western hero is still free to roam but will return to set the world right if and when the need rises. And if the rape of white women was an inevitable, if unfortunate, fact of life on the frontier, perhaps it too contributed to the civilizing process by provoking the righteous and purifying violence of the white male directed against the Indians.

Conrad Richter's The Light in the Forest

If Ford's "The Searchers" represents the remarkable staying power of the Western with its strong anti-Indian bias and fear of miscegenation, Conrad Richter's best-selling novel *The Light in the*

Forest (1953), epitomizes a countervailing tradition of romanticizing the Indian and life in the wilderness, which we will also find in "The Emerald Forest" and "Dances with Wolves." Richter's novel centers around the life of a teenaged boy, Johnny Butler, named "True Son" by the Lenni Lenape who had abducted him eleven years earlier in western Pennsylvania. Richter acknowledges having drawn upon historical works, such as Heckewelder's *Indian Nations* and Zeisberger's *History of North American Indians*, in writing his novel. But, speaking of himself in the third-person, he asserts that his intention was not to write a historical novel but rather "to give an authentic sensation of life in early America. In the records of the Eastern border, the author was struck by the numbers of returned white captives who tried desperately to run away from their flesh-and-blood families and return to their Indian foster homes and the Indian mode of life. As a small boy he himself had tried to run off to Indian country without the benefit of ever having lived among the savages."[12]

Richter's childhood dream of joining the Indians was shared by many other youngsters who grew up with magazine articles, short stories, and novels depicting the exciting lives of Indians and white Indians, and as members of clubs like the Boy Scouts or Campfire Girls. Unlike Archibald Belaney, Richter never went native permanently, yet as an adult he believed that people could do so imaginatively through literature. In his carefully crafted captivity tale, he sought to recreate an imaginative and affectively charged experience in his readers, "an authentic sensation of life in early America." He had full faith in the power of fiction to engage the imaginative faculties of readers in such a way that they could assume the existential position in the world of another person distant in time and space. Richter's understanding of the phenomenology of the act of reading shares a great deal with that of the first novelists, the sentimental writers of the eighteenth century. Through an act of historical anamnesis and identification with literary characters achieved in the act of reading (i.e., through a reverse form of metempsychosis), people could share the intellectual and somatic experience of other human beings.

The Light in the Forest belongs to the venerable tradition of works using the captivity topos to critique aspects of modernity, urbanization, and industrialization. In Richter's own words:

> If the novel has another purpose, it is to point out that in the pride of
> our American liberties, we're apt to forget that already we've lost a

good many to civilization. The American Indians once enjoyed far more than we. Already two hundred years ago, when restrictions were comparatively with us, our ideals and restrained manner of existence repelled the Indian. I thought that perhaps if we understood how these First Americans felt toward us even then and toward our white way of life, we might better understand the adverse, if perverted, view of us by some African, European, and Asian peoples today.[13]

Like Grey Owl and others before him, Richter extolled the freedom and pleasures of life in the woods. A nostalgia pervades the novel, which depicts this way of life precisely at the time it was coming to an end. Richter asks the reader to face the bitter irony that through captivity some persons had found a freedom, while others who considered themselves to be free were in fact unwitting captives of modern capitalism. The epigraph, a quotation from Wordsworth, first sounds this note:

> Shades of the prison-house begin to close
> Upon the growing Boy,
> But he beholds the light, and whence it flows,
> He sees it in his joy.

This theme is addressed more fully in a dialogue between Bejance, an elderly black slave, and Johnny Butler's little brother, Gordie. Bejance had himself been abducted by Wyandotte Indians as a child, but had subsequently been rescued at the age of twenty by an army officer, who became his master. The irony of the situation is not lost on the old man as he responds to Gordie's observation that he is a slave:

"I reckon I am, child," he agreed equably. "And so are you and your brother, though you don't know it yet. Now I know it too well. For nigh onto sixty years I been wantin' to go fishin' in the spring and summer, and huntin' fall and winter. But every spring and summer I had to work in the fields and every fall and winter in the woods. Now when I kain't work in the woods and fields no more, I kain't go out huntin' or fishin' neither. All I'm good for is sit on my bench and braid up hampers for the white folks."

"You're not free like us," Gordie declared.

"No. I'm never free from white folks," the Negro assented. "And neither are you and your brother. Every day they drop another fine

strap around you. Little by little they buckle you up so you don't feel
it too much at one time. Sooner or later they have you all hitched up,
but you've got so used to it by that time you hardly know it. You eat
with a fork and spoon. You sleep in a bed. You own a house and a
piece of land and pays taxes. You hoe all day in the cornfield and toil
and sweat a diggin' up stumps. Piece by piece you get broke in to
livin' in a stall by night, and by day pullin' burdens that mean
nothin' to the soul inside of you."[14]

The ironic equation that Indian captivity leads to a renewed life
of freedom, while life in white, modern capitalist society is a
terrible form of unconscious captivity is found throughout the
novel, which ends on a note of tragic loss as True Son is irrevocably
returned to the white world against his will. The scene recalls the
expulsion from Eden after the Fall: "Ahead of him ran the rutted
road of the whites. It led, he knew, to where men of their own
volition constrained themselves with heavy clothing like harness,
where men chose to be slaves to their own or another's property
and followed empty and desolate lives far from the wild beloved
freedom of the Indian."[15] As we shall see, this same mythic structure informs the film "The Emerald Forest," released three decades later.

Little Big Man

The romanticizing of Indian Life found in *The Light in the Forest*
is extended in Thomas Berger's novel *Little Big Man* (1964), and in
the Arthur Penn film adaptation (1971), yet the same nostalgia for
the Indian's "wild beloved freedom" is not central here. Rather,
Berger parodies the captivity genre, while raising issues of language, narrative representation, and authenticity. The novel is
filled with incidents and forms of phrasing borrowed from earlier
captivity narratives, as well as examples of southwestern humor.
Berger incorporated large amounts of ethnographic detail, which
earned both the novel and the film praise for their convincing
realism.[16] When the film was released, some viewers interpreted it
as a veiled commentary on the Vietnam war, then raging and
playing on the nightly television news broadcasts. Scenes of the
massacre of the inhabitants of Indian villages, including women,
children, and the elderly, recalled recent images of the My Lai
massacre.[17]

Little Big Man is purportedly the transcription of a first-person account spoken into a tape recorder in 1953 by Jack Crabb, an old man living in a retirement home. Crabb claims to be 111 years old and the sole survivor of Custer's Last Stand. He is not your typical narrator for a captivity tale, however, for he is an unreliable narrator. Berger puts his own name on the cover of the novel and thus claims authorship for *Little Big Man* as a work of fiction. Yet inside he creates an editor (one Ralph Fielding Snell) who offers the reader the narrative proper as a direct transcription of the tapes of Crabb's oral account.

Snell describes his role in bringing the tale to the public as little more than a "catalytic function." Yet while he claims that the narrative is a faithful transcription of the tapes, Crabb is not presented as necessarily reliable. His reliability remains in question throughout the text, as doubts on the subject are raised by Snell in the "Foreword by a Man of Letters" and again in his "Editor's Epilogue," where he addresses the reader directly: "So, as I take my departure, dear reader, I leave the choice in your capable hands. Jack Crabb was either the most neglected hero in the history of this country or a liar of insane proportions. In either case, may the Everywhere Spirit have mercy on his soul, and yours, and mine."[18]

For his part, Jack Crabb takes notice of the multitude of conflicting accounts of Custer's Last Stand, or the Battle of the Little Bighorn, including those of a Crow scout, of army officers from nearby fields of action, contemporary newspaper accounts, and the work of twentieth-century historians. Finally, however, he dismisses all of these as unreliable and appeals to his own unique status as the only surviving white eyewitness to authenticate his account. Scars on his body are offered as proof of his having been wounded at Little Big Horn.[19]

Berger's work reflects a growing suspicion in the 1960s of the power of language to recapture the reality of the past. The self-assured confidence in language exuded by Richter a decade earlier has become suspect. Berger seeks to disabuse his reader of the naive assumption that language and narrative representation are neutral agencies, or mirrors, which accurately reflect reality. He leads his reader into a narrative house of mirrors. At the end of the work, the reader is situated in the middle of a series of representations all offered as true, yet because the reader's position is radically decentered and the narrative voice unreliable, it is impossible to distinguish the real from the reflections, facts from talltales.

As Snell notes, "It is of course unlikely that one man would have experienced even a third of Mr. Crabb's claim. Half? Incredible! All? A mythomaniac! But you will find, as I did, that if any one part is accepted as truth, then what precedes and follows has as great a lien on our credulity. If he knew Wild Bill Hickok, then why not General Custer as well? The case is similar when we suspect his veracity at a certain point: then why should he be reliable anywhere?" The reader feels the ground of meaning shifting under him; his sense of center disappears. This state, Berger implies, characterizes the modern Western condition. As Old Lodge Skins observes, whites "do not seem to know where the center of the world is."[20]

Yet while the reader is trapped in a narrative house of mirrors, in an important sense he is also liberated from the constraints of a determined past or identity. Like Jack Crabb, who is able to relive his many lives through his memories (or, if these are talltales, then through his imagination), the reader is invited to suspend his disbelief and skepticism for a brief moment in order to enter into the world of the novel and its imaginative play. Through the story of the life—or, better, lives—of Jack Crabb, the reader is led to reflect on the fluidity and the seeming fickleness of identity. Crabb moves rather easily back and forth between the white and Indian worlds and between his social identities as Jack Crabb and Little Big Man. Moreover, he assumes a series of different occupational identities at different points of his life—white Indian, shopkeeper, gunslinger, con man with a snake oil medicine show, muleskinner, drunkard, and army scout—which he wears rather lightly, putting them on and taking them off as his immediate needs and situations change. It is only the continuity of the narrative voice that ties all of them together, and that voice leads the reader to believe (or at least to imagine the possibility) that Jack Crabb could have assumed all of these identities and done so with a certain personal integrity—and yet this narrative voice is unreliable.

In a humorous yet touching fashion, Berger raises a series of issues of authenticity. Jack's account of how his sister, Caroline, had grossly misread the Indians' intentions toward her, while they had misunderstood her actions and intentions towards them, is a case in point. After a band of drunk Cheyenne Indians killed some members of the wagon train and raped some of the women, Caroline fell under the illusion that she had not been raped because the Indians were "saving her" for later. In fact, Jack recalls, Caroline was a tomboy who had never had any luck with men and the Indians had not realized that she was a woman! The comedy of errors continued when, after sobering up, the Indians brought horses to the survivors as compensation for their actions, yet Caroline assumed that they had returned to purchase her for sexual purposes and mounted a horse and followed them. In sum, the captivity of Jack and Caroline had been self-imposed.[21] If Caroline represents a person literally captured by texts, Jack Crabb is someone who can never be caught in this way—he simply spins another tale and, spiderlike, escapes on the wind.

"A Man Called Horse"

In 1970 Richard Harris brought another white Indian to the screen in "A Man Called Horse." This character was to enjoy such popularity at the box office that two sequels would follow—"The Return of a Man Called Horse" (1976) and "Triumphs of a Man Called Horse" (1982). The first film is a prime example of a seemingly realistic film that actually is a vehicle for a subtext expressing the white male fantasy we have seen before. Directed by Elliot Silverstein, it was based on a short story by Dorothy M. Johnson. Most of the changes made are to the detriment of ethnographic accuracy and in the service of the film's unsavory (but very marketable) sexual and racial subtext. For instance, in a variant of the ruse used in the short story, the white captive adopts the pretense of being crazy and a horse in order to survive; in the film, in a scene of brutal human degradation, Morgan is forced by the Sioux chief to become a pack animal.

"A Man Called Horse" was one of the first Hollywood productions to strive for ethnographic realism, a fact that earned it generally positive reviews when it was released.[22] The film uses Lakota dialogue extensively and presents itself as being based on research in the Smithsonian Institution archives and the letters and paintings of George Catlin and Carl Bodamer, who had witnessed performances of the ritual Vow to the Sun in the late nineteenth century. However, as Ralph and Natasha Friar have caustically noted, "The customs depicted in *A Man Called Horse* were neither Sioux nor Crow. They belonged only to the authentic Hollywood tribe called 'Indian.' "[23]

The scenes in the movie of the Vow to the Sun reproduce paintings and lithographs by George Catlin in close detail, but they are not in the service of representing the spiritual lives of the Indians as much as they are in proving the macho sexuality of the white male. This ceremony was performed among the Mandan, not the

Sioux, but more importantly it was not performed as a rite of initiation into manhood, as the film would have it, but in order to attract the buffalo to the hunters.[24] Yet because the images on the screen largely matched the popular image of the Indian, few reviewers (and, presumably, even fewer moviegoers) questioned the ethnographic accuracy of the film. One reviewer not only found the depiction of the Indians to be realistic, he even felt the film had captured the feelings of all whites upon first encountering the Indians.[25]

Much of the film's vaunted ethnographic realism is, in fact, little more than a slight permutation of earlier racist representations and the white male sexual fantasy associated with the primitive. In the film, Running Deer, the beautiful younger sister of the chief, quickly evinces a sexual interest in the white male captive. (In a casting decision faithful to the white male fantasy and the Pocahontas complex, a Greek actress, Corinna Tsopei, plays Running Deer.) When Black Eagle, a Sioux chief himself, comes to Yellow Hand to purchase Running Deer as his wife, his proposal is bluntly, even rudely, rejected by both of them, yet Morgan's proposal, made shortly thereafter, is immediately accepted and universally hailed by the Sioux.

The message that a white man is more sexually desirable than a red man also finds expression in other scenes. For instance, the dramatic high point of the movie is when Shenkawkan ("Horse") undergoes the painful Vow to the Sun ritual in order to prove his manhood and, thus, to win the hand of Running Deer. But this is part of a ruse to effect his escape; his primary motivation is not physical attraction and sexual desire. He even cynically calls Running Deer "Little Freedom."

Naturally, Morgan passes the ordeal of the Vow to the Sun with flying colors and even has a series of highly auspicious visions while he is hanging and twirling in midair. When he is taken down, a brief wedding ceremony is performed and he is led to his new teepee; a smiling Running Deer follows him in. Then, in an interior shot, as he lays on his back on a buffalo robe, Running Deer mounts him—an act that places the burden of sexual desire and aggression on the female native rather than on the white male, effectively distorting the power relations in the informing fantasy.

Another crucial scene informing the racial and sexual subtext occurs immediately after the new couple have entered their nuptial teepee. As the assembled crowd is leaving the wedding, Yellow Hand spies his wife in the arms of Black Eagle, slipping off into the shadows. On discovering that he is being cuckolded, Yellow Hand takes a suicidal vow never to retreat in battle and to attack the enemy no matter what their numbers might be. This scene contributes nothing to the main story line and would be gratuitous were it not for its crucial contribution to the subtext. Yellow Hand epitomizes the ideal Indian male—young, tall, handsome, powerfully built, and a chief. Yet he is cuckolded—and cuckolded precisely by the character whose marriage proposal for his sister's hand he had rejected, while accepting Morgan's. By calling into question Yellow Hand's ability to satisfy women sexually, the scene symbolically emasculates the Indian male. Given this subtext, need one add that in the film Yellow Hand has no children, while Morgan's virility is quickly proven as Running Deer becomes pregnant? Or that she dies?

In the fullest form of the white male fantasy, the native female lover always dies or is killed. This convenient death allows the white male hero (and, through identification with him, the reader) to enjoy sexual relations with the exotic female Other without having to take responsibility for these. At the same time, the dubious morality of the ruse of marrying a native woman with the intention of abandoning her and any children is avoided.[26]

"Dances with Wolves"

Kevin Kostner's 1990 Oscar-winning "Dances with Wolves," like "A Man Called Horse," portrays the Indian world as superior to the white world, which is irredeemably wicked and corrupt. "Dances with Wolves" is not a captivity narrative proper but the story of how and why John Dunbar, a decorated soldier seeking refuge from the insanity and the horror of the Civil War, voluntarily takes on an Indian identity as Dances with Wolves. Stands with Fist (Mary McDonnell), a white woman living with the Sioux, is not a captive per se; she had been adopted by Kicking Bird, after he found her alone on the plains as a child, the only survivor of an Indian attack on a wagon train. This film merits brief mention as one of the most influential representations of going native in the late twentieth century.

It is a simple story, with three interrelated themes: the value of living in harmony with nature, the need to recognize the humanity of the Other, and the love of a man and a woman. Kostner repeatedly makes the point that racial stereotypes are inaccurate and dangerous even as his film indulges the stereotyping he con-

demns. Few whites come off well in the film—most are portrayed
as ignorant, prejudiced, and brutal, while the Sioux are wise, open-
minded, and humane. Whites are largely written off as incorrigibly
corrupt. Thus, Dances with Wolves does not regret having killed
the cavalry soldiers who were taking him back to be court mar-
shaled, for they were bad and deserved to die. In "Dances with
Wolves," going native is a way to escape the immoral white world.

Rather than writing a complex and nuanced portrayal of human
nature, Kostner gives us a crude modern rendition of the noble
savage handsomely disguised by beautiful photography. As a moral
and sensitive human being, Dunbar has to become Dances with
Wolves to be true to his own nature. Here the figure of the white
Indian and the phenomenon of going primitive is not spiritually
liberating; it is escapist. "Dances with Wolves" displays almost no
interest in Indian religion or the natives' spiritual lives. Going
native is depicted as a secular event, something accomplished
without any social or religious ritual agency. Moreover, it has little
or no spiritual import other than a vague hint of a private communion with nature. Although the Indian world is a world without
spirits, it offers a refuge from the modern world—at least in the
politically correct imagination.

Psychodelic Captives: Dreams, Visions, Hallucinogens, and the Vogue of Native American Religions

The 1960s were a time of great social and political turmoil in the
United States, where profound differences over involvement in the
Vietnam war tore at the social fabric of the nation. It was also
a time of spiritual searching and experimentation, as many persons sought guidance in non-Western and nontraditional religions.
Many experimented with diverse and exotic means of getting in
touch with their inner selves. Alternatively, they explored religious teachings and practices, such as Zen and yoga, which denied an epistemology based upon the self and sensory perception.
Hallucinogenic substances were used in the search for spiritual
truth as persons rejected the negative meanings of the idea of
hallucination ("perception of objects with no reality usu. arising
from disorder of the nervous system") and hallucinosis ("a pathological mental state characterized by hallucinations").[27] Through
their actions, many people affirmed their faith in, if one might
coin a term, hallucignosis. That is, they believed in the human

ability to gain immediate knowledge of spiritual truth through visions and altered states of consciousness.

In the 1960s gurus from India were suddenly everywhere (or so it seemed), offering disenchanted and disaffected westerners access to eternal truths, various forms of meditative practice, and altered psychosomatic states. So, too, American Indian medicine men and shamans were suddenly in vogue. It is not necessary to rehearse the cultural history of the 1960s at length here, but we must take note of significant developments in popular religiosity. For instance, the tremendous popularity enjoyed by the Don Juan series of books by Carlos Castenada, recounting his purported visionary and spiritual experiences under the influence of a hallucinogen and the guidance of a Yaqui Indian shaman, was to affect the telling of captivity tales in print and in films. Whatever their status as fiction or nonfiction, Castenada's works both signaled and contributed to a new openness among many persons toward accepting the reality, validity, usefulness, and accessibility of alternative worlds of meaning. The widespread acceptance of hallucignosis is a hallmark of the religiosity of the 1960s.

The publication in 1964 of an English translation of Mircea Eliade's study of shamanism around the world, *Shamanism: Archaic Techniques of Ecstacy*, did much to legitimate shamanic practices as spiritually meaningful. Whereas American Indian shamans or medicine men had long been ridiculed and dismissed as quacks and fakirs, they came to be seen as repositories of spiritual truths at one with nature. They held the promise of an escape from the existential prison of modern society.

Characters such as Old Lodge Skin in *Little Big Man* introduced the figure of the wise shaman to millions of people at all levels of society.[28] Similarly, novels and films depicted the grandeur, the spiritual dignity, and the promise of American Indian cultures (albeit often in distorted and romanticized forms) for millions of people. More so than in previous generations, white Indians in captivity tales from the 1960s down to the present eloquently defend the value of Indian forms of spirituality and invite people to imagine other ways of being human.

The visionary practices and ritual uses of various hallucinogens among American Indians had, of course, been known for centuries. Alvar Nuñez Cabeça de Vaca, the sixteenth-century author of the first North American Indian captivity narrative, reported that he had himself become a visionary healer and practiced this vocation throughout his journey on foot from Florida to Mexico.[29]

While his narrative created a sensation in Spain, this was due to his recycling of tales of fabulous cities of gold in the New World; his claims concerning visions attracted little interest. In the early nineteenth century, John Tanner, John Dunn Hunter, and other white Indians had also offered testimony concerning the reality of the knowledge gained through dreams and induced visions in Native American culture, but this aspect of their work had little influence or credence in the broader culture. Certainly very few of their readers saw the spiritual lives of the Indians as offering anything of interest or value worth emulating.[30]

Yanoáma: The Story of a Woman Abducted by Brazilian Indians (1969) is the remarkable story of Helena Valero's life for many years with the Yanoáma Indians in the rain forests of Brazil and Venezuela, transcribed and edited from tape recordings made by the Italian ethnographer Ettore Biocca.[31] Biocca was perhaps hyperbolic (he certainly was incorrect) when he announced, "The opportunity of studying an unknown and wild group of Indians through the testimony of a woman prisoner who succeeded in returning to the world of the white men, is a fortunate and exceptional event which, it seems, has no parallel in the history of American ethnology."[32]

Biocca found the former captive, Valero, invaluable as a guide and native informant. He also found the literary form of the captivity narrative to be an efficient way to introduce ethnographic data to the general public. "I decided to collect information on the Yanoáma," he writes, "by means of this woman's lifestory, steering the narrative towards those aspects which I considered most important, without influencing, with appreciations or judgments, her recollections and her confessions."[33] Valero's account is filled with information on the ritual use of hallucinogens, the shamanic practices of the Yanoáma, and memories of raids on neighboring tribes to capture wives, human sacrifice, the killing of widows, and endocannibalism.

It is not necessary to detail Helena Valero's story here. Suffice it to say that it contains many of the narrative elements we have come to expect of this genre—the opening rehearsal of her life before her captivity, her abduction, her harrowing experiences in flight, how her hair was cut and her body painted; tales of hunger, illness, suffering, and of captive infants' brains dashed out; the captive wondering at times whether God was punishing her; and extensive passages providing ethnographic information and detail concerning Yanoáma cultural practices and material life. A few lines sparkle like gems, such as Valero's observation that "when one runs away in the night, it's a long time before morning comes." *Yanoáma* witnesses to the sustained power of the fantasy in the West of discovering a primitive people who have never seen a white person. Biocca promises his reader access to "a world . . . completely new, which no white man certainly had ever seen."[34]

Two years after Biocca's *Yanoáma* appeared, another South American captivity narrative about a white Indian *curandero*, or shamanic curer, was published. F. Bruce Lamb's *Wizard of the Upper Amazon: The Story of Manuel Córdova-Rios* (1971) is based on the oral reminiscences gathered over several months in 1962 from Manuel Córdova-Rios, then seventy-five years old, who had been abducted as a fifteen-year-old at the turn of the century and spent his subsequent life among the Amahuaca.

This work was republished in 1974 in an inexpensive paperback format, with a new introduction by Andrew Weil. Weil explains why he brought the book back into print: "I felt strongly that the book should be re-issued because it contained so much valuable information about the potentials of the human mind. . . . For many readers the most compelling sections of the book will be the descriptions of the use of *Banisteriopsis caapi*, the *yagé* or *ayahuasca* of the Amazon forests. This powerful hallucinogen has long been credited with the ability to transport human beings to realms of experience where telepathy and clairvoyance are commonplace."[35]

According to Weil, *Wizard of the Upper Amazon* is an important document concerning human mental and spiritual capacities. The primary interest is no longer the captive's suffering and the pain he had borne, nor is it his hunting adventures and romps in the rain forest. Córdova-Rios's tale is immensely valuable for us today, according to Weil, because it proves the existence of a universal, if largely untapped, human psychosomatic capacity for experiencing visionary states of shared consciousness with other persons, which promise liberation from the body-as-boundary, individual identity, and individual consciousness:

> These passages [describing collective trance] are the high points of the narrative. They leave us awed at the reality of an experience that seems infinitely worthwhile. The desire to transcend one's own ego boundaries, to share completely, if even for a moment, the consciousness of another person, must be a universal longing. It motivates many of our activities, from taking drugs to making love, and

lies behind the search for new ways of getting close to one another
that is so intense in our society today. . . . To read of "primitive"
Indians achieving what we cannot is both frustrating and exhilarating. Manuel Córdova's experiences suggest that there is hope for the
rest of us.[36]

The accounts of white Indians are precious precisely because, like
the unknown flora and fauna of the rain forest, they hold out the
promise of a possible cure not for any physical disease but for a spiritual one by returning our primordial nature and religiosity to us.

"The Emerald Forest"

John Boorman's 1985 Hollywood film "The Emerald Forest" resonates with *Wizard of the Upper Amazon* in its promotion of
hallucignosis, but it is a modern myth of the Fall cast in romantic
ecological terms. Paradoxically, this storyteller believes modern
myths must be realistic in order to be effective. Thus, as the film
opens, he proclaims disingenuously: "This film was made in the
Rain Forest of the Amazon and is based on real events and actual
characters." True, the inspiration for the film was a filler piece in
the *Los Angeles Times* concerning the abduction of the seven-
year-old son of an engineer by Indians in Brazil, but the film is an
imaginative construct designed to convey several very specific
messages to the audience.

In a diary kept during the making of the film, Boorman provides
useful insight into the way he employed ethnographic data in this
creative project: "20 June 1982. A good day on the story with
Rospo thumbing through his library of ethnographic and anthro-
pological research. He is wonderfully sceptical about these ex-
perts. He is able to suck it all in and sift it through a fine net of
imaginative cynicism. One hopes that a patina of what is poetically true of tribal life will begin to emerge." For Boorman, the
truth is "what is poetically true," not ethnographic realism. Jo-
hannes Wilbert, one of two anthropologists employed as expert ad-
visers on the film, did not appreciate this fact, quitting in frustration over Boorman's willingness to forego ethnographic accuracy
for the sake of the story, cinematography, or a dramatic shot.
Boorman baldly asserts, "Fiction is, after all, merely the truth
liberated from facts. If a story finds a deep-lasting resonance, then
it is probably true, mythologically. . . . Our story must be true and
real, moment to moment, but its value must be in expanding to

include our tribal past—the past we left behind without a backward glance."[37]

"The Emerald Forest" is an instance of modern mythmaking. Originally, the film was conceived as a retelling of the story of man against nature and the conflict between the two sides of human nature. As mythmakers, Boorman and his screenwriter were necessarily *bricoleurs*, constructing their tale from bits and pieces of many other tales—captivity narratives, ethnographies, a newspaper report, documentary films such as Adrian Cowell's "The Tribe That Hid from Man" and "Decade of Destruction," James Fenimore Cooper, Lévi-Straus's *Triste Tropique*, personal experiences, previous films they had made, and many other things besides. According to Boorman, "Movies are the repository of myth. Therein lies their power. An alternative history, that of the human psyche, is contained and unfolded in the old stories and tales. Film carries on this tradition."[38]

In Boorman's hands, Indian captivity becomes a vehicle for telling a modern myth, a cautionary tale about paradise lost through Western hubris and the thoughtless pursuit of material wealth. It is also an impassioned tale of ecology, the need to preserve the world's tropical rain forests, cultural and individual identity, and authentic spirituality. Boorman builds on elements of the captivity genre in telling his tale.

The opening scene replicates that found in innumerable earlier captivity tales—a domestic scene of a happy family on the frontier and the promise of progress through cleared land is suddenly shattered. The Markham family is having a picnic at the future site of a hydroelectric dam on the Amazon River that Bill Markham (Powers Boothe), an American engineer, is building. Large bulldozers are ripping up trees and leveling the ground.

The little boy, Tommy, soon becomes fascinated with an army of ants and wanders into the edge of the forest. There he sees a painted Indian (Wanadi, played by Rui Polonah), hidden in the lush foliage. Wanadi reaches out and touches his nose with a feather; he smiles innocently in response, then runs back to tell his father that he had seen "smiling people" in the woods. His parents believe this report to be a figment of an active imagination. When Tommy returns to play, he is carried off into the impenetrable jungle by the Indians, setting up a ten-year search for him. The scene was designed to call into question the terms of success in contemporary America and to undermine the West's misplaced sense of supreme self-confidence. As Boorman imagined the scene:

The boy's abduction must be inexplicable, must have the mystery of myth. The Markhams are optimistic Americans, successful and sure of their values. It is the arbitrariness of their loss that drives them to search on for ten years. They cannot accept what has happened to them. Only at the end does Bill understand—through his experiences with the tribe—that it was his thoughtless blundering into this world with his bulldozers that triggered the tragedy. Just as in "Deliverance" [an earlier film by Boorman] when the four city men arrive in the Appalachian village and crassly insult the hillbillies, it is a metaphor for their insensitivity to nature. Another river is being damned. Nature, malignantly personified in the mountain men, wreaks its revenge. Here, the Invisible People are the benign manifestations of a savage nature.[39]

Boorman draws a series of sharp contrasts between nature and the noble savage, on the one hand, and technological and industrial progress and civilization, on the other. The village of the Invisible People is a peaceful paradise, where beautiful young men and women cavort in a clear pool at the base of a waterfall, comfortably naked or wearing only penis sheaths or skirts. Life is easy. The white world that is invading the rain forest, on the other hand, is characterized by booze and drunken stupor, senseless violence, greed, and sexual exploitation.

The theme of the Fall structures "The Emerald Forest"—both the biblical Fall that has occurred in the West and the fall precipitated by the introduction of Western knowledge, technology, and the rapacious greed and amorality associated with capitalist forms of progress. A paradisiacal state of innocent sexuality, introduced through the love story of the abducted boy, now a teenaged white Indian known as Tomme (Charley Boorman), and the lovely Kachiri, is contrasted to the rapacious sexual appetites of white men and the commodification of sex. Boorman's goal, however, is not to play to the white male sexual fantasy; he seeks to make a moral and a political statement.

If fallen man is to redeem himself, this escapist fantasy must be rejected. When Wanadi offers Bill a beautiful maiden to meet his natural "needs" and invites him to stay with them permanently, Bill realizes that he must leave the Edenic garden. While Tomme could assume a new identity because he had been abducted as an innocent child, Bill knows that *he* is not innocent. The best he can do is to act morally and try to protect this last patch of paradise, even if that requires righteous violence or dynamiting the dam.

Here, too, though, Boorman introduces a significant and ambiguous twist into his tale. Bill would redeem himself and save the world of the Invisible People by destroying the hydroelectric dam, but we see Tomme leading prayers to the frogs to "sing" a big rain, awakening the mythic Giant Anaconda. As the chirping of the frogs increases in intensity and the rain pounds down, the Amazon River (Giant Anaconda) rises and rushes down on the dam, smashing it to bits just as Bill is about to detonate the dynamite. This is clearly a nod to the power of spirituality—primitive spirituality.

Like *Yanoáma* and *Wizard of the Upper Amazon*, "The Emerald Forest" represents the ritual use of hallucinogens in a positive fashion and affirms hallucignosis. In several crucial scenes of native rituals, Tomme has a hallucinogen blown into his nostril. He then dances until he falls into a trance and assumes the spirit form of an eagle soaring over the rain forest. This spirit form indicates the visionary powers he attains through the ritual use of hallucinogens. Bill, too, is persuaded to take the drug and finds his own spirit animal, a leopard, which races through the forest and attacks a bulldozer—a vision foreshadowing his decision to blow up the dam.

Boorman anticipated that some members of the audience would resist accepting hallucignosis, yet he hoped that the film's realism, constructed through images, sounds, careful characterizations, and plotting, would "seduce and disarm the audience." He claims a professional affinity with the traditional Indian shaman, since they both traffic in magical illusions, visions, and meaning-making. He also reports having experienced the same shared consciousness Weir had found so exciting.[40]

The film ends with the following notice on the screen: "The Rain Forests of the Amazon are disappearing at the rate of 5,000 acres per day. Four million Indians once lived there; 120,000 remain. A few tribes have never had contact with the outside world. They still know what we have forgotten." Once again, in "The Emerald Forest," the Indian is depicted as the repository of a saving knowledge, an understanding of the world and nature that is necessary to save humankind from its own excesses.

This will conclude our brief analysis of selected popular treatments of Indian captivity in the twentieth century. We will now turn to scholarly interpretations of captivity narratives. Scholars, like creative writers and filmmakers, have their own tales to tell and their own agendas to push. Their work is not value free, nor is it without designs on readers. Our goal in *Captured by Texts* has been to understand the significance captivity has had for readers in different times and places and thereby to account for the popularity of the captivity tales over the centuries. Although the basic plot line changes little over time, we have seen that Indian captivity has been narratively cast in diverse ways and to very different effect. Indian captivity narratives have been cast with an informing interpretive frame of Puritan covenantal theology, as sentimental tales of suffering and woe, as historical tales of paradigmatic patriotic men and women, as vehicles of moral didacticism for children, as adventure tales, as expressions of cultural and sexual fantasies, as modern myths of the Fall, and as vehicles for messages of ecological preservation. In the late twentieth century captivity narratives have become grist for the ideological mills of scholars and others who have attempted to harness selected works to their own projects of historical analysis and cultural criticism. In their own work, modern scholars, too, address issues of authenticity, human nature, cultural identity, the integrity of the individual or self, and the meaning of suffering.

Captivity narratives have attracted the interest and attention of scholars in the second half of this century as never before. Captivity tales have been (re)presented to readers in nonfictional studies as proof texts for the existence of unconscious archetypes, as American cultural myths of redemptive violence, as vehicles of feminist discourse, as products of ideological repression, and, in one case, as a clarion call to rally round the social agenda of the evangelical Christian Right. There is no need for us to survey the complete corpus of recent work on captivity narratives. Rather, we will end by returning to the beginning, closing the circle, as it were, with the Mary Rowlandson narrative in order to see how and why this work has once again captured the imagination of a broad spectrum of readers and hermeneuts.

A common way of treating an accumulated body of scholarship would be to survey and critique specific studies and the approaches employed therein. While a bit of this is unavoidable, my main goal is not to determine which authors, if any, have gotten things right or proffered the correct reading of these captivity tales. Instead, I want to reflect on the reasons why captivity narratives have been appropriated as objects of study at this time. I am interested in what was (or is) at stake in the existential stances scholars have themselves assumed in strategically employing captivity tales in their own interventions in cultural and critical discourse.

Richard Van Der Beets and the early Richard Slotkin have sought to explain the seemingly perennial appeal of captivity narratives by pointing to their archetypal content and structure. Influenced by Jungian psychology via Joseph Campbell, Van Der Beets finds the informing monomyth of the heroic initiation to be the key to the deep meaning of such tales. He put the archetypal thesis in its strongest terms, arguing that this initiatory scenario is "an essential structuring mode of such tales," which accounts "in large measure for the remarkable pull the captivities have exercised upon readers, an appeal that transcends sectarian religious feeling, narrow chauvinism, or morbidity. The narratives of Indian captivity are more than cultural indices or curiosities; they touch upon fundamental truths of experience. . . . they belong with those expressions of man which draw and shape their materials from the very wellsprings of human experience."[41]

Van Der Beets's archetypalism is an easy target for one's critical arrows: it is based on a limited and unrepresentative selection of texts; it ignores reception history or the different ways the same texts have been interpreted; it ignores the conscious practices of composition, editing, anthologizing, and reading used by historical agents; and it reduces the strategic theological and ideological uses of the captivity topos to a tertiary status at best. For Van Der Beets, the deep meaning of each and every captivity tale is the same.[42]

This archetypalist reading of the corpus of captivity narratives denies any real meaning to history, even as it denies any real significance to human agency and intention in the acts of narrating or consuming captivity tales. Archetypalism could be (no doubt should be) dismissed as a crude and naive approach to texts such as these, yet for a time it also attracted Slotkin, a well-known, sophisticated, and sensitive cultural historian.[43] What was the attraction of archetypalism for these scholars in the early 1970s?

Archetypalism is an attempt to preserve the Enlightenment assumption of the psychic unity of humankind in the face of divisiveness on many fronts (political, socioeconomic, sexual, gender, racial) and the implications of cultural relativism. It declares cultural differences to be less important than the universal identity of the collective unconscious. At the level of deep meaning, the apparent diversity of the products of cultural creativity bespeak the same fundamental human condition. In the wake of the Vietnam war, with all of the social divisiveness it caused, archetypalism offered a way of reclaiming our shared humanity and, in Slotkin's hands, our national identity. For myself, the trade-off this requires is too great. The devaluation of the human activity of conscious meaning-making in history is unacceptable, as is the inherent denial of human agency. In archetypal interpretations, people are portrayed as unconsciously reproducing and consuming unchanging universal truths, rather than making and remaking meaning consciously.

In recent years the Mary Rowlandson narrative, which has been in almost constant circulation for over three hundred years, has generated a wide variety of readings, ranging from psychological investigations to revisionist feminist readings. Thus, it has been read and reinterpreted by audiences the author could not possibly have imagined. Given this situation, recovering the interests of the author and the original audience for this work, as attempted in chapter 1, is only part of an adequate study of the history of this text. One must also pay attention to the specific ways in which different readers returned to it at specific points in time in order to find (or create) new meaning therein.

The diversity of meanings modern readers have found in their encounters with the Rowlandson narrative is striking. Feminists, for instance, have recently embraced the work for largely political reasons; the aesthetic qualities or literary excellence of the work are never the primary reasons they recommend it to their readers. Rather, its status as the first work of female prose published in North America has commanded the attention of these readers and critics and has led to it becoming a primary site for feminist cultural work. Since women were generally excluded from publicly assuming the role of author in the colonial period, the Rowlandson narrative is an exceptional text. It is not surprising to find it included in a recent revisionist anthology, which seeks to restore women's literature to its rightful place within American literary history. Significantly, each of the four texts anthologized is characterized as "both a tale of exploration beyond the frontiers of woman's sphere and an account of discovery within the unchartered borders of the self."[44] The dual issues of expanding the boundaries of "woman's sphere" and of the self or gender, highlighted here, are pressing at this time due to socioeconomic changes in contemporary American society where the majority of women now work outside the home. These scholars turned to the Rowlandson narrative as part of the contemporary search for new definitions of family and gender roles.

Some scholars have raised serious questions, however, about the voice of this text. Annette Kolodny, for instance, has rightly noted that Rowlandson's narrative was "no doubt composed with her minister husband looking over her shoulder (and later published with an accompanying sermon by him)," yet she does not pursue the full implications of this generative situation for feminist discourse.[45] Some feminists claim that this work preserves an authentic female voice, but others, like Kolodny, argue that the patriarchal Puritan divines stifled this voice and imposed their own orthodoxy on this and other female texts. How the work is characterized depends in part on whether one is more interested in recovering a long-lost female voice or in protesting against the long history of repression in patriarchal society. Given this, can one speak of an authentic female voice here? And what does "authentic" mean to begin with? Is the "voice of the text" the same as authorial voice? Or is it, perhaps, more complex—a composite voice of sorts? Is the voice of the text stable or shifting over time?

Most feminist scholars recommend the Rowlandson narrative to readers as a site where one can find a paradigmatic female model for living meaningfully today. Nancy Woloch has presented the work in summary form as an exercise in the "major revisionist mission" of women's history, which seeks to recover the distinctively female experience of the world, as well as women's past "efforts to gain leverage, exert influence, or assume control—to shape their own destinies and those of others." Woloch's Rowlandson is an exemplar of the frontier woman as a nurturing wife and mother, a pragmatic, shrewd, and adaptive businesswoman with cross-culturally marketable skills, and a heroic survivor.[46]

June Namias, an American historian, reports, "From the moment I read the first paragraph of the narrative of Mary Rowlandson, I felt a sense of amazement, recognition, pain, and sorrow." She describes her subsequent study of captivity narratives as "a personal quest to uncover a part of my own and America's history that had been denied me in my long trail of study through public school and university." Namias finds Rowlandson to be a meritorious role model for women today, one of the female captives who "showed women how they could go on 'alone' without husbands, and still be good mothers, indeed, cultural heroines."[47]

However, Namias does not stress the manner in which Mary fulfilled the societal expectations of a minister's wife even in captivity and thus served as a role model for her contemporaries.

Like most feminists, she virtually ignores the religious dimensions of the texts she works with and is oblivious to the crucial role the devotional forms of praxis played in the women's lives. It is almost as if the theological content of many of these works were an embarrassment to most feminist scholars. Too often, the religious language and metaphors female authors employed are dismissed as largely an artificial overlay, a male interpretive frame imposed on authentic female experience. This position denies these women their dignity as active hermeneuts in their own right who used the symbolic and rhetorical resources available to them to give meaning to their lives.

Namias argues that "the popularity of the captive story came from a fascination with both the other and the self," as it enabled readers to confront various aspects of cultural relativity in family and social relations, gender constructions, and ethnicity. While not entirely wrong, this evaluation is too one-sided and, frankly, too modern in its concerns to represent the motives of earlier generations of readers in reading the captivity tales. The readers of earlier centuries, as Namias sketches them, appear suspiciously modern in their interests and reading strategies. Lamentably, Namias largely ignores the recent work of feminist scholars and others on sentimental literature and, as a result, she ends up often denying women of earlier ages their dignity as moral agents and hermeneuts. "Nineteenth-century values and sentimental fiction encouraged dependence, weakness, cleanliness, and racial superiority" in women, she asserts. "[Consequently], their refusal to take responsibility for their actions appears to have turned some nineteenth-century women into Frail Flowers."[48] This characterization misses the ways in which women actively participated in the sentimental moral economy as real players.

For her part, Frances Row Kestler finds Rowlandson to be "brave and ingenious" and a model for "women all over the world who have to face insurmountable obstacles and to do so with patience, dignity, and faith." Kestler is one of the few feminist scholars to emphasize the religious aspects of this text. She joins with Namias and other feminists, however, in turning to this text in a search for paradigmatic women or "founding mothers." One will be a better person, they all imply, for having read Rowlandson's narrative, for this heroic woman illustrates the condition, character, and potential of all women.[49]

Amanda Porterfield has recently claimed that the Rowlandson narrative represents "the most sustained and profound exploitation of female suffering as a symbol of New England Puritan culture." This exploitation was at the hands of male ministers, she implies, who "made the social implications of Rowlandson's association between female piety and redemptive suffering explicit." Porterfield also denies that the covenantal theology Mary invoked could ever finally be redemptive or (and for Porterfield, this is much the same thing) emotionally satisfying. She suggests that the biblical texts Rowlandson used "are as much a foil against which she shaped her feelings as they are a model of those feelings. Neither her suffering nor her return from captivity are [sic] redemptive, except in the sense that they allowed her to develop and articulate her feelings."[50]

Nancy Armstrong and Leonard Tennenhouse have also found the Rowlandson narrative to be a pivotal text, but this time in terms of the emergence of "the author" as a legitimating or authenticating category. Rowlandson's text is constitutive of the modern moment because the self or subject emerges through the act of writing—the subject in the dual Foucauldian sense of the individual as subject to someone else's control and, simultaneously, as bound to an identity constituted by self-knowledge or conscience.[51] Armstrong and Tennenhouse focus on the effect this narrative had on English readers rather than New Englanders. Whereas Porterfield argues that Mary Rowlandson as a literary figure was constructed largely by men to symbolize New England and the redemptive suffering of the Puritan community, these authors find Rowlandson herself representing the English presence in the New World as a body out of place, an abducted body. In their reading, Mary becomes a symbol of the English nation.

They note that Richardson's *Pamela* shares the same pattern of abduction, captivity, and return as Rowlandson's narrative. In both cases, in composing their tales, the women create a new world where "every literate individual matters," rather than just wealth, class, or bloodline. They argue that although Mary returned to reassume her place in domestic space, through writing and circulating her story she helped to create an imagined community à la Benedict Anderson. "Rowlandson's narrative demonstrates how an individual could acquire value quite apart from wealth and station simply because she was the source of writing." Moreover, "as the first appearance of the author who is an entire world of consciousness and an authentic source of language . . . her narrative can be used to imagine how a new basis for nationality came into being."[52]

These scholars do not concern themselves with Rowlandson's stated reasons for telling her tale. They have a different story to tell, a history that Rowlandson is implicated in—even central to—although unbeknownst to herself. They use the Rowlandson narrative as a way of discussing the origins of modernity and then of calling into question the ideological purposes to which the search for origins has been put. In some respects, my own agenda intersects with theirs, especially in maintaining that the meaning-making activities of humans should be our object of study. "In going back to the origin of the myth of origins," they write, "we hope to provide some insight into the means of that myth's production. . . . [and] to show that modern humanism began in writing and continues to empower and to conceal the power of intellectuals. . . . We would like to make it just a little easier for others to abandon the whole concept of origins as the basis of identity politics and to study, in its place, the discursive practices by which we are made and remade into selves, families, and nations."[53]

Two more readings of the Rowlandson narrative have recently been offered that are as different as one could imagine. One is by an evangelical Christian, the other a postmodernist literary critic. Mark Ludwig, a conservative Christian, recently republished this captivity because, he holds, "Mary Rowlandson has a special message for our generation." Indeed, he champions this work as a "clarion call" to Christians to take up arms in the cultural war being waged for the soul of the United States. In contrast to most modern critics, Ludwig maintains that "it is not the story line or the excitement that won this narrative its fame among the founders of our nation. Rowlandson's is a story of amazing faith and perseverance in the face of adversity, and a great testimony to the faithfulness of God towards those who love him."[54]

In many ways Ludwig's reading of this narrative recalls that of Per Amicum, the author of the original "Preface to the Reader" for this text. Ludwig accepts the internal biblical interpretative frame as the key to the meaning of the events that had befallen Rowlandson. Whereas Slotkin, among others, dismisses the sovereignty, goodness, and faithfulness of God of the work's title as merely the "ostensible subject" of the work, Ludwig finds it central not only for the original Puritan audience but for readers today as well. Rowlandson provides a model for Christians today in the battle against liberals, immorality, homosexuality, abortion, humanism, and cultural relativism. Ludwig's Rowlandson is anything but a figure of "passive forebearance"; she is an exemplar of fierce righteous anger directed toward the hypocrisy of false Christians. Finally, whereas most feminists and postmodern critics find the text's informing theology to be an imposition that represses a more authentic voice, Ludwig lauds Mary precisely for fully and faithfully embracing the Bible as the repository of eternal and literal truth.

Mitchell Robert Breitwieser's *American Puritanism and the Defense of Mourning*, the first modern full-length study devoted exclusively to the Rowlandson narrative, is immediately concerned with issues surrounding the relationship between authorial voice and cultural ideology. Because Breitwieser's understanding and evaluation of the role religion and religious forms of praxis played in the construction of meaning differs fundamentally from my own, a brief exposition of his position is called for.

According to Breitwieser, "[Mary Rowlandson's] life is remarkable by virtue of the narrative she brought into existence, not just because it is the only sustained prose work known to have been written by a woman in the seventeenth century New World, but also because it is among the more intense and unremitting representations of experience as a collision between cultural ideology and the real in American literature before Melville, whose writing often echoes hers." Breitwieser argues that while this text is informed in important ways by the operative Puritan worldview and ideology, it also preserves traces of Mary's individual voice, a voice that resists having the "singularity of her experience" finally and completely repressed or subsumed under Puritan typologies of any sort. "Rowlandson's narrative is a realistic work," he claims, "not because it faithfully reports real events, but because it is an account of experience that breaks through or outdistances her own and her culture's dominant means of representation, and because it is itself a continuation of that breakthrough rather than a fully composed and tranquilized recollection."[55]

Breitwieser seeks to discriminate between the collective, largely patriarchal, voice of Puritan orthodoxy in the text and that of Mary, whose experience outran the culturally available interpretive paradigm. He argues that heretofore we have not adequately appreciated the central role the Puritan repression of public mourning played in the genesis of this particular female text. In his reading, Mary is a heroic figure, an exemplar of the human possibility of resisting theology, ideology, and other forms of repression. Her narrative preserves a witness both to the "hermeneutic violence" of Puritan ideology and to the undeniable pain of "the real." But he seems to suggest that Rowlandson accomplished all of this almost in spite of herself.

Breitwieser argues that Rowlandson's voice, at the points it breaks through the ideological surface of the text, is an important one for us today in the secular postmodern age. If I read him correctly, Rowlandson was the victim of a form of false consciousness. Puritan ideology was a patriarchal construction imposed on the community—and especially on women—that proved finally to be unsatisfying precisely insofar as it forced individuals like Mary to repress or deny their "real" experiences and raw emotions. He argues for "the importance of Mary White Rowlandson's innocent narrative, where countermemory emerges from the silence of being an eternal irony in the heart of the community and teaches those who come after what was really down below." This "countermemory" is the largely unarticulated trace of raw experience ("the real") prior to its subjection to repression or silencing by the machinery of Puritan ideology.[56]

Breitwieser's goal as a postmodern hermeneut is to recover, through a form of close reading that approaches an act of divination, the really real ("what was really down below"), which has been occluded by Puritan cultural ideology and repressed beneath the surface of the text. By reading the "fissures" in the text, much as a diviner might read the cracks in a heated tortoise shell, he claims to know what Mary really experienced in the past but could not express openly.

Breitwieser's characterization of Rowlandson's text as an "innocent narrative" is questionable; it implies that Mary did not have control of her narrative. In his hands, she becomes a passive and largely unconscious actor and author, "a kind of preconscious loam for Puritan theory," enmeshed in structures of power and repression she neither understood nor could openly resist.[57] In chapter 1 I sought to demonstrate how Rowlandson consciously and skillfully used the cultural resources available to her to make sense of the events swirling about her and to chart her actions in captivity. Her text is anything but an innocent or naive text, nor was the biblical interpretive frame retrospectively imposed on her recollections under male pressure. There are clear indications in her text that Rowlandson's specific reading and devotional practices in captivity shaped the contour of her captivity experience as it unfolded in an important way. That is, her experience of captivity was never pretextual, never not already implicated in a complex intertextuality and symbolic world of meaning.

The great diversity found among even the modern readings of the Rowlandson captivity is due in large measure to the existential concerns each reader or scholar brought to his or her encounter with the text. All seek to appropriate this famous work in their own discursive project. Feminists seek to claim this first female-authored text for themselves; Christian fundamentalists find her faith, courage, and absolute reliance on the Bible to be inspirational; and postmodernists seek to recoup the narrative traces of "the real" in her text so that they might believe it is indeed possible to escape the cultural webs of signification we are enmeshed in. For the historian of religions, each of these different readings and re-presentations of Rowlandson's captivity are of interest and import, for each reader-as-hermeneut is searching in his or her own way for authenticity in the world and a way to live a meaningful life.

As a literary topos, artistic theme, and symbolic complex, captivity was (and is) a cultural resource available for appropriation in the ongoing agonistic process of the construction and deconstruction of symbolic worlds of meaning. As we have seen, diverse sorts of cultural work have been conducted around, by means of, and through captivity tales. Captivity tales have often been told in diverse genres of popular literature and film (the jeremiad, the conversion narrative, the sentimental novel, the male adventure tale, the sexual fantasy, the classic western). The internal structural logic of each specific genre (formal and narrative devices, conventional plot lines, stock characters) influenced the telling of captivity tales in predictable ways, yet the captivity topos could never be contained within the boundaries of any genre or literary tradition.

In the preceding chapters I have demonstrated how the captivity topos itself (i.e., the basic element of an individual carried off into an alien world) opened up a discursive and imaginative space in which readers or filmgoers could at times assume, temporarily at least, new identities and contradictory subject positions from those they would otherwise naturally occupy. As a result, although captivity tales have proved to be important vehicles for representing specific theological or ideological positions, the capacity for reversing, inverting, or otherwise reworking them was always present. Because captivity tales are stories of human beings in extremis—people suddenly outside their normal societies, and with the danger (or promise) of undergoing an identity transformation—such tales have fostered in each new generation reflection on issues of individual identity, authenticity, morality, and cultural relativity.

For many persons today, race, ethnicity, nationality, gender, sexual orientation, and religious affiliation are important markers used to classify others and to construct one's own identity. The study of captivity narratives helps us to recognize that identity (cultural and individual) is not given so much as it is created collectively and individually. By historicizing the component parts or markers of the identities found in the past and in the world today, they are denaturalized. As a result, we can regain the freedom to imagine alternative ways of being human and to assume different existential positions in the world without the necessity of denigrating the subject positions and identities others have assumed in order to authenticate our own.

American Indian captivity narratives are not the only works that allow us to do these things, of course. Moreover, they seem to have a built-in limitation since white Indians do not represent all persons. Yet color also needs to be abandoned as an identifying and differentiating marker. White Indians may serve today as one symbol of the stunning human potential to imagine and to assume a new identity. By recognizing the human ability to live fully in different cultural worlds of meaning, we should be able to affirm a plurality of ways of being human in the world.

In the United States, with our national image as a melting pot, we have little difficulty in affirming the possibility of immigrant communities going native and becoming Americans. Yet we are less generous with individuals and selected minority communities who have assumed new identities (e.g., members of religions characterized as cults, homosexuals, transsexuals). Too often we use pathological terms to represent such persons and thereby deny their humanity and value. For instance, in the criminal trial of Patty Hearst, who had been abducted by a group of self-styled urban guerrillas in the 1974 and who later went over and joined them, the defense lawyers claimed that Hearst had been brainwashed. She had taken the name of a martyred compatriot of Che Guevara and assumed a new identity as "Tania" with her captors, yet no one—the lawyers, the press, the jury, psychologists, expert witnesses—recognized identity transformation as a real possibility. The brainwashing defense that was mounted represented Hearst as having been mentally incapacitated and, thus, not legally responsible for her actions. This case is introduced in passing not to judge Hearst's innocence or guilt but as a well-known instance exemplifying our unwillingness, reminiscent of Grey Owl, to accept the fragility of the self and one's identity as a fact, both frightening and exhilarating.[58]

Last Words

In my reading of over three hundred captivity narratives, I came across a number of reports from former captives recalling their initial disbelief and then the shock of recognition when, after having gone native and lived among Indians for years, a white person pointed out to them that they were white, not Indian. These accounts have long puzzled readers, who have found it difficult to imagine that anyone could forget who he or she was or (and for these readers it is much the same thing) their obvious differences. At issue, of course, were (and are) questions of how identity is determined and whether identity is a given (racially, culturally, in terms of sex) or fluid and constructed. Our study of captivity tales suggests that the latter is the case, although societies always seek to naturalize (and, thus, disguise or deny) this fact in one way or another.

I have no problem accepting at face value the accounts of the white Indians mentioned above. From 1971 to 1977 I lived in a city in Japan where I was one of a handful of foreigners. Having married a Japanese, I settled into a new life and culture, used English only in the classroom, and soon was even dreaming in Japanese. In the beginning I was painfully aware of my status as a foreigner (in Japanese, literally an "outsider"), but gradually over time I felt more and more comfortable in my new world. One day, while walking through the downtown shopping district, I heard someone say something I had heard hundreds of times before: "*Ah! gaijin da!*" (Look! A foreigner!). That day, though, I caught myself looking around and saying to myself, "*Eh-h. Doko da?*" (Oh, where?). There was a dual shock of (mis)recognition then. Without realizing it, at some point in time I had crossed over a line, gone native in terms of my own sense of self. That is why I was caught up short when I realized that *I* was still the Other in the eyes of others (*hitome*). My spontaneous question that day—Where was the Other?—has driven these reflections on tales of persons who found themselves with the Other and who faced serious questions concerning the boundaries of self and Other. These questions haunt us all. Where is the Other? Where does our real identity lie? *Doko da?*

NOTES
BIBLIOGRAPHY
INDEX

NOTES

Introduction: Recapturing the Meaning of Texts

1. The literature on the history of the formation and perpetuation of stereotypes and popular images of the American Indian in the West is vast. Those I have consulted will be found in the bibliography.
2. Levernier and Cohen, *Indians and Their Captives*, p. xiii.
3. It is ironic that some Indian groups, especially on the East Coast, adopted "civilized" practices such as holding slaves. This phenomenon, as well as the complex relations of blacks and Indians, has attracted the interest of historians. See Abel, *American Indian as Slaveholder*; Halliburton, *Red over Black*; Hudson, *Red, White and Black*; Katz, *Black Indians*; McLoughlin, "Red Indians, Black Slavery"; Nash, *Red, White, and Black*; and Porter, *Negro on the American Frontier*.
4. Two scholars who have noted that captivity sometimes led to voluntary decisions to remain with the Indians are Axtel, "White Indians," and Ulrich, *Good Wives*. Not all blacks who had the opportunity to stay with the Indians did so. See, for instance, *A Narrative of the Uncommon Sufferings and Surprizing Deliverance of Briton Hammon, A Negro Man* (1760) in *Garland* 8.
5. See Drinnon, *White Savage*, and Fierst, "Return to 'Civilization,'" for information on John Tanner, a famous nineteenth-century white Indian whose troubled life is representative of the difficulties such figures faced. For two examples of many failed attempts by white Indians to return to white society and to readapt to white cultural mores, see John Alexander McClung, *Sketches of Western Adventure* (1832), in *Garland* 50, and Josiah Priest, *The Low Dutch Boy* (1839), in *Garland* 56. In general, authors and audiences in the second-half of the twentieth century have been more sympathetic to the plight of white Indians. See, for instance, Richter's novel *The Light in the Forest* and Johnson's short story "Lost Sister."
6. Severance, ed., *Captivity and Sufferings*, pp. 11, 12. The original 1784 narrative and the 1848 edition may be found in *Garland* 15. For bibliographical information on the various editions of the narrative, see Vail, *Voice*, pp. 324, 331, 355–56.
7. Benjamin, "The Image of Proust," in *Illuminations*, p. 202.
8. For two excellent recent ruminations on the body-in-pain, see Scarry, *Body in Pain*, and Morris, *Culture of Pain*. On the role of pain in initiation rites, see Morinis, "Ritual Experience."

9. See Long, *Significations*, p. 1.

10. See Mott, *Golden Multitudes*, pp. 303–6. This information is repeated in Slotkin, *Regeneration through Violence*, p. 96.

11. For examples of modern South American captivity tales, see Lamb, *Wizard of the Upper Amazon*, and Biocca, *Yanoáma*. Modern adaptations and retellings for new audiences include Manfred, *Scarlet Plume*, a novel loosely based on the Sarah Wakefield captivity among the Sioux in the 1860s; Lenski, *Indian Captive*, an award-winning children's book, reprinted more than twenty times, that retells the Mary Jemison captivity; and, most recently, Keehn, *I Am Regina*, a retelling for children and young adults of the Regina Leininger captivity (1755–63) among the Lenni Lenape. As of 1991, twenty-two titles had appeared in Bantam's "White Indian Series," which the publisher advertises as a "thrilling series [which] tells the compelling story of America's birth against the equally exciting adventures of an English child raised as a Seneca." Moreover, the reader is informed that each volume is designed "to capture the heart and inflame the imagination with tales alive with history, lore, and the unique American experience of the white Indian." This language echoes that found in eighteenth- and nineteenth-century works.

12. Tompkins, *Sensational Designs*, p. xvi.

13. Space limitations and the broad temporal sweep of this study preclude my exploring many other possible differences in reading practices related to factors of gender, age, education, socioeconomic status, and regional variations.

14. Eliade, "Methodological Remarks," p. 89.

15. Silko, *Ceremony*, pp. 2–3.

1. The Captivating Text

1. The dates of Rowlandson's birth and death long remained a point of conjecture. Most earlier studies assumed that Mary had died before the publication of her narrative. Recent research, however, has conclusively shown that Mary Rowlandson was remarried in 1679 to Capt. Samuel Talcott and died in 1711. See David L. Greene, "New Light on Mary Rowlandson."

2. See, for instance, Slotkin and Folsom, *So Dreadfull a Judgment*, p. 303; Vaughan and Clark, *Puritans among the Indians*, p. 32; and Kolodny, "Captives in Paradise," p. 93. Lang has perceptively pointed out that the assumption that Mary died shortly after the death of her husband, Joseph, "encouraged the melodramatic view of languishing Rowlandson, unable to resume a normal life after the Lancaster tragedy" (in Andrews et al., *Journeys in New Worlds*, p. 19).

3. Thus, the sort of worrying found in Slotkin and Folsom, *So Dreadfull a Judgment*, pp. 312–13, is largely irrelevant.

4. For bibliographic information, see Vail, *Voice*, pp. 31–33.

5. Cited ibid., p. 167.

6. In Andrews et al., *Journeys in New Worlds*, p. 19.

7. The Rowlandson narrative has the date as 10 February. This apparent discrepancy is due to the fact that the British still used the Julian calendar at this time. See Vaughan and Clark, *Puritans among the Indians*, p. 33.

8. Ibid., pp. 4, 6, 7.

9. Hambrick-Stowe, *Practice of Piety*, p. 258. The classic study of the devotional meditative techniques in Europe and England that underlay the Puritan practice is Martz, *Poetry of Meditation*.

10. See Ulrich, *Good Wives*, p. 185.

11. Hambrick-Stowe, *Practice of Piety*, pp. 66–68.

12. See, for instance, Breitwieser *American Puritanism*, pp. 77, 121. To give Breitwieser his full due, he does note that this phrase is similar to that found in Job

(see pp. 77–78), yet he takes every use of this phrase to be "Satanic," a reading I cannot accept.

13. Bourdieu, *Logic of Practice*, p. 56. Mary recalls why her son once had assumed an unusual posture for prayer: "Hearing that my Son was Come to this place, I went to see him, and found him lying flat upon the ground: I asked him how he could sleep so? he answered me, that he was not asleep, but at Prayer; and lay so, that they might not observe what he was doing. I pray God, he may remember these things now he is returned in safety" (*Garland* 1:12).

14. See, for instance, *Garland* 1:5. The great changes in the view of many persons concerning the nature of God that occurred within a generation of the publication of Rowlandson's narrative may be gauged by comparing this work, with its heavy emphasis on the wrathful God of the Old Testament, with the manner in which Isaac Watts (1674–1748) recast the Psalms by reading and rewriting the Old Testament deity through the New Testament. In his *Psalms of David Imitated in the Language of the New Testament* (1719), Watts writes, "Where the Psalmist uses sharp invectives against his personal enemies, I have endeavoured to turn the edge of them against our spiritual adversaries, Sin, Satan, Temptation. . . . Where the Psalmist describes religion by the fear of God, I have often joined faith and love to it. . . . Where he talks of sacrificing goats or bullocks, I rather choose to mention the sacrifice of Christ, the Lamb of God" (Cited in Sambrook, *Eighteenth Century*, p. 42).

15. The 1716 account of Thomas Church, the son of Benjamin Church, the commander of the Plymouth troops, seems to have been based on the father's diary and memoirs. It has been conveniently reprinted in Slotkin and Folsom, *So Dreadfull a Judgment*, pp. 393–464. Compared to the Rowlandson narrative, the account of divine providence promised in the title here is made almost in passing. As Slotkin notes, "Indeed, so striking were Church's [military] accomplishments that the orthodox [Cotton] Mather felt constrained to remind his readers that the will of God and the power of Puritan society were, after all, the true determinants of historical movements—since otherwise the reader might conceive an exaggerated sense of the power of individuals to shape events" (p. 370). This was, of course, a constant problem and an inherent contradiction in Puritan thought and society. Mather's works are also available in Slotkin and Folsom, pp. 80–163, 165–206.

16. Of the forty-two persons who had sought refuge in the Rowlandson house before the Indian attack, eighteen were directly related to the Rowlandsons. Besides Mary, there were two of her sisters, a brother-in-law, Mary's three children, and eleven nieces and nephews.

17. Cited in Hambrick-Stowe, *Practice of Piety*, p. 258.

18. See Breitwieser, *American Puritanism*, p. 102.

19. *Garland* 1:A3. See Cohen, *God's Caress*, especially pp. 189, 199. Apparently, some eighteenth-century readers in Europe found it hard to believe that Americans quoted scripture regularly in their speech, prompting one author to protest that this feature in his work was a realistic touch. See Michel René Hilliard d'Auberteuil's footnote in *Mis Mac Rea, Roman Historique* (1784), reprinted in *Garland* 16:10. On how self-censorship operates, see Bourdieu, *Language and Symbolic Power*, pp. 137–59. It is also clear that not all Puritans were able to censor their own speech at all times and in all situations. For an interesting account of the textual traces of uncontrolled verbal exchanges, see Robert St. George, " 'Heated' Speech."

20. Breitwieser, *American Puritanism*, pp. 106, 107, 10, 11, 12.

21. Ibid., p. 8. It is also presumptuous to assume that it is only we today who can recover the "real," which Mary traced discursively and unconsciously, or that what we find in our engagement with this narrative is somehow the first encounter with "what was really down below" the surface of the text.

22. The literature on the Puritan sermon is extensive. For a recent work, see Stout,

New England Soul. The quotation is from the preface by "B.W." to Joseph Rowlandson's sermon (*Garland* 1:35).

23. Cotton Mather also spoke of the people being abandoned to "spiritual plagues." See *Garland* 1:34.

24. Mary's report of the dogs that did not protect her family may also have another intertextual referent—the rhyme for the letter *D* in *The New England Primer:* "A Dog will bite / A Thief at night."

25. The bibliography is extensive, but mention may be made of Carroll, *Puritanism and the Wilderness*; Heimert, "Puritanism, the Wilderness, and the Frontier"; Miller, *Errand into the Wilderness*; Nash, *Wilderness and the American Mind*; Williams, *Wilderness and Paradise in Christian Thought*; and Frederick Turner, *Beyond Geography.*

26. Hambrick-Stowe, *Practice of Piety*, p. 66. The chapter "Puritan as Pilgrim" (pp. 54–90) in this work is especially useful in understanding the centrality of the pilgrimage metaphor in Puritan discourse.

27. Breitwieser, *American Puritanism*, p. 70.

2. Captives of Sin or Captives of Ideology?

1. See Lockridge, *New England Town*; Stout, *New England Soul*; Butler, *Awash in a Sea of Faith*; and Gura, *Wisdom of Words.*

2. Simply denying oneself food does not constitute a religious fast, according to Cotton Mather: "For men to think, that they Serve God, by a Fast wherein they do nothing but Fast from Corporal Sustenance, and they draw not near to God in Devotions all the Day long, 'tis a piece of Ignorance" (*Garland* 1:19).

3. On Duston (or Dustin), see Arner, "The Story of Hannah Duston," and Whitford, "Hannah Dustin."

4. This paradox—that the recognition of one's powerlessness, insofar as one cannot earn grace, resulted in renewed power—has been recognized by Charles Cohen and others in the extant examples of Puritan conversion narratives. Cohen suggests that these narratives "testify indirectly to church members' sense of power, for the plaints of helplessness that predominate in the narratives of preparation subside once vocation has been described" (*God's Caress*, p. 210).

5. Mather's vitrolic hatred of the Indians at this time and the unfortunate consequences of wedding theology to racism are well known (see, for example, *Garland* 3:12). For him, the Indians represented all possible evils and vices, while backsliders among the Puritans came to resemble them (see ibid., pp. 211–12, 251). Thus, for Mather, the Indians were the vices of the people projected large onto the historical stage.

6. Cited in Hambrick-Stowe, *Practice of Piety*, p. 244; *Garland* 3:240–241, 201–2.

7. Mather sought in his own life to turn the regular visitations of death in his family to spiritual effect. In *Meat out of the Eater, Or, Funeral Discourses Occasioned by the Death of Several Relatives* (Boston, 1703), he wrote, "I will do what I can that the Death of my Children, may promote the Death of my Sins." The cultural uses of grief are not uniform over time and space anymore than the understanding and experience of death. For an important study of Western responses to death and how these changed over time, see Aries, *Hour of Our Death.*

8. By the mid- and late seventeenth century, the declining rate of conversion among the Puritans as a percentage of the total population was very noticeable. This had prompted the clergy to open the possibility of baptising the children of full members, a practice increasingly common in the latter decades of

the century. Many historians point to a spreading anxiety at this time as to whether the covenant would be continued with the next generation. This was, no doubt, one of the sources of the interest of Mather and others in the religious education of the children.

9. Lockridge, for example, notes that in the town of Dedham only eight persons were baptised between 1653 and 1657, while no one was admitted over the next five years (*New England Town*, pp. 33–34).

10. For a thorough and sensitive study of the effects of captivity on the Williams family, see Demos, *Unredeemed Captive.*

11. Ibid., p. 60.

12. On "ordering one's conversation aright," see Hambrick-Stowe, *Practice of Piety*, pp. 200–201.

13. *Garland* 5 contains reprints of the 1707 edition, the 3d enlarged edition of 1758, and the 1853 edition. The first two both contain Williams's 5 Dec. 1706 sermon, but the 3d ed. also includes an appendix by his son, Stephen, listing those slain and taken captive in Deerfield. The 1853 edition has replaced the sermon with a thirty-nine-page "Biographical Memoir of The Rev. John Williams, Author of 'The Redeemed Captive.'" The captivity narrative is available in modern editions in Clark, ed., *Redeemed Captive,* and in Vaughan and Clark, *Puritans among the Indians,* pp. 167–226. The latter does not include the sermon.

14. The Hannah Swarton captivity was also reprinted by Mather in a slightly enlarged version in his *Magnalia Christi Americana* (London, 1702). It is available in Vaughan and Clark, *Puritans among the Indians,* pp. 147–57.

15. See Vaughan and Clark, *Puritans among the Indians,* pp. 6, 148.

16. "Humiliations," *Garland* 1:56; Cohen, *God's Caress,* p. 148. Cohen notes that conversion narratives, the genre to which I think Swarton's narrative belongs, "are better understood as documents beginning in speech; their final, written form should not disguise their complex evolution" (p. 19, n. 37).

17. Caldwell, *Puritan Conversion Narrative,* pp. 31, 182.

18. Bercovitch, *Puritan Origins,* p. 8.

19. See, Cohen, *God's Caress,* pp. 76, 239–40.

20. Modern readers too often fail to take seriously the fact that in Puritan society individuals lived in an extended community that extended to the afterworld. Some, such as Breitwieser, have seen expressions by captives of the conviction that they would be reunited with deceased loved ones in heaven as "a sparse promise of consolation." This is an unsupportable reading of Puritan texts, ignoring the many testimonies to the "consolation" that individuals found through such biblical promises. See Breitwieser, *American Puritanism,* pp. 109–11. Driven by his thesis that mourning is a process that will "out" no matter what, Breitwieser misunderstands why Rowlandson is interested in her sister's death and her "inner history." Quite simply, this was because of the cultural belief that the state of her soul *did* affect her eternal condition. Thus, by recalling her sister's conversion and her favorite bible verse, 2 Corinthians 12:9, Rowlandson was seeking public corroboration of her sister's life as a visible Saint, and thus the promise of reunion in the afterlife.

21. *Garland* 4. The author's name on the title page is given as "Dickenson." All references to the author in the scholarly literature use the more common spelling, "Dickinson," as have I in this study.

22. Levernier and Cohen, *Indians and Their Captives,* p. 40.

23. Cited in Vail, *Voice,* p. 127; see pp. 216–18 for more detail.

24. Vaughan and Clark, *Puritans among the Indians,* pp. 94, 22. Jeremy Belknap's copy of this narrative, held in the Boston Public Library, contains this handwritten note: "Said to be *really* written & embellished by Joseph Seccombe, Chaplain of the Garrison at St. George's, afterwards minister of Kingston in N. Hampshire" (cited in Vail, *Voice,* p. 227).

3. Capturing the Audience

1. For a summary of the publishing situation, see Davidson, *Revolution and the Word*, p. 11. For background on the history of the book in America at this time, including publication, distribution, and consumption of texts, see Lehmann-Haupt, *Book in America;* Berthold, *American Colonial Printing;* Oswald, *Printing in the Americas;* Shepard, *History of Street Literature;* Hall and Hench, *Needs and Opportunities;* Resnick, *Literacy;* Joyce et al., *Printing and Society;* Hall, *Worlds of Wonder;* and J. Paul Hunter, *Before Novels.* American booksellers imported most of the fictional reading materials available in North America well into the eighteenth century or, alternatively, brought out American editions (frequently pirated) of English and European fiction. At the same time, there was a ready market in England and on the Continent for some types of American works, which were quickly reprinted there. An instance of the latter case is *A Narrative of the Captivity of Mrs. Johnson* (Walpole, N.H.: David Carlisle, Jr., 1796), which was brought out in a pirated edition the following year in Glasgow. The pirated edition included the following notice: "The Publishers of this Narrative bought it of an American Gentleman who arrived at Greenock in the Bark Hope, a few weeks ago; and as he assured them that there was not a copy of it to be procured in Europe, and that it sold in America for four shillings and sixpence, they deemed it worthy of reprinting" (*Garland* 23: n.p.).
2. This linkage of Pamela and captivity narratives has recently been made by Armstrong and Tennenhouse, *Imaginary Puritan,* pp. 200–216.
3. See Davidson, *Revolution and the Word,* p. 260.
4. Van Der Beets, *Indian Captivity Narrative,* p. 36; Pearce, "Significances," pp. 2, 9.
5. Rowson, *The Inquisitor,* cited in Herbert Ross Brown, *Sentimental Novel,* p. 166. Two useful studies of the female domestic novel and the modern romance novel are Papashvily, *All the Happy Endings;* and Radway, *Reading the Romance.*
6. O'Flaherty, *Other People's Myths,* p. 148.
7. Barnett, *Ignoble Savage,* p. 48; Fliegelman, *Prodigals and Pilgrims,* p. 144.
8. I have found the following works useful in understanding the emergence of the Newtonian-Lockean sensory psychology and epistemology, as well as the attendant developments over the next century and a half, especially the rise of a culture of sensibility: Todd, *Sensibility;* Proby, *English Fiction;* Mullan, *Sentiment and Sociability;* Brissenden, *Virtue in Distress;* Beasley, *Novels of the 1740's;* Sambrook, *Eighteenth Century;* Fliegelman, *Prodigals and Pilgrims;* McKeon, *Origins of the English Novel;* Gillian Brown, *Domestic Individualism;* Barker-Benfield, *Culture of Sensibility;* Nicolson, *Newton Demands the Muse;* Samuels, *Culture of Sentiment;* Hagstrum, *Sex and Sensibility;* Bredvold, *Natural History of Sensibility;* and Gura, *Wisdom of Words.*
9. Barker-Benfield, *Culture of Sensibility,* p. 69. See also Fiering, "Irresistible Compassion."
10. Fliegelman, *Prodigals and Pilgrims,* p. 12.
11. Cited in Brissenden, *Virtue in Distress,* p. 42, n. 60.
12. Barker-Benfield, *Culture of Sensibility,* p. 6. This form of the transmission of knowledge should not surprise us, nor should the fact that developments in science quickly affected literary forms. It is well known, for instance, that secondhand information on Einstein's theories of relativity, which Virginia Woolf gained from acquaintances at Oxford, affected the form of her novels and inspired aspects of her narrative manipulation of time.
13. "Moral Philosophy" (unsigned), *Encyclopaedia Britannica.*
14. As Brissenden has noted, concerning Richardson's works, "The sentiments in

his novels were indeed 'moral and instructive' and they were intended to provide comfort as much for the reader as for the heroine during her trials" (*Virtue in Distress*, p. 100).

15. Cited in Barker-Benfield, *Culture of Sensibility*, p. 9.

16. Dr. Benjamin Slocock read *Pamela* to his congregation from the pulpit. See Beasley, *Novels of the 1740's*, pp. 134, 138.

17. For an introduction to the culture of sentiment and the moral economy of tears in France, see Vincent-Buffault, *History of Tears*.

18. Tompkins, *Sensational Designs*, p. xii.

19. *Garland* 7. The source of these lines is not cited on the title page, but we may assume that most contemporary readers would have readily recognized them as from Addison's *Cato*, 5.2.15–18.

20. In *Before Novels*, J. Paul Hunter convincingly argues that the early novel is indebted to the diverse literature of wonders and remarkable occurrences, including the works of Puritans such as Cotton Mather, while eschewing the earlier reliance on supernatural intervention in history because of the increasing acceptability of rational scientific explanations of the world and of causality.

21. Herbert Ross Brown, *Sentimental Novel*, p. 38.

22. Shaftsbury, cited in Humphreys, " 'The Friend of Mandkind,' " p. 205.

23. See Fiering, "Irresistible Compassion"; Crane, "Suggestions"; and Donald Greene, "Latitudinarianism and Sensibility."

24. Stowe felt that social reformation would come about only through a spiritual conversion in the individual, which would be marked by correct emotional responses to specific situations: "There is one thing that every individual can do—they can see to it that they feel right. An atmosphere of sympathetic influence encircles every human being; and the man or woman who feels strongly, healthily and justly, on the great interests of humanity, is a constant benefactor to the human race. See, then, to your sympathies in this matter! Are they in harmony with the sympathies of Christ? or are they swayed and perverted by the sophistries of worldly policy?" (*Uncle Tom's Cabin*, p. 448).

For more on the ways in which *Uncle Tom's Cabin* participated in the cultural work of the sentimental novel, see Jane Tompkins, "Sentimental Power: *Uncle Tom's Cabin* and the Politics of Literary History," in *Sensational Designs*, pp. 122–46. In the following pages, however, I will suggest by example that the sentimental novel was not exclusively a female literary form but was a culturally available form appropriated by female authors for their own soteriological or religiopolitical purposes.

25. *The Spectator*, No. 418, cited in Barker-Benfield, *Culture of Sensibility*, pp. 62–63.

26. Hume, *A Treatise of Human Nature*, p. 569.

27. Eliot, *Adam Bede*, p. 116.

28. Cited in Davidson, *Revolution and the Word*, p. 43.

29. Thomas Berger followed in this tradition of the fictional ruse of an editor retelling "remarkable" tales in his 1964 best-selling novel *Little Big Man*, a modern fictional captivity.

30. Davidson, *Revolution and the Word*, p. 14.

31. Herbert Ross Brown, *Sentimental Novel*, pp. 86–87.

32. Ibid., p. 78.

33. On the popularization of Ignation and other meditative practices in Protestant circles, see Martz, *Poetry of Meditation*, as well as the more recent work of J. Paul Hunter, *Before Novels*, which links these practices to the novel.

34. Cited in Herbert Ross Brown, *Sentimental Novel*, p. 85. In an important sense, Sterne's understanding of the complicity of the author *and* the reader in the construction of meaning (more precisely, shared meaning) would have helped modern critics to avoid the major weakness of early reader-response and

audience-oriented criticism—an overemphasis on the author's ability to chan-
nel or structure the reader's response. The reader was represented as largely
passive, while the text, as an autonomous object, had the power to generate
specific responses.

35. Brown notes that some sentimental authors even claimed that medical autop-
sies, then a new scientific advance, "proved" the refined sensibility of certain
characters by revealing the delicate lines of his or her sensorium, the organ of
sensibility (ibid., pp. 78–79).

36. Cited ibid., pp. 9, 76.

37. On the kidnapping of children for sale into indentured servantship, see Coldham, " 'Spiriting' of London Children," and Robert C. Johnson, "Transportation of Vagrant Children."

38. On the influence of Scottish commonsense philosophy on Americans, including Jefferson and Benjamin Franklin, and American fiction, see Terence Martin, *Instructed Vision*, Gura, *Wisdom of Words*, and Fiering, *Moral Philosophy*.

39. Speaking to Tom, Matthewsons says at one point, "If I can at all read the
destiny of persons, from their ways of acting and thinking, for all others
are pretending and fallacious, for you, are reserved, by heaven, happier and
smoother hours, and uninterrupted content" (*Garland* 7:38).

40. Lillie Deming Loshe, while recognizing the fictional nature of the work, nevertheless suggests that it is "probably founded on the experiences of Mrs.
Bleecker's husband during an Indian raid" (*Early American Novel*, p. 67). The
work was still classified as nonfiction in the Library of Congress catalogue in
1949 when Vail's *Voice* appeared, although today it is no longer so listed.
Nevertheless, the fictional protagonist's purported dates (1721–1779) continue
to be included in the cataloguing information.

41. I agree wholeheartedly with Tompkins, who has argued that "the power of a
sentimental novel to move its audience depends upon the audience's being in
possession of the conceptual categories that constitute character and event.
That storehouse of assumptions includes attitudes towards the family and
toward social institutions; a definition of power and its relation to individual
human feeling; notions of political and social equality; and above all, a set
of religious beliefs that organizes and sustains the rest. Once in possession
of the system of beliefs that undergirds the patterns of sentimental fiction, it
is possible for modern readers to see how its tearful episodes and frequent
violations of probability were invested with a structure of meanings that fixed
these works, for nineteenth-century readers, not in the realm of fairy tale or
escapist fantasy, but in the very bedrock of reality" (*Sensational Designs*,
pp. 126–27).

42. On this point Porterfield's recent work, *Female Piety*, has opened new avenues
of inquiry. The emphasis on maternal consolation as the wife's primary duty
found in the sentimental novel may be compared with a passage in the Rowlandson narrative where Mary feels little compunction to claim that her first
thoughts while in captivity had always been for her husband or others back
home (*Garland* 1:17).

43. Cited in Herbert Ross Brown, *Sentimental Novel*, p. 77. Jefferson was not, of
course, in favor of most novels and at best held an ambivalent attitude toward
them.

44. Note the description of the proper dress and attitude for receiving an audience:
"In the afternoon Maria received her visitants in a neat little parlour. She was
dressed in a plain suit of mourning, and wore a small muslin cap, from which
her hair fell in artless curls on her fine neck: her face was pale, though not
emancipated, and her eyes streamed a soft languor over her countenance, more
bewitching than the sprightliest glances of vivacity. As they entered, she arose,
and advancing, modestly received their civilities" (*Garland* 20:51).

45. Adam Smith, *Theory of Moral Sentiments*, bk. 1, sec. i, chap. 2.

4. Rebinding the Bonds

1. The author's or editor's stated or purported reason for publishing a given narrative is, of course, not necessarily the actual—or the only—reason for having done so. Nevertheless, even in those instances where one feels confident in saying that an unstated motive was at work, the stated reasons indicate what sorts of motives for publicly telling a given tale were thought to be socially acceptable.

2. See Cvetkovich, *Mixed Feelings*, for a feminist cultural analysis of the sensation novel of the 1860s.

3. The identical sentimental passage is found in David Humphreys, *An Essay on the Life of the Honorable Major-General Israel Putnam* (1788), *Garland* 19:74–75.

4. Filson's text, as well as other major texts that contributed to the popular image of Daniel Boone, have been well treated by Slotkin in *Regeneration through Violence*, pp. 268–354, 394–465. Quotation from p. 269.

5. Lawson-Peebles, *Landscape*, p. 6.

6. Ibid.; Slotkin, *Regeneration through Violence*, p. 272.

7. Slotkin, *Regeneration through Violence*, p. 277. Whereas Slotkin assumes that the "power" and meaning of the text came from its narrative content and archetypal structure, I want to stress the importance of the reading practices the original audience brought to bear on the text and how these were skillfully anticipated and manipulated by Filson.

8. From the sermon entitled "New England's Duty" (1698) by Nicolas Noyes, cited in Bercovitch, "Puritan Errand Reassessed," p. 59.

9. John Cawelti has identified the plot of the male hero bringing order and founding a peaceful society, but then "riding off into the sunset" as the defining characteristic of the classic Westerns of the 1940s and 1950s. There one finds a nostalgic longing for the vanishing frontier, along with the hero's refusal to be assimilated into the new society or to be domesticated (*Adventure*, pp. 246–47).

10. Van Campen himself became the subject of a lengthy heroic biography, written by a grandson, who sought to preserve the family's oral history of the Revolutionary War. See John Niles Hubbards, *Sketches of the Life and Adventures of Moses Van Campen* (1841), in *Garland* 13.

11. Apparently, the real Mrs. Howe was not among those readers who found Humphreys's version of her life "interesting." In *A Genuine and Correct Account of the Captivity, Sufferings & Deliverance of Mrs. Jemima Howe* (1792), Humphreys was himself charged with having misrepresented some of the facts of the case and, more seriously, of having besmirched Mrs. Howe's reputation (*Garland* 19:19).

12. Hume, *A Treatise of Human Nature*, p. 627.

13. Not everyone seems to have been taken with Williamson's tale of woe, afflictions, and the vicissitudes of life. In June 1758 Williamson was imprisoned briefly in Aberdeen at the instigation of some local merchants, who charged him with having libeled them by implying that they were behind the kidnapping of children in the city. More than 350 copies of his narrative were seized by the authorities, threatening the author's livelihood. In prison he was forced to sign a retraction and, as a condition of his release, made to promise to insert this retraction in every copy of his work. After his release, however, the scrappy Williamson went on the offensive again, charging in an expanded edition of his captivity that he had signed the retraction under duress. He also collected and reprinted a number of depositions, sworn before magistrates, to the effect that he had, indeed, been kidnapped as a child and, thus, had not misrepresented the facts. Thus, retelling his tale was a means of attempting to restore his good

name. Later, his text was also used in an effort to affect British foreign policy toward the colonies (1758 ed., *Garland* 9).

14. See Shepard, *History of Street Literature.*

15. James Fenimore Cooper spoke for many members of his generation when, in a laudatory review of Royall Tyler, he quoted the novelist Fielding to the effect that political historians wrote fiction, while novelists, like himself, captured the *real* world in their writing (Davidson, *Revolution and the Word*, p. 220).

16. Larimer had announced that because of considerations of length she had been unable to include the full story of her friend Mrs. Kelly, but she promised to do so in a forthcoming work entitled "Mrs. Kelley's Experience among the Indians." Apparently Fanny Kelly did not appreciate her "friend's" effort to tell her story in print, for in her own account, *Narrative of My Captivity*, she writes: "Some explanation is due the public for the delay in publishing this my narrative. From memoranda, kept during the period of my captivity, I had completed the work for publication, when the manuscript was purloined and published" (*Garland* 85:vi).

   In October 1870, Kelly filed suit against the Larimers in court. The case was contested in various venues until the summer of 1876, when the parties finally settled out of court, with the Larimers paying approximately $2,000 to Kelly. Details of the legal battle between Kelly and Larimer may be found in Farley, "An Indian Captivity" and in the "Epilogue" (pp. 323–32) to the 1990 reprint of Kelly, *Narrative of My Captivity Among the Sioux Indians.*

17. Tompkins, *Sensational Designs*, p. 130.

18. The literature on the cult of motherhood in the eighteenth and nineteenth centuries is extensive. See, for example, Cott, *Bonds of Womanhood*; Ryan, *Empire of the Mother*; Epstein, *Politics of Domesticity*; and Douglas, *Feminization of American Culture.*

19. John Cawelti finds *Seth Jones* to be less successful than James Fenimore Cooper's works insofar as "only a skeletal residue of Cooper's ideal of natural simplicity remains." In this novel the "idea that there is a way of life or a set of moral values associated with nature and opposed to civilization simply doesn't enter the picture. . . . During the heyday of the dime novel the Western developed primarily as a form of adolescent escapism, complete with the simple moral conflicts and stereotyped characters and situations usually found in such literature." Cawelti privileges the classical western form as the norm against which all other works are to be judged and, thus, hybrid works, such as *Seth Jones*, fair poorly as the sentimental elements are dismissed as "adolescent escapism" (*Adventure*, pp. 210–11).

5. Going Native, Going Primitive

1. *History of the Five Indian Nations*, quoted in Axtell, "White Indians," p. 57.

2. Letter to Peter Collinson, May 9, 1753, in Labaree, *Papers of Benjamin Franklin*, 4:481–82.

3. Crèvecoeur, *Letters from an American Farmer*, pp. 208–9.

4. In another case, a former captive claims that the natives called him a god not because of any superior technology he possessed, but because of his talents as an interpreter (*The Surprising Adventures of Ransom Clark* [1839], in *Garland* 54:11).

5. See *A Narrative of the Captivity and Adventures of John Tanner* (1830), in *Garland* 46:100–101, 115–18. This work contains the only reference I know of in a captivity narrative of a marriage proposal from a transvestite (see pp. 105–6). For an example of a forced marriage, see Elias Darnall, *A Journal* (1813), in *Garland* 33:45–46.

6. On the Pocahontas complex, see Dearborn, *Pocahontas's Daughters*; Green,

"Pocahontas Complex"; Hubbell, "Smith-Pocahontas Story"; Mossiker, *Poca-hontas;* and Philip Young, "The Mother of Us All."

7. See "Mr. John Davenport's Narrative," in Elias Darnall, *A Journal* (1813), in *Garland* 33.

8. Other authors reported that Native Americans freely offered sexual favors to them. See, for example, "The Journal of Mr. Charles Le Raye," in Jervis Cutler, *A Topographical Description of the State of Ohio, Indiana Territory, and Louisiana* (1812), in *Garland* 34:184–85,

9. See Mintz, *Prison of Expectation,* for a study of the Victorian family.

10. This popular image of male comaraderie in nature has remained powerful in American culture and, through the mass media and commercial advertisements, has been exported around the world. One thinks, for example, of the subliminal associations of "the Marlboro man" and the popular series of television commercials for Old Milwaukee Beer, which feature a group of male friends on a hunting or fishing outing. They are usually sitting around a campfire as the sun sets, beer in hand, talking and laughing. Women are conspicuously absent as one of the men, speaking for them all, says, "It doesn't get any better than this."

11. The literature on this subject is extensive and growing rapidly. Mention might be made of Ryan, *Empire of the Mother;* Baym, *Woman's Fiction;* Cott, *Bonds of Womanhood;* Welter, "Cult of True Womanhood, 1820–1860"; Kaplan, *Sacred Tears,* and Douglas, *Feminization of American Culture.*

12. Even the nineteenth-century vogue for shaving devices promising a close shave and smooth facial skin came from the value placed on softening men's nature. See McKendrick, "George Packwood."

13. See Heard, *White into Red,* p. 14.

14. For the whole story, see E. N. Wilson, *White Indian Boy.*

15. Quoted in Axtell, "White Indians," p. 86.

16. Juliette Kinzie recalls one of the most striking—and, if the story is true, almost tragic—stories of the effect the content of captivity narratives (oral and written) had on persons. In 1779 when two small children in western Pennsylvania fled to the woods when Indians attacked their home, the small boy was about to kill his little sister, who could no longer run, in order to spare her the horrors of Indian captivity. Kinzie ends her retelling of this story with the comment, "The idea of the little boy that he could save his sister from savage barbarity by taking her life himself, shows what tales of horror the children of the early settlers were familiar with" (*Wau-bun,* in *Garland* 70:276).

17. Torgovnick, *Gone Primitive,* pp. 51, 53.

18. Kasson, *Marble Queens and Captives,* p. 4.

19. After Pamela has just finished recounting how Mr. B. had repeatedly attempted to seduce her and to have his way with her, even taking her captive, Lady Davers responds, "Except one had known these things, one should not have been able to judge of the Merit of your Resistance. . . . It was necessary, Child, on Twenty Accounts, that we, you and his Wellwishers and Relations, should know, that he had try'd every Stratagem, and made use of every Contrivance, to subdue you to his Purpose" (Richardson, *Pamela,* 3:44).

20. Native Americans, of course, imagined their own utopian and eschatological futures in the face of the devastating sociocultural consequences of white incursion. These took the form of the Ghost Dance and similar religious movements.

6. Inside the House of Mirrors

1. John Demos's *The Redeemed Captive* (1994) represents a return to an earlier form of narrative history by a distinguished historian.

2. These numbers are taken from the lists of films compiled in Friar and Friar, *Only Good Indian*, pp. 302–5.
3. John A. Price has roughly divided films depicting Indians into three major periods: 1908–29 witnessed the formation of negative stereotypes of Indians; 1930–48 saw extremely negative representations; since then there has been a gradual process of breaking down these negative stereotypes, while portraying the Indian in a positive light ("Stereotyping").
4. Only recently have questions of the fluidity of cultural, tribal, and individual identity become an important legal issue in Canada and the United States, as native rights movements have begun to bring their grievances and demands before the courts as members of recognized tribes. See, for instance, Jennifer S. H. Brown, *Strangers in Blood;* Canny and Pagden, *Colonial Identity in the Atlantic World;* Peterson and Brown, *New Peoples;* and Zuckerman, "Fabrication of Identity in Early America."
5. Rister, *Border Captives*, pp. viii, ix.
6. Cited in Mechling, "Playing Indian," p. 20.
7. Dickson, *Wilderness Man*, p. 8.
8. In a four-month speaking and promotional tour in England in 1935, Grey Owl delivered over two hundred talks to nearly a quarter of a million people. His book *Pilgrims of the Wild* was selling five thousand copies a month and going through multiple reprintings, while a children's book, *The Adventures of Sajo and Her Beaver People*, did even better (Dickson, *Wilderness Man*, pp. 238, 242).
9. Dickson, *Wilderness Man*, pp. 233–34.
10. For the definition of the "classic western" employed here, see Cawelti, *Adventure*.
11. On the women in John Ford's films, see Movshovitz, "The Still Point."
12. Richter, *Light in the Forest*, Acknowledgments.
13. Ibid.
14. Ibid., p. 50.
15. Ibid., p. 117.
16. See Berger, *Little Big Man*, p. 80, for Jack's appeal to the rational ruse as an explanation for his having gone native. See Tom Milne's review, "Little Big Man."
17. See, for example, Pauline Kael's review in the *New Yorker* and Friar and Friar, *Only Good Indian*, pp. 276–78. Having taught this film, I can report that (not surprisingly) students today do not read the film in this way. On the relationship of westerns and Vietnam War films, see Mortimer, "From Monument Valley to Vietnam."
18. Berger, *Little Big Man*, pp. ix, 440.
19. Ibid., pp. 428–29.
20. Ibid., pp. 440, 91.
21. Ibid., p. 23.
22. See, for instance, Penelope Gilliatt's review, "Back to the Trees," in the *New Yorker*, where she finds the film to be incredibly well-researched; Arthur Knight, "A Man Called Horse," in the *Saturday Review;* Margaret Ronan, "Film: Lo, the True Indian!" in *Senior Scholastic;* and the anonymous review, "Home of the Brave," in *Time*.
23. Friar and Friar, *Only Good Indian*, pp. 206–7. Other early reviewers were also critical of the film's purported ethnographic realism. See, for example, the reviews by Alex Keneas, Dan Georgakas, and Arthur Bell listed in the bibliography.
24. Friar and Friar, *Only Good Indian*, pp. 35–39.
25. Farber, "Short Notices."
26. Other elements of the white male fantasy found in the film include Morgan's becoming chief of the Yellow Hand Sioux band and being a superb warrior. He

also turns back an attacking horde of enemy Indians, avoiding a devastating rout, by organizing the Sioux on the spur of the moment into a British-style defensive line and having them shoot their arrows in unison on his command.

27. *Merriam-Webster's Collegiate Dictionary*, 10th ed.

28. See, for example, "Noble Non-savage: Chief Dan George," *Time* 97 (Feb. 15, 1971): 76.

29. Cabeza de Vaca's narrative is available in Hodge, *Spanish Explorers*. A recent Mexican film, "Cabeza de Vaca," directed by Nicolas Echevarria, has played in fine arts theaters in the United States and aired on PBS stations.

30. For information on how Tanner's editor handled his reports of the accuracy of prophetic dreams and visions, see *Garland* 46:5.

31. A more detailed account is available in Valeros, *Yo soy Napéyoma*.

32. Biocca, *Yanoáma*, p. 7.

33. Ibid., p. 7.

34. Ibid., pp. 34–35, 89, 87, 8. The irony, of course, is that Helena Valero was known to the Yanoáma, and she was certainly not the first white encountered by these people. What Biocca really sought, then, was to be the first white to record his encounter with the Yanoáma. It was not that the Yanoáma could not really "see" any whites; rather, what is essential is that the ethnographer be seen being seen by primitives.

35. Lamb, *Wizard of the Upper Amazon*, 2d ed., Introduction, pp. v, vi.

36. Ibid., pp. vi–vii.

37. Boorman, *Emerald Forest Diary*, pp. 7, 13–14, 97, 7–8.

38. Ibid., p. 22.

39. Ibid., pp. 168–69.

40. Ibid., pp. 211, 88–89.

41. Van Der Beets, *Indian Captivity Narrative*, p. 50.

42. He writes, for instance, "Certain beliefs and acts, unrestricted to a particular time yet found in the particular records of human experience throughout time, tend to have a common meaning and serve similar functions" (ibid., p. 39).

43. Slotkin adopts an archetypal approach in *Regeneration through Violence* (1973), labeling the captivity narrative a "cultural archetype" (i.e., a narrative pattern showing persistence within a single culture rather than worldwide distribution). Slotkin uses the term *archetype* in two different and incompatible ways: (1) in the Jungian-Campbellian sense of a timeless pattern; and (2) in referring to Mary Rowlandson's narrative as the model for later works. He abandoned this approach in the subsequent volumes of his cultural history.

44. Andrews et al., *Journeys in New Worlds*, p. 5.

45. Kolodny, *The Land before Her*, p. 18.

46. Woloch, *Women and the American Experience*, pp. vi, 1–15.

47. Namias, *White Captives*, p. xiv, 8, 10–11, 47.

48. Ibid., pp. 8, 10–11, 47.

49. Kestler, "Mary White Rowlandson," unpaginated "Dedication"; Namias, *White Captives*, pp. 47–48.

50. Porterfield, *Female Piety*, pp. 137, 8, 141.

51. Although I had not read *The Imaginary Puritan* before most of *Captured by Texts* had been completed, this aspect of the authorial condition is what I had sought to suggest by my own title.

52. Armstrong and Tennenhouse, *Imaginary Puritan*, pp. 25, 204, 208, 215. In *Domestic Individualism*, Gillian Brown has argued that the values of domesticity—interiority, privacy, and psychology—informed the development of nineteenth-century American individuality.

53. Ibid., p. 26.

54. Ludwig, *The Captive*, p. vi.

55. Breitwieser, *American Puritanism*, pp. 4, 10.

56. Ibid., p. 70.

57. Ibid., p. 70.
58. For a fuller discussion of the cultural significance of the Hearst case, see Ebersole, "Experience/Narrative Structure" and Timberg, "Patty Hearst." Timberg compares Hearst with Mercy Short, who became embroiled in the outbreak of witchcraft accusations in New England in the 1690s, arguing that both became national symbols of suffering and sin.

BIBLIOGRAPHY

Abel, Annie Heloise. *The American Indian as Slaveholder and Succes-sionist.* Cleveland: Arthur H. Clark, 1915.

Ackernecht, Erwin H. " 'White Indians': Psychological and Physiological Peculiarities of White Children Abducted and Reared by North American Indians." *Bulletin of the History of Medicine* 15 (1944): 15–36.

Adams, Percy C. *Travelers and Travel Liars, 1660–1800.* Berkeley: Univ. of California Press, 1962.

Albanese, Catherine L. *Nature Religion in America: From the Algonkian Indians to the New Age.* Chicago: Univ. of Chicago Press, 1990.

Allen, Phoebe S. "The Double Exposure of Texas Captives." *Western Folklore* 32 (1973): 249–61.

Anderson, Marilyn. "The Pocahantas Legend," *Indian Historian* 12, no. 2 (1979): 54–64.

Andrews, William L., ed. *Journeys in New Worlds: Early American Women's Narratives.* Madison: Univ. of Wisconsin Press, 1990.

Ariès, Philippe. *The Hour of Our Death.* New York: Knopf, 1981.

Armstrong, Nancy, and Leonard Tennenhouse. *The Imaginary Puritan: Literature, Intellectual Labor, and the Origins of Personal Life.* Berkeley: Univ. of California Press, 1992.

Arner, Robert. "The Story of Hannah Duston: Cotton Mather to Thoreau." *American Transcendental Quarterly* 18 (1973): 19–23.

Austerman, Wayne R. "The Ordeal of Jane Adeline Wilson." *Password* 35 (1990): 19–25.

Axtell, James. "The White Indians of Colonial America." *William and Mary Quarterly,* 3d ser. 32 (1975): 55–88; reprinted in his *The European and the Indian.*

———. "The Ethnohistory of Early North America: A Review Essay." *William and Mary Quarterly,* 3d ser. 35 (1978): 110–44.

———. *The European and the Indian: Essays in the Ethnohistory of Colonial North America.* New York: Oxford Univ. Press, 1981.

——. *The Invasion Within: The Contest of Cultures in Colonial North America.* New York: Oxford Univ. Press, 1985.

——. *After Columbus: Essays in the Ethnohistory of Colonial North America.* New York: Oxford Univ. Press, 1988.

Barbeau, C. Marius. "Indian Captivities." *Proceedings of the American Philosophical Society* 94 (1950): 522–48.

Barker-Benfield, G. J. *The Culture of Sensibility: Sex and Society in Eighteenth-Century Britain.* Chicago: Univ. of Chicago Press, 1992.

Barnett, Louise K. *The Ignoble Savage: American Literary Racism, 1790–1890.* Westport, Conn.: Greenwood, 1975.

Bataille, Gretchen M., and Charles C. P. Silet, eds. *The Pretend Indian: Images of Native Americans in the Movies.* Ames: Iowa State Univ. Press, 1980.

Batten, Charles L., Jr. *Pleasurable Instruction: Form and Convention in Eighteenth-Century Travel Literature.* Berkeley: Univ. of California Press, 1978.

Baudet, Henri. *Paradise on Earth: Some Thoughts on European Images of Non-European Man.* New Haven: Yale Univ. Press, 1965.

Baym, Nina. *Woman's Fiction: A Guide to Novels by and about Women in America, 1820–1870.* Ithaca: Cornell Univ. Press, 1978.

——. *Novels, Readers, and Reviewers: Responses to Fiction in Antebellum America.* Ithaca: Cornell Univ. Press, 1984.

Beasley, Jerry C. *Novels of the 1740's.* Athens: Univ. of Georgia Press, 1982.

Behen, Dorothy M. F. "The Captivity Story in American Literature, 1577–1826." Ph.D. diss., University of Chicago, 1952.

Bell, Arthur. "Neigh." *Commonweal* 92 (1970): 318.

Bell, Michael Davitt. *The Development of American Romance: The Sacrifice of Relation.* Chicago: Univ. of Chicago Press, 1980.

Benjamin, Walter. *Illuminations.* Trans. Harry Zohn. New York: Schocken, 1969.

Bercovitch, Sacvan. *Typology and Early American Literature.* Amherst: Univ. of Massachusetts Press, 1972.

——. *The Puritan Origins of the American Self.* New Haven: Yale Univ. Press, 1975.

——. *The American Jeremiad.* Madison: Univ. of Wisconsin Press, 1978.

——. "New England's Errand Reappraised," in John Higham and Paul Conkin, eds., *New Directions in American Intellectual History.* Baltimore: Johns Hopkins Univ. Press, 1979.

——, ed. *The American Puritan Imagination: Essays in Revaluation.* Cambridge: Harvard Univ. Press, 1974.

Bercovitch, Sacvan, and Myra Jehlen, eds. *Ideology and Classic American Literature.* Cambridge: Cambridge Univ. Press, 1986.

Berger, Morroe. *Real and Imagined Worlds: The Novel and Social Science.* Cambridge: Harvard Univ. Press, 1977.

Berger, Thomas. *Little Big Man.* New York: Dial, 1964.

Berkhofer, Robert F., Jr. *Salvation and the Savage: An Analysis of Protestant Missions and American Indian Response, 1787–1862.* Lexington: Univ. of Kentucky Press, 1965.

——. *The White Man's Indian: Images of the American Indian from Columbus to the Present.* New York: Knopf, 1978.

——. "The North American Fronter as Process and Context." In *The Frontier in History: North America and Southern Africa Compared,* ed. Howard Lamar and Leonard Thompson, pp. 43–75. New Haven: Yale Univ. Press, 1981.

Berthold, Arthur Benedict. *American Colonial Printing as Determined by Contemporary Cultural Forces, 1639–1763.* New York: Burt Franklin, 1970.

Bidney, David. "The Idea of the Savage in North American Ethnohistory." *Journal of the History of Ideas* 15 (1964): 322–27.

Bieder, Robert E. "Scientific Attitudes towards Mixed-Bloods in Early Nineteenth-Century America." *Journal of Ethnic Studies* 8 (1980): 17–30.

——. *Science Encounters the Indian, 1820–1880: The Early Years of American Ethnology.* Norman: Univ. of Oklahoma Press, 1986.

Billington, Ray Allen. *Land of Savagery, Land of Promise: The European Image of the American Frontier.* New York: Norton, 1981.

Biocca, Ettore, ed. *Yanoáma: The Story of a Woman Abducted by Brazilian Indians.* London: George Allen and Unwin, 1969. Rpt. as *Yanoama: The Narrative of a White Girl Kidnapped by Amazonian Indians.* New York: Dutton, 1970.

Birkhead, Edith. "Sentiment and Sensibility in the Eighteenth-Century Novel." In *Essays and Studies by Members of the English Association,* 11:92–116. London: Dawson, 1966.

Blackburn, Julia. *The White Man: The First Responses of Aboriginal Peoples to the White Man.* London: Orbis, 1979.

Bloch, Ruth H. "American Feminine Ideals in Transition: The Rise of the Moral Mother, 1785–1815." *Feminist Studies* 4 (1978): 101–26.

——. "The Gendered Meanings of Virtue in Revolutionary America." *Signs* 13 (1987): 37–58.

Boning, Richard A. *The Long Search.* Baldwin, N.Y.: Dexter & Westbrook, 1972.

Boorman, John. *The Emerald Forest Diary.* New York: Farrar, Straus Giroux, 1985.

Bourdieu, Pierre. *Language and Symbolic Power.* Ed. John B. Thompson. Cambridge: Harvard Univ. Press, 1990.

——. *The Logic of Practice.* Stanford: Stanford Univ. Press, 1990.

Bourne, Russell. *The Red King's Rebellion: Racial Politics in New England, 1675–1678.* New York: Oxford Univ. Press, 1990.

Brantley, Richard E. *Locke, Wesley, and the Method of English Romanticism.* Gainesville: Univ. of Florida Press, 1984.

Bredvold, Louis I. *The Natural History of Sensibility.* Detroit: Wayne State Univ. Press, 1962.

Breen, Gertrude. *Indian Captive: The Story of Mary Jemison, by Lois Lenski.* Play no. 31. Chicago: Coach House Press, 1961.

Breen, T. H. *Puritans and Adventurers: Change and Persistence in Early America.* New York: Oxford Univ. Press, 1980.

Breitwieser, Mitchell Robert. *American Puritanism and the Defense of Mourning: Religion, Grief, and Ethnology in Mary White Rowlandson's Captivity Narrative.* Madison: Univ. of Wisconsin Press, 1990.

Brisbin, James S., ed. *Belden, The White; or, Twelve Years Among the Wild Indians of the Plains.* Athens: Ohio Univ. Press, 1974. Rpt. of the 1870 edition.

Brissenden, R. F. " 'Sentiment': Some Uses of the Word in the Writings of David Hume." In *Studies in the Eighteenth Century,* ed. Brissenden, pp. 89–107. Canberra: Australian National Univ. Press, 1968.

——. *Virtue in Distress: Studies in the Novel of Sentiment from Richardson to Sade.* New York: Harper and Row, 1976.

Brown, Charles Brockden. *Edgar Huntly; or, Memoirs of a Sleep-Walker.* Bicentennial Ed. Kent, Ohio: Kent State Univ. Press, 1984.

Brown, Gillian. *Domestic Individualism: Imagining Self in Nineteenth-Century America.* Berkeley: Univ. of California Press, 1990.

Brown, Herbert Ross. *The Sentimental Novel in America, 1789–1860.* Durham: Duke Univ. Press, 1940.

Brown, Jennifer S. H. *Strangers in Blood: Fur Trade Company Families in Indian Country.* Vancouver: Univ. of British Columbia Press, 1980.

Brown, Parker B. "The Fate of Crawford Volunteers Captured by Indians Following the Battle of Sandusky in 1782." *Western Pennsylvania Historical Magazine* 65 (1982): 323–40.

Brown, Richard D. *Knowledge Is Power: The Diffusion of Information in Early America, 1700–1865.* New York: Oxford Univ. Press, 1989.

Brumm, Ursula. "The Art of Puritan Meditation in New England." In *Studies in New England Puritanism,* ed. Winifred Herget, pp. 139–68. Frankfurt am Main: Verlag Peter Lang, 1983.

Buckelew, F. M. *The Indian Captivity as Related by Himself. Life of F. M. Buckelew.* Bandera, Tex.: Hunter's Publishing House, 1925.

Buscombe, Edward, ed. *The BFI Companion to the Western.* London: André Deutsch/British Film Institute, 1988.

Butler, Jon. *Awash in a Sea of Faith: Christianizing the American People.* Cambridge: Harvard Univ. Press, 1990.

Caldwell, Patricia. *The Puritan Conversion Narrative: The Beginnings of American Expression.* New York: Cambridge Univ. Press, 1983.

Calloway, Colin G. "An Uncertain Destiny: Indian Captivities on the Upper Connecticut River." *Journal of American Studies* 17 (1983): 190–210.

——. "The Conquest of Vermont: Vermont's Indian Troubles in Context." *Vermont History* 52 (1984): 161–79.

——. *North Country Captives: Selected Narratives of Indian Captivity from Vermont and New Hampshire.* Hanover, N.H.: Univ. Press of New England, 1992.

——. ed. *New Directions in American Indian History.* Norman: Univ. of Oklahoma Press, 1988.

Campbell, Maria. *The Half-Breed.* Toronto: McClelland and Stewart, 1973.

Canny, Nicholas, and Anthony Pagden, eds. *Colonial Identity in the Atlantic World, 1500–1800.* Princeton: Princeton Univ. Press, 1987.

Carey, Larry Lee. "A Story of the Indian Captivity Narrative as a Popular Literary Genre, ca. 1575–1875." Ph.D. diss., Michigan State University, 1978.

Carleton, Phillips D. "The Indian Captivity." *American Literature* 15 (1943): 169–80.

Caswell, Harriet S. *Our Life Among the Iroquois Indians.* Boston and Chicago: Congregational Sunday-School and Publishing Society, 1892.

Cawelti, John C. *Adventure, Mystery, and Romance: Formula Stories as Art and Popular Culture.* Chicago: Univ. of Chicago Press, 1976.

Charvat, William. *The Profession of Authorship in America, 1800–1870.* Ed. Matthew J. Bruccoli. Columbus: Ohio State Univ. Press, 1968.

Chiapelli, Fredi, Michael J. B. Allen, and Robert L. Benson, eds. *First Images of America: The Impact of the New World on the Old.* 2 vols. Berkeley: Univ. of California Press, 1976.

Clark, Edward W. *The Redeemed Captive: John Williams.* Amherst: Univ. of Massachusetts Press, 1976.

Clark, Robert. *History, Ideology and Myth in American Fiction, 1823–52.* London: Macmillan, 1984.

Clifton, James A., ed. *Being and Becoming Indian: Biographical Studies of North American Frontiers.* Chicago: Dorsey, 1989.

Cohen, Charles L. *God's Caress: The Psychology of Puritan Religious Experience.* New York: Oxford Univ. Press, 1986.

Cohen, Daniel A. *Pillars of Salt, Monuments of Grace: New England Crime Literature and the Origins of American Popular Culture, 1674–1860.* New York: Oxford Univ. Press, 1993.

Coldham, Peter Wilson. "The 'Spiriting' of London Children to Virginia, 1684–1685." *Virginia Magazine of History and Biography* 83 (1975): 280–87.

Coleman, Emma Lewis. *New England Captives Carried to Canada.* 2 vols. Portland, Maine: Southworth, 1925.

Cooper, James Fenimore. *The Wept of Wish-Ton-Wish.* Boston: Dana Estes, 1909.

Corrigan, John. *The Prism of Piety: Catholick Congregational Clergy at the Beginning of the Enlightenment.* New York: Oxford Univ. Press, 1991.

Cortesi, Lawrence. "The Tragic Romance of Jane McCrea." *American History Illustrated* 20 (Apr. 1985): 10–15.

Cott, Nancy F. *The Bonds of Womanhood: "Woman's Sphere" in New England, 1780–1835.* New Haven: Yale Univ. Press, 1977.

Crane, Ronald S. "Suggestions toward a Genealogy of the 'Man of Feeling,'" *ELH: A Journal of English Literary History* 1 (1934): 205–30.

Crèvecoeur, J. Hecter St. Jean de. *Letters from an American Farmer,* London and New York: Dutton, n.d.

Cvetkovich, Ann. *Mixed Feelings: Feminism, Mass Culture, and Victorian Sensationalism.* New Brunswick, N.J.: Rutgers Univ. Press, 1992.

Davidson, Cathy N. *Revolution and the Word: The Rise of the Novel in America.* New York: Oxford Univ. Press, 1986.

——. ed. *Reading in America: Literature and Social History.* Baltimore: Johns Hopkins Univ. Press, 1989.

Davis, Mrs. Elvert M. "History of the Capture and Captivity of David Boyd from Cumberland County Pennsylvania, 1756." *Western Pennsylvania Historical Magazine* 14 (1931): 28–39.

Davis, Lennard J. "A Social History of Fact and Fiction: Authorial Disavowal in the Early English Novel." In *Literature and Society: Selected Papers from the English Institute, 1978.* Ed. Edward Said. Baltimore: Johns Hopkins Univ. Press, 1980.

Dearborn, Mary V. *Pocahontas's Daughters: Gender and Ethnicity in American Culture.* New York: Oxford Univ. Press, 1986.

DeCamp Sweet, J. E. "Mrs. J. E. DeCamp Sweet's Narrative of Her Captivity in the Sioux Outbreak of 1862." *Minnesota Collections* 6 (1894): 354–80.

Demos, John. *The Unredeemed Captive: A Family Story from Early America.* New York: Knopf, 1994.

Derounian, Kathryn Zabelle. "Puritan Orthodoxy and the 'Survivor Syndrome' in Mary White Rowlandson's Indian Captivity Narrative." *Early American Literature* 22 (1987): 82–93.

——. "The Publication, Promotion, and Distribution of Mary White Rowlandson's Captivity Narrative in the Seventeenth Century." *Early American Literature* 23 (1988): 239–61.

Derounian-Stodola, Kathryn Zabelle, and James A. Levernier. *The Indian Captivity Narrative, 1550–1900.* New York: Twayne, 1993.

Dickinson, A. T., Jr. *American Historical Fiction.* 2d ed. New York: Scarecrow, 1963.

Dickson, Lovat. *Wilderness Man: The Strange Story of Grey Owl.* New York: Athenaeum, 1973.

Diebold, Robert, ed. *The Narrative of the Captivity and Restoration of Mrs. Mary Rowlandson.* National Bicentennial Ed. Lancaster, Mass.: N.R., 1975.

Dijkstra, Bram. *Idols of Perversity: Fantasies of Feminine Evil in Fin-de-Siècle Culture.* New York: Oxford Univ. Press, 1986.

Dolbeare, Benjamin. *A Narrative of the Captivity and Suffering of Dolly Webster among the Comanche Indians in Texas.* 1843. Rpt. New Haven: Yale Univ. Press, 1986.

Dondore, Dorothy A. "White Captives among the Indians." *New York History* 13 (1932): 292–300.

Douglas, Ann. "Heaven Our Home: Consolation Literature in the Northern United States, 1830–1880." *American Quarterly* 26 (1974): 496–515.

——. *The Feminization of American Culture.* New York: Knopf, 1977.

Downing, David. " 'Streams of Scripture Comfort': Mary Rowlandson's Typological Use of the Bible." *Early American Literature* 15 (1980): 252–59.

Drimmer, Frederick, ed. *Scalps and Tomahawks: Narratives of Indian Captivity.* New York: Coward-McCann, 1961.

Drinnon, Richard. *White Savage: The Case of John Dunn Hunter.* New York: Schocken, 1972.

——. *Facing West: The Metaphysics of Indian-Hating and Empire Building.* Minneapolis: Univ. of Minnesota Press, 1980.

Dudley, Edward, and Maximillian Novak, eds. *The Wild Man Within: An Image in Western Thought from the Renaissance to Romanticism.* Pittsburgh: Univ. of Pittsburgh Press, 1972.

Eastman, Charles Alexander (Ohiyesa). *From the Deep Woods to Civilization.* 1916. Rpt. Lincoln: Univ. of Nebraska Press, 1977.

Eastman, Edwin. *Seven and Nine Years among the Comanche and Apaches: An Autobiography.* Jersey City: Clark Johnson, 1873.

Ebersole, Gary L. "Experience/Narrative Structure/Reading: Patty Hearst and the American Indian Captivity Narratives." *Religion* 18 (1988): 225–42.

Edgerton, Samuel Y., Jr. *"The Murder of Jane McCrea:* The Tragedy of an American Tableau d'Histoire." *Art Bulletin* 58 (1965): 481–92.

Edkins, Carol. "Quest for Community: Spiritual Autobiography of Eighteenth-Century Quaker and Puritan Women in America." In *Women's Autobiography: Essays in Criticism,* ed. Estelle C. Jelinek, pp. 39–52. Bloomington: Indiana Univ. Press, 1980.

Eliade, Mircea. *Rites and Symbols of Initiation.* New York: Harper & Row, 1958.

——. "Methodological Remarks on the Study of Religious Symbolism." In *The History of Religions: Essays in Methodology,* ed. Eliade and Joseph M. Kitagawa, pp. 86–107. Chicago: Univ. of Chicago Press, 1959.

——. "Initiation and the Modern World." In Eliade, *The Quest: History and Meaning in Religion,* pp. 112–26. Chicago: Univ. of Chicago Press, 1969.

——. "Cultural Fashions and the History of Religions." In Eliade, *Occultism, Witchcraft and Cultural Fashions: Essays in Comparative Religions,* pp. 1–17. Chicago: Univ. of Chicago Press, 1976.

Eliot, George. *Adam Bede.* Boston: Houghton Mifflin, 1968.

Elliot, Emory. *Power and the Pulpit in Puritan New England.* Princeton: Princeton Univ. Press, 1974.

——. *American Colonial Writers, 1606–1734.* Detroit: Gale, 1984.

Emerson, Everett, ed. *American Literature, 1764–1789: The Revolutionary Years.* Madison: Univ. of Wisconsin Press, 1977.

Emerson, Roger L. "American Indians, Frenchmen, and Scots Philosophers." *Studies in Eighteenth-Century Culture* 9 (1979): 211–36.

Epstein, Barbara. *The Politics of Domesticity: Women, Evangelism, and Temperance in Nineteenth-Century America.* Middletown, Conn.: Wesleyan Univ. Press, 1981.

Eramesta, Erik. *A Study of the Word "Sentimental" and Other Linguistic Characteristics of Eighteenth-Century Sentimentalism in England.* Helsinki: Helsingin Liikekirjapaino Oy, 1951.

Farber, Stephen. "Short Notices: 'A Man Called Horse' and 'Flap.'" *Film Quarterly* 24 (Fall 1970): 60–61.

Farley, Alan W. "An Indian Captivity and Its Legal Aftermath." *Kansas Historical Quarterly* 21 (1954): 247–56.

Fielder, Leslie. *The Return of the Vanishing American.* New York: Stein and Day, 1968.

Fiering, Norman S. "Irresistible Compassion: An Aspect of Eighteenth-Century Sympathy and Humanitarianism." *Journal of the History of Ideas* 37 (1976): 195–218.

——. *Jonathan Edwards' Moral Thought and Its British Context.* Chapel Hill: Univ. of North Carolina Press, 1981.

——. *Moral Philosophy at Seventeenth-Century Harvard: A Discipline in Transition.* Chapel Hill: Univ. of North Carolina Press, 1981.

Fierst, John T. "Return to 'Civilization': John Tanner's Troubled Years at Sault Ste. Marie." *Minnesota History* 50 (Spring 1986): 23–36.

Fisher, Philip. *Hard Facts: Setting and Form in the American Novel.* New York: Oxford Univ. Press, 1987.

Fitzpatrick, Tara. "The Figure of Captivity: The Cultural Work of the Puritan Captivity Narrative." *American Literary History* 3 (1991): 1–26.

Fletcher, Angus, ed. *The Literature of Fact: Selected Papers from the English Institute.* New York: Columbia Univ. Press, 1976.

Fliegelman, Jay. *Prodigals and Pilgrims: The American Revolution against Patriarchal Authority, 1750–1800.* Cambridge: Cambridge Univ. Press, 1982.

Flores, Dan L., ed. *Journal of an Indian Trader: Anthony Glass and the Texts Trading Frontier, 1790–1810.* College Station: Texas A & M Univ. Press, 1986.

Franklin, Wayne. *Discoverers, Explorers, Settlers: The Diligent Writers of Early America.* Chicago: Univ. of Chicago Press, 1979.

Friar, Ralph E., and Natasha A. Friar. *The Only Good Indian . . . The Hollywood Gospel.* New York: Drama Book, 1972.

Freeman, John F. "The Indian Convert: Theme and Variation." *Ethnohistory* 12 (1965): 113–28.

——. "Religion and Personality in the Anthropology of Henry Schoolcraft." *Journal of the History of the Behavioral Sciences* 1 (1965): 301–12.

French, Philip. *Westerns: Aspects of a Movie Genre.* Rev. ed. Cinema One Series, vol. 25. London: Secker & Warburg, 1977.

Friedman, Arthur. "Aspects of Sentimentalism in Eighteenth-Century Literature." In *The Augustan Milieu,* ed. Eric Rothstein and G. S. Rousseau, pp. 247–61. Oxford: Oxford Univ. Press, 1970.

Frieman, Larence J. *The White Savage: Racial Fantasies in the Postbellum South.* Englewood Cliffs, N.J.: Prentice-Hall, 1970.

———. *Inventors of the Promised Land.* New York: Knopf, 1975.

Fryd, Vivien Green. "Two Sculptures for the Capitol: Horatio Greenough's *Rescue* and Luigi Perisco's *Discovery of America.*" *American Art Journal* 19, no. 2 (1987): 16–39.

Gardner, Jeanne LeMonnier. *Mary Jemison: Seneca Captive.* New York: Harcourt, Brace & World, 1966.

The Garland Library of Narratives of North American Indian Captivities. 311 titles in 111 volumes. Selected and arranged by Wilcomb E. Washburn. New York & London: Garland, 1976–77.

Gay, Peter. *A Loss of Mastery: Puritan Historians in Colonial America.* Berkeley: Univ. of California Press, 1966.

Geertz, Clifford. *The Interpretation of Cultures.* New York: Basic Books, 1973.

Georgakas, Dan. "They Have Not Spoken: American Indians in Film." *Film Quarterly* 25 (Spring 1972): 26–32.

Gherman, Dawn L. "From Parlour to Tepee: The White Squaw on the American Frontier." Ph.D. diss., University of Massachusetts, 1975.

Gilliatt, Penelope. "Back to the Trees." *New Yorker* 46 (May 9, 1970): 118.

Gilmore, Michael T. *The Middle Way: Puritanism and Ideology in American Romantic Fiction.* New Brunswick, N.J.: Rutgers Univ. Press, 1977.

———. *American Romanticism and the Marketplace.* Chicago: Univ. of Chicago Press, 1985.

Green, Rayna. "The Pocahontas Complex: The Image of Indian Women in Popular Culture." *Massachusetts Review* 16 (1975): 698–714.

Greenblatt, Stephen J. "Learning to Curse: Aspects of Linguistic Colonialism in the Sixteenth Century." In *First Images of America: The Impact of the New World on the Old,* ed. Fredi Chiapelli, 2:561–80. Berkeley: Univ. of California Press, 1976.

———. *Marvelous Possessions: The Wonder of the New World.* Chicago: Univ. of Chicago Press, 1992.

Greene, David L. "New Light on Mary Rowlandson." *Early American Literature* 20 (1985): 24–38.

Greene, Donald. "Latitudinarianism and Sensibility: The Genealogy of the 'Man of Sensibility' Reconsidered." *Modern Philology* 75 (1977): 159–83.

Gura, Philip F. *The Wisdom of Words: Language, Theology, and Literature in the New England Renaissance.* Middletown, Conn.: Wesleyan Univ. Press, 1981.

Haberly, David T. "Women and Indians: *The Last of the Mohicans* and the Captivity Tradition." *American Quarterly* 28 (1976): 431–41.

Hacker, Margaret Schmidt, and Cheryl J. Foote. *Cynthia Ann Parker: The Life and the Legend.* Southwestern Studies Series no. 92. El Paso: Texas Western Press, 1990.

Hadlock, Wendall S. "The Concept of Tribal Separation as Rationalized in Indian Folklore." *Pennsylvania Archaeologist* 16 (1946): 84–90.

Hagstrum, Jean H. *Sex and Sensibility: Ideal and Erotic Love from Milton to Mozart.* Chicago: Univ. of Chicago Press, 1980.

Hall, David D. *The Faithful Shepard: A History of the New England Ministry in the Seventeenth Century.* Chapel Hill: Univ. of North Carolina Press, 1972.

——. "The World of Print and Collective Mentality in Seventeenth-Century New England." In *New Directions in American Intellectual History,* ed. John Higham and Paul K. Conkin. Baltimore: Johns Hopkins Univ. Press, 1979.

——. *Worlds of Wonder, Days of Judgment: Popular Religious Belief in Early New England.* Cambridge: Harvard Univ. Press, 1989.

Hall, David D., and David Grayson Allen, eds. *Seventeenth-Century New England.* Boston: Colonial Society of Massachusetts, 1984.

Hall, David D., and John B. Hench, eds. *Needs and Opportunities in the History of the Book: America, 1639–1876.* Worcester, Mass.: American Antiquarian Society, 1987.

Hall, David D., John M. Murrin, and Thad W. Tate, eds. *Saints and Revolutionaries: Essays on Early American History.* New York: Norton, 1984.

Halliburton, Robert, Jr. *Red over Black: Black Slavery among the Cherokee Indians.* Westport, Conn.: Greenwood, 1977.

Hallowell, A. Irving. "American Indians, White and Black: The Phenomenon of Transculturalization." *Current Anthropology* 4 (1963): 519–31.

Hambrick-Stowe, Charles E. *The Practice of Piety: Puritan Devotional Disciplines in Seventeenth-Century New England.* Chapel Hill: Univ. of North Carolina Press, 1982.

Hanna, Warren L. *The Life and Times of James Willard Schultz (Apikuni).* Norman: Univ. of Oklahoma Press, 1986.

Harris, Susan K. *Nineteenth-Century American Women's Novels: Interpretive Strategies.* Cambridge: Cambridge Univ. Press, 1990.

Hart, James D. *The Popular Book: A History of America's Literary Taste.* New York: Oxford Univ. Press, 1950.

Hatch, Nathan O., and Harry S. Stout, eds. *Jonathan Edwards and the American Experience.* New York: Oxford Univ. Press, 1988.

Heard, J. Norman. *White into Red: A Study of the Assimilation of White Persons Captured by Indians.* Metuchen, N.J.: Scarecrow, 1973.

Heckewelder, John. *History, Manners, and Customs of the Indian Nations Who Once Inhabited Pennsylvania and the Neighboring States.* 1819. Rpt. New York: Arno Press, 1971.

Heimert, Alan. "Puritanism, the Wilderness, and the Frontier." *New England Quarterly* 26 (1953): 261–82.

——. *Religion and the American Mind: From the Great Awakening to the Revolution.* Cambridge: Harvard Univ. Press, 1966.

Heizer, Robert F., and Theodore Kroeber, eds. *Ishi, the Last Yahi: A Documentary History.* Berkeley: Univ. of California Press, 1979.

Herget, Winfried, ed. *Studies in New England Puritanism.* Studien und Texte zur Amerikanistik Bd. 9. Frankfurt am Main: Verlag Peter Lang, 1983.

Hilliard-d'Auberteuil, Michel René. *Miss McCrea: A Novel of the American Revolution.* Trans. Eric LaGuardia. Gainesville, Fl.: Scholars' Facsimilies and Reprints, 1958.

Hinsley, Curtis M., Jr. *Savages and Scientists: The Smithsonian Institution and the Development of American Anthropology, 1846–1910.* Washington, D.C.: Smithsonian Institution Press, 1981.

Hitt, Jim. *The American West from Fiction (1823–1976) into Film.* Jefferson, N.C., & London: McFarland, 1990.

Hodge, Frederick W., ed. *Spanish Explorers in the Southern United States, 1528–1543.* New York: Scribners, 1907.

Hodgen, Margaret T. *Early Anthropology in the Sixteenth and Seventeenth Centuries.* Philadelphia: Univ. of Pennsylvania Press, 1964.

"Home of the Brave." *Time* 95 (May 11, 1970): 103.

Horsman, Reginald. "Scientific Racism and the American Indian in the Mid-Nineteenth Century." *American Quarterly* 27 (1975): 152–68.

Hubbell, Jay. "The Smith-Pocahontas Story in Literature." *The Virginia Magazine of History and Biography* 65 (1957): 275–300.

Huddleston, Lee. *Origins of the American Indians: European Concepts, 1492–1729.* Austin: Univ. of Texas Press, 1967.

Hudson, Charles M., ed. *Red, White and Black: Symposium on Indians in the Old South.* Athens: Univ. of Georgia Press, 1971.

Hulme, Peter. *Colonial Encounters: Europe and the Native Caribbean, 1492–1797.* London and New York: Methuen, 1986.

Hume, David. *A Treatise of Human Nature.* Ed. Ernest C. Mossner. London: Penguin Books, 1969.

Humphreys, A. R. "'The Friend of Mankind' (1700–[17]60)—an Aspect of Eighteenth-Century Sensibility." *Review of English Studies* 24 (1948): 203–18.

Hunter, J. Marvin, ed. *Nine Years among the Indians.* Austin, Tex.: Von Boeckmann–Jones, 1927.

Hunter, J. Paul. *Before Novels: The Cultural Contexts of Eighteenth-Century English Fiction.* New York: Norton, 1990.

Hutton, Paul A. "The Two Worlds of William Wells." *American History* 28 (1983): 33–41.

Jaene, Cornelius J. *Friend and Foe: Aspects of French-Amerindian Cultural Contact in the Sixteenth and Seventeenth Centuries.* New York: Columbia Univ. Press, 1976.

Janeway, Elizabeth. *Powers of the Weak.* New York: Knopf, 1980.

Jansen, Maarten, Peter Van Der Loo, and Roswitha Manning, eds. *Continuity and Identity in Native America: Essays in Honor of Benedikt Hartmann*. Leiden: Brill, 1988.

Jennings, Francis. "Goals and Functions of Puritan Missions to the Indians." *Ethnohistory* 18 (1971): 197–212.

——. "Virgin Land and Savage People." *American Quarterly* 23 (1971): 519–41.

——. *The Invasion of America: Indians, Colonialism, and the Cant of Conquest*. Chapel Hill: Univ. of North Carolina Press, 1975.

Jensen, Joan M., and Darlis Miller. "Gentle Tamers Revisited: New Approaches to the History of Women in the American West." *Pacific Historical Review* 49 (1980): 173–213.

John, Elizabeth A. H. *Storms Brewed in Other Men's Worlds: The Confrontation of Indians, Spanish, and French in the Southwest, 1540–1795*. College Station: Texas A & M Univ. Press, 1975.

Johnson, Dorothy M. "Lost Sister." In *Mid-Century: An Anthology of Distinguished Contemporary American Short Stories*, ed. Orville Prescott, pp. 1–13. New York: Pocket Library, 1958.

Johnson, Robert C. "The Transportation of Vagrant Children from London to Virginia, 1618–1622." In *Early Stuart Studies: Essays in Honor of David Harris Willson*, ed. Howard S. Reinmuth, Jr., pp. 137–51. Minneapolis: Univ. of Minnesota Press, 1970.

Jones, Phyllis M. "Puritan's Progress: The Story of the Soul's Salvation in the Early New England Sermons." *Early American Literature* 15 (1980): 14–28.

Jordon, Winthrop D. *White over Black: American Attitudes toward the Negro, 1550–1812*. Baltimore: Penguin Books, 1969.

Joyce, William L., ed. *Printing and Society in Early America*. Worcester, Mass.: American Antiquarian Society, 1983.

Kael, Pauline. "The Current Cinema." *New Yorker*, Dec. 26, 1970, pp. 50–52.

Kaplan, Fred. *Sacred Tears: Sentimentality in Victorian Literature*. Princeton: Princeton Univ. Press, 1987.

Kasson, Joy. *Marble Queens and Captives: Women in Nineteenth-Century American Sculpture*. New Haven: Yale Univ. Press, 1846–65. *Dialogue* 18 (1984): 82–88.

King, John Owen. *The Iron of Melancholy: Structures of Spiritual Conversion from the Puritan Conscience to Victorian Neurosis*. Middletown, Conn.: Wesleyan Univ. Press, 1983.

Knight, Arthur. "A Man Called Horse," *Saturday Review of Literature* 53 (May 2, 1970): 51.

Knowles, Nathaniel. "The Torture of Captives by the Indians of Eastern North America." *Proceedings of the American Philosophical Society* 82 (1940): 151–225.

Koehler, Lyle. *A Search for Power: The "Weaker Sex" in Seventeenth-Century New England*. Urbana: Univ. of Illinois Press, 1980.

Kolodny, Annette. *The Lay of the Land: Metaphor as Experience and History in American Life and Letters.* Chapel Hill: Univ. of North Carolina Press, 1975.

——. "Turning the Lens on 'The Panther Captivity': A Feminist Exercise in Practical Criticism." *Critical Inquiry* 8 (1981): 329–45.

——. *The Land before Her: Fantasy and Experience of the American Frontiers, 1630–1860.* Chapel Hill: Univ. of North Carolina Press, 1984.

——. "Captives in Paradise: Women on the Early American Frontier." In *Women's Personal Narratives: Essays in Criticism and Pedagogy,* ed. Lenore Hoffman and Margo Culley, pp. 93–111. New York: Modern Language Association, 1985.

——. "Among the Indians: The Uses of Captivity." *New York Times Book Review,* Jan. 31, 1993, pp. 26–29.

Kroeber, Theodora. *Ishi in Two Worlds: A Biography of the Last Wild Indian in North America.* Berkeley: Univ. of California Press, 1961.

Kupperman, Karen Ordahl. "Nature's 'Rude Garden': English and Indians as Producers and Consumers of Food in Early New England." *Comparative Civilizations Review* 1 (1979): 64–78.

——. *Settling with the Indians: The Meeting of English and Indian Cultures in America, 1580–1640.* Totowa, N.J.: Rowman and Littlefield, 1980.

Labanee, Leonard W., et al., eds. *The Papers of Benjamin Franklin,* vol. 4. New Haven: Yale Univ. Press, 1961.

Lamb, F. Bruce. *Wizard of the Upper Amazon: The Story of Manuel Córdova-Rios.* 2d ed. Boston: Houghton Mifflin, 1974.

Landsman, Gail H. "The 'Other' as Political Symbol: Images of Indians in the Woman Suffrage Movement." *Ethnohistory* 39 (1992): 247–84.

Lankford, George E. "Losing the Past: Draper and the Ruddell Indian Captivity." *Arkansas Historical Quarterly* 49 (1990): 214–39.

Lawrence, Christopher. "The Nervous System and Society in the Scottish Enlightenment." In *Natural Order: Historical Studies of Scientific Culture,* ed. Barry Barnes and Steven Shapin, pp. 19–39. Beverly Hills: Sage Publications, 1979.

Lawson-Peebles, Robert. *Landscape and Written Expression in Revolutionary America: The World Turned Upside Down.* Cambridge: Cambridge Univ. Press, 1988.

Leach, Douglas Edward. "The 'Whens' of Mary Rowlandson's Captivity." *New England Quarterly* 24 (1960): 352–63.

Legates, Marlene. "The Cult of Womanhood in Eighteenth-Century Thought." *Eighteenth-Century Studies* 10 (1976): 21–39.

Lehmann-Haupt, Hellmut. *The Book in America: A History of the Making and Selling of Books in the United States.* New York: Bowker, 1951.

Lenski, Lois. *Indian Captive: The Story of Mary Jemison,* 15th ed. Philadelphia: Lippincott, 1941.

Levernier, James A. "Indian Captivity Narratives: Their Functions and Forms." Ph.D. diss., University of Pennsylvania, 1975.

Levernier, James, and Henning Cohen, eds. *The Indians and Their Captives.* Contributions in American Studies, no. 31. Westport, Conn.: Greenwood, 1977.

Lewalski, Barbara Kiefer. *Protestant Poetics and the Seventeenth-Century Religious Lyric.* Princeton: Princeton Univ. Press, 1979.

Lewis, James R. "Assessing the Impact of Indian Captivity on the Euro-American Mind: Some Critical Issues." *Connecticut Review* 11 (1989): 14–26.

Lincoln, Charles H., ed. *Narratives of the Indian Wars 1675–1699.* New York: Scribners, 1913.

Lockridge, Kenneth A. *A New England Town: The First Hundred Years.* New York: Norton, 1970.

———. *Literacy in Colonial New England: An Enquiry into the Social Context of Literacy in the Early Modern West.* New York: Norton, 1974.

Long, Charles H. *Significations: Signs, Symbols, and Images in the Interpretation of Religion.* Philadelphia: Fortress Press, 1986.

Loshe, Lillie Deming. *The Early American Novel.* Lancaster, Pa.: New Era Printing, 1907.

Lowance, Mason I., Jr. *The Language of Canaan: Metaphor and Symbol in New England from the Puritans to the Transcendentalists.* Cambridge: Harvard Univ. Press, 1980.

Ludwig, Mark, ed. *The Captive: The True Story of the Captivity of Mrs. Mary Rowlandson among the Indians and God's Faithfulness to Her in Her Time of Trial.* Rev. ed. Tucson: American Eagle Publications, 1988.

Luft, Martha Levy. "Charles Wimar's *The Abduction of Daniel Boone's Daughter by the Indians,* 1853 and 1855: Evolving Myths." *Prospects* 7 (1982): 300–314.

Lynch, James. "The Iroquois Confederacy and the Adoption and Administration of Non-Iroquoian Individuals and Groups Prior to 1756." *Man in the Northeast* 30 (1985): 83–99.

McKendrick, Neil. "George Packwood and the Commercialization of Shaving: The Art of Eighteenth-Century Advertising or 'The Way to Get Money and Be Happy,' " in Neil McKendrick, John Brewer, and J. H. Plumb, eds., *Birth of a Consumer Society: The Commercialization of Eighteenth-Century England* (Bloomington: Indiana Univ. Press, 1982).

McKeon, Michael. *The Origins of the English Novel, 1600–1740.* Baltimore: Johns Hopkins Univ. Press, 1987.

McLoughlin, William G. "Red Indians, Black Slavery, and White Racism: America's Slaveholding Indians." *American Quarterly* 26 (1974): 367–85.

McLoughlin, William G., and Walter H. Conser, Jr. "The First Man

Was Red—Cherokee Responses to the Debate over Indian Origins, 1760–1860." *American Quarterly* 41 (1989): 243–64.

Mailloux, Steven. *Interpretive Conventions: The Reader in the Study of American Fiction.* Ithaca: Cornell Univ. Press, 1982.

Manfred, Frederick. *Scarlet Plume.* Lincoln: Univ. of Nebraska Press, 1983.

Marsh, R. O. *White Indians of Darien.* New York: Putnam, 1934.

Marshall, David. *The Surprising Effects of Sympathy: Marivaux, Diderot, Rousseau, and Mary Shelley.* Chicago: Univ. of Chicago Press, 1988.

Martin, Calvin, ed. *The American Indian and the Problem of History.* New York: Oxford Univ. Press, 1987.

Martin, Terence. *The Instructed Vision: Scottish Common Sense Philosophy and the Origins of American Fiction.* Bloomington: Indiana Univ. Press, 1961.

Martz, Louis L. *The Poetry of Meditation: A Study in English Religious Literature of the Seventeenth Century.* New Haven: Yale Univ. Press, 1954.

Meade, James. "The 'Westerns' of the East: Narratives of Indian Captivity from Jeremiad to Gothic Novel." Ph.D. diss., Northwestern University, 1971.

Mechling, Jay. "Playing Indian and the Search for Authenticity in Modern White America." *Prospects* 5 (1980): 17–33.

Medlicott, Alexander, Jr. "Return to the Land of Light: A Plea to an Unredeemed Captive." *New England Quarterly* 38 (1965): 202–16.

Meek, Ronald L. *Social Science and the Ignoble Savage.* Cambridge: Cambridge Univ. Press, 1976.

Melvoin, Richard I. *New England Outpost: War and Society in Colonial Deerfield.* New York: Norton, 1989.

Michaelsen, Robert S. "Red Man's Religion/White Man's Religious History." *Journal of the American Academy of Religion* 51 (1983): 667–84.

Miller, Perry. *The New England Mind: From Colony to Province.* Cambridge: Harvard Univ. Press, 1953.

———. *Errand into the Wilderness.* Cambridge: Harvard Univ. Press, 1956.

Milne, Tom. "Little Big Man." *Focus on Film* 6 (1971): 3–7.

Minter, David. " 'By Dens of Lions': Notes on Stylization in Early Puritan Captivity Narratives." *American Literature* 45 (1973): 335–47.

Mintz, Steven. *A Prison of Expectation: The Family in Victorian Culture.* New York: New York Univ. Press, 1983.

Mitchell, Sally. "Sentiment and Suffering: Women's Recreational Reading in the 1860's." *Victorian Studies* 21, no. 1 (1977): 29–45.

Mogen, David, Mark Busby, and Paul Bryant, eds. *The Frontier Experience and the American Dream: Essays on American Literature.* College Station: Texas A & M Univ. Press, 1989.

Monical, David G. "Changes in American Attitudes toward the Indian as

Evidenced by Captive Literature." *Plains Anthropologist* 14, no. 44, pt. 1 (1969): 130–36.

Morgan, Edmund S. *Visible Saints: The History of a Puritan Idea.* New York: New York Univ. Press, 1963.

Morinis, Alan. "The Ritual Experience: Pain and the Transformation of Consciousness in Ordeals of Initiation." *Ethos* 13, 2 (1984): 307–33.

Morris, David B. *The Culture of Pain.* Berkeley: Univ. of California Press, 1991.

Morrison, Kenneth M. " 'That Art of Coyning Christians': John Eliot and the Praying Indians of Massachusetts." *Ethnohistory* 21 (1974): 77–92.

———. "The Wonders of Divine Mercy: A Review of John Williams' *The Redeemed Captive.*" *Canadian Review of American Studies* 9 (1979): 56–62.

Mortimer, Barbara Anne. "From Monument Valley to Vietnam: Revisions of the American Captivity Narrative in Hollywood Film." Ph.D. diss., Emory University, 1991.

Mossiker, Frances. *Pocahontas: The Life and Legend.* New York: Knopf, 1976.

Mott, Frank Luther. *A History of American Magazines, 1741–1850.* New York: Appleton, 1930.

———. *Golden Multitudes: The Story of Best Sellers in the United States.* New York: Macmillan, 1947.

Movshovitz, Howard. "The Still Point: Women in the Westerns of John Ford." *Frontiers* 7, no. 3 (1984): 68–72.

Mullan, John. *Sentiment and Sociability: The Language of Feeling in the Eighteenth Century.* Oxford: Clarendon Press, 1988.

Murdock, Kenneth Ballard. *Literature and Theology in Colonial New England.* Cambridge: Harvard Univ. Press, 1949.

Murphey, Murray G. "The Psychodynamics of Puritan Conversion." *American Quarterly* 31 (1979): 140–47.

Mussell, Kay. *Women's Gothic and Romantic Fiction: A Reference Guide.* American Popular Culture Series. Westport, Conn.: Greenwood, 1981.

Namias, June. "White Captives: Gender and Ethnicity on Successive American Frontiers, 1607–1862." Ph.D. diss., Brandeis University, 1989.

———. *White Captives: Gender and Ethnicity on the American Frontier.* Chapel Hill: Univ. of North Carolina Press, 1993.

Nash, Gary B. "The Image of the Indian in the Southern Colonial Mind." *William and Mary Quarterly,* 3rd ser. 29 (1972): 197–230.

———. *Red, White, and Black: The Peoples of Early America.* Englewood Cliffs, N.J.: Prentice-Hall, 1974.

Neale, Steve. *Genre.* London: BFI, 1980.

Nicholson, Marjorie Hope. *Newton Demands the Muse: Newton's Op-*

ticks and the Eighteenth-Century Poets. Princeton: Princeton Univ. Press, 1946.

Obeyesekere, Gananath. *The Apotheosis of Captain Cook: European Mythmaking in the Pacific.* Princeton: Princeton Univ. Press, 1992.

O'Flaherty, Wendy Doniger. *Other People's Myths: The Cave of Echoes.* New York: Macmillan, 1988.

O'Gorman, Edmundo. *The Invention of America: An Inquiry into the Historical Nature of the New World and the Meaning of Its History.* Bloomington: Indiana Univ. Press, 1961.

Okin, Susan Miller. "The Making of the Sentimental Family." *Philosophy and Public Affairs* 11 (1982): 65–88.

Oswald, John Clyde. *Printing in the Americas.* New York: Hacker Art Books, 1968.

Pagden, Anthony. *The Fall of Natural Man: The American Indian and the Origins of Comparative Ethnology.* Cambridge: Cambridge Univ. Press, 1982.

Papashvily, Helen Waite. *All the Happy Endings: A Study of the Domestic Novel in America, the Women Who Wrote It, the Women Who Read It, in the Nineteenth Century.* New York: Harper & Brothers, 1956.

Parker, I. Pierce. *Antelope Bill.* Minneapolis: Ross & Haines, 1962.

Patterson, Mark R. *Authority, Autonomy, and Representation in American Literature, 1776–1865.* Princeton: Princeton Univ. Press, 1988.

Pearce, Roy Harvey. "The Significances of the Captivity Narrative." *American Literature* 19 (1947): 1–20.

——. "The 'Ruines of Mankind': The Indians and the Puritan Mind." *Journal of the History of Ideas* 13 (1952): 200–217.

——. "The Metaphysics of Indian-Hating." *Ethnohistory* 4 (1957): 27–40.

——. *Savagism and Civilization: A Study of the Indian and the American Mind.* Rev. ed. Baltimore: Johns Hopkins Univ. Press, 1967.

Peckham, Howard. *Captured by Indians: True Tales of Pioneer Survivors.* New Brunswick, N.J.: Rutgers Univ. Press, 1954.

Peckham, Howard, and C. Gibson, eds. *Attitudes of Colonial Powers towards the American Indian.* Salt Lake City: Univ. of Utah Press, 1969.

Perdue, Theda. *Slavery and the Evolution of Cherokee Society, 1540–1866.* Knoxville: Univ. of Tennessee Press, 1978.

Person, Leland S., Jr. "The American Eve: Miscegenation and a Feminist Frontier Fiction." *American Quarterly* 37 (1985): 668–85.

Peterson, Jacquelin L., and Jennifer S. H. Brown, eds. *The New Peoples: Being and Becoming Métis in North America.* Winnipeg: Univ. of Manitoba Press, 1985.

Pettid, Edward J., S.J., ed. "Olive Ann Oatman's Lecture Notes and Oatman Bibliography." *San Bernardino County Museum Association Quarterly* 16 (1968): 1–39; rpt. under separate cover, n.p., 1969.

Pettit, Norman. *The Heart Prepared: Grace and Conversion in the Puritan Spiritual Life.* New Haven: Yale Univ. Press, 1966.

Piercy, Josephine K. *Studies in Literary Types in Seventeenth-Century America (1607–1710).* Hamden, Conn.: Archon Books, 1969.

Place, J. A. *The Western Films of John Ford.* Secaucus, N.J.: Citadel Press, 1974.

Porte, Joel. "In the Hands of an Angry God: Religious Terror in Gothic Fiction." In *The Gothic Imagination: Essays in Dark Romanticism,* ed. G. R. Thompson, pp. 42–64. Pullman: Washington State Univ. Press, 1974.

Porter, Donald Clayton. *Senecca Warriors.* White Indian Series no. 22. New York: Bantam, 1991.

Porter, H. C. *The Inconstant Savage: England and the North American Indian, 1500–1660.* London: Duckworth, 1979.

Porter, Kenneth W. *The Negro on the American Frontier.* New York: Arno Press, 1971.

Porter, William Sydney (O'Henry). "The Ransom of Red Chief." In *The Best Short Stories of O. Henry,* pp. 188–201. New York: Modern Library, 1945.

Porterfield, Amanda. *Female Piety in Puritan New England: The Emergence of Religious Humanism.* New York: Oxford Univ. Press, 1992.

Pratt, Mary Louise. *Imperial Eyes: Travel Writing and Transculturation.* London and New York: Routledge, 1992.

Price, John A. "The Stereotyping of North American Indians in Motion Pictures." *Ethnohistory* 20 (1973): 153–71.

Pritchard, Kathleen H. "John Vanderlyn and the Massacre of Jane McCrea." *Art Quarterly* 12 (1949): 360–66.

Proby, Clive T. *English Fiction of the Eighteenth Century, 1700–1789.* London and New York: Longman, 1987.

Prucha, Francis Paul. *Americanizing the American Indians: Writings by "Friends of the Indian," 1800–1900.* Cambridge: Harvard Univ. Press, 1973.

Radner, John B. "The Art of Sympathy in Eighteenth-Century British Moral Thought." *Studies in Eighteenth-Century Culture* 9 (1979): 189–210.

Radway, Janice A. *Reading the Romance: Women, Patriarchy, and Popular Literature.* Chapel Hill: Univ. of North Carolina Press, 1984.

Railton, Stephen. *Authorship and Audience: Literary Performance in the American Renaissance.* Princeton: Princeton Univ. Press, 1991.

Renville, Mrs. Mary Butler. *A Thrilling Narrative of Indian Captivity.* Minneapolis: Atlas Company's Books and Job Office, 1863.

Resnick, Daniel P., ed. *Literacy in Historical Perspective.* Washington, D.C.: Library of Congress, 1983.

Reynolds, David. *Beneath the American Renaissance: The Subversive Imagination in the Age of Emerson and Melville.* New York: Knopf, 1988.

Richardson, Samuel. *Pamela.* Shakespeare Head Edition. Oxford: Oxford Univ. Press, 1930.

Richter, Conrad. *The Light in the Forest.* 1953. Rpt. New York: Bantam, 1975.

Richter, Daniel K. "War and Culture: The Iroquois Experience." *William and Mary Quarterly,* 3d ser. 40 (1983): 528–59.

Riley, Glenda. *Women and Indians on the Frontier, 1825–1915.* Albuquerque: Univ. of New Mexico Press, 1984.

Rister, Carl Coke. *Border Captives: The Traffic in Prisoners by Southern Plains Indians, 1835–1875.* Norman: Univ. of Oklahoma Press, 1940.

——. *Comanche Bondage: Beale's Settlement and Sarah Ann Horn's Narrative.* Glendale, Calif.: Arthur H. Clark, 1955.

Rogers, Mary F. *Novels, Novelists, and Readers: Toward a Phenomenological Sociology of Literature.* Albany: State Univ. of New York Press, 1991.

Ronan, Margaret. "Film: Lo, the True Indian!" *Senior Scholastic* 96 (May 4, 1970): 24–25.

Rosentiel, Annette. *Red and White: Indian Views of the White Man, 1492–1982.* New York: Universe Books, 1983.

Ross, Danita. "The Indian Captivity of Clara Blinn: Who Was to Blame for Her Death?" *American West* 25, no. 3 (1988): 44–47.

Ross, Harry J. "Trapped by Society, Imprisoned in the Wilderness: Captivity in American Literature, 1680–1860." Ph.D. diss., Northwestern University, 1989.

Rountree, Helen C., ed. *Powhatan Foreign Relations, 1500–1722.* Charlottesville: Univ. Press of Virginia, 1993.

Rousseau, G. S. "Nerves, Spirits, and Fibres: Towards Defining the Origins of Sensibility." *Blue Guitar* 2 (1976): 125–53.

Russell, Jason Almus. "The Narratives of the Indian Captiviies." *Education* 51 (1930): 84–88.

Ryan, Mary P. *The Empire of the Mother: American Writing about Domesticity, 1830–1860.* New York: Haworth Press, 1982.

Sahlins, Marshall. *Islands of History.* Chicago: Univ. of Chicago Press, 1985.

Said, Edward W., ed. *Literature and Society: Selected Papers from the English Institute, 1978.* Baltimore: Johns Hopkins Univ. Press, 1980.

St. George, Robert. "'Heated' Speech and Literacy in Seventeenth-Century New England." In *Seventeenth-Century New England,* ed. David D. Hall and David Grayson Allen (Boston: Colonial Society of Massachusetts, 1984), pp. 275–322.

Salisbury, Neal. "Red Puritans: The 'Praying Indians' of Massachusetts Bay and John Eliot." *William and Mary Quarterly,* 3d. ser. 31 (1974): 27–54.

——. "Review: *The Indians and Their Captives.*" *American Indian Culture and Research Journal* 3 (1979): 79–82.

——. *The Indians of New England: A Critical Bibliography.* Bloomington: Indiana Univ. Press, 1981.

——. *Manitou and Providence: Indians, Europeans, and the Making of New England, 1500–1643.* New York: Oxford Univ. Press, 1982.

Sambrook, James. *The Eighteenth Century: The Intellectual and Cultural Context of English Literature, 1700–1789.* London and New York: Longman, 1986.

Samuels, Shirley, ed. *The Culture of Sentiment: Race, Gender, and Sentimentality in Nineteenth-Century America.* New York: Oxford Univ. Press, 1992.

Sanford, Charles L. *The Quest for Paradise: Europe and the American Moral Imagination.* Urbana: Univ. of Illinois Press, 1961.

Saum, Lewis O. *The Popular Mood of Pre–Civil War America.* Westport, Conn.: Greenwood, 1980.

Sayre, Robert F. *Thoreau and the American Indians.* Princeton: Princeton Univ. Press, 1977.

Scarry, Elaine. *The Body in Pain: The Making and Unmaking of the World.* New York: Oxford Univ. Press, 1985.

Schaeffer, C. E. "The Grasshopper or Children's War—A Circumboreal Legend?" *Pennsylvania Archaeologist* 12 (1942): 60–61.

Scheick, William J. *The Half-Blood: A Cultural Symbol in the 19th-Century American Fiction.* Lexington: Univ. Press of Kentucky, 1979.

Schick, Frank L. *The Paperbound Book in America: The History of Paperbacks and Their European Background.* New York: Bowker, 1958.

Schwandt, Mary. "The Story of Mary Schwandt. Her Captivity During the Sioux 'Outbreak'—1862." *Minnesota Historical Society Collections* 6 (1896): 461–74.

Scobey, David. "Revising the Errand: New England's Ways and the Puritan Sense of the Past." *William and Mary Quarterly,* 3d ser. 41 (1984): 3–31.

Seaver, James E. *A Narrative of the Life of Mrs. Mary Jemison.* Ed. June Namias. Norman: Univ. of Oklahoma Press, 1992.

Segal, Charles M., and David C. Stinebeck, ed. *Puritans, Indians, and Manifest Destiny.* New York: Putnam's, 1977.

Seelye, John. *Prophetic Waters: The River in American Life and Literature.* New York: Oxford Univ. Press, 1977.

Selement, George. "Publication and the Puritan Minister." *William and Mary Quarterly,* 3d ser. 37 (1980): 219–41.

——. *Keepers of the Vineyard: The Puritan Ministry and Collective Culture in Colonial New England.* Lanham, Md.: Univ. Press of America, 1984.

Severance, Frank, ed. *The Captivity and Sufferings of Benjamin Gilbert and His Family, 1730–83.* Cleveland: Burrows Brothers, 1904.

Sheehan, Bernard W. "Indian-White Relations in Early America: A Review Essay." *William and Mary Quarterly,* 3d ser. 26 (1969): 267–86.

——. *Savagism and Civility: Indians and Englishmen in Colonial Virginia.* New York: Oxford Univ. Press, 1973.

Shepard, Leslie. *The History of Street Literature*. Detroit: Singing Tree Press, 1973.

Sheriff, John K. *The Good-Natured Man: The Evolution of a Moral Ideal, 1660–1800*. Tuscaloosa: Univ. of Alabama Press, 1982.

Shweder, Richard A. *Thinking through Cultures: Expeditions in Cultural Psychology*. Cambridge: Harvard Univ. Press, 1991.

Sieminski, Greg. "The Puritan Captivity Narrative and the Politics of the American Revolution." *American Quarterly* 42 (1990): 35–56.

Silko, Leslie M. *Ceremony*. New York: Viking, 1977.

Silver, Rollo G. "Financing the Publication of Early New England Sermons." *Studies in Bibliography* 11 (1958): 163–78.

Simmons, William S. "Cultural Bias in the New England Puritans' Perception of Indians." *William and Mary Quarterly*, 3d ser. 38 (1981): 56–72.

Sinclair, Andrew. *The Savage: A History of Misunderstanding*. London: Weidenfeld and Nicolson, 1977.

Slotkin, Richard. *Regeneration through Violence: The Mythology of the American Frontier*. Middletown, Conn.: Wesleyan Univ. Press, 1973.

———. *The Fatal Environment: The Myth of the Frontier in the Age of Industrialization, 1800–1890*. Middletown, Conn.: Wesleyan Univ. Press, 1985.

Slotkin, Richard, and James K. Folsom, eds. *So Dreadfull a Judgment: Puritan Responses to King Philip's War, 1676–1677*. Middletown, Conn.: Wesleyan Univ. Press, 1978.

Smith, Adam. *The Theory of Moral Sentiments*. Ed. D. D. Raphael and A. L. Macfie. Indianapolis: Liberty Classics, 1982. Rpt. of the Oxford Univ. Press ed. of 1976.

Smith, Clinton. *The Boy Captives*. Hackberry, Tex.: Frontier Times, 1927.

Smith, Dwight L. "Shawnee Captivity Ethnography." *Ethnohistory* 2 (1955): 29–41.

Smith, Henry Nash. *Democracy and the Novel: Popular Resistance to Classic American Writers*. New York: Oxford Univ. Press, 1978.

Smith, James Morton, ed. *Seventeenth-Century America*. Chapel Hill: Univ. of North Carolina Press, 1959.

Smith, Jane F., and Robert M. Kvasnicka, ed. *Indian-White Relations: A Persistent Paradox*. Washington, D.C.: Howard Univ. Press, 1981.

Smith, Robinson V. "New Hampshire Persons Taken as Captives by the Indians." *Historical New Hampshire* 8 (Mar. 1952): 24–36.

Socolow, Susan Migden. "Spanish Captives in Indian Societies: Cultural Contact along the Argentine Frontier, 1600–1835." *Hispanic American Historical Review* 72 (1992): 73–99.

Solberg, Winton U. *Redeem the Time: The Puritan Sabbath in Early America*. Cambridge: Harvard Univ. Press, 1977.

Speck, Frank G. "The Grasshopper War in Pennsylvania: An Indian Myth

That Became History." *Pennsylvania Archaeologist* 12 (1942): 31–34.

Speck, Gordon. *Breeds and Half-Breeds.* New York: Clarkson N. Potter, 1969.

Spence, Clark C., and Mary Lee Spence. Prologue. In Fanny Kelly, *Narrative of My Captivity Among the Sioux Indians.* Lakeside Classics, no. 88, pp. xxiii–lviii. Chicago: Donnelley, 1990.

The Spiritual Exercises of St. Ignatius. Trans. Anthony Mottola. Garden City, N.Y.: Doubleday, 1964.

Stanford, Ann. "Mary Rowlandson's Journey to Redemption." *Ariel* 7 (1976): 27–37.

Stannard, David E. "Death and Dying in Puritan New England." *American Historical Review* 77 (1973): 1305–30.

——. *The Puritan Way of Death: A Study in Religion, Culture, and Social Change.* New York: Oxford Univ. Press, 1977.

Starna, William A., and Ralph Watkins. "Northern Iroquois Slavery." *Ethnohistory* 38 (1991): 3–57.

Starr, G. A. "Only a Boy: Notes on Sentimental Novels." *Genre* (Winter 1977): 501–27.

Stauferr, Helen, and Susan Rosowski, eds. *Women and Western American Literature.* Troy, N.Y.: Whitson, 1982.

Stearns, Carol Z., and Peter N. Stearns, eds. *Emotion and Social Change: Towards a New Psychohistory.* New York & London: Holmes & Meier, 1988.

Stearns, Peter N. *Jealousy: The Evolution of an Emotion in American History.* New York: New York Univ. Press, 1989.

Stern, Peter. "The White Indians of the Borderlands." *Journal of the Southwest* 33 (1991): 262–81.

Stout, Harry S. *The New England Soul: Preaching and Religious Culture in Colonial New England.* New York: Oxford Univ. Press, 1986.

Stowe, Harriet Beecher. *Uncle Tom's Cabin; or, Life Among the Lowly.* New York: Harper & Row, 1965.

Strecker, Fredrick. *My First Years as a Jemisonian.* Rochester, N.Y.: Fredrick Strecker, 1931.

Street, Brian V. *The Savage in Literature: Representations of "Primitive" Society in English Fiction, 1858–1920.* London: Routledge and Kegan Paul, 1975.

Strong, Pauline Turner. "Captive Images: Stereotypes that Justified Colonial Expansion on the American Frontier Were a Legacy of a Seventeenth-Century War." *Natural History* (Dec. 1985): 51–56.

Swagerty, W. R., ed. *Scholars and the Indian Experience: Critical Reviews of Recent Writing in the Social Sciences.* Bloomington: Indiana Univ. Press, 1984.

Swanton, John R. "Notes on the Mental Assimilation of Races." *Journal of the Washington Academy of Sciences* 16 (1926): 93–502.

Sweet, David, and Gary B. Nash, eds. *Survival and Struggle in Colonial America.* Berkeley: Univ. of California Press, 1981.

Taves, Ann, ed. *Religion and Domestic Violence in Early New England: The Memoirs of Abigail Abbot Bailey.* Bloomington: Indiana Univ. Press, 1989.

Thacker, Christopher. *The Wildness Pleases: The Origins of Romanticism.* New York: St. Martins, 1983.

Thomas, G. E. "Puritans, Indians, and the Concept of Race." *New England Quarterly* 48 (1975): 3–27.

Thomas, Keith. *Religion and the Decline of Magic.* New York: Scribners, 1971.

——. *Man and the Natural World: Changing Attitudes in England, 1500–1800.* London: Allen Lane, 1983.

Timberg, Bernard M. "Patty Hearst and Mercy Short: An Analogue Critique." *Journal of American Culture* 6 (1983): 60–64.

Torgovnick, Marianna. *Gone Primitive: Savage Intellects, Modern Lives.* Chicago: Univ. of Chicago Press, 1990.

Todd, Janet. *Sensibility: An Introduction.* London: Methuen, 1986.

Tompkins, Jane. *Sensational Designs: The Cultural Work of American Fiction, 1790–1860.* New York: Oxford Univ. Press, 1985.

Trelease, Allen W. *Indian Affairs in Colonial New York: The Seventeenth Century.* Ithaca: Cornell Univ. Press, 1960.

Turner, Frederick. *Beyond Geography: The Western Spirit against the Wilderness.* New York: Viking, 1980.

Turner, John W. "*Little Big Man*: The Novel and the Film." *Literature/Film Quarterly* 5 (1977): 154–63.

Turner, Victor. *The Ritual Process: Structure and Anti-Structure.* Chicago: Aldine, 1966.

Tuveson, Ernest Lee. *The Imagination as a Means of Grace: Locke and the Aesthetics of Romanticism.* New York: Gordian Press, 1974.

Tyler, Royall. *The Algerine Captive.* Ed. Don L. Cook. New Haven: College & Univ. Press, 1970.

Ulrich, Laurel Thatcher. *Good Wives: Image and Reality in the Lives of Women in Northern New England, 1650–1750.* New York: Oxford Univ. Press, 1982.

Usner, Daniel H., Jr. "American Indians in Colonial History: A Review Essay." *Journal of American Ethnic History* (1992): 77–85.

Vail, R. W. G. *The Voice of the Old Frontier.* Philadelphia: Univ. of Pennsylvania Press, 1949.

Valeros, Helena. *Yo soy Napéyoma: relato de una mujer raptada por los indígenas yanoami.* Comp. Renato Agagliate and D. Emilio Fuentes. Caracas: Fundación La Salle de Cinecias Naturales, 1984. Monografía no. 35.

Van Der Beets, Richard. "A Surfeit of Style: The Indian Captivity Narrative as Penny Dreadful." *Research Studies* 39 (1971): 297–306.

——. "The Indian Captivity Narrative as Ritual." *American Literature* 43 (1972): 548–62.

——. "'A Thirst for Empire': The Indian Captivity Narrative as Propaganda." *Research Studies* 40 (1972): 207–15.

——. *The Indian Captivity Narrative: An American Genre.* Lanham, Md.: Univ. Press of America, 1984.

——, ed. *Held Captive by Indians.* Knoxville: Univ. of Tennessee Press, 1973.

Van Kirk, Sylvia. *Many Tender Ties: Women in Fur-Trade Society, 1670–1870.* Norman: Univ. of Oklahoma Press, 1983.

Vaughan, Alden T. *American Genesis: Captain John Smith and the Founding of Virginia.* Boston: Little, Brown, 1975.

——. *New England Frontier: Puritans and Indians, 1620–1675.* Rev. ed. Boston: Little, Brown, 1979.

——. *Narratives of North American Indian Captivity: A Selective Bibliography.* Garland Reference Library of the Humanities, vol. 370. New York: Garland, 1983.

Vaughan, Alden T., and Edward W. Clark, eds. *Puritans among the Indians: Accounts of Captivity and Redemption, 1676–1724.* Cambridge: Harvard Univ. Press, 1981.

Vaughan, Alden T., and Daniel K. Richter. "Crossing the Cultural Divide: Indians and New Englanders, 1605–1763." *Proceedings of the American Antiquarian Society* 90 (1980): 23–90.

Vincent-Buffault, Anne. *The History of Tears: Sensibility and Sentimentality in France.* London: Macmillan, 1991.

Waite, Terry. *Taken on Trust.* New York: Harcourt Brace, 1993.

Waller, Susan. "The Artist, the Writer, and the Queen: Hosmer, Jameson, and *Zenobia.*" *Woman's Art Journal* 4 (Spring–Summer 1983): 21–28.

Walsh, Susan. "'With Them Was My Home': Native American Autobiography and *A Narrative of the Life of Mrs. Mary Jamison.*" *American Literature* 64 (1992): 1–18.

Washburn, Wilcomb E. *The Indian in America.* New York: Harper & Row, 1975.

——. Introduction. In Alden T. Vaughan, *Narratives of North American Indian Captivity: A Selective Bibliography,* pp. xi–lviii. New York & London: Garland, 1983.

Watkins, Owen C. *The Puritan Experience: Studies in Spiritual Autobiography.* London: Routledge and Kegan Paul, 1972.

Wauchope, Robert. *Lost Tribes and Sunken Continents: Myth and Method in the Study of American Indians.* Chicago: Univ. of Chicago Press, 1962.

Weimann, Robert. *Structure and Society in Literary History.* Baltimore: Johns Hopkins Univ. Press, 1984.

Welter, Barbara. "The Cult of True Womanhood: 1820–1860." *American Quarterly* 18 (1966): 151–74.

——. *Dimity Convictions: The American Woman in the Nineteenth Century.* Athens: Ohio Univ. Press, 1976.

White, Lonnie J. "White Women Captives of Southern Plains Indians, 1866–1875." *Journal of the West* 8 (1969): 327–54.

White, Mrs. N. D. "Captivity among the Sioux, August 18 to September 26, 1862." *Collections of the Minnesota Historical Society* 9 (1901): 395–426.

Whitford, Kathryn. "Hannah Dustin: The Judgement of History." *Essex Institute Historical Collections* 108 (1972): 304–25.

Williams, George H. *Wilderness and Paradise in Christian Thought.* New York: Harper, 1962.

Wilson, E. N. *The White Indian Boy.* Yonkers-on-Hudson: World, 1919.

Wilson, Raymond. *Ohiyesa: Charles Eastman, Santee Sioux.* Urbana: Univ. of Illinois Press, 1983.

Winans, Robert B. "The Growth of the Novel-Reading Public in Late Eighteenth-Century America." *Early American Literature* 9 (1975): 267–75.

Witthoft, John. "The Grasshopper War in Lenape Land." *Pennsylvania Archaeologist* 16 (1946): 91–94.

Wolff, Cynthia Griffin. *Samuel Richardson and the Eighteenth-Century Puritan Character.* Hamden, Conn.: Archon Books, 1972.

Woloch, Nancy. *Women and the American Experience.* New York: Knopf, 1984.

Wood, Patricia Dillon. *French-Indian Relations on the Southern Frontier.* Ann Arbor: UMI Research Press, 1980.

Young, Mary Elizabeth. *Redskins, Ruffleshirts, and Rednecks: Indian Allotments in Alabama and Mississippi, 1830–1860.* Norman: Univ. of Oklahoma Press, 1961.

Young, Philip. "The Mother of Us All." *Kenyon Review* 24 (1962): 391–441.

Zagari, Rosemarie. "Morals, Manners, and the Republican Mother." *American Quarterly* 44 (1992): 192–215.

Zolla, Elémire. *The Writer and the Shaman: A Morphology of the American Indian.* New York: Harcourt, Brace, Jovanovich, 1973.

Zuckerman, Michael. "Pilgrims in the Wilderness: Community, Modernity, and the Maypole at Merry Mount." *The New England Quarterly* 50 (1977): 255–77.

——. "The Fabrication of Identity in Early America." *William and Mary Quarterly* 3d ser. 34 (1977): 183–214.

INDEX